Labour and
Gold in Fiji

Labour and Gold in Fiji

by

’Atu Emberson-Bain

CAMBRIDGE UNIVERSITY PRESS
Cambridge, New York, Melbourne, Madrid, Cape Town,
Singapore, São Paulo, Delhi, Mexico City

Cambridge University Press
The Edinburgh Building, Cambridge CB2 8RU, UK

Published in the United States of America by Cambridge University Press, New York

www.cambridge.org
Information on this title: www.cambridge.org/9780521363723

First published 1994
First paperback edition 2002

A catalogue record for this publication is available from the British Library

National Library of Australia Cataloguing in Publication Data
Emberson-Bain, 'Atu.
Labour and gold in Fiji.
Bibliography.
Includes index.
1. Emperor Gold Mining Company Ltd.   2. Gold miners – Fiji –
History.   3. Gold mines and mining – Fiji – Vatukoula – History.
4. Industrial relations – Fiji – History.   5. Vatukoula (Fiji) – Social
conditions.   I. Title.
331.76223422099611

Library of Congress Cataloguing in Publication Data
Emberson-Bain, 'Atu.
Labour and gold in Fiji / by' Atu Emberson-Bain.
        p.   cm.
Includes bibliographical references and index.
1. Gold miners – Fiji – History.   2. Gold industry – Fiji – History.
I. Title.
HD8039.M74F43   1993
338.2'741'099611–dc20   93-12431   CIP

ISBN 978-0-521-36372-3 Hardback
ISBN 978-0-521-52321-9 Paperback

Foreword

I have a high regard for Dr 'Atu Emberson-Bain personally and intellectually, and for her work on labour relations in the Fijian gold-mines. Her background and intellectual formation give her unusual advantages for the analysis of such an 'intermediate' and transitional society as that of the Vatukoula miners, and she has used her opportunities well. Her book is of wide interest to those concerned with the economic and social problems of Third World countries.

It will be obvious to any reader that there can be no question as to Dr Emberson-Bain's thorough and meticulous scholarship. The book is a very substantial contribution, indeed probably definitive for its theme. It is well organised and clearly written, the great mass of empirical data is ably marshalled. Dr Emberson-Bain shows herself well aware of the current comparative literature, e.g. on African mining communities, and handles it well; her theory is not obtrusive, but relevant.

For the Pacific region, socioeconomic studies seem to have concentrated mainly on the problems of primary producers, farmers or fishermen, in their relations to the intrusive market economy; on petty entrepreneurs; and on the drift from the land to such quasi-metropolitan centres as Suva or Port Moresby or Noumea. I think Dr Emberson-Bain's book is a pioneer study of a discrete community living and working in a relatively isolated company town. As such it should be of much interest to readers in a number of related disciplines concerned with the changing social structures of Pacific Islanders, and beyond that to those interested in the Third World generally.

Oskar Spate
Australian National University

Dedication

For my mother, Betty Emberson-Bain, and in loving memory of my grandmother Matilda Emberson: two women who, in different ways, continue to be an inspiration to me.

Contents

List of Illustrations
Vatukoula: A Photo Essay (chapter 8)

List of Maps

List of Tables

List of Appendices

Acknowledgements

The genesis of this book was a doctoral thesis in history at the Australian National University in Canberra, and it was through that university's generous four-year scholarship that I was able to begin my voyage of discovery into the mine labour market of Fiji. In some respects this voyage began even before the shaky beginnings of the thesis, when in the seminar room of the Institute of Commonwealth Studies, University of London, I was captivated by the stimulating debates of a group of UK-based South African historians, including Shula Marks, Charles van Onselen, Harold Wolpe and Stanley Trapido. This experience as a young postgraduate in the late 1970s is one that undoubtedly fuelled my interest in labour history and influenced my decision to research the history of Fiji's goldmining industry.

Research for this book in its earlier thesis form was undertaken in Fiji and Australia, where I was assisted by many institutions and individuals, particularly staff of the Melbourne University Archives of Business and Labour; the Australian National University Archives of Business and Labour; the National Library of Australia, Canberra; the Mitchell Library, Sydney; and the Research Library of the Sydney Stock Exchange. I would like to make special mention of the Fiji Government, which in the early 1980s granted me unrestricted access to the records of the Colonial Secretary's Office accommodated at the National Archives, including open files inside the thirty-year period and confidential files. My thanks go to the archivist, Setareki Tuinaceva, and staff, especially Margaret Patel, whose support has remained solid throughout the ten years spanning both thesis and book endeavours.

For their generous intellectual support and encouragement, and for helping me to develop my analytical and writing skills, I am indebted to Oskar Spate and Dorothy Shineberg, who were my thesis supervisors, and to Donald Denoon, Gyan Pandey and John Merritt, who offered me constructive criticism on early drafts. To Oskar Spate I wish to record a special gratitude, not least for his intolerance of clumsy language and of 'too many nails being hammered into one hole'.

The post-thesis phase of writing this book was undertaken while I was employed as a lecturer in the School of Social and Economic Development of the University of the South Pacific, and involved several months of new research in Fiji and at the Public Record Office, London. Aside from fairly substantial revision to the original text, three entirely new chapters were written, subsequently cut back to one, to address developments in the post-colonial period. I am grateful to Wadan Narsey of the University of the South Pacific, who generously read and commented on the post-colonial economic sections, and also to Barbara Hau'ofa, who painstakingly read through two entire drafts to give me the benefit of her incisive editing skills. I am also grateful to my family in the UK for making possible my research at the Public Record Office and to the University of the South Pacific for financing a number of additional visits to Vatukoula. Research and library staff at the Reserve Bank of Fiji and the Bureau of Statistics obligingly assisted me on numerous occasions, as did Josephine Deo, Koresi Tabete, Sashi Prasad, Urmila Prakash and Mohini Singh by typing an assortment of drafts.

Space does not permit me to name the many company staff, union and government officers and others who kindly agreed to be interviewed or gave me valuable assistance. I derived much benefit from discussions with Ruskin Ward and Bill Cornwall (Emperor staff), Sakiasi Waqanivavalagi, Navitalai Raqona, Sairusi Waininima, Mesake Cirimaiwasa, Kavekini Navuso and Aliferети Waqa (FMWU), the late Dr Timoci Bavadra (deposed Labour–NFP Coalition Prime Minister), Tevita Fa (legal counsel to the Nasomo people), Mahendra Chaudhry (FTUC), the late Sir Robert Taylor (Economic Adviser and Financial Secretary, Government of Fiji 1947–52), R. D. Patel (former Member of Legislative Council), Karl Fleischman (former Inspector of Mines), Father Richard Keelan (Xavier College, Ba), and the late Herbert Murray (former member of the Mining Board). I am grateful to Peter Walker (Acting Principal Engineer, Mines) for sharing his technical knowledge of the mining industry and for answering endless questions, to David Greenbaum (former government Economic Geologist), Alfred Simpson (Assistant Director of Mineral Development), Nevil Ebsworth (former Principal Engineer, Mines), Peter Rodda (Principal Geologist, Information), and Raja Ram (former Chief Labour Officer), who helped me in various ways. The Ministry of Information, Department of Mineral Resources and the Fiji Times kindly made available most of the photographs that are included in this book, and Asaeli Lave and Sylvia Low laboured to produce quality products. Paul Geraghty (Fijian Dictionary Project), Amelia Rokotuivuna, Viniana Buitora and Ann Nacola generously assisted with Fijian translations.

I would like to express special thanks to Emperor Gold Mining Co. Ltd and in particular, its Managing Director, Jeffrey Reid, for granting me access to the enormous volume of correspondence files and other private records of the Emperor, Loloma and Dolphin mining companies of Vatukoula. The company facilitated my research by providing office space and also made accommodation available during the field trips I undertook between 1982 and 1983 with a young baby in tow. In the Blatchfords I had a special Sydney 'family', who gave me a wonderful home away from home, shared their rich memories of life at Vatukoula in the 1940s and 1950s, and facilitated contact with other retired company staff living in Australia. I am well aware, and can only regret, that company staff who helped make this book possible may not agree with my conclusions.

Notwithstanding the company's generosity, I should mention that the wide-ranging discussions and (informal) interviews I had with miners and their families at Vatukoula were generally constrained by the realities of life in a company-run town. Given these circumstances, I am enormously indebted to the many workers who succumbed to my persistent proddings and agreed to share their experiences and views, which often included vivid recollections of the early days of labour recruitment, mine work and life in the mining town. I am especially grateful to the Vatukoula relations I discovered I had and came to know, the Corrie family, who provided me with boundless hospitality, humour and information. To the elders and people of Nasomo, may I also express my appreciation.

Without doubt, however, my greatest debt is to my family for whom this journey of mine has almost certainly been a joyless trial. Sitiveni's support and love have been far more than I ever deserved, and three little people, Siale, Anga'ae fonu and Melino, who have popped up at odd intervals along the way, have in different ways, and to different degrees, endured more dislocation (as well as the sharp edge of a deranged mother) than is probably healthy for them. My brother, Ashley, and mother were at different stages of the project persuaded into the unenviable roles of research assistant and companion to me. My parents, Kenneth Bain and Betty Emberson Bain, have contributed critical comments, proofing assistance and crucial moral support. Last, but perhaps most important of all, have been the very special support of two surrogate mothers for my children, Rosa Mavoli Lewalewa, who accompanied me on my thesis fieldwork in Fiji and endured long cold months in Australia away from her family, and Viniana Buitora, who loyally bore the brunt of the second, post-thesis phase of my obsession with Vatukoula. Without them, this book would not have materialised.

'Atu Emberson-Bain
Suva

List of Abbreviations

ADB	*Australian Dictionary of Biography*
BHP	Broken Hill Proprietary Co. Ltd
C/L	Commissioner of Labour
CO	Colonial Office
CP	Council Paper
CS	Colonial Secretary
CSO	Colonial Secretary's Office
CSR	Colonial Sugar Refining Co. Ltd
cwt	hundredweight
DC	District Commissioner
DMS	Director of Medical Services
DO	District Officer
dwt	pennyweight, unit corresponding to one-twentieth of a troy ounce
EGM	Emperor Gold Mining Co. Ltd
EML	Emperor Mines Ltd
ETI	Emperor Timber Industries Ltd
FAB	Fijian Affairs Board
FECA	Fiji Employers' Consultative Association
FMD	Fiji Mines Development Ltd
FMWU	Fiji Mineworkers' Union
FS	*Fiji Sun*
FT	*Fiji Times*
FT & H	*Fiji Times & Herald*

GM	General Manager
ILO	International Labour Organisation
IOM	Inspector of Mines
IOM & ME	Inspector of Mines & Mining Engineer
JCC	Joint Consultative Council
Leg Co	Legislative Council, Fiji
LGMNL	Loloma (Fiji) Gold Mines No Liability
MB	Mining Board
ML	mining lease
MMSA	Methodist Mission Collection, Fiji National Archives
MP	Medical Practitioner
MR	Mineral Resources Division Library, Fiji Government
MSE	Melbourne Stock Exchange Mining Collection
NFP	National Federation Party
NLTB	Native Land Trust Board
NUM	National Union of Mineworkers
OAGF	Officer Administering the Government of Fiii
PC	Provincial Commissioner
PIM	*Pacific Islands Monthly*
PP	Parliamentary Paper
PRO	Public Record Office
RCAF	Roman Catholic Archives of Fiji
SFA	Secretary for Fijian Affairs
SMH	*Sydney Morning Herald*
SML	special mining lease
SNA	Secretariat for Native Affairs
TNC	transnational corporation
TPP	Tavua Power Proprietary Co. Ltd
Vat.	Vatukoula
WMC	Western Mining Corporation

A NOTE ON CURRENCY

Fiji currency is used in the text unless indicated otherwise. Pounds, shillings and pence were replaced by dollars and cents on 13 January 1969.

EQUIVALENTS

1 ounce	=	approx. 30 grams
1 acre	=	approx. 0.4 hectare
1 ton	=	approx. 1 tonne
1 lb. (pound)	=	approx. 500 grams
1 pint	=	approx. 600 millilitres
1 foot	=	approx. 30 centimetres
1 dwt	=	approx. 1.555 grams

ORTHOGRAPHY

In Fijian b is pronounced mb, as in number; c is pronounced th as in that; d is pronounced nd as in find; g is pronounced ng as in singer; q is pronounced ng as in finger.

A NOTE ON TERMINOLOGY

In line with company practice after the Second World War the term 'Part-European' has been used in this book to describe persons of mixed (commonly Fijian and European) descent. The terms 'half-caste' (typical of the pre-war years) and 'Euronesian', both of which are frequently found in company correspondence (and which are retained here when they appear in quotations) were used interchangeably with 'Part-European'. The term 'Indian' does not refer to workers recruited from India. It was used by the mining companies (in accordance with colonial convention) to describe Indo-Fijians. 'Indian' remains the official classification today. While the term is problematic, it is used in the text to avoid confusion.

Glossary

buli	government-appointed district chief
dalo	taro, a staple root crop
Degei	chiefly ancestral god in the form of a snake, believed to live in the Nakauvadra mountain range
galala	literally meaning free, but generally used to refer to the independent or 'free' farmer usually living outside the village and exempt from communal obligations
kumala	sweet potato
lālā	the conscription of goods and services (tribute) by a chief
leqa	trouble(s)
loloma	gift, offering, greetings, love
luveniwai vaka viti	traditional healer or medicine
mana	special powers, believed to be divinely ordained, held by chiefs or others in authority
masi	beaten bark cloth made from the paper mulberry tree
Matanagata	face of the snake, traditional Fijian name for Vatukoula
matanivanua	spokesperson or herald (traditionally male) for a chief
mataqali	the primary, patrilineal social division of a village
ratu	man of chiefly rank
roko tui	head of provincial administration; sometimes also a title given to persons of rank
rourou	green leafy vegetable (from the *dalo* plant)
soqosoqo	association or group
tabu	sacred or sacred thing, taboo
tabua	sperm whale's tooth used in ceremonial presentations or exchanges
taralala	popular Fijian dance in pairs

taukei	indigenous Fijian landowners
teitei	food garden
tui	chief
turaga ni koro	government appointed village headman, not necessarily a chief
turaga	chief, man of rank or status
vale ni mate	house of death, hospital
vanua	land; political grouping or association of villages under one chief
Vatukoula	rock of gold
vulagi	visitor, outsider, alien, foreigner

In the Beginning

(A legend from Saivou, Ra)

During the late nineteenth century, some time after the fortified village of Nakorowaiwai had been under gun attack, the ancestral god Navosavakadua spoke to two elderly brothers, one of whom was called Taivesi, whose great grandfather was the Tui Naliwane of Nacareva, Nasova, in Navuni. Navosavakadua instructed the brothers to undertake a journey to Matanagata. They were to carry a sack of putrid soil that contained the remains of those who had been killed at Nakorowaiwai and to bury them in a hilly place called Tolevu, not far from Matanagata. Under no circumstances were they to look around or behind them.

The two men went on their way and eventually arrived close to the designated area. However, the younger brother was unfortunately suffering from yaws of the foot, and when he trod on some thorny grass he collapsed in pain. He cried out to his brother, who was walking ahead of him, 'Alas, I am finished. My legs are giving way. I feel weak. Something is happening here. Turn around. There is an old man (spirit) who has fallen out of the ivi tree, and he is staring at me from behind. Turn around, I can't walk. Let's pour the soil out here.' The older brother turned back and they both set to work to bury the soil.

On their return journey, as they reached Drauniivi, the brothers met Navosavakadua. They were severely reprimanded for their disobedience. 'You two have not returned from Tolevu as you were told,' he chided. 'You have buried the soil in the wrong place. Why did you stamp on it? You have both been foolish. Because of what you have done, the soil will be dug up before the time is right. The soil was to have brought great wealth to our government and people. It was to have provided for our people.'

And so it came to pass: the riches of the soil at Matanagata were discovered and enjoyed by others.

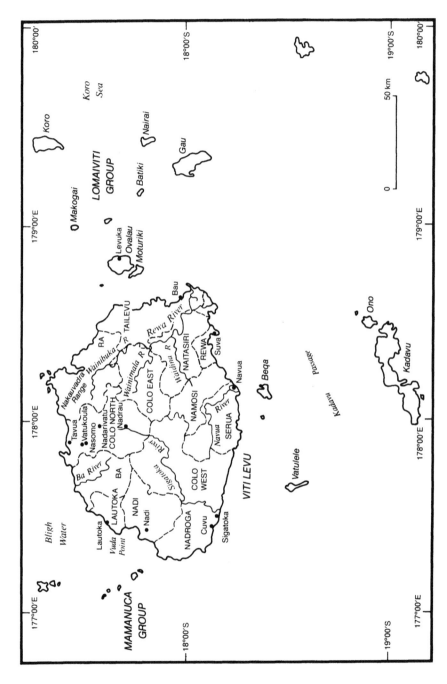

Pre-1945 provincial boundaries, Viti Levu

Introduction:
Rock of Gold, Face of the Snake

... both [Oceanic and Insular history] have their besetting dangers. That of the Oceanic, whether in its older geopolitical or in its new socio-economic trend, may reduce the human story to the unrolling or the interactions of grey impersonal forces ... As for the Insular, its practitioners may on occasion not see the Ocean for the Islands, may be content to be marooned in the tight but so safe confines of their little atoll of knowledge, regardless of the sweep of the currents which bring life to the isles. [O. H. K. Spate 1978 : 34]

Fiji's islands flank the Pacific epithermal arc known as the Rim (or Ring) of Fire, which hosts an impressive range of precious metal deposits. Embracing more than 80% of the world's volcanoes, the Rim stretches from New Zealand, through Tonga, Vanuatu, the Solomon Islands, Papua New Guinea, South-east Asia and down the west (Pacific) coast of North, Central and South America. In Tavua, in the north-west of Viti Levu, Fiji's largest island, the beautiful landscape on the fringe of the Nakauvadra mountain range, and a tapestry of sugar-cane and other farming settlements, skirt the cavity of an extinct volcano. In this collapsed caldera, which sprawls across a diameter of more than ten kilometres, nestles the gold town of Vatukoula, literally 'rock of gold'. The town is a by-product of over half a century of goldmining activities in an area rich in legend and spiritual symbolism. It is traditionally known, not as Vatukoula, but as Matanagata, 'the face of the snake'. The 57-year-old Emperor mine is described as 'a typical high grade bonanza style' orebody with its gold-bearing ore present in thin, highly shear zones. Visible free gold is a fairly common occurrence, and since it began production in 1934 the mine has produced over 4 million ounces of gold.

The story that follows is about the making and undoing of a working class. It is a reconstruction of the tortuous history of indigenous mine labour, exploring the singular features of the country's only company mining town, and examining

1

the various forces that have shaped its character over half a century. The operations of an Australian monopoly, currently represented by a partnership of Emperor Gold Mines Ltd (EML) and the transnational Western Mining Corporation (WMC), form a vital background.

The goldmining industry has special significance in Fiji's labour and economic history. For the first time, indigenous Fijians were required to form the core of an industrial work-force. Labour was drawn from all 14 provinces of the country and, in keeping with the Pacific-wide tradition of recruitment for plantation and mining labour economies, was for more than a decade migrant and indentured. Today, what was once a frontier outpost supporting a few hundred itinerant labourers has been transformed into one of the country's larger urban enclaves: with the nearby township of Tavua, it boasts a combined population of at least 8000.

Although Fiji contributes only a fraction of the world's gold supply, the exploitation of its gold resources by a foreign monopoly highlights the dominant and predatory role of international capitalism in another corner of the Third World. From the earliest years, as the industry carved a harsh and uncertain destiny for thousands of men, women and children, there appeared an obvious human cost. The legacy lingers. Even today Vatukoula still encapsulates the captive labour settlement, manifesting the paradoxical blend of solidarity and conflict that so often pervades communities whose working and social lives are interwoven and which are locked into a relationship of extreme dependence on their employers.

The account that follows is a contribution to the region's limited reserves of 'working-people's' history. Its theoretical framework is not explicit, but is intended to provide a thematic structure. I seek to address questions that I believe are both relevant and necessary to understanding the processes of working-class formation and control. The work comes in the wake of continuing criticism about the state of Pacific historiography. Among the charges are: that mainstream scholarship 'often amounts to simplistic storytelling'[1] and it 'rarely ventures beyond a timid empiricism';[2] that it has failed to produce a 'people's history'[3] and it is still waiting to be 'decolonised'.[4]

On the positive side, Pacific historiography is no longer dominated by imperial historians, but is 'firmly rooted in the islands and not in Europe'. This is, as several Pacific historians have noted, a logical and necessary development given the circumstances of political decolonisation. The end of empire demanded active, if still voiceless, 'natives' and an adjustment to a long-reigning intellectual tradition of Eurocentric bias.[5] Yet along with the new 'islander' history have emerged fresh criticisms. One of these is the proliferation of specialised ethnographic studies, dubbed 'Insular history' by Oskar Spate for their sparing attention to the broader external forces, which have so decisively influenced Pacific Islands.[6]

---

[1]   Leckie 1983 : 54.
[2]   Durutalo 1983 : 9.
[3]   Denoon 1973 : 3-28.
[4]   Durutalo 1985 : 117-56.
[5]   Spate 1978; Howe 1979 : 81-2 & 1984 : xii-xiii; and Leckie 1983 : 12-13.
[6]   Spate 1978 : 32-4; Howe 1979 : 81-90 & 1984 : xiv.

The writing of broader-based, thematic and sometimes even people's history located within the region's political economy is a relatively recent and limited development. Although this has laid the discipline open to charges of superficiality or ideological myopia,[7] the trend has edged the boundaries of regional scholarship beyond the narrow and largely uncritical focus of empiricist ethnographies. Hempenstall's *Pacific Islanders under German rule* and his collaborative work with Rutherford on colonial resistance, Ralston's comparative study of nineteenth-century 'beach communities', and Newbury's portrait of Pacific labour reserves are among the better examples, not to mention Spate's superlative 'Oceanic' *magnum opus*. Howard's survey of the impact of mining on indigenous peoples reaches beyond the region to include Brazil, North America and the Philippines.[8]

A number of recent works, notably Moore, Leckie and Munro's wide-ranging edited essays on Pacific labour history and Bennett's comprehensive history of the Solomon Islands, have enhanced our understanding of the region's labour processes and worker experiences.[9] Yet, regrettably, labour history remains poorly serviced, long dealing with few subjects outside the nineteenth-century Melanesian labour trade and the Indian indenture system. In Fiji, the conspicuous shortage of studies on indigenous Fijian agricultural or industrial labour contrasts with a significant body of scholarship on Indian sugar-workers. With few exceptions, such as work by Narsey and Knapman,[10] economic or labouring histories have also tended to be ethnically specific. It is a pattern that has logically derived from ethnic compartmentalism in the colonial and post-colonial economy, whereby particular industries have historically been identified closely, if not always exclusively, with one or other of the major ethnic categories.

On reflection, the neglect of Fijian labour history would seem to be less an academic oversight than the product of dominant political ideologies. As Leckie comments, there is a 'current fascination with chiefly structures, as part of the wider interest in Pacific elites' and 'Pacific scholarship has never been particularly enthusiastic about studying society from the "bottom up".'[11] Related to this, and pervading the establishment history of Pacific Islanders, is an ideology of pan-Pacific nationalism, which propagates values of consensus, cultural homogeneity and social unity in respect of traditional social systems. The 'reality', according to its visionaries, is that 'even colonially modified customary political systems have in some Pacific states, the capacity to link leaders and their supporters through kinship, reciprocity and mutual obligations'.[12]

Such a perspective denies social relations of exploitation, dominance and conflict, which has scarcely been conducive to a flourishing trade in histories of the indigenous working and producing classes. At the political level, in culturally heterogeneous societies such as Fiji, 'Pacific Way' ideology has acted both as

[7] See, for example, Leckie 1983 : 50-1 in respect of Howe's general Pacific history 1984; and Robertson 1985 : 157-63 in regard to Hempenstall & Rutherford 1984. Leckie (1983) provides an expansive critique of Pacific history.
[8] Hempenstall 1978; Hempenstall & Rutherford 1984; Ralston 1977; Newbury 1980; Spate 1979, 1983 & 1988; Howard 1988.
[9] Moore, Leckie & Munro 1990; Bennett 1987.
[10] Narsey 1986 : 87-161 and 1988; Knapman 1987. Also see Sutherland 1984.
[11] Leckie 1987 : 1.
[12] Meleisea & Schoeffel 1984 : 103.

a stimulus to ethnic consciousness and solidarity and as a check against the development of alliances based on cross-cultural class interests and sympathies.

Howard maintains that the Pacific Way epic has 'tended towards romanticisation of Pacific societies', and 'like similar ideologies in other parts of the Third World, it serves to justify the dominant position of the neo-colonial indigenous elite'.[13] Present circumstances in Fiji appear to lend special weight to this thesis. The military coups of 1987 claimed a new pre-eminence for Fijian culture as a politically charged construct with a legitimating ideological function. Indigenous rights purportedly justified the usurpation of political power by the military. Since 1987, constitutional changes that refurbish the supremacy of the chiefs and penalise commoners (including the resurrection of customary law) have been rationalised by reference to traditional cultural norms. Democracy and democratic processes have suddenly become a 'foreign flower'—encased in thorns.

In the current political environment, labour research and writing are unlikely to be looked upon with favour. This is particularly so if they draw unwelcome attention to the anti-labour and anti-union policies of the military-backed, post-coup administrations; and to the links between these policies and the growth-led development 'religion' persuasively marketed by international institutions such as the World Bank and the International Monetary Fund (IMF). Exposing the contradictions inherent in official posturing on indigenous rights is likely to win even fewer friends. Also likely to be inhibited is the development of a Marxist discourse already retarded by an unsympathetic, even hostile, intellectual climate, which sporadically spits out attacks against the proponents of 'missionary Marxism', 'Eurocentric palaeo-Marxism', or 'a simplistic Marxism with a blinkered emphasis on conflict'.[14]

The paucity of labour studies in Fiji also appears to stem from the continuing influence of pluralist theory in the historiography. The conceptualisation of plural societies, originally argued by J. S. Furnivall in respect of colonial societies, per-ceives communal (racial or ethnic) distinctions as the principal social contra-diction. They, above all else, explain the cleavages, tensions and conflict in society. Although developments of the model since Furnivall's original blueprint in 1948 have acknowledged the analytical relevance of social class, the latter has been incorporated only as a dimension of cultural or ethnic plurality. As such, its role in influencing social attitudes and behaviour is still seen as ancillary rather than central.[15]

The influence of a pluralist perspective on Fijian historiography has been re-inforced by the 'protectionist' thesis, which continues to be the orthodox inter-pretation of Fiji's colonial experience. In essence, the view is that colonialism sought to 'preserve' or 'protect' the indigenous Fijians and their social system from the ravages of the monetary economy.[16] Significantly, preservation embraces

---

[13] Howard, Plange, Durutalo & Witton 1983 : 253. See also Howard 1986 : 2-4. Durutalo (1985 : 152) has similarly argued that this brand of 'islander-oriented' history represents 'the islands' ruling class ideology dressed up under another guise'.
[14] Meleisia & Schoeffel 1984 : 94-5, 103.
[15] Furnivall 1948. Important contributions to the debate include Smith 1965; Kuper & Smith (eds) 1969; Rex 1959 and 1971 : 401-13; van den Berghe 1967; Cross 1971 : 477-94; Kuper 1971 : 594-607; Leftwich, 1974 : 125-85.
[16] Exponents of the 'protectionist' thesis include Scarr 1984; Macnaught 1982; Legge 1958; Gillion 1962 & 1977; Ali 1980; Watters 1969; and Knapman 1987.

the notion of 'paramountcy of Fijian interests'. Durutalo points out that such 'paramountcy' is used in 'an implicitly ethnicist sense in an attempt to consciously or unconsciously avoid the issue of class analysis, especially the emergence of and struggle between social classes within Fijian indigenous society itself'.[17] Together, pluralist and protectionist theories have enjoyed a persuasive allure, making it little wonder that there should be no more than an inchoate literature on the development of a Fijian (wage-earning) labouring or working class.

Misconceptions about the nature of Fiji's traditional social relations and the impact of colonialism have therefore continued to enjoy a high profile in the literature. The substance and effects of early colonial land and labour policies are prominent among these misconceptions. In general, Fijians have been portrayed as a homogeneous group of comfortable landowners basking in 'affluent subsistence', and under little, if any, compulsion to take on wage employment: a kindly fate attributed to enlightened imperial management. They have been generally ignored as an agricultural or industrial work-force because of the belief that conditions for capitalist class formation did not really exist.

To be sure, Fiji's early experience of imperialism was uncharacteristic in some respects. Land dispossession did not occur on a large scale, and labour for the capitalist economy established an early reliance on imported Melanesian and Indian workers. The procurement of indigenous reserves under short-term contract did not necessarily lead to or derive from severed ties with the land. In the mining industry the transformation of a migrant and unstable labour system into a permanent settlement of proletarianised workers was slow; and there were, for many years, fluctuations in the regional distribution of labour, suggesting that mineworkers enjoyed a measure of economic independence. Indeed, dependence on employment at the mines was neither uniformly established nor consistently maintained at least until much later in the colonial period.

Against this, however, there is ample evidence to discredit the protectionist thesis and its implied apology for the colonial experience. The Fijian link with the land was by no means universally secure; and movement to the mine, like other, labour markets was not nearly as circumscribed a process as official sources (and the 'protectionist' school) would have us believe. The 'protectionist' principles of nineteenth and early twentieth-century colonial policy at no stage precluded the utilisation of indigenous labour reserves. Nor did they really shelter Fijian workers from the punishing conditions endured by their Indian and Melanesian counterparts. Together, these different sources of labour shared the common fate of bonded service under annual contract. They were collectively subject to the regulation of coercive labour laws, including the infamous Masters and Servants Laws. As in other parts of the British Empire, these laws were supported by the most virulent of penal sanctions.[18]

Economic pressures associated with intruding capitalist forces provided a major impetus to Fijian labour migration during the colonial period. Despite state controls

---

[17]   Durutalo 1985 : 126. Other critiques of the 'protectionist' thesis, including discussion of the pragmatic considerations that underpinned British colonial policy, can be found in Bain 1985 & 1988; and Sutherland 1984.

[18]   For more detailed discussion of the conditions of Fijian indenture and early colonial labour laws, see Bain 1988 : 119-36.

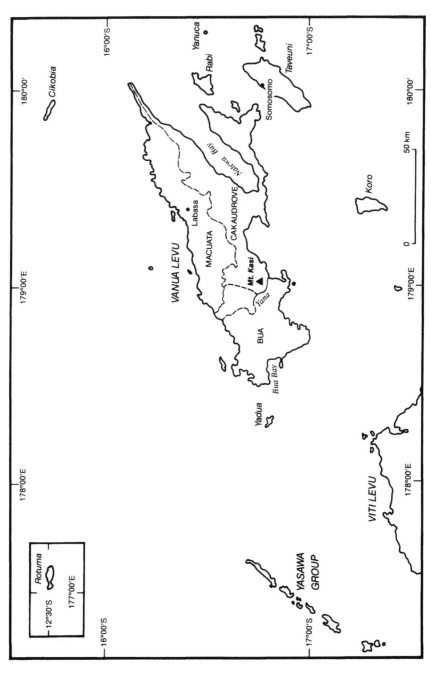

Pre-1945 provincial boundaries, Vanua Levu

on land alienation legislated in particular during the first Gordon administration (1874–80), Fijians lost the major proportion of cash crop arable to foreign interests. Equally significant was the compulsory production of a narrow range of export crops, which trapped farmers within the orbit of unpredictable international markets. The devastating impact of this typical feature of the commodity-producing colonial economy was felt in the depression years of the late 1920s and 1930s. By the formative years of mining, the uneven nature of capitalist development— in particular, its regional, production and infrastructural biases—was becoming increasingly visible, compounding the effects of (fertile) land alienation. An outstanding feature of the mine labour system was that it contained significant elements of economic as well as extra-economic coercion.

There were two early indicators of both the extent and consequences of Fijian incorporation into the colonial labour market. Within eight years of the establishment of colonial rule the numbers of Fijian plantation labour (about half of whom were indentured) totalled more than 4000, representing 25% of the able-bodied, indigenous male population. There was also a high incidence of village absenteeism. A number of factors, including over-recruitment and the failure of some employers to return time-expired workers to their homes, lay behind the depletion of village labour reserves. The impact was felt in serious disruptions to food production and other communal work, which ensured the sustainability of the traditional system. By the 1920s the problem had reached acute proportions, with the result that some districts were entirely stripped of their able-bodied men.[19] The trend continued with the onset of mining.

Social dislocation of this scale was not an intended consequence of colonial 'native' policy, but resulted largely from its contradictions. At the heart of these were the conflicting aims of meeting short-term labour requirements and satisfying broader political and economic imperatives. The state had to ensure its own reproduction and hegemony as well as the long-term reproduction of a cheap and abundant labour supply. Both were best achieved through the selective retention of pre-capitalist structures. Although official ideology projected the 'preservation' of the traditional social system as a philanthropic gesture, material conditions required the policy as a matter of expediency. In particular, some form of labour regulation was necessary if the political and economic costs of a fully proletarianised work-force were to be averted. Far from unique to Fiji, the institutional checks on proletarianisation along with their rationalisation have been a feature of many of the 'developing' countries of Asia, Latin America, Africa and the Pacific.

The migrant labour system sponsored by the state and inherited by the mining industry appeared to satisfy this complexity of needs, albeit with practical imperfections. The system sprang from the articulation of the capitalist and pre-capitalist modes of production, a relationship that accorded the former a dominant status and parasitic role. It prescribed for the indigenous rural economy an essentially *bantustan* function, permitting employers to pay less for their immediate labour costs and to evade reproductive labour costs for successive generations. As in

---

[19]   Bain 1988 : 134–5, 125, 129.

other British colonies where indigenous social formations were retained, this was possible because the village economy was expected to supplement the earnings of the single male earner and to support his dependants. Curtain's study on Papua New Guinea reveals useful parallels in the rationale and mechanics of the migrant labour system, as does the expansive trailblazing historiography of Southern Africa.[20]

The role of Fijian chiefs introduced a crucial dimension to the regulatory processes of the colonial labour market, and in the mining industry infused a feudal element into capitalist relations of production. The chiefs' position on labour migration was never one of unequivocal support or opposition, and their ambivalence reflected a continuous reassessment of the effects of labour withdrawal on the communal system over which they presided. With sustenance for the chiefly system coming from tributary and community-directed labour, the attitudes of chiefs were also influenced by the extent to which the labour demands of capitalist industry conflicted with their own claims.

Exercised sometimes unpredictably, the prerogative of chiefs to recall labour posed problems for European employers of Fijian labour from the outset. However, this apparent obstructiveness was matched by a willingness to collaborate with settlers and other employers. Labour for the short-lived sandalwood trade at the turn of the century, for example, had been supervised by local chiefs, who succeeded in establishing a degree of control over the trade goods exchanged for the labour services of their people. As with land, the greater pressure for labour that marked the transition to plantation agriculture in the 1860s had expanded the opportunities for accumulating trade goods, firearms, ammunition and money, and the control chiefs were able to exercise in the labour market. By the time of Cession to Britain in 1874, the bribery of chiefs had become a common means of procuring labour and, as the pioneering work of Peter France shows, chiefs were not loath to use direct force to raise labour quotas.[21]

Following the African example, set by imperial administrators such as Nigeria's Lord Lugard and Natal's Sir Theophilus Shepstone, colonial rule in Fiji paved the way for further and formal accommodation of the chieftaincy.[22] Chiefs were incorporated into the system as paid administrators, tax-collectors and custodians of the communal system with its inbuilt mechanisms of social control. As instruments of labour supply and control their role diversified, although in a rather more regulated way than before Cession. Chiefs acted as strike-breakers in the sugar industry and as sponsors of colonial suppression of populist movements such as the Viti Kabani.[23]

[20] Curtain 1984 : 117-41. Examples of the Southern African literature include Wolpe 1972 & 1975; van Onselen 1976; Marks & Rathbone 1982; Perrings 1979; Legassick & de Clercq 1984.
[21] France 1969 : 24-5; Ward 1972 : 93-5, 106 (n.3) & 107-8; Derrick 1950; 166; Chapman 1964 : 212. The role of chiefs as suppliers of labour for the sandalwood trade extended well beyond Fiji. See Shineberg 1967; and Moore, Leckie & Munro 1990.
[22] For the rationalisation of integrating traditional chiefs into colonial management in Nigeria and Natal, see Perham 1960 : 141 and Welsh 1971 : 22. More broadly, K. L. Gillion (1962 : 7) notes that 'The preservation of local customs and the utilisation of local political machinery are colonial practices as old as Ancient Rome or Egypt, for they originate in the need to maintain order and to win the support of the local population with a minimum of expense and dislocation'.
[23] Durutalo 1985 : 135, 141; Robertson 1985 : 159-60.

Incorporation, with its trappings of educational, financial and other privileges, its patronage and powers, gave the chiefs a vested interest in the colonial system, as well as making them accountable and subordinate to it.[24] By the inception of mining, the foundations for a collaborative relationship with mining capital over the management of Fijian labour were well laid. Significantly, the Colo interior, which was to furnish the industry with its first labourers, was coerced into accepting British colonial rule in the 1870s by a military campaign led by Eastern and coastal chiefs.

Certain features of the mine labour process in Fiji might appear to raise conceptual problems for a class analysis. In the first instance, the erratic and essentially transient nature of early sources of labour militated against the emergence of a Fijian proletariat in the full material and ideological sense of the term. The concept of social class is, however, a diffuse one, and, as Raymond Williams reminds us, Marx's notion of the economic base or substructure was never perceived as an immutable structure. Rather, it was a complex and changing process, which was intrinsically contradictory, a definition that could hardly be said to conflict with the early structural irregularities in Fiji's mine labour market.[25]

Similarly, as writers such as Rodolfo Stavenhagen, Harold Wolpe and Issa Shivji have shown, the orthodox conceptualisation of the 'working class' has generally proved irrelevant to the analysis of non-Western agrarian societies. In such cases the relationship between metropolitan capitalism and traditional (subsistence or redistributive) social formations may not necessarily result in the development of Western-type classes.[26] This is because the sale of labour power is not the only means available to the majority of people for obtaining subsistence. Yet, while the category of the migrant worker might not constitute a social class because of a continuing reliance on subsistence farming, labour is none the less sold in return for wages and in circumstances that are highly favourable to industrial capital.[27] Finally, we can draw inspiration from E. P. Thompson's emphasis on the 'historical' as opposed to the 'structural' nature of social class, a definition concisely portrayed in the title of his seminal work *The making of the English working class*.[28]

Like the absence of total land expropriation, the predominance of communalist loyalties among different ethnic categories of labour has also seemed to justify a rejection of a class analysis in Fijian history writing. The notion of a class-consciousness derived from and determined by capitalist production relations has been difficult to reconcile with social behaviour, industrial organisation and political alignments defined along ethnic lines. In the early decades of gold-mining, communalism was conspicuous as an ideological force, and ethnic cleavages undoubtedly impaired the development of class-based, even occupational, resistance.

---

[24] Nayacakalou 1975 and Durutalo 1985 : 138, 140, 142–3.
[25] Williams 1973 : 5–7.
[26] Stavenhagen 1975; Wolpe 1972 : 425–56, and in Oxaal, Barnett & Booth 1975 : 241–50; Shivji 1975 : 10–18, 1–9.
[27] Stavenhagen 1975 : 91.
[28] Thompson 1980 : 8.

But, as we shall see, the strength of communalism diminished significantly from around the mid-1950s, and even before then traditional values were increasingly displaced by perceptions and loyalties that were symptomatic of a new cross-cultural industrial experience. The protracted emergence of a class (or even an occupational) identity and class conflict does not, in any event, invalidate a Marxist analysis. In this context it is worth noting Williams's observations that by 'determination' Marx meant 'a process of setting limits and exerting pressures' for which people's activities rather than a pre-existing external force' were responsible; and that the consciousness or organisation of wage labour (superstructure) was not a 'simple reflection or reproduction' of the material base but 'a related range of cultural practices'.[29]

The story that unfolds below shares none of the romantic notions of the Pacific Way perspective. Quite the reverse, it suggests that contradictions, tensions and conflict were deeply embedded in the relationship between mineworkers and the Emperor group of companies, as well as within the Fijian social system, between mineworkers and chiefs. The primary source of corporate prosperity was, and continues to be, its labour force: the men who burrow into the bowels of the earth and the others, both women and men, whose productive and reproductive labour produce bars of gold bullion for export. Production relations between capital and labour were from the beginning based on exploitation and power, and as elsewhere in the colonial labour market, a system of racial and ethnic differentiation underpinned this. The system did not lapse with the end of colonialism, and among its many ramifications was the creation of a highly dependent work-force with a communal consciousness. Over all there would appear to be much to support Durutalo's general observation that 'capitalist exploitation and class domination in Fiji has depended upon the selective reproduction of communal (racial/ethnic) divisions in the political, cultural and economic spheres'.[30]

An important factor in the chain of exploitation of Fiji's gold resources has been the unique conditions of the international gold market, which derive from the metal's special value as an international monetary asset. While its monetary role as a means of exchange within countries has progressively declined, gold has long been prized as a store of value and as an international reserve. It still commands an investment value that reflects its widely perceived role as a buffer against inflation, financial crisis, political instability and instability in the national currencies that have served as international means of exchange and stores of value.[31]

The distinctive marketing conditions for gold at the time Fiji began production were based on the pricing system laid down by the 1934 United States Gold Reserve Act following the end of gold's convertibility with the pound sterling in 1931. Until the late 1960s this legislation fixed an official price of $US35 per fine ounce, redeemable from the American Federal Reserve Bank. Together with an 'unlimited market', this arrangement was beneficial to producers, at least

---

[29]   Williams 1973 : 4–5.
[30]   Durutalo 1985 : 132.
[31]   Aliber 1977.

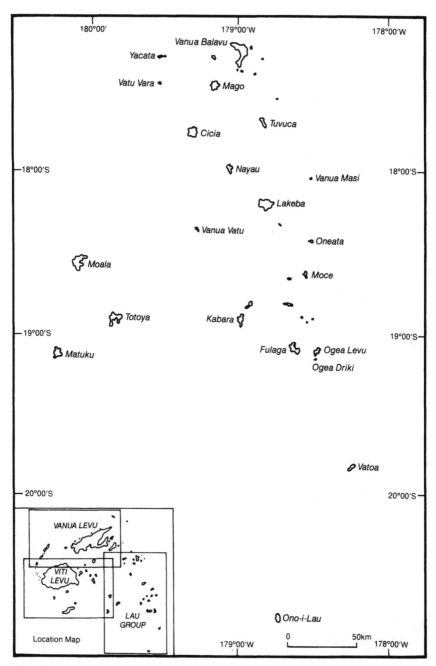

The Lau Group

in the short term. As Duncan Innes points out, it shielded them from the vagaries of the open market, guaranteeing a pre-arranged return irrespective of 'market fluctuations and restrictions'. An unlimited market meant that 'the threat of over-production did not exist, while the existence of a fixed price meant that capitalists could plan production on the basis of assured returns on the sale of the commodity'.[32]

But in the long term the shackling of gold by a static nominal price effectively meant a declining real value. It made producers particularly susceptible to cost increases because these could not be transferred to buyers. Rising production costs threatened profit margins and, as Innes observes, the special marketing conditions for gold therefore had 'contradictory implications for the future development of the industry' in general.[33] Compounding these problems for Fiji was the handicap of currency parities. With Fiji's currency tied to the metropolitan currency, sterling, a strong sterling in relation to the US dollar reduced the domestic value of its gold exports below the official price. According to Narsey, colonial currencies were generally depreciated in terms of gold from around 1932 as the Bank of England 'deliberately pushed sterling *downward*'.[34] This appeared to work to beneficial effect for Fiji gold producers, who enjoyed a steady upward price swing (in Fiji pounds) through the second half of the 1930s. The devaluation of sterling in 1947 brought an even sharper (31%) increase in the unit price for Fiji gold, followed by a further 16% rise after sterling was again devalued in 1967 (see Appendix A).

But, apart from these few spells of buoyancy, instability in the price for Fiji gold was minimal. Over the first 30 years of operations at Vatukoula, it rose by only 79% from £7 13s. 10d. in 1936 to £13 15s. 7d. in 1965. Cost inflation was considerably higher, the wages and salaries bill alone rocketing by 500% for the Vatukoula group between 1938 and 1964 (see Appendix B). The introduction in 1968 of a two-tier system for gold sales (which gave private transactors licence to deal on the free market) permitted much higher returns for gold, but the volatility of prices in the face of unrelenting cost inflation continued to erode profit margins. The small contribution to world gold stocks that derived from the operations of an Australian group of companies underscored its inability to influence world gold prices after, as before, 1968.

In such circumstances the stringent control of labour costs offered one of the most important means of countering the disadvantages of the pricing system as well as offsetting rises in other (particularly capital) costs. In the Fiji mining industry this became increasingly important as an economic strategy from the 1950s, as less profitable operations forced the closure of two of Vatukoula's mines. As we shall see, the gold price hikes of the 1970s and 1980s did not lift the downward pressure on mine wages and other labour conditions.

The examination of labour resistance in this study is premised on the dialectic of capitalist development and thus the conflicting interests of mineworkers and the Vatukoula mining companies (as well as the state). Hyman refers to this

---

[32]   Innes 1984 : 48-9.
[33]   Innes 1984 : 48.
[34]   Narsey 1988 : 301.

as the 'permanent and unbridgeable conflict of interest between workers and employers'.[35] While the relationship in the case of Fiji's mining industry has been complicated, even obscured, by ethnic contradictions, these derive largely from the nature of the labour process itself. Oral and documentary evidence point overwhelmingly to production relations as the primary source of conflict. This highlights the limitations of pluralist theory, which tends to confuse the outward manifestation of social conflict with its source or root cause, failing to recognise that ethnic tensions or violence are symptomatic of a deeper economic or social alienation rather than merely a mark of communal consciousness. As critics of the theory claim, the descriptive tools of the pluralist provide a static and superficial model, contributing little to our understanding of the continuously changing forces that determine the form and expression of social relations.[36]

Given that more than half a century of mining operations is under review, it is not surprising that the protest of Fiji mineworkers has changed in form, scale and level of radicalism; nor that company and state strategies of control have done likewise. Whether overt or covert, coercive or co-optive, the latter have generally been aimed at moulding a tractable labour force in order to safeguard the accumulation process. The post-colonial period brings this dialectical relationship into sharper focus. In this context the study shares Jeff Crisp's view that distinctions between 'political', 'industrial' and 'economistic' action by the working class represent a 'mystifying categorization of labour resistance'. 'Industrial' (work-place-related) or 'economistic' (wage-related) struggles should not, he argues, be tagged 'apolitical in either motivation or effect'. Since both are components of the struggle for 'progressive political change', they can be ascribed a political function.[37]

While the institutionalisation of industrial relations in Fiji following the Second World War helped to strengthen the controls over mineworkers, such mechanisms as unionisation and dispute machinery have not always succeeded in constraining either employer repression or labour militancy. Hyman states that 'trade unions do not normally seek to expropriate the employers, or employers to smash the unions',[38] but industrial conflict at Vatukoula has seen both extremes at different historical junctures. For the mineworkers, this has had a ruinous effect.

This work draws on a wide range of documentary and oral sources, addressing a number of questions that have a relevance beyond Fiji's own experience of mining development. One specific issue addressed is the role of the colonial and post-colonial state: a political structure reflecting the (sometimes competing) interests of capital and to a large extent the traditional élite. It is responsible for 'creat(ing) the structures of the underdeveloped economy at both the levels of production and exchange', which have underlain the process of capitalist class formation.[39] But no general labour study, even when confined to a single

---

[35]   Hyman 1975 : 193 n.
[36]   Walter Rodney's work (1977 a & b) on Guyana highlights the structure (and impact) of colonial relations that underlie communally articulated attitudes and behaviour.
[37]   Crisp 1984 : 12.
[38]   Hyman 1975 : 193.
[39]   Mamdani 1976 : 142.

industry, can hope to cover every aspect of the labour market and its broader social context, least of all exhaustively. The infancy of labour, and in particular mining, history in Fiji makes this survey especially prone to limitations.

Two specific areas have been only briefly probed. First, as an influential factor in the processes of labour mobilisation and control, the precise role of the church has not been assessed, largely on account of the limited written records available in the Methodist and Catholic missions. Second, while attention is drawn to the impact of the migrant system on village labour resources, its more lasting (structural) effects on social and economic organisation have not been investigated. The changing roles and status of women both within the labour-supplying rural communities and in the Vatukoula township itself are among the questions that could usefully be explored in future studies.

In addition, it needs to be noted that as a study of labour protest, this work places greater emphasis on the more visible and institutional manifestations of resistance or, as Cohen observes of early African labour history, 'the more evident forms of protest (predominantly strikes, unionisation, and overt political activity)'.[40] In his work on Ghanaian mineworkers, Crisp highlights two shortcomings of such an approach: the 'activities, attitudes and aspirations of the rank-and-file worker' can in the process be neglected; and researchers are encouraged 'to ignore the vitality of working class resistance in periods when trade unions and radical political parties do not exist, are banned, or have been transformed into instruments of labour control'.[41] Through informal exchanges with rank-and-file mineworkers, a deliberate attempt has been made in this work to tap the consciousness and actions of workers outside the formal boundaries of institutional protest. Undoubtedly, though, there is scope for more comprehensive treatment.

More broadly, in the absence of a solid body of social history on Fiji mining, there is a temptation to attempt a complete historical overview that brings the subject as much up to date as possible. The highly charged industrial and political environment of the country since the 1987 military coups acts as an additional pressure in this direction. But such an ambitious endeavour has its problems, not least the methodological one of juggling a collection of oral and documentary sources whose balance as well as type have inevitably changed over time. It is important to stress that while the time frame of the study extends to the threshold of the 1990s, research and analysis of Vatukoula's corporate operations are focused on the activities of the Emperor group of companies (as distinct from Western Mining) until 1983.

Lastly, this book has a purpose beyond contributing to Fijian labour history. In particular, it aims to share with those who have worked and lived in the gold town of Vatukoula an interpretative account of its past. It is a history that consciously focuses on the ordinary working lives, experiences and struggles of the community as much as it gives more abstract consideration to the mechanics of the labour market, and the intentions and consequences of state and company policies. All these aspects are, of course, interrelated, and their treatment is ac-

---

[40]   Cohen, cited in Crisp 1984 : 11.
[41]   Crisp 1984 : 11–12.

cordingly integrated. But this second purpose could broadly be described as 'political', the essence and rationale of which are perceptively captured by Donald Denoon: 'So long as people cannot relate their experience to the rest of the world, and cannot connect their past to the present, they cannot help seeing future changes as a set of strange and baffling problems.'[42]

In this would seem to lie the virtue of historical inquiry and reconstruction. It can only be hoped that what follows does justice to the obligation implied for the historian.

---

[42]   Denoon 1973 : 20.

1   Making and Managing a Monopoly 1930–50

Until the early 1930s Fiji's export economy was based on commercial agriculture. It was from the three primary cash crops of sugar, copra and bananas that the colony won most of its export earnings and generated other, domestic forms of state revenue. The discoveries of payable gold deposits on Vanua Levu in November 1929 and on Viti Levu in 1931 induced a radical change in the structure of exports. In 1934 two gold-fields were proclaimed at Tavua and Mt Kasi, and a third followed at Vuda in Western Viti Levu three years later.

Gold's meteoric rise to the rank of second export meant it eclipsed copra and bananas, though not sugar, as pillars of Fiji's international trade. This transformation owed its origins to the depression of world commodity prices that occurred from the late 1920s. While this severely dislocated cash-crop production, it enhanced the market value of gold; and for Fiji this was improved with the devaluation of sterling that occurred as Britain (and some other countries) left the gold standard in 1931. With the new gold-pricing system established by the United States government in 1934, the price of the precious metal advanced from $US20.67 to $US35 per ounce. The price spiral triggered a surging tide of mining activity, not least in South Africa, such that between 1930 and 1937 total world production leapt from 21,000,000 to 35,000,000 fine ounces.[1]

By the Second World War, Fiji's 'economic welfare' had become 'increasingly dependent on [the] gold industry'. In 1941 the colony produced gold worth £1,128,884 and, in addition to the employment of some 2000 men, gold contributed over £100,000 in direct (tax and royalty) revenue. The government derived approximately 10% of its 1943 revenue from the industry, most of which was used to finance the war. It was probably a conservative amount compared with earlier years, when nominal and relative values of gold exports were considerably

---

[1]   Sayers 1976 : 483.

higher, averaging as much as 42% of total domestic exports between 1939 and 1941. Gold claimed £5.5 million in foreign exchange earnings (compared with £8.3 million for sugar) during the war years, while state tax and royalty earnings amounted to £710,735. Tax revenue from the industry rose both in volume and as a proportion of gold earnings in the post-war period until the early 1950s (see Appendices C, D and E).

Industrial expansion through goldmining during the Depression offset the ill-effects of low primary commodity prices and market uncertainties, including rural unemployment, diminished national revenue and dislocation of the indigenous communal system. Apart from the attendant expansion of trade, shipping and domestic agricultural production, and the creation of a new source of tax revenue, the establishment of the industry promised to resuscitate the colony's ailing job market: to create employment opportunities for the hundreds of Fijians unable to meet either their tax obligations or the other cash demands (both communal and personal) of their increasingly diversified needs.

For the imperial government, another colonial source of gold was welcome. The abandonment of the gold standard did not diminish its economic and strategic importance. The persistence of a gold exchange standard for the United States until 1971 preserved the convertibility of dollars into gold, and upheld the dollar as the main reserve currency for Western countries, including Britain, after 1934. The sterling area that Britain established in 1931 in turn locked her colonial territories into sterling. Preparations for war with Germany from the late 1930s demanded that Britain acquire supplementary reserves of gold and, even when war had broken out, she was in favour of continuing production in her colonies where this was possible.

In the sterling area, colonial gold supplies became increasingly important as a means of earning dollars once rubber and tin production in Malaya were disrupted in 1942. They were no less important after the war was over, because of the huge debt Britain had accumulated to the United States, the continuing scarcity of dollars, and what Narsey describes as the US challenge to 'Britain's imperial preferences and colonial markets'. The Bretton Woods agreement, which reorganised aspects of the international monetary system in the wake of the Second World War, paved the way for sterling's return to convertibility with the US dollar in 1947 and confirmed the dollar as the most important international reserve currency.[2]

The role of the colonial state in the early years of Fiji's mining industry was as crucial to the emergent monopolistic structure of mining capitalism as it was to the relations of production and control. By contrast, in explaining the monopolistic tendencies of gold production, historians of mining in places as far flung as South Africa and Papua New Guinea have identified other factors as being more decisive catalysts. The geological formation of disclosed ore bodies, high development costs and the marketing conditions for gold have been prominent among these.[3]

---

[2] I am grateful to Wadan Narsey for drawing my attention to Britain's pre-war planning and post-war predicament as likely influences on the adjustments made to her colonial goldmining policies during the 1930s and 1940s. For quotation, see Narsey 1988 : 303.

[3] Johnstone 1976 : 13-14; van Helten 1978 : 2; O'Faircheallaigh 1983; and Innes 1984 : 53.

Although this argument may well be valid, there are empirical objections to applying it without qualification in Fiji's case. For one thing, the creation of a monopoly at Tavua occurred well before cheap outcrop mining was replaced by the large-scale underground mining of low grade ore, which required the economies of concentrated ownership. The logic of mining capitalism did dictate the early integration of mine management and control by the Associated Mining Companies of Vatukoula. However, rationalisation of this kind was only one, albeit a critical, factor in the historical process by which they came to acquire hegemony in the country's principal gold-field as well as an unchallenged monopoly in the industry at large.

The central argument of this chapter is that although several factors may be identified to explain the decline of competitive mining, the intervention of the state, both in response to a powerful mining lobby and by virtue of colonial (and imperial) economic policy, was fundamental. Official policy purposefully destroyed the competitive basis of mining capitalism and fostered conditions that would permit a monopoly from about 1937. It also helped to create conditions of extraordinary profitability for the Emperor group, although, as we shall see, the bonanza years of the 1930s and 1940s were more directly attributable to the group's production, financial and labour strategies. These were in turn decisively influenced by the group's capital structure.

GOLD FEVER: COMPETING FOR CLAIMS 1932-37

For sixty years before the discovery of the Mt Kasi orebody in the Yanawai district of Vanua Levu, cursory and sporadic prospecting of the area had revealed traces of alluvial and outcrop gold. Local folklore furnished the occasional tale of successful panning in the Yanawai late in the nineteenth century; and by 1908 the scale of prospecting activity justified the introduction of Fiji's first mining ordinance. In the district of Tavua, situated in the sugar belt of Viti Levu, the first reported discovery was made by one Baron A. B. de Este as early as 1872. Here, too, subsequent prospecting and geological investigations indicated favourable prospects for both alluvial deposits and lode formations. Not until November 1932, however, did an aged, peripatetic Scot and seasoned prospector, Bill Borthwick, strike the first payable deposit in the foothills of the Nakauvadra mountain range eight miles inland from Tavua.[4]

These two discoveries at the height of the Depression placed the colony on the threshold of unprecedented industrial development. Discoveries did not, however, immediately (or necessarily) translate into viable industries, and the scarcity of finance and technical expertise, by no means peculiar to Fiji, paved the way for the early intervention and high profile of large-scale foreign capital. The Tavua case encapsulated this trend. The initial grubstaking of Borthwick by a local (European) hotelier and property-owner with no real background in mining soon conceded to the Emperor group, astutely marshalled by Edward G.

---

[4] Details of Borthwick's background, prospecting accomplishments and destitute lifestyle following his discovery can be found in Bain 1985 : 122 n.5.

Theodore. Just as the 'small-scale digger was the key figure in the winning of the precious metal' in South Africa,[5] Borthwick's strike was to lead to the historic discovery of the Emperor, Loloma and Dolphin mines. It generated little in the way of personal fortune and a good part of his remaining life was spent in isolation and penury.

In the competitive scramble for gold in the Yanawai after 1929, a number of physical, climatic and geological characteristics of the Yanawai field posed obstacles even for large mining concerns. Prospecting and mining activities were hazardous and more costly than in other parts of the colony, for the field was situated a few miles inland in inaccessible country some 1300 feet above sea-level. It was subject to high rainfall throughout the year, and equipment and machinery had to be transported by boat to the river mouth and hauled by tractor upstream through thick forest to the mine site. The low grade composition of the Mt Kasi ore (averaging 4/5 dwt/ton) and the shallow nature of its lode formation compounded the high cost of sustained activity.

The entry of Australian capital in the early 1930s brought with it a collection of well-known, even controversial or dubious, personalities. The redoubtable 'Red Ted' Theodore, one-time Labor Premier of Queensland and Federal Treasurer of Australia, was to make the most important single impact on the development of Fiji mining. Theodore's interest in Australian mining was longstanding; but his most publicised association with it had been unravelled as the somewhat sordid Mungana affair of 1930–31. The collapse of his political career led him into successful business exploits, notably the establishment with Frank Packer of Consolidated Press of Australia in 1932. This, together with his mining venture in Fiji from 1933, represented the culmination of his career. The nickname 'Red Ted', earned for Theodore's active participation in the Queensland labour movement, sat uneasily as he proceeded to construct a financial empire, to dominate Fiji's goldmining industry and to maintain a powerful and lucrative position as managing director of the Associated Mining Companies of Vatukoula. His appointment by the (Australian) Commonwealth Government as Director-General of Allied Works during the Second World War largely restored his reputation. Nevertheless, by the time he became 'the mystery man of Fiji' the charge that he had 'lost touch with the working class' seemed quite plausible.[6]

As a giant of Australian journalism, Packer's career was hardly less controversial. As one leading paper commented, he often seemed to be 'a caricature of the unreconstructed nineteenth century capitalist; robber baron and press baron rolled into one'. With his strong anti-labour sentiments, his 'substantial' influence within 'non-labour political circles' and his reputation as a 'buccaneer businessman',[7]

[5] Richardson and van Helten 1982 : 77.
[6] The description of Theodore as 'the mystery man of Fiji' is given in the *Sydney Morning Herald* (SMH) 5 Sept. 1945. The charge that he had 'lost touch' with the Australian working class was levelled by the left wing of the Queensland labour movement and cited in Murphy 1978 : 326. For biographical background and details of the Mungana Affair, see Murphy 1978 : 293-340. The Queensland newspapers also give blow-by-blow accounts of the Mungana court hearings, in which the Crown charged Theodore and three others, including former Premier of Queensland William McCormack, with 'conspiracy, causing damage to the estate of our Lord the King'. See *Queenslander* 30 July 1931, 3 March & 7 April 1932 and *Brisbane Courier* 24 Feb. 1932.
[7] Frank Packer, 'Stormy Figure of Australian Journalism', *Canberra Times* 2 May 1974; SMH 4 July 1974.

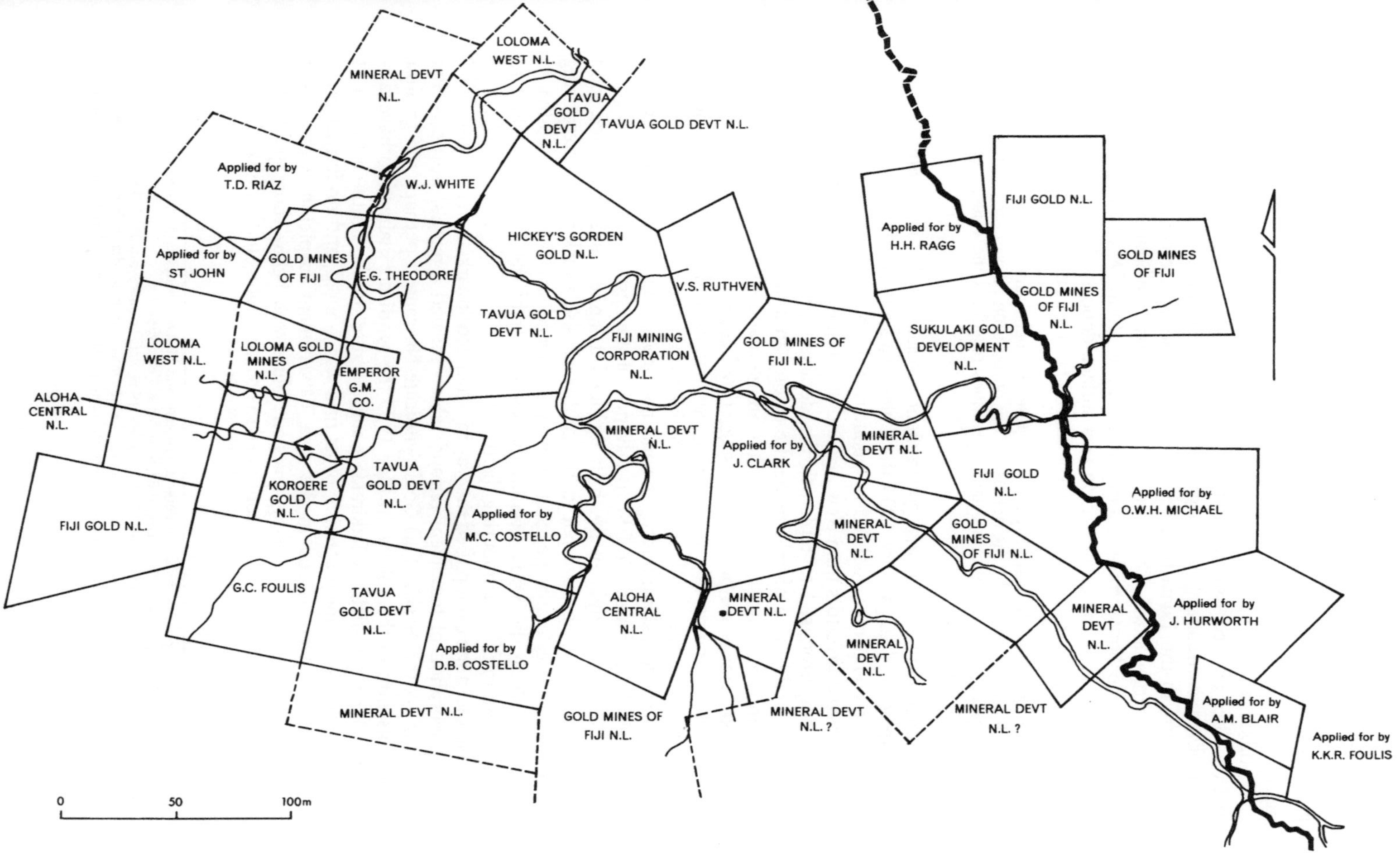

The Tavua gold-field, 1935

Map labels (rotated text):

FIJI GOLD N.L.
GOLD MINES OF FIJI
Applied for by H.H. RAGG
SUKULAKI GOLD DEVELOPMENT N.L.
GOLD MINES OF FIJI N.L.
GOLD MINES OF FIJI
FIJI GOLD N.L.
Applied for by O.W.H. MICHAEL
GOLD MINES OF FIJI N.L.
MINERAL DEVT N.L.
Applied for by J. HURWORTH
Applied for by A.M. BLAIR
Applied for by K.K.R. FOULIS
MINERAL DEVT N.L. ?
MINERAL DEVT N.L.
MINERAL DEVT N.L. ?
MINERAL DEVT N.L.
MINERAL DEVT N.L.
V.S. RUTHVEN
GOLD MINES OF FIJI N.L.
Applied for by J. CLARK
MINERAL DEVT N.L.
MINERAL ● DEVT N.L.
ALOHA CENTRAL N.L.
GOLD MINES OF FIJI N.L.
TAVUA GOLD DEVT N.L.
LOLOMA WEST N.L.
TAVUA GOLD DEVT N.L.
HICKEY'S GORDEN GOLD N.L.
FIJI MINING CORPORATION N.L.
TAVUA GOLD DEVT N.L.
Applied for by M.C. COSTELLO
Applied for by D.B. COSTELLO
MINERAL DEVT N.L.
W.J. WHITE
E.G. THEODORE
EMPEROR G.M. CO.
TAVUA GOLD DEVT N.L.
TAVUA GOLD DEVT N.L.
MINERAL DEVT N.L.
Applied for by T.D. RIAZ
GOLD MINES OF FIJI
Applied for by ST JOHN
LOLOMA GOLD MINES N.L.
LOLOMA WEST N.L.
KOROERE GOLD N.L.
G.C. FOULIS
ALOHA CENTRAL N.L.
FIJI GOLD N.L.

0   50   100m

Packer's close association with Theodore was a measure of how far to the (political) right Theodore had moved.

Theodore arrived in Fiji with a small party of miners late in May 1933 and in December entered into the first of a series of option agreements that were eventually to score control over the gold-rich area. The syndicate formed to purchase his interests in the Tavua field represented the formidable collaboration of four Australian personalities: Theodore, Packer and two Melbourne magnates with interests in the liquor trade, racing and mining, John Wren[8] and P. F. Cody. By the end of 1934 the confirmation of a surface deposit of extraordinarily rich telluride on Loloma had vindicated Theodore's faith and persistence.

> To sum up, I would advise you to acquire the necessary capital to develop this mine. It is, without doubt, the richest surface proposition I have ever had the privilege of sampling and must produce large quantities of gold if the values persist to any degree of depth.[9]

In October 1934 the colonial government proclaimed the Tavua and Mt Kasi mining areas, and in January 1935 the Theodore syndicate floated the Loloma and Koroere companies. Assisted by publicity of high values, these two developments attracted investors from New Zealand and Britain as well as from Australia. If goldmining promised to replenish the depleted colonial coffers, the steady rise in the world price of gold made the colony an attractive gamble to foreign financiers and speculators. A frenetic trade on international, particularly Australian, stockmarkets sent share prices up to staggering heights. Over the following year they spawned innumerable prospecting companies and syndicates, including several 'wild cat' ventures. All joined a veritable rush to the colony (see Appendices F and G) as reckless share-trading in some mushroom companies became evident in the sale of £1 shares for £30 in advance of any significant development.[10] Prospecting at the height of the rush included a limited and short-lived local component. As one observer put it, 'the gold fever' also struck some enterprising Indians who were 'madly pegging all over the place'. Indeed, they dominated prospecting along the Vuda river to the south-west of the Tavua field and to a lesser extent in the neighbouring district of Nadi.

The Mt Kasi mine exemplified the way in which stockmarkets were manipulated by the publication of fraudulent reports, which inflated a mine's prospects. But the 'salting' by the Nasivi (Fiji) Gold Syndicate NL caused perhaps the greatest public sensation in the colony. In May 1935 the syndicate claimed to have discovered a new gold-field at Rakiraki, a sugar centre on the north-east coast of Viti Levu. Its request for protection of its find was granted, and no further prospecting licences were issued in the area. Government suspicions were raised only after independent sampling revealed values well below those publicised. But the value of syndicate shares continued to rise, prompting further investigation,

---

8 The extent of Wren's political influence both in Victorian and Federal politics is discussed in Hardy 1975, and McConville 1981. See also *SMH* 24 Dec. 1983, 9 Jan. & 26 Feb. 1984.

9 Report by T. R. Victor, Loloma Gold Mines NL, Fiji, 13 Dec. 1934, Vat./Loloma Syndicate 1934-35.

10 Details of share trading speculation and mine 'salting' during the gold rush are drawn from the annual reports of the Mining Board, confidential government reports, and correspondence files of the Melbourne Stock Exchange. Also see Dunkin 1947-48 : 384.

which eventually confirmed the falsity of reported values.

The gold rush proved mercurial, with a sharp rise and fall in the number of prospecting rights and licences issued between 1934 and 1937. After peaking in August 1935 the 'phase of feverish speculation' and associated prospecting activity receded abruptly. A confidential despatch to the Secretary of State for the Colonies from the Governor, Sir Murchison Fletcher, captured the change in atmosphere:

> The general position may perhaps be described as one of suspended animation. The feverish excitement of the summer has been replaced by a feeling of uncertainty, if not of depression, and during the past three months share prices, which had been forced to ridiculous figures, have fallen by some £3,000,000 . . . it is all to the good that the brief spell of wild speculation has been followed by a return to sanity.[11]

By the end of 1937 there were only five companies with producing mines or actively engaged in prospecting. The major activities in the Tavua area were restricted to the four mines owned and directed by the Theodore group, although these were operated by separate companies. All mining leases, apart from a 30-acre block retained by Borthwick's grubstaker, Pat Costello, and managed by another Australian company, Aloha Central, were held by what became known as the 'magic circle'. Similarly, the Mt Kasi mine remained for its brief lifetime under the control of a single Australian group, the only interest to hold a mining lease on the Yanawai field. Other companies either ceased to operate or withdrew from the area.

The decline in competitive exploration and the hegemony attained by the Emperor group over the most profitable proven lode formations cannot be explained simply by the latter's superior capitalisation, its rationalisation of joint production (which did not take effect until the late 1930s) or the failure of other ventures to find payable deposits or to overcome the topographical or climatic difficulties. The close alignment of state objectives with the interests of large-scale mining concerns and the sustained representation that Theodore achieved for his companies provided the vital impetus to the foundation of monopolistic conditions.

THE LAND QUESTION

With the expansion of mineral discoveries and exploitation in Britain's empire, the ownership of mineral wealth emerged as a crucial but delicate question, shrouded in political calculations and engineering that were generally of doubtful propriety. Britain's wish to lay claim to the ownership of her colonies' subterranean wealth was particularly complicated by the fact that surface land-rights had been vested in traditional owners. Fiji and the Gold Coast were among those mineral-producing colonies where this problem arose. In these cases the imperial ideology of protectionism, supported to some extent by the 'generous' if expedient pres-

---

[11]   CSO/confidential file.

ervation of indigenous land-rights, appeared to be seriously compromised by a mining policy that was emphatically expropriative.

Within the Colonial Office the drive for ownership was justified on a number of questionable grounds: considerations such as state expenditure on infrastructural development and the need to regulate mineral concessions and exploitation. In addition the case rested spuriously on more explicit 'protectionist' sentiments. For Lord Hailey (one-time Commissioner of the Southern African High Commission Territories), state ownership of minerals in the many colonies bound by communal land-tenure systems was deemed the only way of checking the 'profligate' tendencies of indigenous élites who failed to exercise responsibly their control over the disposal of royalty income. He cited the Gold Coast as a case in point, where the 'most unhappy consequences' had resulted from the large-scale mineral concessions granted by the native owners. By the early 1940s the Crown had established sovereign rights over mineral wealth in only some colonies, including Kenya, Tanganyika, Uganda, Nyasaland and Fiji. In other colonies, such as Malta, Cyprus, Jamaica (in respect of base metals) and the Gold Coast, private and corporate interests or native landowners enjoyed partial or exclusive claim to mineral rights and/or royalties. In certain parts of the Gold Coast, mineral rights were 'jealously guarded' by native landowners.[12]

In 1944 the Minerals Sub-Committee of the London-based Colonial Economic Advisory Committee stressed the desirability of mineral rights being uniformly vested in the Crown. Its proposals were twofold: that mineral rights be reserved for the Crown first 'in any *future* alienations of Crown or public land' and second over 'land *already* alienated or otherwise not held by the Crown' (my emphasis). The second instance was recognised to be politically contentious and likely to require 'private negotiation' or 'legislation' with the possibility of compensation. Addressing the House of Lords in 1945, the Secretary of State for the Colonies, the Duke of Devonshire, acknowledged that 'It would obviously be entirely contrary to the principles of equity for such a re-acquisition to be made without compensation'. Ultimately, the main challenge facing the imperial and colonial governments was how the Crown could, at minimum cost, acquire and safeguard mineral rights over which it laid perfidious claim.

Questions of cost and political sensitivity or impropriety did not prove unduly deterring. Compensation to private holders, it was argued, could be minimal where little or no mining was under way. Conveniently, outside British Guiana, Trinidad and the Gold Coast, the absence of mining activities was the general rule in Britain's colonies. The Crown could, it was conceived, possibly get away without paying any compensation in those territories 'where minerals have not been worked, and where there has been no reason to suspect their existence'. In those colonies where 'political reasons' looked likely to obstruct the ideal formula of uncompensated dispossession, a 5% stake in government royalties, 'more if political objections are insuperable', was considered an acceptable concession to private title-holders.

No such obstruction appeared to exist in the British Solomon Islands Protectorate in the Western Pacific. Here, following the discovery of payable ore, the absence of any recognised claim to mineral rights by the indigenous landowners appeared to pave the way for a straightforward and inexpensive purchase of the land by the state. For a mere £120 (or 2s. per acre), 'the usual price paid by the Protectorate Government to native owners for unimproved land', a total of 1200 acres containing rich alluvial deposits on the island of Guadalcanal was bought in advance of being declared a mining area.

Colonial Office mining policy in respect of Fiji had grave and enduring repercussions for indigenous landowners, with a clear contradiction emerging between land and mining policies, the one at least partially safeguarding indigenous land-rights and the other explicitly threatening them. Through the 1934 Mining Ordinance the dispossession of Fijians was sanctioned, thereby exposing the spurious nature of officially proclaimed 'inalienability' of land and Fijian 'paramountcy'. Alienation was fashioned on the inestimable wealth that would accrue to the colony and its people from mineral development, an argument that disguised the attendant deprivation of Fijian landowners. Moreover, state patronage or protection as expressed in the mining laws was conspicuously directed towards European landowners and mining concerns. Far from being protected, Fijian economic interests were subordinated to the specific needs of the mining industry and the general economic objectives of the colonial state and imperial government.

Ownership of the land at Vatukoula was hotly disputed. According to the official record, the area on which active prospecting began at Tavua was owned by the Australian sugar monopoly, the Colonial Sugar Refining Co. Ltd (CSR), and the Crown. Oral tradition told otherwise: that a local clan held claim to the settlement of Matanagata at the heart of the proclaimed field. A few years before Borthwick's strike, a group of five families headed by their chief, the Tui Nubu, had relocated their village from the hills to Matanagata on the coastal plain. The uninhabited area was, their descendants claimed, part of their ancestral homeland, and they had moved there 'to look for gold' under the stewardship of a controversial Methodist minister, the Reverend A. D. Lelean.[13]

The imperatives of colonial mineral policy and the rationale of colonial law could not accommodate such a claim to ownership, however legitimate. Accordingly, like its neighbouring village of Nasomo, the settlement was officially proclaimed illegal around 1930. A protracted legal battle validated the CSR's claim to the land and confirmed the status of the traditional owners to be that of mere squatters. Disinheritance did not lead to eviction following the beginning of mining operations, but instead to an offer by Theodore of employment and permanent residence. More significantly, it meant relinquishment of any claim to surface or subterranean rights, which of course obviated the need for further intervention by the colonial government.

It was in the Yanawai field, where Fijian land-rights were founded on a more secure and legally recognised basis, with a total of some 2000 acres of metalliferous land at Mt Kasi being held by the CSR and Fijian landowners, that legislative manoeuvres were required. Radical changes were effected to the 1908 Mining

---

[13]   For a profile of Rev. Lelean, see Macnaught 1974 : 14.

Ordinance in order to circumvent the costly requirement that any land needed for mining purposes (with the exception of unoccupied Crown land) be bought by the state. The controversial expropriation of Fijian land, which new draft legislation endorsed in 1934, was handled deftly. Under direction from the Mining Board Chairman, C. A. Holmes, the colonial government was urged to assume control of any needed native land by absorbing it within the conveniently elastic category of Crown land.

This strategy had the dual advantages of sparing the state the cost of compensation and minimising the risk of inciting Fijian opposition. As Holmes cautioned, the alternative of tampering with the Native Lands Ordinance would not only create an awkward precedent but was likely to be hampered by the landowners' refusal to surrender control. It was deemed political and economic sense to dispossess the indigenous people through the colony's mining legislation.[14]

In order to permit land alienation as mining leasehold, the legal provisions for state acquisition of land were drastically changed. Three mutually supporting clauses in the new ordinance endorsed expropriation of any land required for the exploitation of mineral resources. All precious metals and minerals were declared the property of the Crown; any land could be proclaimed a mining area by the Governor; and the Governor-in-Council could, without granting compensation for subterranean wealth, assume control of any land considered necessary for public purposes.

The administration was sensitive to the dubious legitimacy of its claim to 'ownership' of mineral wealth. Although it anticipated that Fijians would probably be ignorant of the implications of the mining bill (notably clause four, claiming all metals and minerals for the Crown), and would not therefore contest it, it none the less prepared for a backlash from the landowners. The prepared defence echoed the broad arguments of the Colonial Office: the Fijians had laid no claim to the subsurface value of land they had ceded to Britain in 1874, nor was there any record of their own attempts to capitalise its mineral wealth. Not so confident of the credulity of European landowners, the government contrived to secure an easy passage for the bill by other means. Under Fletcher's instructions, the unofficial European members of the Legislative Council were denied access to all correspondence and minute papers relating to the land question.[15]

There was another important change to the colony's mining legislation directly linked to the contentious issue of ownership. This affected compensation in the form of royalty and rent payable upon the alienation of land. By repealing clause 23 of the 1908 ordinance, which stipulated that royalty be paid to landowners, and instead allocating both subsurface rent (i.e. fees for mining leases) and royalty to general revenue, the state withdrew from Fijian landowners the right to any compensation for the exploitation of their mineral wealth. In draft form the 1934 regulations provided for the payment of 25% of royalty revenue to landowners; but pressure from the Legal Committee of the Imperial Institute—interestingly in conflict with the more generous policy advanced by the Minerals

---

[14]   CSO/confidential file.
[15]   CSO/confidential file.

Sub-Committee of the Colonial Economic Advisory Committee—seems to have influenced the decision to revoke this by the time the bill was in its final form. While local support for the concession remained, if only as a contingency against intractable Fijian opposition, imperial directives won the day. The only compensation was the payment of surface rent, which was already required by the Native Lands Ordinance in respect of all land leases.

The new ordinance struck another blow at Fijian landowners and in so doing helped to minimise the early production costs of the mining industry. Lease or licence holders were, without paying royalty compensation, permitted to clear land and utilise the timber resources of 'unimproved', unalienated (i.e. Fijian-owned) land. The concession was discriminatory, for it did not apply to holders of mining leases over 'alienated' (i.e. European or Crown) land. The colonial government had in fact already moved towards approving uncompensated and unauthorised deforestation of native land before 1934. Anxious to expedite mining development, it had extracted approval from local landowners in the Mt Kasi mine area in 1931 for a road to be built through their land. The telegram-conveyed bargain offered in return was a pledge that 'If mining operations prove successful Government will purchase mining area from owners for development purposes . . . Natives and Colony will benefit greatly by opening up of land as mining area.'[16] The 1934 ordinance proved the promise to be an empty one. The land did not have to be bought, and the owners received neither financial benefit from the proclamation of a gold-field nor compensation for deforestation.

A MONOPOLISTIC MINING POLICY

Political intervention also took the form of fostering conditions congenial to the emergence of an industrial monopoly. This was demonstrated above all in the systematic removal of smaller mining concerns that did not withdraw voluntarily as the gold rush petered out. The mining policy of the early 1930s principally sought to curb speculation and centralise administrative control. Fletcher's near-obsessive preoccupation with the problem of speculation reflected a firm belief that practitioners of the trade had no legitimate claim to the benefits of the prospector. A situation of rampant speculation had developed on the Tavua field, and the situation at the Yanawai was little better. Licence applicants adjacent to the Mt Kasi strike were regarded as mere fortune-hunters 'without capital, and it was evident that their intention was merely to acquire rights which they could later sell to the highest bidder'. Even Mt Kasi itself was associated with the shady saga of exaggerated values and manipulation of the share market.

It was the loss of 'legitimate' revenue that was considered the most undesirable feature of speculation. By 'transfer[ring] Crown property to Australian speculators', Fletcher alleged, 'men of straw without means or mining experience' were levying between 10% and 20% of capital invested. Accordingly, in 1934, he introduced the first of a series of initiatives designed to tighten state control over mining

---

16   CSO/confidential file.

transactions, insisting that future applications for prospecting licences in the Yanawai area be referred to him personally. A year later he brought in compulsory registration and stamp duty on all agreements. The vociferous opposition of European Legislative Council members, particularly those with personal mining interests, was defeated by the use of the official majority. It was a manoeuvre specifically authorised by the Secretary of State for the Colonies.

The centralised administration of the mining industry in fact extended to limiting the jurisdiction of the Mining Board. In policy matters the Board functioned only in an advisory capacity, while decisions over the issue of titles required the Governor's endorsement. In January 1936 Fletcher made an abortive bid to strengthen the powers of his office further by legislating for his appointment as Chairman of the Mining Board. Although the move was pre-empted by the European Council Members, the new Mining Ordinance enacted the following year awarded the Governor discretionary power of appointment of the Chairman and members of the Board.

Discrimination in favour of large corporations was actively promoted through various provisions in the mining law: the enormous size of the proclaimed areas (the Tavua field originally being 105,000 acres and the Yanawai 50,000 acres); the inflated fees and high capital requirements; and the large land-holdings alienated under prospecting or mining title. Colonial Office support for the strategy was unqualified. Indeed, it urged a policy of 'encouraging larger mining interests and gradually eliminating smaller interests'. To this end it pressed that small, speculative licences should be terminated on expiry and subsequent applications 'rigorously scrutinised'; that licences 'cover as large an area as practicable' and be confined to 'reputable and well-equipped companies'. The activities of the individual prospector were further curtailed by a recommended increase in licence fees.[17]

The effects were numerous. Huge single (prospecting) holdings of 500 acres were granted, while combined holdings over adjacent areas ran into thousands of acres because restrictions on the size of tenements could be circumvented by different members of a family or syndicate applying for separate titles. Two extreme cases were those of Whitehall Securities Co. Ltd, which in 1934 held licence over 2400 acres; and Mineral Developments (Fiji) Ltd, which at one stage held 14 areas totalling 6000 acres. Even Mineral's director acknowledged that this was 'in itself the size of a goldfield'. The raising of licence fees within proclaimed areas had an almost immediate effect. The majority of applications in the Tavua area were withdrawn, while some of the more persistent candidates found their requests rejected by the Mining Board.

Overall, the stringent capital requirements laid down after 1935 combined to make it more than likely that the small operator would be forced to sell out part or all of his title to a large company better able to meet the conditions. The 1934 mining regulations increased royalty from 1s. per ounce of gold to what the Inspector of Mines described as the 'iniquitous extortion' of a 5% levy on the gross value of gold produced. While this further penalised those running

---

[17]   CSO/confidential file.

on small profit margins or at a loss, regulation 79, empowering the Governor-in-Council to reduce royalty, was used to the exclusive advantage of the large Theodore and Mt Kasi companies.

Such initiatives were opposed in certain quarters of the colonial administration, notably by J. C. Grieve, Temporary Inspector of Mines (1935-37). They also drew vocal criticism from the colony's only English language daily newspaper, the *Fiji Times and Herald*, which represented European settler interests. Offended by official discrimination against the pioneer, the paper attacked the mining legislation for its assault on the small prospector, arguing that this had conspired to frustrate the industry's development. In particular, official policy had confined enterprise to the exploitation and development of the original discoveries. The paper struck a solemn note of warning:

> There is a saying that if one watches the pennies the pounds will look after themselves. Protect the prospector and his discoveries, and thousands of pounds for development will flow in of its own accord. Deprive prospectors of the just rewards of their prospecting and mining in Fiji will wither at its very roots.[18]

Nor were Fijian landowners oblivious of the discriminatory provisions of the mining laws. By no means passive victims, their access to information was, however, limited, and their challenge lacked the co-ordinated support necessary to make any real impact on official policy. In 1935, for example, a deputation was dispatched from the village of Navuso in Naitasiri to the Provincial Commissioner. Somewhat deferentially, it inquired if 'the interests of natives who owned most of the land in the Colony, were being watched carefully by the Government, in connection with the discovery of gold in Fiji'. The matter was taken up with the Mining Board, whose reply, inexplicably dated three years later, declared only that there were already 'adequate safeguards' for 'native' interests in the existing legislation.[19] The more controversial question of royalties was raised in a motion to the Council of Chiefs by the Buli Nadi, Rusiate Levula, in 1936. Significantly, this requested 'remuneration to natives in such cases where gold is found on their land.' Evidently the motion was defeated, for it did not appear among the formal resolutions that year.

It was little wonder that the larger mining companies did not share the antipathy towards Fiji's mining legislation. Pacific Gold NL in fact responded with alacrity, declaring that 'The Government of Fiji is to be congratulated on its promptness in taking action to protect the good name of the Colony and the interests of the investors'. Theodore also welcomed the legislation as 'liberal' in content and 'sympathetic' in application. A gratuity of £5000 made over to the government following the enactment of the ordinance was a timely gesture from his syndicate. Overall, the support of 'reputable' mining capitalists such as Theodore and Sir Colin Fraser, who according to Fletcher had declared that Fiji's policy was 'much sounder' than that applied in Australia, possibly explained the Governor's defiant attitude towards his critics. In August 1935 he confidently announced: 'I have

---

[18]   *FT & H* 6 Feb. 1937. See also *FT & H* 26 Jan. 1937 and Letter to Editor 10 Feb. 1937.
[19]   Provincial Commissioner Naitasiri to Acting Secretary for Native Affairs, 23 Nov. 1935; and Chairman Mining Board (Charlton) to Adviser on Native Affairs, 24 June 1939, SNA N50/16.

every intention of retaining complete control.'[20]

The colony's early mining policy undoubtedly helped to establish hegemonic conditions for the Theodore interests. From 1937, however, as Britain prepared for war with Germany, and more particularly after the Second World War, adjustments to imperial (and accordingly colonial) mining policy prompted a new phase of struggle in order to safeguard these conditions. The 1937 Mining Ordinance hinted at what was to come. In a decisive turnabout, the government declared its aim 'to encourage and assist the prospector and the "small man" by all reasonable means'. What followed were cuts in prospecting and mining fees, the introduction of various production incentives including the temporary remission of import duties, reduced assay fees and free technical advice, and the payment of subsidies to selected prospectors and small-scale operators. For the first time, a financial reward was offered for the discovery of payable mineral deposits. This unprecedented assistance to the 'small man' was now seen as crucial for the expansion of the industry. By 1940 it had resulted in a 'marked increase in the prospecting activity'.[21]

The change in policy brought Fiji more into line with other British colonies and dominions, such as Australia, where prospectors benefited from various forms of government technical assistance. Yet its sponsorship of the pioneer miner still fell short of territories such as Tanganyika, British Guiana and Southern Rhodesia, which extended direct financial aid (including small loans) to prospectors, small producers and those engaged in development work. In Southern Rhodesia a post-war scheme for the rehabilitation of ex-servicemen involved a state take-over of 'dormant mines', its purchase of machinery, and its provision of loans and training in mine management.[22]

From 1945 the Theodore monopoly appeared to come under more serious threat from the new trend in Fiji's mining policy. As a Labour home government prepared to review and adjust its colonial policies, the mining industry did not escape the net. The thrust of Britain's strategy for mineral exploitation changed radically from a policy of expediting maximum short-term production levels in order to meet the contingencies of the imperial war effort, to a longer-term vision of planned development aimed at lengthening the life of producing mines and thus enhancing the revenue returns to colonial coffers. Towards the end of the war the Colonial Economic Advisory Committee had argued the case against indiscriminate mining monopolies. Only in exceptional circumstances did it approve of exclusive concessions (that is giving one company the right to mine all minerals or all the deposits of a particular mineral). A general recommendation of a minimum 'dead rent' on mining leases, paid regardless of output and aimed at 'prevent[ing] companies from taking up more land than they are able or willing to work', backed this up.

---

[20] MSE/Prospectus for Pacific Gold NL; Theodore to Members of Loloma Syndicate, 26 Oct. 1934, Vat./Loloma Syndicate 1934-35; Address by Governor to Legislative Council, 1 Nov. 1935; Fletcher minute, 25 Sept. 1935, CSO F111/21.

[21] Prospecting licences granted for 1940 more than doubled those for 1939. For background to the changes and their details, see Mining Ordinance 1937; Leg. Co. Debates Oct. 1937; Report on Subsidies to Selected Prospectors, Appendix T CSO F131/30.

[22] Memorandum prepared by the Mineral Resources Division of the Directorate of Colonial Geological Surveys (n.d.) c. 1950 CSO F111/60.

In Fiji the Colonial Office was taken at its word, and in 1946, to the dismay of the Theodore group, the colonial government responded keenly to the interest of two Canadian mining companies, Pioneer Gold Mines BC and South Pacific Mining Co. The extension of the group's monopoly, including its bid for 3250 acres worth of fresh prospecting licences, was blocked on the grounds that it was likely to retard an increase in gold output and was thus inimical to national economic development. More directly, the Mining Board noted disapprovingly the group's tendency to 'acquire as much land as possible without increasing [its] rate of production'.

The appointment of Sir Alexander Grantham as Governor appeared to be a particular irritant for the Associated Companies. The Governor's decision to uphold the verdict of the Mining Board elicited an unflattering opinion from Theodore's right-hand man and general manager, Nils Nilsen:

> Although I get along very well with Grantham he would not set the world on fire with any original ideas and abides strictly to regulation red tape methods. He does not appear to have any guts and is just guided by usual Government procedure. Personally I think the Government here today is the weakest and most unrealistic we have had since I have been here.[23]

Far from dispirited, still less deterred by the obstructiveness of the post-war administration, Red Ted took the case direct to the Colonial Office. His submissions found favour with the home government, and the Mining Board was instructed to revoke its decision. The group won exclusive rights or 'protection' in the desired area for three years. For local mining officials, this overruling caused confusion as well as offence, not surprisingly, given that it demonstrably contradicted official policy. To Grantham's mind, on the other hand, the Secretary of State had simply been fooled. 'Clauson's letter', he spat, 'leaves me cold. He has been gullible enough to accept as gospel truth all that Mr T told him.'[24]

Other guidelines laid down by the Colonial Economic Advisory Committee proved equally vexatious. In particular, a new royalty formula advocated abolition of the flat *ad valorem* rate practised in Kenya, Nigeria, Sierra Leone, the Uganda Protectorate, British Guiana, Tanganyika and the Solomon Islands as well as Fiji. Along with Tanganyika, Fiji was a chosen guinea pig, and from 1949 a sliding scale of payment (tying royalty to the profitability of a mine) replaced the fixed levy, which calculated royalty as a proportion of revenue. The change was deliberately aimed at fostering long-term planning; at discouraging high grading and short-term profiteering; and at commanding a more proportionate return to the colony from the deposits of rich ore being mined, namely 'adequate compensation for the loss of ... irreplaceable assets'. In all these respects the policy pierced the heart of the production and financial policies pursued by the Theodore group in Fiji. Although Emperor, as a more marginal mine, stood to gain, the new system hit the rich Loloma and Dolphin mines, which had been quietly making fortunes for a small group of investors. Loloma's levy immediately rose

---

[23] Nilsen to Theodore, 14 June 1946, Vat./Correspondence EGT/NEN.
[24] Governor (Grantham) minute, 1 April 1946; and extract of a confidential letter from Sir Gerard Clauson (Colonial Office) to Sir A. Grantham, Governor, c. May 1946, CSO F111/4/145.

by more than 100% (from £13,479 to £30,185 p.a.) while Emperor's dropped by 42% (from £26,560 to £15,344).[25]

The Colonial Office guidelines were formally backed in a Memorandum on Colonial Mining Policy, published as a white paper in December 1946. This did not emerge without considerable debate and disagreement both before and after its adoption. As during the war, the battle lines were drawn between the Colonial Office and the Treasury, discreetly backed by the Bank of England. The royalty question was contested trenchantly, largely on account of fundamental differences in priorities. For the Treasury and the Bank the need to maintain maximum levels of gold output in order to feed Britain's dollar-earning capacity was no less urgent once the war was over. The drastic fall in colonial gold production from 2,500,000 ounces to 1,300,000 ounces highlighted 'the desirability of producing as much gold as possible at the present moment'. It dictated a royalty system that was more sympathetic to the interests of the more profitable mining companies working higher grade ore, a provision expressed somewhat more euphemistically as 'tax easement on higher production'.

Both the Bank and the Treasury strongly opposed the alternative formula optimistically advanced by the Colonial Office for uniform adoption in its colonies. One of its aims, to promote the mining of low-grade ore, was particularly disputed as a strategy for long-term development. The proposed formula, like the concession system in the Gold Coast, was, they claimed, destined to subvert rather than achieve this objective. For although it might assist low-grade mines and encourage the development of new mines, it would work against the 'economic exploitation' of the higher-grade mines, given the general inclusion of low-grade ore in their reserves. Paradoxically, it could well invite mining companies to deliberately retard their production levels (and thus profits) in order to circumvent the higher royalty levies. In the final analysis the main bone of contention for the Treasury was that royalty based on profits was obstructive to increased production of high-grade ore and would thereby 'cut across the need for stepping up output in the immediate future'.[26] In Fiji, these cautionary words proved almost prophetic.

The protest of the Emperor group was loud and unrelenting against a system of 'double taxation' that placed local mining 'on a comparable basis with the South African colonies'. The companies' counter-demand was not only for retention of the old system, but also for a reduction in the royalty rate from 5% to 3%. Even after the Colonial Office had rejected their call for legislative repeal, they appealed in both the Legislative Council and Executive Council, ably represented by several European members, including Sir Hugh Ragg, who had his own mining interests. Management did not itself withdraw from the front line, and with Nilsen at the helm was able to set up discussions with senior government officials, including the Colonial Secretary, the Acting Governor and the Governor.

Nilsen was no diplomat and his dealings with the government were, as usual, marked by ultimatums. In early 1950 he advised the administration that, due to such onerous taxation, Emperor would be 'compelled' to abandon its plans

---

[25] Royalty was assessed at 1.5% of total revenue where (profit) yield did not exceed 12.5%, and at 12% where the yield was more than 12.5% (plus 0.25% of each 1% by which it exceeded 12.5%).
[26] Kahn to Eastwood, 30 July 1947, PRO CO 852/950/1.

for prospecting outside Vatukoula. He continued through the following decade to talk of 'putting pressure on the government', perceiving the prudence of raising the spectre of a complete close-down whenever the group sought financial favours. While irritating to officials, the belligerent manner and bull-dozing technique of 'Bruiser', as he was aptly nicknamed, proved a successful combination. Certainly, the later successes of the mining lobby in the royalty battle owed much to his personal efforts.

MERCHANTS AND MINERS: POLITICAL ALIGNMENTS AND AGENTS

The transition from competitive to monopolistic conditions occurred in just a few years. The speed and success owed much to the working relationship between the colonial state and mining capital. Undoubtedly the Associated Companies were well represented by their own men, Theodore and Nilsen most notably. But in the years before the war the mining lobby functioned with remarkable agility under the management of a small caucus of prominent Europeans with diverse business interests and political influence: men such as Sir Maynard Hedstrom, Sir Henry Scott, and, to a lesser extent, Robert Crompton and Sir Henry Marks.

The growth of the goldmining industry offered the Australian merchant companies that dominated Fiji's commercial sector—Morris Hedstrom, Burns Philp and W. R. Carpenter—opportunities for expanded trade and shipping. A township at Tavua to service the mining community drew their retail market into a previously unpenetrated part of the colony. In the wake of the Depression the volume and range of imported plant, equipment and materials offered a welcome boost for Morris Hedstrom. The company was appointed shipping and forwarding agent for the Theodore group in 1935; hired to transport Fijian contract labour from the outer islands; and granted monopoly trading rights in the mining town. As Hedstrom acknowledged, the commercial relationship between Morris Hedstrom and the mining companies was a close one with the latter being important customers.[27] To similar advantage, Burns Philp acted as agent for the Vatukaisia Company (forerunner to Mt Kasi Mines Ltd) in the Yanawai.

This mutuality of interests was bolstered by a shared employment strategy aimed at discouraging the 'unfriendliness' of competing for or 'stealing' labour. On invitation, the Theodore group joined Morris Hedstrom, Burns Philp and other firms in an informal agreement not to poach each other's skilled workers. Such interference with the market had decided advantages: it inhibited the mobility and undermined the bargaining power of a crucial section of the labour force otherwise, by virtue of its scarcity, able to command competitive wages.

The political influence of the 'small handful of legal and commercial obligarchs' (or the 'Big Four' as they were caricatured by Colonial Secretary Juxon Barton) was well established. The first impressions of Governor Sir Arthur Richards in

---

[27]   J. M. Hedstrom to Theodore, 26 March 1933, Vat./Emperor General Correspondence March–Dec. 1935.

1937 conveyed strong disapproval of the 'stranglehold' they had successfully maintained over the colony for some 20 years.

> As I begin to settle down here things take on a more solid shape. It is a peculiar Colony—*sui generis* indeed. The presence of a resident European population, their long isolation from the world and the limitation even of recent contacts to NZ & Australia has bred a particular insularity of its own. A few big men have obtained a stranglehold of the place—they have won their way to the top and mean to stay there. The under-dog is under-paid and powerless. A few men control everything behind the scenes and even Govt has been run with a strong bias.[28]

Sir Maynard Hedstrom and Sir Henry Marks were both large landowners and closely associated with the Morris Hedstrom firm, Hedstrom as its founder and managing director and Marks as a principal shareholder and director. Marks was founder and head of the merchant company Henry Marks & Co. Ltd, which had been taken over by Morris Hedstrom in 1920. A 'very able and quite unscrupulous' man, as he was described by Barton, Hedstrom had various other merchandise and shipping interests, while Marks, as a landlord in the capital, enjoyed a significant income from 'rack renting his wretched wood and iron hovels'. Sir Henry Scott's political career was complemented by a flourishing legal practice, although it was alleged he had never passed a law examination. He made 'his money out of land deals, money lending transactions and Indian litigation'.[29] In his legal capacity, he represented Hedstrom, Marks and the CSR. A longtime resident, Robert Crompton was another director of Morris Hedstrom and as a practising lawyer represented Hedstrom and Marks as well as the company.

The close business association of Hedstrom, Scott and Crompton was strengthened by social ties and intermarriage between the Hedstrom and Crompton families. Apart from the many years that they had served as members of the Legislative Council, their influence on colonial policy was assured by appointment to the Executive Council and Crompton's part in drafting the early mining legislation. Scott was not nominated to the Legislative Council after 1937, but won an elected seat and remained until 1939 an unofficial member of the Executive Council, 'a suitable place for the Emeritus Professors of the art of political log-rolling'.[30] Together, the four men posed a formidable cabal, which guaranteed for the dominant merchant and agricultural concerns command over the direction and character of official policy: 'They have their differences, they have them still,' Barton quipped in 1938, 'but collectively they worked together and I doubt

---

[28] Colonial Office Dawe to Boyd minute, 24 April 1937, CO83/218/85197.
[29] Juxon Barton (CS) Extract, 1 Jan. 1938, CO83/222/85034. For outline of Marks's other business interests, see *PIM* 20 Feb. 1931.
[30] Governor to Secretary of State for Colonies telegram, 31 Jan. 1939, CO83/224/85197. Hedstrom was a member of the Legislative Council for about 30 years and served for nearly the same number of years on the Executive Council. Scott began his 30-year career in the Legislative Council in 1908 and his appointment to the Executive Council spanned some 25 years. He also acted as Attorney-General six times. Marks was one of the first European members to be elected to the Legislative Council in 1904 (also an Executive Council member). Crompton replaced Hedstrom in the Executive Council in 1934, was a fully fledged member between 1941 and 1944 and, among other legislation, drafted the Mining Amendment Bill of 1935. Details of the careers of the four men are to be found in *PIM* Feb. 1931, July 1933, June 1938, Nov. 1944, Aug. 1946, June 1951; Governor's Addresses 1 Nov. 1935 and 1 June 1956; the Fiji Government Civil Lists; CP No. 23, 1935; and Colonial Office despatches.

if in any small Colony there were such astute individuals. In short they terrorised the Civil Service, so far as I can make out, from top to bottom.'[31]

With the establishment of a mining industry, the mandates of Hedstrom, Scott and Crompton were diversified further, spirited by personal interests acquired in several prospecting and mining ventures. A director of three of the companies controlled by the Theodore group—Koroere Gold NL, Emperor Gold Mining Co. Ltd (EGM) and Loloma (Fiji) Gold Mines NL—as well as Pacific Gold NL, which operated in Tavua, Rewa, Matuku Island and Wainivesi, Hedstrom had, in addition, large shareholdings in a number of other companies, including Koroere Pacific Gold, Tavua Gold Development Ltd and Mineral Developments (Fiji) Ltd.

Scott, too, held a sizeable stake as director of four large mining companies— Tavua Gold Options Ltd, Tavua Gold Development, Mineral Developments and Mt Kasi—and owned shares in all of these as well as others, several thousand in the case of Mt Kasi. He had a number of connections in Australian mining houses, including Sir Colin Fraser, and in his legal capacity represented no less than 13 mining companies, including the Theodore group. He was probably the butt of Grieve's cynical observation that: 'One of the most profitable occupations in Suva since mining began, must have been that of the lawyer . . . I have been told the lawyers' services, also included expediting Government decisions.'

The speculative interests of Marks and Crompton were not as extensive but still significant. Marks directed one mining company, East Reefs Consolidated NL, and invested in a number of others. Crompton represented several companies including the discredited Nasivi (Fiji) Gold Syndicate NL, and held shares in Mt Kasi Mines Ltd, Mineral Developments (Fiji) Ltd, and Tavua Gold Development Ltd. His position on the Executive Council and contribution to the framing of mining law in the early 1930s would have made him an attractive 'investment', like Scott, for the many mining ventures seeking legal advice and favours.[32]

So persistent were the 'Big Four', especially Hedstrom and Scott, in bidding for political favours that Grieve suggested that they held the key to Fiji's 'strange' and 'unorthodox mining policy'. Fletcher himself conceded that Scott was well placed through his membership of the Executive Council to influence the government's mining policy, but Grieve was less temperate: 'all the errors which have arisen were caused by a series of unfortunate misconceptions of mines and mining, developed perhaps, by the intentional efforts of selfish individuals (unofficial) interested in the gold mining activities in the Colony'.[33]

Hedstrom's services to the Emperor group not only relieved it of tiresome formalities, such as licence applications, but also guaranteed it expeditious and generally successful submissions on such matters as tax concessions and (racial) job reservation. On numerous occasions he enjoyed private discussions with the Governor. Privy to government decisions as a member of the Executive Council, he was able to keep the companies closely informed of contemplated action contrary to their interests. In 1935, for example, he was able to intercept moves that could have cost the group dearly: cancellation or suspension of one of its

---

[31] Juxon Barton (CS) Extract, 1 Jan. 1938, CO 83/222/85034.
[32] The Melbourne Stock Exchange records and confidential files of the Colonial Secretariat contain details of all four men's mining interests.
[33] IOM to Chairman Mining Board memo, 23 Sept. 1945, CSO F111/21.

prospecting licences and a blanket prohibition on the cheaper consignment of gold by mail.[34]

Scott's long involvement in framing and interpreting local labour legislation was also put to judicious use as the group embarked on its experiment with Fijian indenture. His efforts surpassed Theodore's expectations. Save two obligatory improvements in the rations schedule and the provision of medical care in accordance with section 17 of the 1891 Labourers' Medical Care Ordinance, official approval was given for the companies to 'ignore the [stricter] provisions of the Fijian Labour Ordinance of 1875' and to recruit under the Masters and Servants Ordinance. This extraordinary concession did not have the support of the Mining Board.

State subsidisation of the early infrastructural development of the Tavua gold-field also owed something to the skills of Hedstrom and Scott. The case for a government wharf at Vatia, 17 miles from the mines, rested on the public interest it would serve and the tax revenue contributed by the mining companies, but, as Barton advised the Colonial Office, 'private interests' were paramount. The mining companies nevertheless clinched a respectable deal. The government undertook to construct (at their expense) a wharf and pipeline at Vatia and to build and pay for three miles of connecting road at an estimated cost of £5500. It was to hold a three-year option to retain or refund at cost price the wharf and pipeline; and during this period would be responsible for the maintenance and administrative costs of the wharf. The companies were not required to pay wharfage fees, and priority would be given to them until the government option was exercised.

The early capitalisation and control of the Mt Kasi mining venture testified to further links between merchant and mining interests. Although the overwhelming majority of shareholders in Mt Kasi Mines Ltd hailed from Australia and to a lesser extent Canada and New Zealand, the original prospecting syndicate that made the strike included four prominent staff members of the local branch of the Australian-owned Burns Philp (SS) Company Ltd. When in 1930 the syndicate was transformed into a public company, Vatukaisia Mining Co. Ltd, one of them, local manager Alan Mackenzie, was appointed a director. He retained this office when Mt Kasi Mines Ltd was incorporated and, together with another of the four, held a combined total of 8800 shares in 1935.[35]

Through the successive stages in its reconstruction, then, the foundation for co-operation between a principal mining concern and another of the large trading and shipping houses was secured. Mackenzie's appointment as 'agent in Suva' for the Vatukaisia Company consolidated the link and undoubtedly increased the financial benefits that accrued to Burns Philp. He became a chief spokesman in matters of mining policy and legislation, urging the amendment of restrictive clauses of the 1908 Mining Ordinance in 1931, and spearheading the push for

[34]   Hedstrom to Theodore Confidential, 7 June 1935, Vat./Loloma Syndicate 1934-35; Hedstrom to Theodore, 5 July 1935; Managing Director to Hedstrom, 2 Jan. 1936; and Hedstrom to Theodore, 8 Jan. 1936, Vat./ Emperor General Correspondence March-Dec. 1935; CSO/confidential files. For fuller discussion, see Bain 1985 : 90-3.

[35]   Details of the reconstruction, capitalisation and prospecting/mining activities of the Mt Kasi venture until its liquidation in 1948 can be found in the Sydney Stock Exchange classification M145; and CSO F111/56.

tariff reduction in 1932. With the formation of Mt Kasi Mines Ltd late in 1933, Scott's efforts to secure it favourable operating conditions, particularly through reduced customs dues and secure mining titles, came to match Hedstrom's lobbying for the Theodore group.

BONANZA YEARS FOR THE 'MAGIC CIRCLE' 1933-50

> Talking of gold-mining I cannot—make up my mind about Tavua (the Emperor and Loloma group). I suspect that it has no depth, that the values are not continued as they go down but tend to die away—in fact they are shaped like a boat tapering down to the keel. The reports are very clever and I have no doubt contain all the information which a mining expert would require for judgement. Theodore—ex Federal Treasurer of Australia and one of the ablest men in the Antipodes—is not such a fool as to suppress anything. Who runs may read—but so few can read. If the mantle of Elijah were upon me I would prophesy five or six prosperous years and then collapse. On the other hand the mines may prove the great success everyone hopes they will. In mining chance must ever play a large part, but I hazard a guess that on the information at present in the hand of Theodore their life will be short— if merry.

The capital structure of the Emperor group of mining companies was striking for its concentration of shares in the hands of a small group of business associates. Of the 1,900,000 shares issued to provide the holding company Emperor Gold Mines Ltd (EML) with a subscribed capital of £A950,000, 950,000 were distributed among the original partners and shareholders of its operating company Emperor Gold Mining Co. Ltd (EGM)—Theodore, Wren, Cody, Packer and a few others— and 900,000 were taken up by a Melbourne company, Wallace H. Smith & Co., which was represented on the boards of both Emperor and Loloma. The small balance of 50,000 shares, a mere 2.6%, was offered for public subscription.

Emperor's two sister companies shared the structural features of its capitalisation as well as a number of its investors. Loloma (Fiji) Gold Mines NL was financed on a more modest scale of £A206,250, but over 70% of its 825,000 issued shares was retained by the Theodore, Wren and Cody-based partnership; 150,000 shares were allotted to a group of London financiers through Melbourne magnates Messrs E. L. & C. Baillieu; and the 9% balance of 75,000 registered for the public on the Australian state stock exchanges. Until 1947, when it was reconstructed as a public company (Dolphin Mines Ltd) and Emperor acquired all its issued shares, the entire capital of Fiji Mines Development, which operated the richest of the three mines, was privately subscribed. Theodore, Wren, Cody and Packer together held about 80% of its 10,000 issued shares.

In the two public companies this concentration of ownership gave the holding interests considerable speculative advantages. Shares could be and were bought just prior to dividends being declared or sold at a premium in anticipation of a decline in profits.[36] The reconstruction of the Emperor interests in 1935, notably the incorporation of EML as a parent company to acquire EGM's 100,000 £1

---

[36] In 1939, for example, Nilsen brought 2000 shares in Loloma because the company proposed paying high dividends from the following year. Nilsen to Theodore, 6 Dec. 1939; and Nilsen to Theodore, 3 Jan. 1940, Vat./Confidential to 1940.

shares, also scored them an early windfall. Instead of a direct transfer of shares or capital between the companies, the transaction was executed indirectly by way of a dummy company with the unlikely name of TSP Investments Ltd of Singapore. The triangular exchanges enabled Theodore and his colleagues to make a handsome profit. As the Acting Commissioner of Stamp Duties wryly observed: 'It would appear that Theodore and Company have sold to themselves their own shares for £100,000 and bought them back from the T.S.P. for £600,000 the cash and shares being supplied by the Emperor Mines Limited.' Its mission accomplished, TSP went into liquidation, leaving Theodore, Packer, Wren and Cody to share out 95% of its £600,000 sale price.[37]

Yet inherent in a financial structure that minimised public shareholding there were potential difficulties in raising additional capital. This had important implications for production and financial policies, discouraging long-term planning, encouraging a high rate of profit repatriation through the payment of large and frequent dividends, and dictating the tight control of labour costs. As J. van Helten argues in respect of Wernher Beit of South Africa, the 'immobility of share capital . . . made it all the more vital that capital invested . . . should be utilised to its very utmost'.[38] The Emperor group's expansion into two ancillary industries during the late 1930s helped to offset the disadvantages of holding little mobile capital. The incorporation of the Tavua Power Proprietary Co. (TPP) and the establishment of a lime quarry at Tau (albeit some 85 miles from the mines) strengthened its monopoly on gold production and created sources of self-generating revenue through loans and cross-investment. Diversification through the provision of power, compressed air and water, and the substitution of expensive imported lime were also beneficial in reducing mining and treatment costs.

The speed with which the group pursued these initiatives was probably designed to forestall similar plans by others. Although abortive, the attempt by Sir Charles Marr to exploit local sources of hydroelectric power threatened to undermine the group's hegemonic position in the Tavua basin. A prominent Australian politician who had held key portfolios, including Defence and Home and Territories, Marr was a director of the two major competitors of Theodore's companies on the Tavua field: Mineral Developments (Fiji) Ltd and Tavua Gold Options Development Ltd.[39]

Another early consolidation of the Theodore interests occurred in 1938, when Koroere Gold NL merged with Emperor. Koroere was originally capitalised at £A150,000 and had among its directors Theodore, Wren and Hedstrom. The company's sale garnered for its beneficiaries £25,000 in 50,000 10s. shares in EML. Its early prospecting and mining operations had produced a low tonnage and a marginal grade of ore, which did not 'warrant(ed)' the capital outlay needed to install and operate a separate mill and to finance deep ground exploration. For Emperor, too, the merger proposition was a rational one, not simply because

[37]   Acting Deputy Commissioner of Stamp Duties, Memorandum of Mining Board, MR/Bunch 2 MB 7/136 Pt 1; Vat./Emperor General Correspondence March–Dec. 1935; CSO/confidential file.
[38]   van Helten 1978 : 7. van Helten (1978 : 11) discusses the economic advantages of diversification in circumstances where capital is fairly immobile.
[39]   For details of Marr's political career, engineering background and mining interests in New Guinea as well as Fiji, see ADB File 750 C3 Sir Chas Wm Clanan Marr.

of the economies of shared production costs, but because proven lodes within its leases extended into the Koroere area.

Once the Emperor and Loloma mines became established producers, the possibility of replacing 'joint management' by 'common ownership' was raised. A single mine amalgamating their leases and operated by one company promised many savings, including an end to the costly duplication of capital expenditure on plant and equipment. It would also improve managerial efficiency. The contiguity of leases was itself a reason for a merger, for as development expanded the underground workings of the two mines, the ore-bearing formations disclosed on Loloma began to encroach upon the Emperor lease. There were early signs of the reverse happening too. Yet the two mines continued under separate ownership until Loloma had mined out all its richest disclosed ore by the late 1950s, thus confining economies to shared technical expertise, senior management, some plant and equipment, and indirect labour costs, in particular community services. Dolphin ore was treated by the Emperor mill when it began producing in 1940, and ore from all three mines was treated by one mill from 1944. This went 'a long way towards giving some of the advantages of a merger', including a reduction in milling costs, especially for Loloma, thereby making possible the inclusion of lower grade ore in its reserves.[40]

Taxation was probably the most important single factor advising against complete amalgamation of capital before the 1950s. The 1940s saw a rise in taxation, peaking at 31.25% (or 6s. 3d. in the £) by 1945. However, during the 1930s rates remained relatively low, rising only from 5% to 7.5%. Even when the levy was doubled in 1941 (to 15%), Theodore admitted that it was 'comparatively light', and that it put local mining interests 'in a much more favourable position in the matter of taxation than most other parts of the British Empire'. The royalty system in practice until 1949 in particular encouraged capital diffusion because it was tied to gross revenue rather than to net profits. This was especially beneficial for the high-grade Dolphin and Loloma mines, which, though extremely profitable, received (declared) annual revenues that were relatively modest.

Dolphin was the most spectacular as a mine of small tonnage, but few overheads and very rich ore. At the peak of its production its total labour strength numbered less than 100, and from the beginning of operations until its reserves were mined out in 1954, it milled only 120,803 tons of ore. Yet these produced a staggering average of 30.67 dwts/ton and yielded about 166,455 fine ounces of gold. Loloma, too, was a rich though small mine, producing in its best years only about one-sixth of Emperor's tonnage and employing just a few hundred men. Between 1938 and 1945 it mined and treated some 200,000 tons of ore with an impressive yield of around 260,000 fine ounces. Its high grade of ore similarly compensated for a smaller throughput and for the heavier costs of mining at depth and treating sulphur-telluride ore. In the first three years of production Loloma produced ore averaging nearly 29 dwts/ton, and until the early 1950s when, in preparation for closure, it began to mine out its reserves, the value of its ore was consistently

---

[40] Loloma's operating costs dropped from 90/3 per ton to 49/11.8 between 1944 and 1945. Emperor bore most of the burden of treating its sulphide ore, treatment costs between Emperor, Loloma and Dolphin being divided on the basis of 10:2:1. See Annual Reports 1943-45; Vat./EGM Dept Memos 1941-May 1944.

high. Even when its head grade dropped to one of its lowest in 1953, it was still a handsome 21.07 dwts.

By contrast, Emperor's ore was low grade (averaging about 6–7 dwt/ton between 1935–50) but extensive. It was also predominantly oxidised and therefore amenable to the simpler treatment process of cyanidisation. Another deflationary cost factor was that until the mid-1940s its ore was mostly extractable by open-cut mining methods. In the first ten years of production (1935–45), the mine treated some 1,200,000 tons of ore for 380,000 ounces of gold valued at around £A3,800,000 (see Table 1.1 for production data on all three mines).

From the published accounts of Loloma and Emperor it is possible to get an indication of their profit margins. This being so, it should be noted that declared costs, tonnage, gold output and ore grades were not always accurate. For example, in order to sustain desired levels of profitable production, both companies pursued a policy of regularising their gold output, in Emperor's case at 4000 ounces per period. It is known that this policy was adopted at least in the late 1930s. It entailed the accumulation of substantial bullion reserves and the issuing of 'conservative' accounts of fine gold recovered and ore tonnage treated during the 'clean up' period before the end of each four-weekly period. As well as being legally risky the policy soon became an administrative headache with an undeclared reserve of 6000 ounces built up within the first year. By the end of 1939 a directorate decision was accordingly taken to reduce the reserve by treating lower-grade ore on both mines.[41]

The manipulation of production accounts was also achieved by artificially raising certain operating costs. This was done by EGM in 1939–40, for example, in order to avoid declaring a profit margin that had been unexpectedly boosted by an unforecast rise in the price paid for Fiji gold. The manoeuvre was proposed locally by Nilsen, but was endorsed by the company's Australian directors, who urged only that care be taken to inflate depreciation, mine development and the income tax reserve, rather than ordinary working costs; this because the latter's discrepancy with previous years might provoke awkward questions from shareholders. Management was also authorised to make any further (cost) adjustments necessary to meet the higher costs of production anticipated during the war; and to raise by 1000 ounces the output publicised for Loloma in Australia 'in order to bring in a little more cash'.

As the Australian government prepared in 1942 to limit profit distribution to a maximum of 4% return on capital during the war years, immediate plans were triggered 'to shape Loloma Company's policy in such a way as to show a net profit not exceeding £20,000 for the 1942–43 financial year'. In order to carry this out, all bullion produced to July 1942 was lodged in the previous year's accounts and only sufficient to meet running costs (including taxation) declared at subsequent four-weekly periods. Although the company subsequently decided to revert to 'normal production policy', the introduction of a Commonwealth tax on dividends paid out of Fiji mining profits and the expectation that sterling would be devalued, thereby improving the price received for Fiji

---

41   Managing Director to Nilsen confidential memos, 23 March 1938 and 23 Oct. 1939, Vat./Emperor General Correspondence Aug.–Dec. 1939.

Making and Managing a Monopoly 1930-50   41

Table 1.1 Gold output, value and profits, 1935–51
A. Emperor Gold Mining Co. Ltd (EGM)

Year	Tons of ore treated	Grade, dwts gold per ton	Gold ounces won	Value of gold output £ (F)	Declared operating profits (before taxation, depreciation, & mine development) £ (F)	Profit rates (profits expressed as a % of revenue)
1935 to 1937	60,878	10.85	29,989	233,077	(1936/37) 47,249	—
To June 1938	74,631	6.58	22,483	175,526	(1937/38) 113,259	—
1938/39	178,941	6.39	52,394	430,928	244,021	56.6
1939/40	165,214	6.90	53,375	499,908	314,024	62.8
1940/41	147,058	7.94	52,562	504,980	307,804	60.9
1941/42	123,181	8.62	45,721	433,582	237,647	54.8
1942/43	125,214	7.94	41,119	394,590	165,308	41.8
1943/44	151,499	4.15	25,736	245,163	57,056	23.2
1944/45	113,074	6.99	33,461	321,887	142,371	44.2
1945/46	149,155	7.61	48,795	468,427	184,366	39.3
1946/47	138,761	8.73	53,632	514,866	201,945	39.2
1947/48	148,370	7.76	55,417	532,482	156,040	29.3
1948/49	137,181	8.89	54,440	556,375	192,580	34.6
1949/50	137,386	8.73	55,140	683,346	333,468	48.7
1950/51	147,130	8.32	56,381	785,384	367,697	46.8
Totals/(average p.a.)	1,997,673	(7.76)	680,645	6,780,521		(44.7)

Table 1.1 (cont'd)
B. Loloma (Fiji) Gold Mines NL

Year	Tons of ore treated	Grade, dwts gold per ton	Gold ounces won	Value of gold output £ (F)	Declared operating profits (before taxation, depreciation, & mine development) £ (F)	Profit rates (profits expressed as a % of revenue)
1937/38	18,036	27.92	22,074	171,256	108,975	63.6
1938/39	27,767	29.50	37,208	304,975	208,426	68.3
1939/40	32,342	30.45	48,006	455,012	333,509	73.2
1940/41	33,308	28.15	45,150	434,217	309,823	71.3
1941/42	28,962	26.65	37,040	348,096	223,116	64.0
1942/43	17,323	21.47	17,748	176,345	93,011	52.7
1943/44	9,013(a)	25.37	16,004	153,513	80,293	52.3
1944/45	31,003	14.47	19,934	191,369	103,524	54.0
1945/46	12,410	42.91	23,046	221,241	137,838	62.3
1946/47	19,831	22.38	22,384	214,894	124,268	57.8
1947/48	19,405	27.95	25,042	240,491	140,640	58.4
1948/49	19,787	30.07	25,340	262,969	192,233	73.1
1949/50	19,384	21.56	24,652	304,592	197,297	64.7
1950/51	19,499	29.98	25,981	362,633	283,426	78.1
Totals/(average p.a.)	308,070	(27.0)	389,611	3,841,607		(63.8)

Table 1.1 (cont'd)
C. Fiji Mines Development Ltd (Dolphin)

Year	Tons of ore treated	Grade, dwts. gold per ton	Gold ounces won	Value of gold output £ (F)
1940	3,577	21.80	3,196	30,526
To June 1941	4,200	24.60	4,398	42,081
1941/42	14,597	30.05	16,706	158,066
1942/43	4,667	32.46	9,720	92,527
1943/44	1,996	37.40	3,585	34,396
1944/45	8,282	34.70	12,619	121,147
1945/46	8,916	33.90	12,379	118,838
1946/47	9,968	29.71	14,287	137,158
1947/48	10,194	26.84	12,980	124,620
1948/49	11,240	NA	18,735	203,918
1949/50	12,833	NA	23,904	303,851
1950/51	12,102	NA	17,128	238,968
Totals/(average p.a.)	102,572	(30.1)	149,637	1,606,096

Note: Data for June 1948–June 1951 have been estimated by taking an average of the figures for January to December of those years.
(a) This tonnage was for less than half a year's production, a restriction imposed because of the anticipated completion of the combined mill. The gold yield for 1943–44 was disproportionately high because Loloma had accumulated auriferous material that could be treated.
NA = not available.

Source: Vat/Associated Mining Companies Production Statistics to June 1948 and Statistics Relating to Activities of the Associated Companies from Jan. 1935 to Dec. 1964; Loloma & Emperor Annual Reports 1949–51 and Profit and Loss Accounts 1937–50.

gold, led to restrictions on bullion exports for Loloma and Emperor for some years during and after the war. The companies' comfortable profit margins made this possible.[42]

A key feature of the group's financial policy was the priority given to profit distribution over reinvestment in development and exploration necessary to prolong the life of the mines. By September 1941, only a year after it had come into production, Dolphin was in a position to propose the payment of four dividends amounting to £2 per share over the following financial year. Surging profits enabled returns to surpass even these expectations and an aggregate £50,000—comprising £30,000 in dividends and £20,000 in (£2) bonus shares out of a net profit of £68,120—was dispersed among 22 shareholders who had subscribed a mere £10,000. Remaining funds were used to help finance Theodore's goldmining venture in Guadalcanal in the Solomon Islands and to acquire an interest in TPP Ltd.[43]

The scale of distribution by Loloma was conservative by comparison yet still impressive. Like Emperor, the company early announced its intention to pay quarterly dividends. Between May 1938, when it declared its first return, and September 1941 it repatriated an aggregate £A660,000 in dividends. With the total face value of its issued capital repaid by 1939, Loloma's annual rate of return in the first five years of production averaged as much as 64% (see Table 1.2). Its fervour dampened to some extent during the war years by the disruption to production and the Commonwealth's tax penalties, it was significant that by the end of the 1943-44 financial year the company had distributed a total of £A701,250, a return of 17s. per 5s. share. Over the same period it reinvested less than £A200,000 in development and exploration. The average ratio of dividends to development as a proportion of profits between 1937 and 1944 was 42 : 12 (see Table 1.2).

Though Emperor was undoubtedly the poor relation of the three mines, its shareholders also shared in the boom. It was, the chairman of the holding company noted in 1938, 'no mean achievement' to have brought 'a mine the size of Emperor up to the dividend stage in a little over three years'. The company paid £A570,000 in dividends between 1938 and 1941, representing an average 15% rate of return per annum (or if the non-productive first three years are included, 8.5%). As a proportion of profits, this far exceeded the capital reinvested to expand the mine's ore reserves (see tables 1.3 and 1.4).

Another production strategy appeared to stem from the financial structure of the group: the mining of ore well above its pay limit or minimum payable grade. As the 'temperature chart' of mining policy, the pay limit was of critical importance to the economics of mining. It referred to an ore grade level that generated sufficient revenue to cover the range of costs intrinsic to the production and marketing of gold, including mining, milling and development.[44] A succinct

[42] Managing Director (Theodore) Memorandum on the Policy of the Company for financial year 1942/43 and other correspondence in Vat./Correspondence EGT/NEN July 1941–Nov. 1944; Minutes of EGM Directors' Meeting, 28 Sept. 1942, Vat./Emperor Confidential Feb. 1942–June 1944; Vat./Correspondence EGT/NEN.

[43] Vat./Fiji Mines Period Reports Finance, etc. 1940–42; FMD Annual Report August 1942; Emperor Annual Report 1941; other miscellaneous correspondence in unclassified company files.

[44] Wilson 1972 : 39.

Table 1.2 Comparative trends in distributed and reinvested profits Loloma (Fiji) Gold Mines NL, 1937–51

Year	Operating profits £ (A)	Dividends £ (A)	Dividends as % of profits	Rates of return to shareholders (% of issued capital of £206,250)	Cost of investments £ (A)	Development expenditure £ (A)	Development expenditure as % of profits
1937/38	122,597	82,500	67.2	40	31,000	24,427	19.9
1938/39	234,480	123,750	52.7	60	31,000	17,342	7.3
1939/40	375,197	247,500	65.9	120	31,000	35,002	9.3
1940/41	348,552	165,000	47.3	80	41,000	46,839	13.4
1941/42	251,006	41,250	16.4	20	74,375	40,728	16.2
1942/43	104,637	—	—	—	74,647	19,083	18.2
1943/44	90,329	41,250	45.6	20	176,918	—	—
1944/45	116,464	—	—	—	187,577	14,056	12.0
1945/46	155,067	—	—	—	211,892	19,069	12.2
1946/47	139,803	—	—	—	270,250	10,766	7.7
1947/48	158,221	20,625	13.0	10	664,408	20,419	12.9
1948/49	216,262	37,812	17.4	18.3	836,096	25,973	12.0
1949/50	221,957	48,125	21.6	23.3	962,264	431	0.1
1950/51	318,852	103,125	32.3	50	1,152,053	24,829	7.7

Source: Calculations based on data available in Loloma (Fiji) Gold Mines NL Balance Sheets, Working and Profit and Loss Accounts, Appropriation Accounts 1938–51.

Table 1.3   Emperor Mines Ltd Profit distribution, 1935-51

Year	Total Returns to Shareholders		Issued capital £ (A)	Rate of return (as % of issued capital)	Rate of return (as % of original capital)
	Dividends £ (A)	Returns of capital £ (A)			
1935/36	—	—	950,000	—	—
1936/37	—	—	950,000	—	—
1937/38	—	—	950,000	—	—
1938/39	190,000	—	950,000	20	20
1939/40	190,000	—	950,000	20	20
1940/41	142,500	—	950,000	15	15
1941/42	47,500	—	950,000	5	5
1942/43	—	—	950,000	—	—
1943/44	—	142,500	950,000	15	15
1944/45	—	—	807,500	—	—
1945/46	—	237,500	807,500	29.4	25
1946/47	—	—	570,000	—	—
1947/48	—	—	574,200*	—	—
1948/49	—	191,400	574,200	33.3	20.1
1949/50	—	—	382,800	—	—
1950/51	—	287,100	382,800	75	30.2
1951/52	—	—	95,700	—	—

* The increase in issued capital here resulted from the purchase of the Costello Mines Ltd mining lease (ML9) for £4200 in 14,000 fully paid 6s. shares.

Source: Calculations based on figures given in Emperor Annual Reports 1937-52.

description of the implications of the pay limit is provided by Duncan Innes: 'The lower the pay limit, the more ore becomes available in the reserves for profitable production and the longer the mine's lifespan; conversely, the higher the pay limit, the less ore is available in reserves and the shorter the life of the mine.'[45]

Favourable gold prices and labour-intensive production, particularly in the formative years of mining, made the pay limit of the Vatukoula mines low, facilitating the mining of low-grade ore. This did not, however, deter the Associated Mining Companies from opting for selective mining (or high grading). The ore mined at Loloma varied between 25 and 30 dwts/ton even though the minimum payable grade was 5 dwts at least into the early 1940s. In 1940 management observed that even mining ore of 15 dwts/ton would still guarantee 'a substantial profit'; but with one exception the company never extracted ore of less than 20 dwts/ ton until the mine's reserves were being mined out more than a decade later. For a period during 1943, low-grade oxidised ore averaging as little as 3.8 dwts/ ton yielded Emperor 'a small margin of profit'. In general, however, the company mined ore between 6 and 7 dwts that was well in excess of its pay limit of 2 dwts/ton (see Table 1.1).

The practice had severe repercussions. As production costs and therefore the pay threshold rose during and after the war, ore that could previously be included

---

[45]   Innes 1984 : 49.

Table 1.4 Comparative trends in distributed and reinvested profits Emperor Gold Mining Co. Ltd (EGM)

Year	Operating profits £ (F)	Total returns to shareholders (dividend payments and returns of capital) by Emperor Mines Ltd £ (F)	Returns to shareholders as a % of profits	Development expenditure £ (F)	Development expenditure as a % of profits
1935–June 1936	NA	Nil	Nil	17,219	—
1936/37	47,249	Nil	Nil	21,692	45.9
1937/38	113,259	Nil	Nil	22,838	20.1
1938/39	244,021	168,889	69.2	29,873	12.2
1939/40	314,024	168,889	53.7	51,852	16.5
1940/41	307,804	126,667	41.1	51,470	16.7
1941/42	237,647	42,222	17.7	47,140	19.8
1942/43	165,308 } 222,364	Nil	} 56.9	43,825	26.5
1943/44	57,056	126,667		2,592	4.5
1944/45	142,371 } 326,737	Nil	} 64.6	17,548	12.3
1945/46	184,366	211,111		37,156	20.1
1946/47	201,945	Nil	} 30.9	39,634	19.6
1947/48	156,040 } 550,565	Nil		56,118	35.9
1948/49	192,580	170,133		43,028	22.3
1949/50	333,468 } 701,165	Nil	} 36.3	46,224	13.8
1950/51	367,697	255,202		101,843	27.6

Source: Calculations based on data available in EGM Co. Ltd Profit & Loss Accounts & Balance Sheets and EML Annual Reports 1937–51.

in the reserves was rejected because it was no longer economical to mine. Thus, with its object of maximising returns in the short term, and securing quick returns for a small group of investors, mining above the pay limit forfeited the country revenue and undermined the prospects for a lasting industry. It was also one of the factors underlying the frantic drive for higher output during the 1950s and 1960s. As we shall see, the mine work-force bore the brunt of this imperative.

The declining rate of dividends characteristic of the 1940s was not simply a measure of reduced profits resulting from the wartime interference with production. It was due, above all, to new financial policies adopted to counter higher taxation on distributed profits. Particular hostility was reserved by the group for the (Australian) Commonwealth tax initiatives, because these were not applied to Australian mining companies operating within Australia, New Guinea or the Solomon Islands. With dogged determination the group sought first to defeat and then to amend the tax legislation, Theodore making a personal submission to Prime Minister Chifley in 1947. In the face of defeat the companies settled for two solutions. In Emperor's case the directorate took the decision to repatriate the bulk of its profits by way of reductions in its capital. Between 1944 and 1945 alone it returned £A380,000 to its shareholders under this form of tax-free distribution. This reduced the face value of its 10s. shares to 6s. and at the same time brought total distribution (from 1935) up to nearly £A1,000,000 (see Table 1.3).[46]

More modestly capitalised Loloma was driven to an alternative means of escaping the clutches of Australian tax law, since under Victorian company law a no-liability company could not repay capital unless operations were winding up. Loloma's solution took the form of accumulating a substantial reserve of surplus funds, which were then invested outside the Fiji mining industry. In this way, as its dividend payments all but lapsed from 1941 to 1948, the (cost) value of its investments rose dramatically from £A41,000 to £A664,408 (see Table 1.2). The shift was significant on two levels. First, it enabled the company to resume tax-free distribution of profits within a few years, because a proportion of its dividends could be declared out of income from Australian rather than Fiji mining. Second, the pattern and scale of its investments emphasised the lack of any long-term commitment to mining in Fiji. Although some initial investment took place in the colony, principally through the purchase of government war bonds and shares in TPP, the bulk of Loloma's surplus was directed towards Australian mining, banking and other ventures that even included loans to the Commonwealth Government during the post-war period.

The logic of making returns of capital and building up an undistributed surplus was not easily accepted by Emperor and Loloma shareholders, and in December 1946 both directorates faced harsh criticism for their failure to declare dividends. Irritated by the Australian press's 'exaggerated' account of opposition to the companies' financial policy, Theodore was not disposed towards a review. Two further reductions of Emperor's capital aggregating £A478,500 were thus made in lieu

---

[46]   The only tax payable on a return of capital was by the parent company itself. Local Secretary EGM Melbourne to Nilsen (Private & Confidential), 18 June 1948, Vat./Emperor Budget Estimates, Finance, etc. Current File; Emperor Annual Reports 1944 & 1946.

of dividends in 1948 and 1950, bringing the total return of capital issued in 1935 to £A858,000 or 90%. Loloma continued to garner its reserve, with the value of its Australian holdings alone soaring from £A94,000 to £A474,000 between 1947 and 1948. In one particular investment (the long-established Great Boulder Gold Mines) it purchased a 30% ownership stake. Theodore, Wren, Cody and Nilsen became directors. Loloma's Australian investments continued to rise substantially through the early 1950s, with the total amount sunk into ventures outside Fiji mining grossing £1 million by mid-1951.

The first fifteen years of operations by the Theodore group were thus highly profitable. As early as 1941 the combined production of the three mines had surpassed the annual output of Great Boulder and had pushed the mining industry towards the top of the colony's export charts. There was no single explanation for this rapid and, for some, unexpected rise to fortune. Two important factors were the monopoly that the group held over the Tavua field, including the rich ore bodies of Loloma and Dolphin, and the extensive outcrop of oxidised ore at Emperor, which did not, at least in its early stages, entail heavy mining and treatment costs. There was a buoyant price for gold; and production and financial policies together ensured that short-term profits were maximised and returns to shareholders generally high. But a hallmark of profitable mining was undoubtedly the system of cheap, indigenous labour. The following chapters seek to demonstrate this.

2   Mobilising Mine Labour 1934-50: Who, Why and How?

THE 'CHOSEN RACE'

> Although a somewhat indolent agriculturalist, the magnificent physique of the Fijian makes him particularly suitable for work in the mines; and if he is able, and willing, to continue in this form of employment I am sure that a great deal will have been done to enable him to occupy a position in the production of this Colony more comparable with that of indigenous natives elsewhere. [Acting Governor, Fiji to Secretary of State for Colonies, 27 May 1936, CSO F111/31 Pt1]

The search for a large and cheap supply of unskilled labour was an integral part of the process of rationalising the production of gold. A low-cost structure was necessitated above all by the fixed international pricing system and the high capital costs of bringing a mine into production and keeping it viable. Labour cost control was also logical to the process of capital accumulation, given that the 'directing motive, the end and aim of capitalist production, is to extract the greatest possible amount of surplus value, and consequently to exploit labour power to the greatest possible extent'.[1] The need to 'control the *supply* of labour' was a prerequisite of the valorisation process.[2] The mission was to be accomplished in the Fiji mining industry only with some difficulty on account of the continuing existence (in some respects the strength) of pre-capitalist political and economic structures. As the following sections show, however, it would be an oversimplification to cast the traditional social formation as a structural impediment. Paradoxically, the system was, like the colonial state, consigned a crucial role in the process by which a mine labour supply (and working class) was created.

---

[1]   Marx 1901 : 321.
[2]   Crisp 1984 : 2. Legassick & de Clercq (1984 : 144-5) discuss Marx's notion that it is in the interests of capital to have a surplus labour supply (or industrial reserve army).

From the beginning the labour supply for the Tavua, as for the Mt Kasi gold-field was heavily dominated by ethnic Fijians. By 1936 about 2000 had been absorbed into the nascent industry, nearly 80% of its unskilled labour strength. At Tavua, 'free' Indians provided an accessible and plentiful source of seasonal labour. They were concentrated in the sugar industry, where since 1920 they had been employed chiefly as tenant farmers or mill labourers. This 'quite intelligent' source of labour formed an economical and convenient reservoir despite its high turnover. Despite these advantages the Emperor group adopted a policy of discouraging the use of Indians in any working capacity, putting a total ban on their employment underground until the late 1940s. Until after the Second World War, numbers rarely exceeded 100.

The common perception of Indian workers as more truculent than their Fijian counterparts stemmed from a characteristic radicalism and political consciousness rooted in their long and bitter experience of indenture. Nilsen's advice to Theodore following a Fijian labour strike in 1938 typified the contemporary stereotype: 'Personally, I do not care for Indian labor as they are always a source of trouble. Occasionally there may be trouble with the Fijians but it soon blows over.' Indian agitation for political and land reform predated the inception of mining and was intensified by industrial struggles in the sugar industry during the late 1930s and 1940s. In search of a docile and compliant work-force, the group accordingly refrained wherever possible from signing on this category of labour, even to alleviate the periodic shortages of Fijians before and during the war.

Perhaps the most important reason for the embargo, however, was the 'gentle-men's' agreement with the CSR. While this laid down general guidelines for col-laboration over the employment and wage rates of all local labour—a policy of mutual advantage for it 'minimise[d] the risk of labour playing off one Company against the other'—it specifically committed the mining companies to restricted employment of Indians. As the previous chapter has shown, concessions of this kind were part of a broad pattern of reciprocal gestures that cemented the unequal relations between labour and capital.

The employment of Rotumans offered a more suitable alternative, and the first group was introduced at Vatukoula about the mid-1930s. They were highly regarded for their industry and application to mine work. Their regular attendance—'only being absent when sick or after obtaining leave for a real reason'[3]—contrasted with the high rate of absenteeism to which Fijian workers became prone. Rotumans were collectively classified with Part-Europeans (Euronesians or half-castes) in respect of jobs and earnings, and typified as 'better and more reliable worker[s] than the average Fijian and than most of the Euronesians'. Their alleged intellectual limitations, however, confined them to positions of minor responsibility.

The qualities attributed to Rotuman labour were better explained by material than biological factors. Before the mid-1930s land scarcity and population pressure had already set in train a flow of surplus labour to the mainland of Viti Levu. Together with the vast distance separating work-place from home, the irregular shipping services and the cost of a return visit, such economic and demographic

---

[3]   D. T. Mitchell, Mine Superintendent to General Manager EGM Confidential, 20 July 1948, Vat./unclassified.

factors encouraged more permanent settlement. The link between worker dependence and dependability (including low turnover) was not lost on Colonial Secretary Barton. In 1938 he observed: 'Generally, I am informed, Polynesian labour is more reliable than Melanesian, & obviously it is easier to deal with natives who cannot go home for the week end.'[4]

Other government officials offered a similarly candid rationalisation. The Rotuman, one District Commissioner said, was 'a steady and much valued worker in regular employment, more particularly away from his own island'. The higher status and earnings of Rotumans in the mines' occupational and wage structure reinforced their 'naturally law-abiding and docile' disposition. In fact it was the opposition of Fijian mineworkers to their privileges that brought consignments of Rotuman labour to a temporary end in 1938. Not until the 1950s did they come to represent a significant proportion of the work-force; and this took place under very different circumstances for mining capital.

The recruitment of Fijians in preference to other ethnic categories was of singular importance. Although the reservoir of Fijian labour had been tapped with some success by incoming traders, settlers and plantation capital during the nineteenth and early twentieth centuries, the choice deviated from the convention of deploying the indigenous people as a discretionary labour reserve that supplemented imported foreign supplies. The mine labour system was also distinctive in that for the first time the Fijian village economy and social system were shackled with the responsibility of providing an industrial as opposed to an agricultural work-force. As we shall discover, this incorporation of Fijian labour power into the new industry was both a manifestation and a consequence of the disruptive and dislocating effects of colonial capitalism. Such forces were not always conspicuous, but they unleashed a steady process of proletarianisation.

The domination of the pre-capitalist village economy by metropolitan capitalism had created the conditions by which labour could be 'freed' for the mining industry; and the world Depression of the late 1920s and 1930s proved to be an important catalyst in this process. The circumstances were far from peculiar to Fiji which, along with many other colonial possessions, bore the brunt of economic and social changes: the erosion of independent and self-sustaining indigenous economies through such processes as land alienation and the destruction of traditional markets or craft industries; the redirection from food production and other traditional economic activities to the servicing of metropolitan markets with cheap (i.e. undervalued) cash crops and other primary commodities; the uneven regional nature of capitalist 'development' (as in the Gold Coast and Nigeria); its racial (white settler) bias designed to eliminate 'native' competition (as in South Africa and Uganda); and the establishment of cheap labour reserves, often a direct result of the poverty or economic dependence generated by one or more of the above. The impoverishment associated with the pre-capitalist mode of production was, like the retention of the system, no accident. It was directly linked to the reproduction of capitalist relations of production that had a vested interest in both.

---

[4] CS (JB) to Governor, 10 Nov. 1938, CSO F 36/39/1.

As in the nineteenth century, the attitudes and policies of the colonial state in Fiji betrayed an ambivalence about the extent to which the indigenous economy and social institutions should be tailored, even suppressed, to meet the needs of metropolitan capital. A keen awareness of the dangers and costs of economic and social disintegration was persistently weighed against the need to secure and safeguard favourable conditions for capital accumulation. The articulation of traditional and capitalist systems and the political formula of indirect rule represented both a pragmatic solution to these conflicting demands and a compromise. In the mining industry, one symbol of this (articulated) relationship was the migrant labour system, which appeased the chiefly élite while serving the broader goals of social control and capital reproduction.

Although its 'protectionist' policy brought the state into conflict with various forms of capital, bent on a destructive strategy that would satisfy short-term labour needs, it was not designed to hinder the interests of employers. In the long run it proved its credentials both as a politically expedient strategy and as economically beneficial to corporate and settler interests. The preservation of the chiefly system and its integration into the broader structure of colonial management co-opted rather than alienated this traditional ruling class. In the mining industry, as we shall see, this directly bolstered company efforts to control working class organisation and militancy.

Equally important, the policy of 'protectionism' permitted the exploitation of Fijian mine labour while ensuring its long-term reproduction. The independent access of workers to land and to a traditional system of social support enabled the companies to pay them at rates below the full cost of their reproduction. Mine wages for migrant male labour could be assessed according to the barest subsistence needs of an individual worker, while the reproductive costs of family subsistence and welfare, as well as a worker's own security in old age, times of sickness or other disability, and periods of unemployment and recuperation, were conveniently transferred to the pre-capitalist rural economy and in particular to women within it.[5]

The draining of male labour from the villages, as well as the latter's responsibility for subsidising the labour costs of industry, spearheaded the underdevelopment of the traditional economy. The demands inflicted upon women within the gender division of labour were also intensified. A singular feature of the articulation process, moreover, was that the subsidisation of certain reproductive labour costs for the mining industry did not depend on the continuance of the migrant system. The function of the village as a sanctuary for the ill, the old and the redundant (and even as a place for rest and recuperation during holidays) would long outlive transition to family-based recruitment and an urban proletariat. Even in respect of direct earnings, stringent wage control until the 1950s demanded ongoing support from the indigenous economy.

This parasitic role of capitalism and the conditions that made it possible were

---

[5]   This theory has been tested against the conditions of various migrant labour economies. See Wolpe 1972 & 1975; Johnstone 1976; Legassick 1974, 1977; Legassick & Wolpe 1977; Trapido 1971; Marks & Rathbone 1982; Stichter 1985; Perrings 1979; Burawoy 1976; Parpart 1983; Southall 1983; Deere 1976; Meillassoux 1981; Mies 1984.

disguised by 'protectionist' theory. This depicted the well-worn image of an affluent subsistence economy comfortably catering for the needs of ethnic Fijians and which the state was committed to preserving. Official ideology celebrated the discretionary and temporary basis on which Fijians entered the labour market, claiming that cash earnings were not crucial to their livelihood. All Fijians were 'landowners who can support themselves from the produce of their lands. There is no economic necessity for them to work for long periods as wage earners.'[6]

The argument's utility was not lost on Theodore, who in 1936 assured his co-directors that the communal system independently assured a mine labourer of his social and economic well-being. With a currency in the Empire at large, this ubiquitous stereotype provided the moral justification for an exploitative practice. It gave colonial employers (including the state) licence to grant nominal wages to 'discretionary' workers, because, like other indigenous peoples, they were ostensibly able to 'fall back on subsistence cultivation' when the labour market contracted or commodity prices collapsed.[7]

In fact, conditions in the traditional economy were seldom idyllic. Labour migration to the mines was often a response to poverty. For those living in the interior of the two main islands, in particular, work was sought in order to acquire the means of subsistence. In this respect the dichotomy between official ideology and the material reality of the South African system of apartheid—the disjunction between the state's rationale of separate (but equal) development and conditions of structural poverty in the African reserves—portrays a striking parallel with Fiji. Fiji had its own equivalents of the black South Africans for whom land pressure and a declining quality of reserve land in the early twentieth century forced movement 'into "white" labour areas to make up the deficit between their needs and crop production'. Though land hunger and rural poverty were far more severe in Southern Africa, First's conclusion that 'the fundamental assumption (of an affluent subsistence economy)... is a faulty one' seems equally true for Fiji.[8]

An arbitrary and discriminatory definition of Fijian subsistence—which classified as luxuries what were seen as necessities for European workers—compounded the downward pressure on Fijian wages. Even after recruitment of married men with families began, the wage schedule remained unaltered. In essence the burden of supporting dependants was considered adequately recompensed by the supply of one extra half-ration. The spurious distinction was repeatedly drawn between 'native' and European living standards—or the frugal needs and wants of the 'tropical worker' compared with those of his European counterpart, as it was put by Major Orde Browne to the Colonial Office.[9] A serious flaw in this argument lay in its failure to accommodate what has been described in respect

---

[6] Recruitment of Native Labour Correspondence July 1934–April 1935, Miscell. No. 450 Confidential, Fiji & Western Pacific No. 35.

[7] Lord Hailey, Colonial Economic Advisory Committee, 19 Dec. 1944, PRO CO 852/617/11. Official and company theories attesting to an affluent subsistence economy have been reinforced by historical writing on Fiji mining. See for example Plange 1985 : 100.

[8] First 1982 : 17.

[9] G. M. Orde Browne, Labour Adviser to Secretary of State for Colonies Memorandum 'The Colonial Labourer and Post-War Conditions', 11 Dec. 1941, PRO CO 852/369/1.,

of India as 'the social and cultural requirements, that have historically become a part of working class life'.[10] In Fiji the point was put incisively to the Legislative Council by the 1st Native Member, Ratu Sukuna, in 1938:

> The Fijian's living expenses are apparently lower because he uses less imported foods and clothing. The European standard of living is high because his society demands a high standard of living...The Fijian is born to a standard of living in which he is demanded by his society to contribute towards the needs of his clan so that, in effect, his expenses are considerably higher than people unacquainted with Fijian custom would believe...[11]

For all types of Fijian mine labour, contemporary ideologies thus conveniently rationalised returns that fell well short of daily and generational reproduction costs.

Although ambivalent, the colonial government declared an early preference for the use of Fijians, partly because of the impact of the Depression. Plummeting commodity prices consigned many provinces to debt; tax payments fell seriously into arrears; and rural unemployment rose alarmingly. The glutting of the mine labour market guaranteed a regular tax income to the state, the more so because responsibility for payment was transferred from the beleaguered provincial councils to the mining companies, which then reclaimed through wage deductions the payments advanced. Employment at the mines also promised to spare the central government much of the cost of rural infrastructural development, including social services. For, in addition to their ordinary taxes, Fijians were charged with subsidising the maintenance of water supplies, schools and transport through the payment of an absentee tax as well as directly through cash remittances and compulsory wage deductions organised by their chiefs.

Economic pressures were not always sufficient to meet the labour requirements of the mining industry. Above all, non-economic factors were crucial to the structural transformation that took place in the mine labour market after the Second World War. Giovanni Arrighi's insights on the process of African proletarianisation in Rhodesia are helpful in understanding the broader purpose behind political intercession in the Fiji labour market. At the heart of this was the fact that a notion of price was intrinsic to employer references to labour supply. The various arguments that had contrived an artificially low Fijian wage, thus crucially underpinned complaints of labour shortages. In turn the failure of economic factors to produce adequate labour was a failure to do so at what Arrighi terms the desired 'customary level of wages' (i.e. providing for a bachelor's subsistence).

Arrighi's conclusion is equally relevant: 'as changes in wages were no longer to be the equilibrating factor in the labour market, political mechanisms became of crucial importance in closing gaps between supply and demand'.[12] Implicitly, then, the colonial state, like other forces of extra-economic coercion operating within the mining sector of Fiji's colonial economy, have to be seen as determinants not only of labour supply but of the pattern of labour cost control that applied to Fijian mineworkers.

---

[10] Nathan 1987 : 799.
[11] Fiji Leg. Co. Debates, 27 April 1938.
[12] Arrighi 1973 : 184.

Internal migration to the Vatukoula and Mt Kasi mines affected all 14 of the colony's provinces to varying degrees. Initially the labour needs of the Emperor group were satisfied at minimum cost and with little difficulty by the reservoir of village labour power in the surrounding districts of Colo North. But about 1935 the group was compelled to look farther afield for a significant proportion of its Fijian labour. Its expanding activities, and the competing demands of the many syndicates and companies that descended upon the area during the gold rush, diminished its supply, encouraged a high turnover, and inflated wage rates. Drawing first on the neighbouring provinces of Ra, Tailevu and Colo East, the group soon moved into more distant parts of Fiji, notably Bua, Macuata and Cakaudrove on the island of Vanua Levu, Lomaiviti and Lau to the south-east, and the Yasawa Islands to the north-west. Tailevu and Ra became the largest donors and together with Colo East and Naitasiri (amalgamated after the war), the two provinces continued to dominate the Fijian work-force in the post-war years and increasingly through the 1950s and 1960s. On the Yanawai field the closest provinces of Bua, Macuata, Cakaudrove and Lau were similarly established as the predominant sources of labour until the Mt Kasi mining company ceased operations in 1946.[13]

ECONOMIC FOUNDATIONS OF A FIJIAN LABOUR SUPPLY

> Now the Fijians are endeavouring to enter into the field of production where it is possible to find markets for cash crops. He finds himself, in many areas, economically strangled as his good lands are leased to the C.S.R. Co. who sub-let them to the Indians or are leased out direct to Indian cane farmers. In many cases the sugar fields extend to the adge[sic] of the village and the alienation of these lands is a long story and those of us who have been in positions of authority for long periods must accept responsibility for this condition. The Fijian has, in certain areas only a limited area of suitable land available for food crops but the balance which is fairly extensive is of little use at the present time. [R. N. Caldwell, for SFA to Financial Secretary, 17 April 1948, CSO F37/307]

The flow of labour into the mining industry from the provinces contiguous to the two main mining areas was facilitated by conditions of economic dependence and sometimes impoverishment. The land question lay at the heart of this. Although colonial policy had retained for ethnic Fijians over 80% of the colony's land area (totalling 4.5 million acres), British 'protectionism' took little account of the quality of unalienated holdings and the level of infrastructural development, particularly accessibility to markets. Alienated land comprised a high proportion of the more fertile and accessible littoral, including land suited to sugar-cane cultivation, leaving to the supposed beneficiaries of colonial policy the rugged hinterland and about 5% of arable land. It was a practice by no means unique

---

[13]   Provincial labour data is drawn from Vat./Native Affairs Camps Reports 1935- ; and Associated Companies Labour Strength in Provinces, 1935-70.

to Fiji, being paralleled in the region in the New Hebrides, the Solomon Islands Protectorate, Australia and French-controlled New Caledonia, and beyond, in Southern Rhodesia, South Africa and Kenya.

The allocation of 'reserve' land for Fijians, criticised as 'over-protective', included less than 5000 acres suitable for cane production. A large proportion of this required a 'fairly high level of capitalisation and costly technical experiment to become productive'.[14] Despite opposition from the colonial-created Council of Chiefs, Fijians continued to be dispossessed under provisions of the 1940 land legislation: the Crown could appropriate the holdings of landholding units (*mataqali*) declared to be extinct and could reclaim any land believed to be unoccupied at the time of Cession to Britain.

The hinterland regions tended to suffer most from low productivity, the area inland from the south-western coast of Viti Levu being but one example. Its plight was simply but evocatively depicted by Ratu Sukuna:

> There are patches of fertile land but all too small and I have often wondered how peasant farmers living in these arid areas managed to exist. Under the covering of red clay and rocky soil, soapstone appears to exist all over this area. Erosion and poor parched grass are common features.

Much later in the 1950s a soil and land use survey lent further credence to this uncommonly frank view of Fijian land holdings. It concluded that out of a total land area of 3,967,761 acres in Viti Levu and Vanua Levu, a mere 468,237 acres or 11.8% could be considered 'potentially useful for arable purposes'; and that unalienated land included 'large areas of waste and forest land'.

The enduring myth of a protective land policy also ignored glaring inequalities in individual access. Two features of this were the wide variation in the size of landholding units and the system of rental distribution. Under the 1940 Native Lands Trust Ordinance the state deducted 25% of rentals to cover administrative costs and allocated a further 30% to its 'chiefly civil servants'.[15] In units comprising many households the distribution of the balance (45%) reduced per capita incomes to mere 'pocket money'.[16] Such anomalies gave rise to discrepancies in the wealth acquired from the land. But, more important, they helped to produce conditions of landlessness and wage labour dependence in some places. Unequal access to and control of land represented a structural distortion in the rural economy that laid the foundations of underdevelopment, as well as capitalist class formation.[17]

Attempts by the growing number of Fijians after the First World War to participate in the production of sugar-cane, sometimes as *galala* or independent farmers, were often thwarted by the shortage of suitable land. Population growth aggravated the problem. The development was viewed with circumspection in the Colonial Office, concerned above all about its political implications. As the Secretary of State warned the Governor:

---

[14] Stanner 1953 : 245.
[15] The term 'chiefly civil servants' is used by Macnaught 1974 : 3.
[16] Stanner 1953 : 245.
[17] See Southall 1983 : 73-88 for development of this argument in respect of the Transkei in South Africa.

You will no doubt agree that this growth of land consciousness amongst the Fijians will require to be watched and guided if complications with the Indian settlers are to be avoided. Both races have their importance in the economy of the Colony and developments which may tend unduly to foster aspirations will require guidance.

Compensation for 'permanent and unexhausted improvements' as a precondition of land reclamation was one particular obstacle facing potential canefarmers. As the District Commissioner Ra observed in 1936, it was 'unfortunate' that 'in many cases where there is a genuine desire on the part of the native owners to plant cane the value of the improvements precludes them from taking the land back'. Similarly, prospective *galala* had to give evidence of sufficient capital; while Fijians seeking to grow cane on communal land (i.e. without individual title) were generally not eligible for credit from the CSR to buy livestock and implements. The company in any event had reservations about the wisdom of 'investing' in contracts with ethnic Fijians from the early 1930s in view of 'seditious' elements, which it believed to be operating in Western Viti Levu. Symptomatic of social as well as economic change, the *galala* movement was also actively opposed by some chiefs. By settling outside the traditional social unit, independent farmers were beyond the chiefly sphere of influence and tribute, paying a commutation fee in compensation for the services withdrawn from the community.

Mine labour reserves I: the cases of Colo North, Ra, Tailevu, Naitasiri and Colo East

A remote hinterland, the tiny province of Colo North had the unenviable reputation of being the 'poorest in Fiji' and the notoriety of being the most recalcitrant. It had spurned the advances of Christian evangelists in the nineteenth century and had been the last outpost of resistance to the political ambitions of the Bauan 'kingdom'. Its economic history told a tale as wretched as its post-contact experience of political suppression and religious conversion. Population density was low, but the only fertile coastal belt and inland arable pockets were under lease to the CSR. Significant rental income derived from just one district, while the remaining six were condemned to large tracts of mainly unproductive land.

Isolation from coastal markets and the rugged undeveloped terrain made the marketing of small surpluses a laborious task. It was, the District Commissioner remarked with more curiosity than concern,

> very stimulating to meet a man—and often women—carrying on his shoulders a few shillings worth of produce, 20, 30 and even 40 miles over mountain country to the markets of Ba and Tavua, journeys which for 3/-s or 4/-s necessarily involve a 3 days' absence from their homes in the case of places like Navatusila in Colo North.[18]

The impoverishment of the province was exacerbated by the Depression, and by 1930 wage labour was already the main source of provincial revenue. An expanding reservoir of unemployed taxpayers had difficulty in obtaining cash for the 'minimum requirements' of 'taxes, clothes, soap and kerosene'. In many

---

[18] DC Colo North & East (Reay) to CS, 11 April 1938, CSO F13/1 Pt2.

cases, the District Commissioner reported, it was 'quite common to find a village entirely without a light at night, a certain indication of poverty'. Such was the gravity of the situation in 1932 that about 272 men—more than half the total number of taxpayers—were gaoled for failing to pay their taxes that year.

The origins of mine labour migration from Ra, Tailevu, Naitasiri and Colo East also lay in such factors as their limited avenues for commercial agriculture and the scarcity of cane-suited land within 'economical' reach of the CSR tramline. These conditions created pools of labour well in excess of the CSR's demands for mill labour and the temporary jobs available as government wharf or road labour. Fijian commercial farming in Ra was confined to banana production, small-scale experiments with tobacco and maize farming and some rice cultivation. Only 13% of its arable land was alienated, but a mere 8% of its total land area was considered to be of this quality, while as much as 74.3% was 'potentially useless'. Only in three out of its 18 districts was cane cultivated by Fijians, and this area amounted to barely 100 acres.

The establishment of a mining settlement opened up a new market for food crops in Ra as for parts of North Tailevu and Colo East. Transport problems, however, led to considerable wastage and the prices offered by the mining companies for staple crops often compared unfavourably with those of other local markets. The need for employment, on the other hand, drew large numbers out of their districts and even away from the province. In 1934 about 60% of Ra's taxpaying population was declared absent. The figures continued to be high throughout the decade, and with the outbreak of war rose higher still. By the late 1930s provincial revenue derived mainly from the wages of unskilled labour in the sugar and mining industries.

In Tailevu, too, the economic conditions of the 1930s sapped its ability to produce a surplus adequate to meet tax and other cash needs and led to high rates of absenteeism. Fijian holdings of unalienated arable land were larger than in Ra, but aggregated only 21% of the province's total land area. For districts such as Bau, where land scarcity was critical, and the banana-producing regions, the Tavua goldfield offered a vital and accessible avenue of employment. In Naitasiri and Colo East, a trivial 8.6% of land was suitable for arable cultivation. In both areas there was a dependence on banana production for export, which caused declining incomes and deteriorating living standards during the depression years.

Mine labour reserves II: the copra provinces

The provinces of Lau, Bua and Macuata, the Yasawa Islands and the Savusavu district of Cakaudrove, where copra was the mainstay of Fijian commercial agriculture, also languished under conditions of economic decline and rural impoverishment. All these areas were drawn into the mine labour market during the 1930s and early 1940s.

In Bua, a small province of less than one thousand taxpayers, large areas of quality land had been alienated as freehold to European settlers and the bulk of the remaining fertile valley areas leased out to Indian rice, tobacco and maize farmers. Land retained was essentially confined to 'barren hills and unfertile country'. In the neighbouring province of Cakaudrove existed a similar situation, with 'Only odd patches of nuts on the coast, the formerly untravelled Natewa Bay, and the bush-covered mountains belong[ing] to the natives'.[19]

In Lau unequal land distribution limited the ability of some districts to participate in copra production, forcing men into indentured service on European estates even before the Depression. 'Except for the Chiefs and Tongans', the District Commissioner reported in 1934, 'few people possess holdings capable of producing more than about 4 cwts. of copra a year'.[20] Dependence on copra in both Lau and the Yasawa Islands was exacerbated by infrequent shipping and the high freight charges that applied to scattered island groups far from the commercial centres of Suva and Levuka. In remote outposts such as these, producers were commonly at the mercy of one trading firm or buyer and obliged to accept monopsony prices for their own produce as well as the consumer goods they bought. Likewise, in the copra districts of Cakaudrove, isolation from markets demanded that produce be carried several miles to the nearest store where the lowest prices were paid. Unequal terms of trade were by no means confined to Fiji, and reflected a pattern of capitalist development reproduced in many pockets of colonial penetration.[21]

Both in Lau and Bua the sale of *bêche-de-mer* and trochus shell supplemented incomes but did not reduce the dependence on copra. For Bua, the sugar industry in Ra also offered a small market for food crops, but reliance on decrepit boats and competition with Chinese traders limited the ability to exploit this. A like situation existed in Macuata where the sugar centre of Labasa provided an outlet for surplus food crops: the distance of the supplying villages from town, the absence of roads, high freight costs and competition with Indian traders were major disincentives.

Hurricanes and to a lesser extent droughts posed additional threats to the viability of commercial agriculture. The devastation of coconut trees along with food crops and houses reduced families to destitution, with the seven-year gestation for coconuts lengthening the wage labour cycles into which men were forced. Coupled with the slump in copra prices, natural disasters slashed rural incomes in the 1930s, creating reservoirs of labour that could not be absorbed by the estates, government road contracts or cane harvesting. These areas became the chief labour pools for the Yanawai and alternative reserves for the Tavua gold-field.

The economic stress in Bua exemplified conditions that were highy favourable to mining interests. As it began operations in 1931, the Mt Kasi Mining Co. found the province grappling with serious food shortages triggered by two hurricanes and a drought (in 1929 and 1930) and the highest provincial tax rate in the colony. Over two years later the stark reality of living conditions was captured in an official report:

> The standard of living in Bua is very low. Few villages have bread, and tea, milk and meat are rare luxuries. The furniture of a house is extremely simple usually

---

[19]   DC Taveuni Report in SNA Annual Report 1937, CP No. 42, 1938.
[20]   DC Lau (Sukuna) Annual Report 1934, CSO F15/Pt1.
[21]   One good example was the South African reserves, such as the Transkei. See Southall 1983 : 82–4.

consisting of a box of clothes, a lamp, a few iron pots, plates and cups, two or three spoons and a fork... Most of the hill villages have been without kerosene for months, their light at nights being only the fire.[22]

In the same year a report of Ratu Sukuna poignantly described the effects of natural disasters and the copra market depression on the living standards of Lauans.

> Now most of the people are back on native foods. There are families with just one change of clothes between them. Others cannot buy even soap. Houses are unlit at night. Villages (even Lomaloma) find it necessary for want of kerosene to dispense with Evening Services. No longer are happy, holidy-making Lauans to be met with in the streets of Levuka and Suva. These days they are seen there only as labourers.[23]

As for Fijians from other copra districts and the banana regions, the combined blows of land shortages, falling commodity prices and mounting costs of basic items of food and clothing set the scene for the indenture of Lauans as mine labour from the early years of the industry.

TAXATION AS A DETERMINANT OF WAGE LABOUR

Although economic adversity and natural disasters undermined the economic and social autonomy of Fijians, they did not of themselves produce a mining proletariat. Even when the pressures to take on wage employment were most acute, mine labour remained erratic in supply and mobile. For those areas where export crops could be grown as an alternative to wage labour, price improvements at least offered the choice of a return to the land; and this occurred briefly in the mid-1930s for mineworkers recruited from banana districts, and in 1942 and in the post-war years for labour originating in the copra regions. The proportional and absolute decline in the contributions of Lau, Bua and Macuata to the Vatukoula work-force after the war can largely be explained in terms of recovery in the copra market, notably the sevenfold price increase between 1938 and 1949.

An important instrument of labour mobilisation was the colony's direct taxation system. This political mechanism predated Cession and had proved especially effective in areas where adequate agricultural means of production did not exist. From 1913 Fiji's colonial government demanded from Fijian males between the ages of 16 and 60 annual cash contributions to revenue in the form of both a provincial rate and a government tax of £1.[24]

The rate was something of a misnomer, for it took no account of individual resources. Men with five or more dependants enjoyed concession rates, but in all other respects it was recognised for what it was: a 'head tax'.[25] There the

---

[22] DC Bua Annual Report 1932, CSO F11/1.
[23] Extract from DC Lau Annual Report 1932, CSO F15/1 Pt1.
[24] Native Taxes Ordinance, No. II 1913. In 1948 the age threshold was raised to 18 years. (Fijian Regulation No. VII, 1948). See Bennett (1987 : 162) for a similar tax levied on able-bodied males in the Solomon Islands Protectorate.
[25] Report of R. S. McDougall on Fijian Administration Finances, CP No. 35, 1957.

tax burden did not rest. There were other levies, including an education rate, land survey fees, and reimbursement of the cost of government food relief distributed during hurricane and other disasters. For those employed or otherwise absent from their homes for more than a year an absentee tax or commutation rate (generally set at £1) had to be paid in lieu of compulsory communal services; while for the thousands of Christian converts an informal but more or less obligatory tithe was solicited by the church. The colonial tax system integrated Fijians formally and firmly into the cash economy.

As demands for mine labour expanded during the 1930s, the full weight of the system was brought down upon them. An iniquitous structure that took no account of disparities in provincial (and district) wealth in determining per capita levies, it dealt a particularly savage blow to those areas that already relied on wage labour for cash incomes, thus compounding the disability of restricted or inadequate landholdings. In Colo North the general pattern between 1935 and 1939 was, with few exceptions, one of small but steady increases, including fees for education and land surveys. This occurred in spite of the high incidence of defaulting and imprisonment.

The establishment of the mining industry was unquestionably regarded as something of a panacea for the province. Reports by its District Commissioner, C. S. de Reay, observed with disarming frankness that 'But for the necessity to go out to earn these taxes many Fijians would not bother to leave home, their dependants would be deprived of what have now become necessities (clothing, soap, kerosene etc.), and industry would go short of labour'.[26] Beyond Fiji, taxation had long proved successful in countries such as South Africa, Kenya, Uganda and, in the Pacific, in German (and subsequently Australian) controlled New Guinea in bringing 'able-bodied' male 'natives' within the clutches of the monetary economy. Reay's recognition of the vital service that taxation rendered the colonial labour market struck a similar chord in Kenya, where it was admitted to be 'the only possible method of compelling the native to leave his reserve for the purpose of seeking work'; and in New Guinea where the native tax system in the early decades of the twentieth century gave the colony 'the dubious distinction of a unique fiscal system which was manipulated almost entirely for non-fiscal ends'.[27]

Tax demands were also tested against the resilience of (export) agricultural districts, bringing new areas into the orbit of wage labour relations because of falling commodity prices. In Savusavu, for example, it was estimated that two tons of copra were needed from each taxpayer in order to raise the basic (government and provincial) taxes in 1933. To do this, a taxpayer needed eight acres of coconut land, but many Fijians did not have this, 'in other words he is being taxed more than his property is worth'.

The harmful social effects of the system, which obliged an increasing number of men to leave their villages for distant centres of employment for at least two or three months of every year, caused an anxiety within the establishment that

[26]   DC Colo North Annual Report 1936, CSO F13/1 Pt1.
[27]   J. Ainsworth, colonial government official, Kenya, cited in Curtain 1984 : 124–5.

was reminiscent of the nineteenth-century dilemma over Fijian plantation labour. Long spells of separation from the village 'interfered' with home life, taught bad habits and induced a general restlessness. The 'overtaxation of the Fijian', it was charged, was 'breaking up the native life'; the withdrawal of able-bodied men left the 'old men and the women and children [to] pick up a poor living for themselves while the village work is entirely neglected'.

Reform (which included a reduction in the basic tax) did not tamper with the structural inequalities of the system, legitimised on the peculiar grounds that income levels varied within as well as between provinces. Survey fees continued the trend, with uniform rates being applied within each province, irrespective of the varying amounts of work done in each district and the differing sizes of landholding units. Ultimately, practical considerations were paramount. As the Provincial Commissioner Lau admitted in 1937 in respect of his province, where an additional £4000 had to be raised: 'The method of collection is not equitable, as small landowners and large landowners will pay the same, but it is the simplest form from an accounting point of view, and the only one which will ensure full payment.'[28]

Failure to pay taxes was a criminal offence bringing a fine or a prison term, and Fijians were tried for default before native courts. The reports of district officers habitually noted the wide gulf between provincial estimates and receipts, and the high rate of prosecutions. In 1936 25% of Tailevu's taxpayers were prosecuted and nearly all its 'native prisoners' the following year were tax offenders. In Ra there were as many as 54% defaulters in 1940; while in the colony at large 38% (over 3000) of the total number of cases heard before the district and provincial courts in 1948 were against tax offenders.[29]

The colonial administration was not oblivious of the fact that financial difficulty was the principal cause of tax debts. As the Provincial Commissioner Tailevu recorded in 1936:

> Some of the people of the Province find it difficult to earn money. It seems that those who have the means do not neglect to pay their native Provincial Rates and that the balance outstanding is a fair indication of the inability of some of the natives of the Colony to earn money . . .

Paradoxically, tax defaulting was often met by attempts to increase annual levies and there was generally an upward trend in direct taxation from the late 1930s. In Naitasiri the annual levy more than doubled between 1937 and 1949 (from £1 12s. to £3 10s.), and in Colo East, which amalgamated with it in 1945, the rise was scarcely less marked (from £1 18s. to £3 10s.). Though in Ra taxes stabilised during the 1940s, and in Tailevu fluctuated only slightly, both provinces experienced significant proportional increases over the same period.

Higher import duties increased indirect tax obligations following the outbreak

---

[28] PC, J Goepel note, Lau Provincial Report July 1937.
[29] The fine for failure to pay the provincial rate was originally set at 5s. in 1912. In 1927 it was raised to £2 and an imprisonment term of three months introduced for default in payment. The maximum fine was again raised in 1948 to £5, and although the prison term was reduced to one month provision was made for this to be inflicted in addition to the fine.

of war; and from the mid-1940s there was the additional pressure on Fijians of contributing to education costs, notably teachers' salaries. This effected a steep rise—on average over 30%—in provincial rates throughout Fiji between 1944 and 1950 (see Table 2.1). It was, the Secretary for Fijian Affairs admitted, 'extremely doubtful whether any further increase can reasonably be borne by the people of the poorer provinces'.[30]

Table 2.1 Provincial rates (per capita), 1945-50
(£ s.d.)

	1945	1946	1947	1948	1949	1950
Ba	2. 0.0	2.12.0	2.13.0	2.13.0	2.15.0	3. 0.0
Bua	2.15.0	2.15.0	2.12.0	2.19.0	2.18.0	3. 0.0
Cakaudrove	2.10.0	2. 5.0	2. 5.0	3. 0.0	3.10.0	3.10.0
Kadavu	2.10.0	2. 5.0	2.10.0	2.10.0	3. 0.0	3. 0.0
Lau	2. 5.0	2. 5.0	2.10.0	2.15.0	2.15.0	3. 2.0
Lomaiviti	2. 3.0	2. 3.0	2.14.0	2.11.0	2.16.0	3. 0.0
Macuata	2.10.0	2.10.0	2. 8.0	2. 8.0	3. 0.0	3. 5.0
Nadroga & Navosa	2. 2.0	2. 3.0	2. 5.0	2. 8.0	2.10.0	2.10.0
Namosi	2.10.0	2. 5.0	2. 5.0	2.15.0	3. 5.0	3. 5.0
Naitasiri	2. 0.0	2. 5.0	2. 5.0	3. 0.0	3.10.0	3. 5.0
Ra	2. 2.0	2. 2.0	2. 2.0	2. 7.0	2.10.0	2.13.0
Rewa	1.12.0	1.17.0	2. 0.0	2.15.0	2.15.0	2.15.0
Serua	2.10.0	2. 0.0	2. 5.0	2.15.0	3. 0.0	3. 5.0
Tailevu	1.16.0	2. 0.0	2. 0.0	2.10.0	2.11.0	2.10.0
Average	2. 4.8	2. 4.10	2. 6.9	2.13.2	2.18.2	3. 0.0

Source: Secretary for Fijian Affairs Annual Reports for 1949 (CP No. 2, 1951) and 1950 (CP No. 5, 1952).

The mounting tax burdens placed on Fijian farmers, especially in the banana districts, reduced the real value of their produce and increased the opportunity cost of continued cash-crop production. For the mining industry, on the other hand, such misfortunes promoted a flow of labour. Tight control of Fijian wages during the 1930s and 1940s (occasionally incurring a fall in real earnings) prolonged the periods of employment required to raise taxes and protect living standards. In this way the pattern of Fijian taxation should also be seen as an important element in the process of labour stabilisation at Vatukoula. More broadly it emphasises the need to analyse trends in taxation, as other political devices, in the context of the wider political economy and specifically in relation to colonial mining policy and metropolitan demands for gold.

SOCIAL AND CULTURAL INFLUENCES

A feature of the early history of goldmining was the extent to which the traditional social system (and in particular the chiefs who presided over it) were successfully

[30] SFA Annual Report 1949, CP No. 2, 1951.

integrated into the process of labour mobilisation. As evidenced earlier, incorporation was not without precedent; nor was it devoid of contradictions in attitude or action. This being said, the perceived benefits—both personal and communal—of supplying batches of men under contract, led to an extraordinary degree of collusion by chiefs in the mine labour market. It established the traditional ruling class as a crucial intermediary between the mining companies and their Fijian workers.

In spite of the conservationist platform of nineteenth-century 'native' policy, the principles governing indigenous social relationships were emphatically altered. The chiefs who were traditionally vested with control over the distribution and use of resources (including labour), acquired new powers, which were safeguarded by the colonial state. Exactions of tribute and service to the community became compulsory and backed by the force of law. Unauthorised absconding became a criminal offence; and the checks and balances of a stratified social structure were removed.[31]

The programme of village and district work drawn up annually by the colonial-devised provincial councils formally regulated the productive labour resources of the pre-capitalist economy. Certain months of the year were set aside for compulsory housebuilding and repairing, the weeding of roads, the planting of food, and other tasks designed to keep villages productive and sanitary. In addition all Fijian males between the ages of 14 and 60 (unless exempt by payment of a commutation fee or deemed physically unfit) were obliged like their counterparts in other British, Belgian, French and Portuguese colonies to perform certain 'public works'. Annual *lala* (tribute) in the form of several days' labour (or cash in lieu) to both district chiefs and village headmen had likewise to be paid. For three months of each year, dubbed the 'free' months, men were at liberty to earn money for their taxes and domestic needs.

The application of penal sanctions to enforce personal *lala* to chiefs, labour services to the community and 'public' works undermined the voluntary and reciprocal aspects of the relationship between chief and commoner. The demands made upon the labour time of commoners were also extended. The formula defied the prevailing wisdom of international labour forums and directly contravened the Forced Labour Convention, ratified and brought into effect in Britain by 1932. Significantly, Fiji's compliance with the convention (under the Forced Labour Prohibition Ordinance of 1933 and subsequently under the 1947 Labour Ordinance) was compromised by excluding any form of compulsory communal work from the meaning ascribed to 'forced labour'.[32]

As in other British colonies the appointment and payment of official chiefs as custodians of the communal system and as tax-collectors made them accountable

---

[31] According to Cyril Belshaw, traditional Fijian society 'had within it many elements of mobility and flexibility, and was weak in elements of formal co-ordination. Modern administration has emphasized authority and has created, in certain limited spheres, autocratic community discipline as an organizational goal, imperfectly achieved in practice.' Belshaw 1964 : 125. See also Nayacakalou 1975 : ch. 3; and France 1969 : ch. 7.

[32] Compulsory 'public works' and communal labour backed up by fines or imprisonment were also legislated elsewhere in the Pacific, for example in the Gilbert & Ellice Islands, where, according to Barrie Macdonald (1982 : 195), 'a diligent search through the ILO's conventions revealed a convenient escape clause which permitted compulsory labour for "minor communal services" '.

to the colonial administration rather than to their own people. Their designation as curators of traditionalism also, ironically, placed them under pressure to become directly involved in the recruitment of wage labour for the colonial economy. Commoners often undertook employment at the mines in response to the 'social levy': to meet the cash demands of traditional occasions and transactions as well as the social, educational and health services of the rural community—water tanks, schools, churches, roads and boats for the transportation of produce. It was the duty of official chiefs to ensure that the burden of rural welfare services was responsibly shouldered, and that in the process their constituencies remained solvent. During the Depression years, when this was rarely possible, ways of reducing local debts had to be found. In these circumstances chiefs became further drawn into the mine labour market, playing seemingly contradictory roles as promoters of the encroaching capitalist economy and agents of their own demise.

It did not immediately become apparent that this was a course of political suicide, and it did have tangible short-term gains. Indeed, the incorporation of chiefs enabled them to extend their power base beyond the traditional domain, acquiring a significant degree of control over the distribution of communal labour outside the subsistence economy and the terms on which this was sold. Chiefs determined when and how large a party of men should be sent to the mines; they negotiated the terms of engagement with the employer or recruiter on behalf of the contracting labour; and they decided what proportion of monthly pay-packets labourers were permitted to receive for their own use.

Wage deductions authorised by chiefs, commonly between 50% and 100% of gross earnings, were accumulated to fund communal projects, with personal remuneration to a labourer regarded as a privilege rather than an entitlement. A letter from Ratu Sukuna to Theodore in July 1936 illustrated this well:

> Under the influence of the wealth of the Gold Mining area, the Lauans with you find that money is a necessity and their Chief considers that they might now be allowed to draw 5/- [less than one-tenth of their earnings] a month per male. May this be arranged please?[33]

The financial rewards of collaboration in the mine labour market did not go unrecognised. Indeed, the promise of customary *loloma* or gratuities, permitted in practice if not by law, sometimes encouraged chiefs to send men to the mines rather than into the fields to cut copra, even when the latter was a quicker method of clearing community debts. An economic motive also lay behind some protests against unauthorised and indiscriminate recruitment of labour. The situation was by no means unique to the mining industry, extending, for example, to the market in stevedore labour during the 1930s where: 'It appears as if the Bulis and Chiefs are sometimes anxious to get more than a reasonable share of the money earned by the people . . . Some Bulis when approached send mere boys and weaklings who are unsuitable for the work.'

---

[33] Sukuna to Theodore, 4.7.36, Vat./Native Affairs Camps Reports 1935- .

News travelled of the *loloma* paid by the Emperor group to local chiefs; and one *buli* at least took umbrage at being overlooked:

> rumours have reached me of the present or bonuses received by those Bulis of the Districts, whose men have come to work in the Mining Centres. If this is true then I earnestly implore you to allow me to receive that gift, just as you have done to the others. I should be very pleased to receive it.
>
> A good number of my men have now left my District to work in your Mining Districts of Matanagata.
>
> I beg you Sir to kindly excuse me for taking upon myself the liberty to write to you concerning the matter; for I feel that I ought to be the recipient of such a gift!
>
> Hoping you will oblige me by fulfilling my petition.[34]

Mine work under conditions of deferred and community-targeted earnings offered few material attractions for the labourers themselves. But alongside the contract system was a rising tide of 'voluntary' migratory labour, villagers who without the consent of their chiefs made their own way to the mines and other centres of employment thus circumventing the controls of the contract system and its financial deprivation. Promoted by the International Labour Organisation (ILO) after the Second World War, 'voluntary' labour was misleadingly projected as untarnished by the coercive features of the contract system.

The concept of 'free' or 'voluntary' labour was ideologically charged, above all belying the oppressive weight of economic pressures that underlay the 'free' market and had replaced the various forms of non-economic coercion (including taxation) associated with a forced labour economy. In Fiji the voluntary tide of labour was symptomatic of growing social as well as economic dislocation, highlighting one of the contradictions of colonial native policy. Ostensibly designed to cement the institutions and values of traditional society, native policy in fact acted as a catalyst of social change by creating internal tensions.

Voluntary migration was in some measure a product of these tensions. Even before goldmining began, the prospect of wage employment encouraged many young and able-bodied men to abandon the disciplined and exacting life of the village. Once established, the Tavua gold-field offered an alternative avenue such that by 1937 'much of the denudation of the village population' was considered to be due to this traffic. The case of Koroboya village in the hills just above the field typified the problem, with its men moving down to the mines during the 'work' months and returning home during the 'free' in order to avoid communal work. Only the old men, women and children remained.

The communal work programme had its critics, even within the colonial administration, notably C. S. de Reay, District Commissioner of Colo North (later the colony's first Commissioner of Labour). For Reay the high incidence of prosecutions for failure to perform communal services signified a decisive social protest, which contributed to the drain on rural manpower. It was proof that 'the native works reluctantly under the present system of control'. But opposition of this kind within the government's own ranks was not about to bring a change

---

[34] Buli Waima (Colo East) to Theodore, 18.8.36, Vat./Native Affairs Camps Reports 1935-

in policy, particularly when pitted against objections of chiefs that threatened to be politically destabilising. While articulated as a concern for the hardship it brought to the community, the opposition of chiefs was also dictated by self-interest. The loss of labour power meant not only that food production, house-building and other welfare services were detrimentally affected, but also that they suffered a personal loss in diminished *lala*. Their objections similarly addressed the steady erosion of their authority and influence within the colonial administration, begun during the first decade of the twentieth century.[35]

The 1945 Fijian Affairs Ordinance and its supporting (1948) regulations marked the sensitivity of the colonial state to such 'irritation' and 'protests'. The overhaul of the colony's native administration had become imperative, for it was considered 'urgently necessary to broaden the base of Native support and collaboration upon which every Colonial Government must stand and to give reality to Native responsibility for Native Affairs'.[36] The legislation represented a fresh commitment to regulating the social and economic activities of Fijians in accordance with the nineteenth-century principles of indirect rule. The restrictions imposed on movement outside the village were justified on the grounds that 'overcrowding' was not conducive to good moral and physical health, which was 'far more important in the public welfare than the right of free movement'.

Concern at the 'moral deterioration' of urban Fijians, however, disguised real fears that the large-scale migration to the town centres was a bid for freedom from 'tribal discipline and from the obligation to perform social services'. It was intolerable that Fijians should be allowed to revel in the (alleged) decadence and indolence of urban life 'when they should be doing useful work in their own villages'. The effect of the legislation was to lend a new strength and legitimacy to the chiefly system: to consolidate a traditional class structure conducive to social stability and continuing colonial control.[37]

THE STATE INTERVENES

The future of the Fijian under the rapidly changing conditions of the Colony, particularly his employment in large numbers on the gold fields, is a matter that has exercised my mind for some time past. Two grave dangers appear to face the Fijian under the present conditions that are depleting the villages of their able-bodied men. They are the health of the race and the lowering of its moral standards. With villages left to the care of the aged, the women, and the children, living conditions are deteriorating and insanitary villages the result. These in turn will undoubtedly materially affect the health of the community.

---

[35] Examples of the innumerable formal protests by chiefs against out-migration can be found in the proceedings of the Council of Chiefs for 1923, 1933, 1936, 1938, 1940 & 1942; and the Provincial Council Reports for Tailevu 1938 & 1939, Ra 1936, Lomaiviti 1937, Bua 1935 and Namosi 1936.

[36] Governor (P. E. Mitchell) to Secretary of State for Colonies, 16 July 1943, CP No. 24, 1943.

[37] The Criminal Offences Code prohibited unauthorised visits by Fijians (lasting more than 7 days) to the main town centres or industrial areas unless they were registered landowners, had been resident for five years, or were in 'permanent employment' in those areas. An offender was liable to repatriation and a fine or (in default) a prison sentence.

> On the mine fields, at the mills, and on plantations, but more particularly the first, large numbers of virile men are living in lines or barracks, as at Tavua, with a few native villages in more or less close proximity. It would be absurd to maintain for a moment that the moral standards of these men and the women with whom opportunity permits them to associate will not suffer. [Ag SNA (Monckton) memo Feb. 1937 CSO F36/11 Pt2]

Colonial policy was not easily wedded to the idea of a permanent work-force, despite the economic advantages of directing surplus labour to the mines. As in other places (the Northern Rhodesian copperbelt, for instance) the creation of a large industrial proletariat was not the preferred alternative. First, the removal of Fijians from the restraining influences of traditional society raised the awkward prospect of finding alternative means of social control. Second, the low-cost structure of Fijian labour was seen as largely reliant on the continued vitality of the pre-capitalist economy. The regulation of the labour market thus had both an economic and social purpose of mutual advantage to the colonial state and capital: it was a means of 'prevent[ing] a class of Fijians divorced from tribal associations and dependent for their livelihood on the economic conditions of the labour market'.[38]

Such sentiments were paralleled in East, West and Southern Africa as well as the Pacific. So too were the corrective measures they initiated such as the retention of customary social structures, some form of landed base and legislated controls on the movement of labour, including terms of contract. The reserves or *bantustans* and related pass laws of South Africa, Zambia and the territories of Basutoland, Bechuanaland and Swaziland were two such institutional devices. In New Guinea, where villages were frequently closed to recruitment in the inter-war years and other legislative controls brought the contract system under government management, a Commission of Inquiry into Native Labour rationalised the migrant labour system in terms almost identical to that of the Fiji administration. The establishment of permanent settlement at the plantations was opposed on the grounds that: 'from peasant proprietors as they are now, they would become landless labourers dependent for their living on the wages planters paid to them'.[39]

Within the British imperial establishment, concern over the political dangers posed by unrestrained proletarianisation was pointedly voiced by Lord Lugard in his introduction to Orde Brown's *African Labourers* in 1933:

> the problem of today is to ensure that service with Europeans shall not result in the premature disintegration of native society. For the illiterate worker who has lost faith in the approval or anger of his forebears, who has renounced his tribal loyalties and his claim to a share in the family or clan land and the ready help of his fellows in time of need, has now no motive for self-control and becomes a danger to the state.[40]

More than a decade later, these anxieties had not dissipated. In fact, in the context of Britain's post-war strategies for colonial development, the need to

---

[38] Fiji Colonial Report 1931, CO 83/228.
[39] Curtain 1984 : 130, 117–37.
[40] This is cited in Phillips 1977 : 16.

restrict the time spent by Africans at the mines or any other centre of wage employment in order 'to prevent the decay of tribal life and the loss of . . . home traditions and surroundings'[41] was arguably even more relevant. Addressing the House of Lords in 1945 the Secretary of State for the Colonies stressed the undesirability of long-term employment: 'Absence for too long periods of too large a proportion of the male population from their homes may lead to a breaking down of local custom and authority, to a loosening of home ties, and so on. All those things need to be carefully considered.'[42]

In Fiji the state's commitment to preserving the structures and *modus operandi* of Fijian society had a decisive impact on the new mining industry. Although market conditions on the whole favoured its early labour needs and the migrant system was officially backed, the demands of compulsory village and district work introduced a basis for conflict. Communal demands on the labour of Fijian mineworkers induced high turnover that raised production costs and reduced efficiency. Both the Tavua and Mt Kasi companies perpetually complained, and bitterly, of this interference, insisting from the earliest stages that the industry required labour that would stay more than a few months, providing some 'continuity of employment'. Turnover at Mt Kasi in the mid-1930s was around 30% a month, and there were often more extreme weekly fluctuations. According to the company, 'almost all the Fijians use the mine merely as an opportunity to acquire ready money quickly, and, when the immediate need is satisfied, leave the mine without warning'.

The argument was to some extent ideological. High turnover was not only a product of the conflicting demands of the indigenous and mining capitalist modes of production. It was also a mark of labour dissatisfaction or protest over unappealing conditions and the difficulties of adjustment to an unpleasant and hazardous occupation. This was particularly true of underground work, which was widely disliked, partly for superstitious reasons: *Na gauna ga keimami na curu kina ki na qara ni keimami sa bulu* ('the only time you go underground is when your body is buried'). Complaints from the mining companies nevertheless swiftly acquired the force of ultimatums, with Theodore warning that it would be 'uneconomical . . . to rely upon Fijians for our main labour force' and the Mt Kasi company delivering a more direct threat that it would be 'get(ting) rid of its Fijian labour altogether if the position cannot be remedied'.

From mid-1936, as the gold rush receded and the two interests secured virtual monopolies over the main mining areas, formal state intervention appeared both logical and necessary. It was not, however, without difficulties. Efforts to secure a more stable supply of mine labour flew in the face of intensifying protest from the chiefs to curb movement out of the villages; they stirred the residual forces of conservatism within the administration itself; and they rebuffed prevailing international opinion on labour recruitment. An international labour convention adopted in 1936 urged that the social, political and economic welfare of recruited labour be adequately safeguarded; and the Colonial Office had drawn this to

---

[41] Lord Harlech, House of Lords Debate, 15 May 1945.
[42] Duke of Devonshire, House of Lords Debate, 15 May 1945.

the attention of the Fiji administration as early as 1934, when the convention was still in its draft stages. Responding, the government clung fiercely to one of the most enduring myths of official wisdom:

> the number of natives recruited for contract service is small, and there are no large movements of labour which might have serious sociological effects upon the race. There is no economic necessity for the natives to become wage-earners for long periods, and no pressure of any description is placed upon them to enter into contracts of service . . .[43]

It was article four of the Recruiting of Indigenous Workers Convention that was especially relevant to Fiji's new mining industry. This recommended that before any new economic development likely to involve labour recruitment was approved, steps be taken:
(a) to avoid the risk of pressure being brought to bear on the populations concerned by or on behalf of the employers in order to obtain the labour required;
(b) to ensure that, as far as possible, the political and social organisation of the populations . . . and their powers of adjustment to the changed economic conditions will not be endangered by the demand for labour; and
(c) to deal with any other possible untoward effects of such development on the populations concerned.
The Colonial Office was assured that the effects of the 'voluntary' flow of mine labour would be closely watched and, if necessary, controlled under the Native Regulations.

Reassurances to the home government did not accurately reflect the local situation, or even the preoccupations and policies of the colonial government. As the Acting Secretary for Native Affairs soberly observed in 1937, only two years after the Emperor mine had come into production, the diversion of Fijian labour was indeed threatening to unleash the type and scale of social dislocation to which the government had been alerted. In the absence of a consensus on how to deal with the problem there was, however, tacit agreement that Fijian employment was not itself a contentious issue. Pressure for the prohibition of 'indiscriminate recruiting' remained just that; and quantitative restrictions on engagements were not enforced. A proposed formula that the number of men leaving their villages during the 'working' (i.e. communal work) months be limited to 25%, in practice proved 'the exception rather than the rule'.

Another corrective measure that was put forward stemmed from the belief that the industry's labour demands could jeopardise the very survival of the Fijian social system. But the revision of the labour laws and the native regulations nevertheless failed to elicit sufficient support. Steps taken to alleviate food shortages and arrest the deterioration in living conditions were not to 'hamper the employers of labour' and it had to be remembered that an adequate labour supply was a *sine qua non* of mining. Other senior officers, such as Colonial Secretary Barton, exhibited little of this ambivalence and few if any anxieties. The proposals for

---

[43] OAGF to Secretary of State for Colonies, Recruitment of Native Labour Correspondence July 1934–April 1935, Miscell. No. 450 Confidential, Fiji & Western Pacific No. 35.

stricter control simply ran counter to what Barton perceived to be an ineluctable process of social change. The progressive disintegration of the communal system was merely a part of this, and further regulations could have the undesirable effect of intercepting the free flow of labour. Barton's private admission to the Governor was that article four of the Recruiting of Indigenous Workers Convention made him feel 'a little nervous' at its likely hindrance to economic development.

Actions, in any event, spoke louder than words; and the colony's labour and native legislation remained unchanged. Even specific measures proposed by the chiefs—an increase in the absentee tax, tighter restrictions over indenture including the need for a *buli's* permission and a reduction in the number of months that a Fijian male could be legally absent from his village—were rejected or ignored. The labour laws, notably the Masters and Servants Ordinance with its biting penal sanctions, were a continuing testimony to the political strength of European capital, in particular the planters and the CSR; and while official policy stood committed in theory to regulating migration to the mines, the demands of the mining companies were ultimately met.

State intervention in the mine labour market took explicit form in the practical assistance given by administrative officers as unofficial recruiters; the introduction of informal recruitment schemes in a number of provinces; the *de facto* modification of native policy to permit and encourage the stabilisation of labour; the attempts to involve official chiefs in recruitment; and the support for Fijian indenture under the controversial and largely discredited conditions of nineteenth-century labour law. The combined effect of these measures was to transform an irregular and arbitrary pattern of supply, which allowed Fijians a certain degree of freedom to withdraw their labour, into a more rationalised system of mobilisation and control.

The warning from Mt Kasi was not taken lightly, and once it had resolved that it was vital to 'keep Fijian labour on the job and not let others in', the colonial administration acted quickly and decisively. Directives were issued to European district officers to ensure that the mine had a regular supply of Fijian labour, including some (of the more skilled men) committed to at least one year's service. From July 1936 a series of recruitment schemes was introduced into the provinces of Bua and Cakaudrove. These were based on a regular rotation of labour, 80 men every three months in the first of Bua's ventures. A tactical compromise, the incorporation of local chiefs into the management of the schemes ensured their smooth running. As the Acting Secretary of Native Affairs remarked laconically: 'If labour can be arranged through the chiefs—the chiefs will not call them back.' Among the more conspicuous trends in Bua's successive experiments were the move towards a more centralised recruitment organisation (albeit nothing resembling the elaborate organisation of the South African mining industry); the vesting of greater powers in co-opted chiefs (who were promoted from overseers to organisers); and adjustments in the communal work programme to accommodate fluctuations in the demand for mine labour.

At the Tavua field the role of local chiefs, particularly their employment as professional recruiters, was neither as extensive nor as formalised. Between 1934 and 1937 a two-man team comprising a chief and the son of a local European planter was assigned the task of procuring labour from the large island of Vanua

Levu. But, on the whole, chiefs appear to have participated only on an informal basis. Officers of the district administration acted in a similar capacity—following up requests for labour, advising the companies where and when men were available, and generally assisting in the organisation of group recruitment and labour transportation. While District Commissioner of Lau, Ratu Sukuna acquired in the correspondence of the colonial secretariat the dubious designation of unofficial 'recruiter' for Theodore's mines. This was not very different from the recruitment process in post-war Portuguese Mozambique for the South African mines, of which Ruth First says: 'The Portuguese Authorities net the fish, while the mines just take delivery.'[44]

The 'netting' function of Fiji's colonial government was exemplified in February 1936 following an outburst of communal violence that left the Vatukoula mines stricken by a sudden and critical labour shortage. Theodore's personal entreaty to the local District Commissioner 'to do all that can reasonable [sic] be done to cooperate with my companies in replacing labour' led to prompt refurbishment. With the co-operation of the Native Assistant Commissioner and Native Stipendiary Magistrate of the Yasawa Islands, the officer arranged for a total of 80 'Yasawa boys' to be dispatched by provincial boat to Tavua. Many were married, and copra production and housebuilding, it was admitted, demanded their services at home. Another 188 men were sent by the Roko Tui Macuata from Vanua Levu.

With the assistance of the colonial government the Emperor group tested a number of strategies to reduce the mobility of mine labour and to diversify the provincial composition of its Fijian work-force. Migrant labour under contract offered to solve the twin problems of periodic shortage and a highly mobile labour supply. Though recruitment from farther afield was more expensive on account of transport and other costs, the policy had a number of advantages. The group was assured of longer-serving labour at fixed wages and improved labour discipline because groups of between 20 and 100 men came under the direct management of their chiefs. The distance from home and the irregular shipping services connecting Viti Levu with the outer islands also made it more difficult for men to abscond. From 1936 the Associated Companies accordingly began to indenture Fijian labour under written contract for between six and 12 months.

While brief, the indenture experiment was significant as a measure of the state's support for Fiji's large mining interests. Contracts were permitted under the Masters and Servants Ordinance despite its long-condemned effects on the donor districts of plantation labour, the censure of its penal provisions in other colonies, and the illegality of its general application to Fijian labour. (See Appendix H.) Over this matter the Colonial Office was not in the dark, but clearly willing to turn a blind eye. In spite of its own efforts to have the labour laws in its colonies reformed, it saw fit to accommodate the questionable manoeuvrings in Fiji. It was all a 'rather awkward' matter 'because for some time employers with a good deal of affinative [sic] acquiescence by the government have been breaking

[44] First 1982 : 10.

the law by engaging Fijians as plantation labourers under the Masters and Servants Ordnc'.[45]

Yet formal indenture proved less popular as a method of recruitment than unwritten contracts of group employment. This latter alternative offered employers the benefits of immobilised labour, such as fixed wages and enhanced control, while sparing it the official scrutiny of contracts and other liabilities under prevailing labour law. Terms of engagement had neither the scope of formal contracts in respect of minimum housing standards or medical provisions, for example, nor indeed the force of law. Workers thus had no legal claim to 'protection' under the labour legislation. For these reasons, as well as for others, the system was cheaper: there were fewer expenses, lower transport costs and no obligatory tax advances. In August 1936 the Emperor group estimated that the cost of recruiting Fijian labour under written contract averaged £5 7s. 6d. per head (exclusive of rations and wages). In sharp contrast, the engagement of Yasawa men under informal contracts in February the same year cost it approximately 12s. 6d. per head.

Under the 1912 Employment Ordinance it was obligatory for labourers indentured from districts outside their own to have their return fares paid by their employers, whatever the length of service. Private arrangements such as those Theodore negotiated with Ratu Sukuna circumvented this requirement, enabling Lauan labour to be returned at the group's expense only if a minimum of six months employment was undertaken. A single fare was all that was paid for men who engaged for three to six months, which meant that they had to meet the cost of both transport and food for the duration of the voyage home themselves, the trip to Lau lasting about a week.

The use of government or provincial boats, approved at the discretion of officers or chiefs, afforded the companies a further convenience. In the case of Lau, they were in a strong enough bargaining position to insist on the vessels making regular trips as a condition of employing its labour. For time-expired workers it was a raw deal. The numerous commitments and limited carrying capacity of provincial boats meant delays in returning home, and almost certainly diminished or no savings by the time they got there. For those on six-month to 12-month contracts and thus fortunate enough to have their return fare paid, the cost of board and lodging in Suva was deducted by the group if the end of a contract did not coincide with a scheduled shipping run home.

The recruiting services rendered by chiefs and local officers did not escape the watchful eye of the colonial secretariat. But although they flouted international conventions and even deviated from practice in other areas of the British Empire, such as East Africa, where chiefs were 'rigorously forbidden' and officials 'absolutely forbidden' to recruit, their activities were not unduly curtailed. Article nine of the ILO Recruiting of Indigenous Workers Convention No. 50 (1936) prohibited recruitment by public officers for private concerns, unless the labour was required for public works. Article ten forbade chiefs or 'other indigenous authorities' to

---

[45] Illegible minute, 23 April 1931, CO 83/194/12. For discussion of the Masters and Servants laws and their controversial application to Fijian labour, see Bain 1988 : 128-9.

'act as recruiting agents'; to 'exercise pressure upon possible recruits'; or to 'receive from any source whatsoever any special remuneration or other special inducement for assistance in recruiting'. The colonial government agreed to apply the convention in February 1937, but no supporting legislation was introduced for ten years.

Article nine of the Convention caused some ripples of disquiet among offending officers, but it was argued that they were tacitly permitted to direct taxpayers seeking work to places of employment. In fact, it was precisely against this more subtle use of authority that the International Labour Conference had warned: 'the position of the administrative officer is such that his wish is often equivalent to a command, and if . . . generally permitted . . . would not be far removed from compulsion to labour'. Furthermore, a recruiting function was deemed incompatible with the task of labour supervision.[46]

Not until the enactment of the 1947 Labour Ordinance, which expressly prohibited any form of recruitment by chiefs or government officers, did the colonial government become sensitised to the tenuous grounds on which the defence of its role in the labour market rested. But there the problem was not solved. The fine distinction between guidance and active procurement (or canvassing) had to be made, and, to this end, district officers were instructed to use their 'discretion' to ensure that neither chiefs nor public officers used 'their rank or authority to induce Fijians to engage with a private employer'. In either case the idea of detaching rank from a person of rank (or authority) was about as fanciful as the notion of separating wetness from water.

Recourse to indenture, whether formal or informal, was not the only or indeed the most effective remedy to the problem of turnover. Time restrictions on the employment of single male workers could be outwitted by employers applying for their exemption from communal duties, paying the obligatory commutation fees, and then reclaiming these from workers by wage deductions. A beginning to a longer-term solution was to provide housing for married recruits and their families, for labour could then legitimately remain in employment for an indefinite period. Initially, at least, housing was made available to married members only if they committed themselves to a minimum six-month indenture.

For a number of reasons the provision of housing became a compelling alternative. First, changing production techniques—in particular the greater emphasis on mechanised underground mining—demanded a more skilled work-force. Second, accompanying wives could conveniently provide unpaid reproductive services, thereby subsidising the cost of married labour. They were expected to maintain *teitei* (food gardens), prepare meals, wash clothes, keep homes, compounds and barracks clean (thus assisting the industry in its battle against sanitation-related disease) and to cater to the emotional and sexual needs of workers. As Chapter 4 shows, resident wives were also preferred to unmarried female visitors, most of whom came under suspicion for prostitution and venereal disease. On the Zambian (Northern Rhodesian) copper mines, the practice of

---

[46]   The Regulation of Certain Special Systems of Recruiting Workers Report, ILC 20th Session Geneva, 1936.

family settlement was already enabling the Anglo-American mining group to reap the rewards of the 'more efficient, healthier, more contented' married worker, who 'remains longer than the single native'.[47] The presence of miners' wives, it was found, also 'discouraged prostitution, gambling, fights and general disorder'.

The social, economic and production benefits of family recruitment were thus considerable; and while data on the economics of family recruitment are unfortunately incomplete, the policy's benefits would seem to have far outweighed the companies' nominal expenditure on extra rations, married housing and development of the town's rudimentary social and recreational infrastructure. As the following chapter shows, there was also little adjustment to wages before 1950 and most benefits, such as sick pay and superannuation, remained beyond the reach of ethnic Fijian mineworkers.

As early as 1936 the Theodore group embarked on a modest housing programme. It did so with the blessing of the local administration and the tacit approval of the metropolitan government, whose Colonial Labour Committee had recently recommended that the family unit become the basis for labour recruitment in the 'more primitive' territories. Yet the release under Fijian labour law of married men who took their immediate dependants to Vatukoula compromised regulations aimed at restricting entry to the labour market, protecting community living standards, and conserving the communal system itself. Labourers took only their wives—the unit vital for the reproduction of labour—and possibly their children, but not members of their extended family towards whom they also had responsibilities. In this way, social as well as economic dislocation was implicitly sanctioned.

For the mining companies the contradictions inherent in colonial policy presented few problems. Overall, official policy helped to bring about a degree of labour stabilisation in the early years; while in the long term it laid the foundations of permanent employment. By 1938 all married men housed at Vatukoula had been employed for a minimum of 18 months to two years. Assured that the government's wish was to 'facilitate . . . the permanent departure from the communal system of Fijians who are offered skilled employment and training of a more or less permanent character', the group was given more concrete support when, in 1940, the commutation rate for single men was reduced by 10s. and total exemption was granted to married men with dependants.

As economic conditions deteriorated during the late 1930s, active recruitment, such as the contract system and other non-economic devices aimed at stabilising labour, became less necessary. Plunging copra prices forced European plantations to close and scores of Fijian agriculturalists and workers (particularly from the Yasawa Islands, Kadavu and Lau) swamped the mines. Faced with a rising surplus and the tiresome fact that 'although they are turned away they still continue to come back seeking work', the companies could take comfort from the fact that, if needed, 'there [were] hundreds awaiting employment' in the villages. Such conditions facilitated stringent wage control and encouraged longer periods of service. This would become the predominant trend of the future.

---

[47] Parpart 1983 : 35.

THE LABOUR CRISIS OF THE 1940s

From the end of 1941 various factors that had combined so well to satisfy the labour needs of the mining industry were thrown off course. An improvement in the copra price of £18 a ton prompted large numbers of Fijian as well as Part-European workers to leave the mines. With the colony drawn into international combat, the offer of higher wages and other more favourable terms of employment in government defence works, the CSR, firms such as Morris Hedstrom, and ancillary jobs for the American forces ('chiefly through taking in [their] washing'!) lured still more away to the main centres of Suva and Nadi.

Beyond the inevitable dislocation to labour supply caused by military recruitment, the effects of a more competitive labour market were crippling for the industry. Having lost nearly half its expatriate staff at the beginning of the war, the Emperor group was faced in 1942 with the withdrawal of 1345 employees, 1219 of whom were Fijian. By the following year its total work-force was reduced to 873. More generally, the situation deteriorated as restrictions were placed on the importation of necessary materials and equipment, shipping services were disrupted, and power was rationed. All were blamed for the falling rate of production, this by as much as one-third between April and June 1942. Shortly afterwards the group was forced to reckon with the possibility of a partial close-down.

The importance of gold production to colonial and imperial interests dictated direct state intervention. It was considered imperative to forestall the immediate loss of revenue and the deleterious long-term effect on economic development of a shut-down of operations. An improvement in Britain's purchasing power of dollars at a crucial time of combat was also regarded as necessary. The colonial government accordingly took steps to boost the industry's fast dwindling labour supply. The classification of goldmining as 'essential' to the war effort legitimised its involvement in an area which the Governor privately acknowledged to be the responsibility of the mining companies, as well as the use of recruitment methods more akin to conscription. For the duration of the war, at least a few hundred Fijians were 'forced' to accept employment at the mines.[48]

While supporting the continued production of gold during the war the Colonial Office was unwilling, with the apparent exception of the Nigerian tin mines, to condone any initiatives that exercised compulsion on 'natives' to do mine work. Fiji's request in 1942 that it 'countenance an extension of definition of essential industry for which labour can be ordered to work' was therefore rejected. But the absence of legal powers 'to order men not engaged in mining to engage in it' did not prove inhibiting. Encouraged by the home government's agreement that it could 'persuade labour [excluding those on military duties] to return to mines voluntarily', the Governor adopted the position that: 'If . . . there is anything we can do to induce men to stay at the mines or go back to them we should do it.'[49] Contrary to a ruling by the Colonial Office, mineworkers (numbering

---

[48]   CSO/confidential file.
[49]   CSO/confidential file.

over 100 on a single occasion) who had been drafted into the defence services as part of the mines territorial company were released on the government's orders. Men who subsequently applied for defence work were rejected. To make this watertight, it became obligatory for all mine employees to have the Governor's permission before they could enlist in the forces.

In December 1942 officers responsible for administering the provinces of Colo North, Ra, Colo West and Nadroga in the western and central districts of Viti Levu received instructions aimed at safeguarding existing supplies and mobilising more labour for the mines. Time-expired contract labour at Nadi airport was one possible source of supplementary labour power and it was decided 'to encourage some of these returnees after a reasonable period at home to seek employment at the Mines'. The general message of the Adviser on Native Affairs was a simple one: 'that officials should use your best endeavours whenever opportunities occur to persuade the existing labour to remain at the mines, as well as to help in securing labour when required'.[50] Specific labour requests from the mines management were handled directly by Reay, now the Commissioner of Labour, in liaison with Ratu Sukuna and Fijian representatives from selected provinces.

The significance of this political pressure went beyond the labour supply it successfully generated and the liberal interpretation given to Colonial Office despatches. Saddled with its own problem of maintaining adequate numbers for the war effort, the government had conducted a recruitment campaign that, by the end of 1942, had 'just about skinned the villages'. 'Nearly all native labour', Reay admitted, could be 'classed as conscript, for we get them by instructing Rokos to use their influence as chiefs to send them in.'[51] Reports from numerous provinces bemoaned the serious depletion of labour reserves along with its economic and social consequences. In Bua only 302 out of 1013 able-bodied males between the ages of 18 and 60 remained in the villages; while in Ra, where the largest Fijian population in the central district was to be found, dislocation appeared to be even more shattering: the Roko Tui Ra was unable to comply with orders to supply men to the mines because not 'a single man' could be mustered.

Labour shortages at Vatukoula persisted into the late 1940s in spite of the steady reduction in defence work, government assistance over recruitment and two wage adjustments. The problem at Loloma and Dolphin remained 'very acute', and although the total work-force for the three sister mines had climbed to around 1200 by December 1945, and the demand for surface workers was met, underground and open-cut labour was still about one-third below requirements. The austerity of post-war conditions, in particular soaring living costs, slowly pushed numbers closer to pre-war levels, but gains were soon offset by the combined bogeys of buoyant copra prices, competitive wages outside the industry and a mine strike in 1947.

If the prominent feature of the mine labour market during the late 1940s was

50   CSO/confidential file.
51   Reay to Theodore, 31 Dec. 1942, Vat./Correspondence EGT/NEN July 1941–Nov. 1944.

the perennial shortages of Fijian and Part-European labour, the problem found inspired solution in changes made to the racial and ethnic distribution of workers during the following decade. This was closely linked to the pressing matter of labour costs. The crisis of the 1940s did not, in any event, appear to impede the structural transformation taking place in the mine labour market. The steady displacement of short-term migrant labour by a growing proportion of semi-permanent and permanent workers had begun around the late 1930s. By 1939, within five years of active mining on the Tavua field, a sample of nearly 500 Fijian workers revealed that 15% had been in continuous employment for periods ranging from between six months and five and three-quarter years (an average of one and a quarter years) and 25% for at least two and three-quarter years. Ten years later, management estimated that approximately one-third of its Fijian workers were married and settled at the mines with their families.

The proletarianisation of mine labour was embryonic, yet these early years of goldmining witnessed the successful application of a number of strategies designed to meet the need for more stabilised workers. The political as well as the economic and social factors that have been discussed were crucial in preparing the ground for a more complete transition by the 1950s.

3 Employment and Earnings

RACE, ETHNICITY AND THE ORGANISATION OF MINE LABOUR

Unlike other costs of production over which the mining industry had little influence, labour costs offered an important means of maintaining optimum conditions of accumulation. The gulf between the value of gold production and the value of labour power was the basis of labour exploitation. But levels of surplus value varied according to the ability of mining capital to minimise returns to labour and maximise its productivity. These in turn were influenced by conditions in the labour market, political pressures and the demands made by labour itself.

In addition the opportunities for accumulation were enhanced in a colonial economy serviced primarily by non-white indigenous labour. The traditional socio-economic system could be utilised in ways that allowed a higher rate of labour exploitation and safeguarded production relations generally. As Chapter 5 demonstrates, a significant ideological dimension to this role rested in the propagation of traditional values of deference to persons in authority. But while exploitation assumed a racial form, racial/ethnic relations were not coincident with class relations. The work-force included white (European) workers, who, while privileged, also contributed as exploited labour to the valorisation of mining capital.

In the heyday of operations at Vatukoula, labour costs represented a small if significant proportion of production costs. The period between 1938 to 1948, however, witnessed a 109.8% increase in labour costs from £121,610 to £255,221. Over the same period, workers also received a rising proportion of the gross value of production, from 18.1% to 28.2% (see Appendix B). While inimical to the interests of capital, these trends were decidedly conservative beside those of the post-war period, in particular following the formation of the mineworkers union in 1948. Further, annual increases of 10% (labour costs) and 1% (wages as a proportion of revenue) were slight, especially compared with increases in other production costs and the improving skill profile of mineworkers. The pattern was not one shared by all sections of the work-force. A range of devices intensified the exploitation of Fijian labour, and higher labour costs were caused mainly by wage adjustments to non-Fijian, especially European, labour. Over the same period the ratio of European to Fijian employees scarcely changed, from 1:10.5 to 1:9.8.

At the same time the total wages and salaries bill for all three of the Emperor group of companies declined between 1941 and 1945 on account of the shrinking size of the wartime work-force. The threat to production posed by labour shortages led to heightened exploitation of those workers who remained at the mines or who were effectively forced back. In essence the falling aggregate return to mine labour in the form of wages and salaries (from £161,847 p.a. to £138,163 p.a.) coincided with a noticeable rise in labour productivity or per capita output (from 126.6 tons p.a. to 154.2 tons p.a.) (see Appendix I).

Strategies of labour-cost minimisation during the 1930s and 1940s were directly influenced by the supply of labour and the structure of production. The abundance of labour until the early 1940s facilitated tight control of Fijian wages, while the predominance of surface (open-cut) mining, especially at Emperor, lent itself to labour-intensive mining methods and tolerated an oscillating system of low-skilled and therefore cheap migratory labour. To great profit, the Associated Mining Companies were able to capitalise on the large reserves of unskilled Fijian labour subject to reduction in its turnover. Another function of low-cost Fijian labour (as well as its overall subordination within the work process) lay in the sparing efforts of the group to provide formal or technical training. Until after the Second World War this was popularly regarded as of little value, and experience (or on-the-job learning) was projected as the most important method of ensuring safe working habits. Evidently this alternative was not perceived as an impediment to productivity, and its adoption in lieu of a training programme was probably also influenced by conditions of labour surplus and migrancy as well as the limits placed on occupational mobility for non-European mineworkers.

The changes that occurred in the labour market from the early 1940s effected shortages in all classes (skilled and unskilled) and ethnic categories of mineworkers with the exception of Indian labour. Over the same period, open-cut mining on the Emperor mine progressively gave way to underground stoping. This transition inflated production costs through the introduction of new plant and greater mechanisation, necessitating a more skilled workforce, as well as the more complicated and costly process of extracting semi-sulphide rather than oxidised ore. Both developments demanded occupational changes to guarantee economies in labour costs.

The opportunity to achieve this lay at the heart of the mine labour system where a racial division of labour and earnings provided a blueprint for exploitation. This transcended the inherently exploitative nature of capitalist production relations. Formalised in broad divisions within which Fijians were classified as unskilled labour, Part-Europeans and Rotumans as unskilled and semi-skilled workers, and Europeans as skilled operators and supervisors, the mines' occupational formula combined elements of racial specificity with racial hierarchy.

So, too, their structure of earnings and social life categorised and stratified mine-workers according to racial and ethnic origin.

Institutionalised racism was a pivotal force of the plantation and mining colonial economies of Africa, Asia, the Caribbean, North and South America and the Pacific, its precise forms varying less in substance than degree. The variant of Fiji's mining industry was never immutable, although its basic principles proved enduring. This blend of flexibility and consistency held the key to its success in the long term, permitting the modifications demanded by ever-fluid conditions of production. The racial and ethnic differentiation of wages and work was not altered significantly until the 1950s and 1960s, but, as we shall see, the years during and after the Second World War witnessed important adjustments to the structure of employment.

Born out of imperial notions of cultural superiority and paternalism, racialist values legitimised divergent forms of social and economic discrimination. These were not confined to the mining industry. In fact their ubiquity, like their sanction by the colonial authorities, encouraged the mines to adopt a system of accumulation based on the intensive exploitation of non-European labour. The projection of racialist stereotypes in defence of labour division, and particularly the exclusion of non-Europeans from certain jobs demanding skill and responsibility, habitually took the form of caricatures. The view of Inspector of Mines Grieves was that:

> [The Fijian was] . . . careless, unreliable, inclined to take unnecessary risks and is mentally lethargic.
> [The Indian was] . . . probably the most suitable of the local coloured folk—whilst methodically reliable under routine conditions has . . . a tendency to carelessness and risks, and although mentally alert, he is of an excitable disposition and thus becomes untrustworthy in dangerous moments.
> [The Part-European] was . . . unreliable, quarrelsome and addicted to late hours in his intemperate habits. Physically he is slow and clumsy with a tendency to indolence. He lacks initiative and ambition, requires to be under constant control in most occupations. As a tradesman, where he is extensively used in the Colony, he lacks precision, and the ability to control men; hence he seldom rises from a subordinate position. Where sudden, prompt decisions are vital, he would probably fail through mental inalertness and . . . relative to Europeans he suffers from an inferiority complex . . . [he was to be regarded as] of very doubtful suitability.

The crude conclusion of Grieve's argument was that 'it is the white man's prerogative to assume all positions demanding extreme reliability in a dark man's land'.[1]

The role of a racialist ideology in shaping not only attitudes but the very principles of job classification in the mining industry raises questions about the compatibility of a system of discrimination with the process of capital accumulation. As early as the 1960s these questions attracted attention among South African scholars, spawning considerable debate between liberal and Marxist social scientists.[2] The liberal argument has essentially been that an institutionalised

---

[1] IOM to Chairman Mining Board, 31 Dec. 1935, CSO F111/25.
[2] For the liberal school of pluralists writing on South Africa, see Horwitz 1967; van den Berghe 1967; Kuper & Smith 1969; Houghton 1967; Wilson & Thompson 1969, 1971; Wilson 1972; Adam 1971; Rex 1971 : 401–13. For good examples of Marxist scholarship on this aspect of South African history, see Trapido 1971 : 309–20; Wolpe 1972 : 425–56; Wolpe 1970; Simons & Simons 1969. For more recent contributions to the debate, see Marks & Rathbone 1982; Wolpe 1988.

job colour bar is 'dysfunctional' to the rational development and growth of a capitalist economy.[3] It is a notion that had far-reaching implications for the conceptualisation of class relations and class struggle in South Africa.

In Fiji the relationship between occupational discrimination and capitalist development emerged as a contentious issue within the colonial administration. For some, the economic irrationality of excluding non-Europeans from certain jobs brought the practice into serious disrepute. In 1934, as the mining industry cut its first teeth, Governor Fletcher reasoned:

> Man for man the European is undoubtedly to be preferred, but it is a question of cost. The whole of the tropical world, apart from White Australia or protected territories such as Honolulu, depends for its prosperity upon cheap labour, and it is essential that Fiji should be in a position to compete... what we have to do is to translate the difference [i.e. relative efficiency] into terms of money.

Fletcher's opinions were shared by the Theodore group, which found a valuable ally in its efforts to defy the *de facto* reservation, under the 1934 Mining Regulations, of winder engine driving in the early 1930s. Writing to Hedstrom in December 1935, Theodore complained that it would be 'an onerous and unnecessary burden if we were compelled to employ only European certificated engine drivers'. Two years later the mining regulations were amended so that only drivers on principal winding plant were required to be 'fully certificated'. On all three types of winches (air, diesel and electric-motor driven) the government accepted that 'of necessity [drivers had] to be drawn from the ranks of workers of mixed descent, native Fijians, and the like'.[4]

The repudiation of Fletcher's theory by the government's own public works department reflected a number of considerations. First, it was a 'false economy' to employ less-efficient, non-European labour, for Indians were reputedly careless and in need of supervision. Second, there were decided disadvantages in tapping only one (ethnic) source of labour. As the Commissioner of Works put it, 'the present system [of deploying both white and non-white labour] acts as a check in more ways than one and conduces to a greater output than would be possible if only one class of driver were employed'. The view evidently claimed some support within CSR management, which also pointed out the risks of Indian labour militancy as an argument against the total displacement of Europeans.

In the final analysis, economic rationalisation in both the sugar and the mining industries dictated a guarded policy of local substitution. Even for Fletcher himself, proposals for local substitution were not as radical as they appeared, and he did not reject the racist assumptions that underpinned the job colour bar. He denounced only its indiscriminate application and, more important, he supported a system of discriminatory earnings. Ideology did not, then, hinder economic development because, on the grounds of its (alleged) relative inefficiency and unreliability, unskilled local labour could be deployed at lower wage rates to do the skilled work of Europeans.

---

[3] Johnstone 1976 : 203–5.

[4] For comparison with amendments made to mines and works legislation in New Guinea around the same time, see Newbury 1975 : 32–3.

While labour substitution gained increasing currency in Fiji, a new wave in metropolitan thinking began to lap corrosively at the shores of the colonial colour bar. In 1945 the watchdog eye of the House of Lords was cast critically over its continued application in Britain's territories. As Nigeria's Minerals Ordinance came up for review, Lord Ammon placed the case of Northern Rhodesia squarely before the House. Criticising the fact that the white wage was 'from forty to fifty times as great as that paid to the coloured worker', he argued that Britain had a responsibility in the African colonies to provide Africans with training opportunities. It was necessary that they be equipped 'to fill positions of responsibility and authority' and that they should not remain 'confined to the lowest conditions and terms of work', as 'hewers of wood and drawers of water'.[5]

As with the Christian missionary lobby the arguments against institutionalised discrimination in Africa and India were influenced by pragmatic as well as moral considerations. Both kinds of objections were synthesised in the case put forward by the Episcopal Synod of South Africa:

> We affirm that the effect of colour prejudice is cruel, wasteful and dangerous: cruel, for it deprives those who are its victims of the opportunity of making full use of their capacities and talents, and so causes frustration and despair; wasteful, for it deprives the community of the skill of many which would otherwise be used for the benefit of all; dangerous, for unjust treatment meted out by one section of the community to another creates fierce and ever-increasing resentment, with results that no one can foresee . . .[6]

No consensus was reached in the House of Lords, and although lip-service disapproval was registered against the colour bar, the fault was generally held to lie with the white trade union movements. Prohibitive legislative measures were regarded by Lords Rennell, Hailey and Harlech as futile. Ammon's sentiments nevertheless appear to have filtered through from London to the colonial governments, having found favour with the Colonial Office. The 1946 Memorandum on Colonial Mining Policy adopted an emphatic position: 'provision should be made for the indigenous populations to fit themselves for the highest technical and administrative posts'. All colonial governments were instructed to take the necessary steps to implement the recommendations of the 1944 International Labour Conference at Philadelphia on the Prohibition of Colour and Religious Bars and other Discriminatory Practices.[7]

The force of international opinion was not enough to dislodge a system that had served colonial capital so well. In the Fiji mining industry, racialist structures and attitudes persisted. The economic logic of discrimination, as we shall see, derived from the peculiarities of the mines' employment structure. The attempt of the colonial administration to introduce trade testing in 1946 was aborted under pressure from the mining and sugar companies. This meant that the classification of non-European (especially Fijian) labour, whose skills were not formally recognised, as 'ordinary' labour was able to continue. Even in circumstances

---

[5] House of Lords Debate, 15 May 1945.
[6] Ibid.
[7] PRO CO 852/757/4.

of declining safety standards and an accelerating rate of mining accidents, the group was reluctant to invest in a more formal training scheme. In the late 1940s, a government-sponsored and substantially subsidised programme of classes in areas such as mechanical engineering, mining practice, milling and ore treatment, and carpentry was restricted mainly to those of 'boss boy' or 'leading hand' status. A 10s. per term fee was extracted for the privilege of a once-weekly course of instruction.

Institutionalised discrimination was effective as a means of labour control as well as being economically rewarding. The creation of an aristocracy of labour was assisted by positive discrimination in favour of Rotumans, who were allocated to Fijian-held jobs at higher rates of pay, and for whom a more diverse range of jobs, including lower-ranking supervisory ones such as leading hand and junior boss, was available. The policy was not without contradictions, for the classification of Rotumans as Part-Europeans, like the privileges afforded Part-European workers, inflated the cost of 'native' labour and had a destabilising effect on production relations, contributing to early industrial unrest.

Yet this unique convention of the mines, like the even more costly practice of supporting an élite European work-force, was advantageous for the conservative influence it exercised on one section of the working class. The disciplinary function performed by Rotuman community elders compounded this. Overall the system served as a drawing card to this favoured category of labour. As the group's mines superintendent observed in 1948, the practice

> has been, and will continue to be a success. It has given the Rotumans a feeling of importance, for at Vatukoula they enjoy better conditions than elsewhere. This is appreciated by Rotumans who endeavour to live up to their improved status. In fact the leaders of their community, in disciplining their less responsible members, point out that they must behave themselves or they may be the cause of all the Vatukoula Rotumans losing all or part of their privileges. This, I think, is the main reason why it will always be possible to attract this class of labour to the field . . .[8]

A further observation needs to be made. Unlike South Africa or Papua New Guinea, the absence of a suitable and sizeable local European labour supply absolved the mining industry of political pressure to construct a formal and legalised system of job reservation that explicitly prohibited the employment of non-Europeans in certain (mainly skilled) categories of work. Nor was it obliged to adopt a South African-type 'civilised labour policy' aimed at shielding unskilled Europeans from unemployment and preserving their higher wage levels. In spite of this the industry adopted from its infant years an informal job colour bar, applying it to a more ethnically diversified work-force than that existing in South African mining.

Thus the system both compared and contrasted with the South African paradigm. As in South Africa, the reliance on expensive immigrant whites as skilled and supervisory labour 'was in direct conflict with the cost-minimising strategies dictated by the imperatives of profitable production', although the proximity of Australia and New Zealand to Fiji lessened the burden of carrying such costs.

---

[8]   D. T. Mitchell, Mine Superintendent to GM Confidential, 20 July 1948, Vat./unclassified.

So, too, the South African 'solution to this contradiction' held true, resting in the various mechanisms of 'native' exploitation and the sparing and judicious use of whites.[9] But, unlike its South African model, the job colour bar in the Fiji mining industry did not derive to any extent from the demands of the white working class but from the mining companies themselves. Arguably this gave the Fiji industry a greater measure of control in managing the system. As we have noted the progressive modification of this over time had little real impact on the principle of occupational stratification. It made even less of a mark on the racialist structure of earnings that supported it.

What is argued, then, is that discrimination ultimately assisted rather than hindered the quest for a surplus in the mining industry: that it bolstered the exploitative relations of production. As with South African mining, a theory attesting to the dysfunction of ideology upon capitalist expansion does not stand up to scrutiny.

COLLABORATION IN THE LABOUR MARKET

Between 1934 and 1948 the exploitation of Fijian mineworkers took various forms. Principally it consisted in the stabilisation of their wages at very low levels with declining real value; in their categorisation as unskilled labour despite their deployment in skilled work; in the restrictions imposed on their occupational and wage mobility; and in their exclusion from or token participation in the occupational benefits that represented the non-cash component of earnings. In sum, Fijians were the main victims of an elaborate system of job and wage discrimination in the industry.

The first fifteen years of mining witnessed a prolonged and highly successful period of wage control by the Theodore group. The surplus of labour during the Depression years and until the war imposed severe constraints on the bargaining power of Fijian labour. So, too, the migrant and contract basis of employment precluded any sustainable form of industrial organisation and militated against change either in the structure of earnings or in the form of wage adjustments within it. Yet these factors do not fully explain why Fijian wages scarcely rose between 1936 and 1948. Faced with wage demands during and after the war and opposition to the discriminatory system of earnings voiced as early as 1938, the mining companies enjoyed a seemingly unassailable strength.

Briefly during 1935, at the zenith of the colony's gold rush, the competition for mine labour enabled Fijian mineworkers to demand and strike for higher wages and better rations. On the Tavua field they extracted from the group competitive weekly rates of 16s. for unskilled and 25s. for skilled work. The unskilled wage was matched by only one other company on the field; the skilled wage was surpassed by just one (see Table 3.1). This display of strength by local mine labour was observed with some alarm within the colonial administration,

---

9   Richardson & van Helten 1982 : 81.

inciting fears of the damaging effects it might have on wages outside the industry. It prompted a proposal to establish the distinctive African-style central recruiting bureau that would eliminate competition for labour and standardise and control wages and ration scales.[10]

But the Fijian advantage in the mine labour market was short-lived; and as the gold rush receded it became apparent that drastic measures would not be necessary. By early 1936 the major mining companies operated a uniform daily rate, and within a year the Emperor group was no longer forced to compete for labour at least with other mining concerns. A number of other conditions constructed a sturdy defence against working-class pressures. Monopsonistic conditions of recruitment, as well as the state's co-operation in mobilising labour and controlling the terms of indenture, permitted reduction in the basic (Fijian) wage rate to between 12s. (surface) and 15s. (underground) a week. Collusion with other employers (especially the sugar monopoly, the merchant companies and the state) over rates of pay and conditions of employment offered additional means of wage regulation.[11] Details of the CSR's unskilled rates were solicited before a first Fijian mine wage schedule was drawn up in 1936.

A shortage of Part-European artisans around the late 1930s, however, strained this informal wage collaboration. Commenting on the case of a resigning (Part-European) blacksmith, Emperor's chief engineer advised Theodore that 'although [the General Manager] agrees that [the man] is worth more than 14s 0d per day, he is unable to make an increase by reason of an agreement amongst employers in Fiji that no half-caste is to receive more than 14s 0d per day'.[12] The payment of periodic bonuses to a prized worker was one way of circumventing wage restrictions without jeopardising labour control. But the companies also acknowledged that some of the CSR's conditions, particularly its housing facilities and overtime rates, were in fact superior to their own; and that these discrepancies were a major reason for the defection of workers. The expansion of recreational facilities, improvements to housing and wage (and benefits) adjustments for Part-European workers in the 1940s may well have been intended to overcome this problem.

In a bid to preserve the low cost structure of Fijian labour, the colonial state played a critical role. The rate paid to road labour, for example, was established 'after conferring with the various agricultural interests', while in 1936 a motion tabled in the Council of Chiefs urging a higher rate for unskilled Fijian labour was firmly rejected. An increase in the daily wage for road labour could not be granted, the Governor insisted, since 'it would handicap the Colonial Sugar Refining Co. and other planters, and probably result in the Colony being unable to compete with other tropical countries in the world's markets'.

In another respect official attitudes hammered the commitment to collective wage control. Following Britain's ratification of the Minimum Wage-Fixing

---

[10] DC Colo North to CS, 3 Aug. 1935, CSO F36/16.
[11] E. S. Smith (Inspector) to N. E. Nilsen, 19 Aug. 1943, CSR 142/2906; Chief Engineer EGM to Mr Turley c/- M. H. personal, 16 Sept. 1940, Vat./Confidential to 1940; GM to Manager Lautoka Mill Private Out, 30 May 1933, CSR 142/1092. See Chapter 2 for further details.
[12] Potter, Chief Engineer to Managing Director, 19 June 1939, Vat./unclassified.

Table 3.1 Rates of wages (per week) in the goldmining industry, 1935 (£ s.d.)

Company	Av. no. of men employed during 1935	EUROPEAN Skilled	EUROPEAN Unskilled	PART-EUROPEAN Skilled	PART-EUROPEAN Unskilled	FIJIAN Skilled	FIJIAN Unskilled	CHINESE Skilled	CHINESE Unskilled	INDIAN Skilled	INDIAN Unskilled	Hours worked per week
Fiji Mining Corp. NL	28	7. 0. 0	—	—	—	—	0.15. 0	—	—	1.10. 0	—	45
Concessions: Europeans provided with quarters. Fijians with quarters and rations.												
Gold Mines of Fiji NL and Fiji Gold NL	73	6. 5. 0	—	—	—	0.18. 0	0.13. 6	1.15. 0	—	1. 1. 0	0.16. 6	44
Concessions: Europeans provided with quarters. Fijians and Chinese with quarters and rations. First aid dressings provided.												
Mt Morgan Developments Ltd	44	6. 0. 0	3.10. 0	—	—	1. 4. 0	0.15. 0	—	—	2. 0. 0	1. 1. 0	50
Concessions: Europeans and Indians provided with quarters. Fijians provided with quarters and rations.												
Loloma West Ltd	43	6. 5. 0	—	—	—	—	0.16. 0	—	2.10. 0	—	1. 5. 0	46½
Concessions: Drill superintendent allowed £2 per week boarding allowance. Europeans provided with quarters. Fijians with rations and medicines.												
Aloha Central GMNL	36	6. 0. 0	—	—	—	—	0.13. 6	1.17. 6	—	—	—	47
Concessions: Europeans provided with quarters, lighting and medicine. Fijians and Chinese with quarters, rations and medicines.												
East Reefs Consolidated NL	20	10.10. 0	—	2. 0. 0	—	0.17. 6	0.15. 0	—	—	—	—	44
Concessions: Each class is provided with quarters, rations, tobacco, soap and medicines.												
Vatukaisia Mining Co. Ltd	60	5. 0. 0	—	2.10. 0	—	2.10. 0	0.15. 0	1.10. 0	—	—	—	48
Concessions: Each class is provided with quarters, rations and medicines.												
Mineral Developments (Fiji) Ltd	61	8. 6. 0	5.17. 0	—	4. 0. 0	1. 0. 0	0.13. 6	—	1.10. 0	1. 7. 6	—	48
Concessions: Europeans provided with quarters and medicines. Fijians, Chinese and Indians provided with quarters, rations and medicines. Part-Europeans provided with quarters and medicines.												
Tavua Gold Developments Ltd	86	7. 7. 8	4.11.11	—	2. 0. 0	0.18. 6	0.11. 0	1.16. 8	—	1. 5. 0	—	48
Concessions: Europeans and Part-Europeans provided with quarters and medicines. Fijians, Chinese and Indians provided with quarters, medicines and rations.												

Table 3.1 (cont'd)

Company	Av. no. of men employed during 1935	EUROPEAN Skilled	EUROPEAN Unskilled	PART-EUROPEAN Skilled	PART-EUROPEAN Unskilled	FIJIAN Skilled	FIJIAN Unskilled	CHINESE Skilled	CHINESE Unskilled	INDIAN Skilled	INDIAN Unskilled	Hours worked per week
Pacific Gold NL	15	6. 6. 0	—	—	—	1.10. 0	0.13. 6	—	—	—	—	44
Emperor Gold Mining Co. Ltd	224	6.10. 0	4. 0. 0	3. 5. 0	1.10. 0	1. 5. 0	0.16. 0	—	—	—	—	47
Loloma (Fiji) Gold Mines NL	71	6.10. 0	4. 0. 0	3. 5. 0	1.10. 0	1. 5. 0	0.16. 0	—	—	—	—	47
Koroere Gold Mines NL	55	6.10. 0	4. 0. 0	3. 5. 0	1.10. 0	1. 5. 0	0.16. 0	—	—	—	—	47
Mt Kasi Mines Ltd and Kasi Developments Ltd	133	6. 0. 0	3.10. 0	4. 0. 0	2.10. 0	—	0.15. 0	—	—	—	—	48

Concessions (Pacific Gold NL): Fijians provided with quarters and rations. First aid kit provided on all jobs.

Concessions (Koroere Gold Mines NL): Europeans provided with free quarters and meals at 22s. per week. Insurance against accident and compensation paid by the company. Fijians provided with quarters, rations and medical attention. Part-Europeans provided with quarters, rations and part medical expenses and insurance against accident and compensation paid by company.

Concessions (Mt Kasi Mines Ltd and Kasi Developments Ltd): Free quarters to all Europeans. Free rations to all Fijians.

Source: CSO F36/29.

Machinery Convention of 1928 the administration succeeded in delaying the passage of local legislation. It was not, quipped the CSR, a change of heart that lay behind the decision five years later to ratify the convention, but rather the increasing difficulties of withstanding pressure from the Colonial Office. Although there seemed 'little hope that it can again be shelved', the company was placated by the reassuring forecast of the Acting Governor: the legislation would be applied with restraint and was likely to become a 'dead letter' because wage-fixing machinery was used only at the government's discretion.

As we have seen, state intervention in the mine labour market took coercive form in the early years of the war. Its effect was to annul the market advantage mineworkers had acquired; to deny them the 'freedom' to choose where to sell their labour; and to sanction their employment at uncompetitive wages of lower real value. Wage regulation was evidently as much a political convention as it was a function of a mining monopsony. This dual advantage made a marked impression on the pattern of mine earnings.

THE STRUCTURE OF MINE EARNINGS

It was not only the wage returns to mine labour that differentiated Fijians from other ethnic groups, but the very structure of their earnings. Rations and free housing represented two principal non-cash supplements to wages; and the practice of the Emperor group was to include the value of these in its overall estimation of Fijian earnings. In spite of the apparent problems this poses for analysing inter-racial/ethnic earnings, there are sound reasons for rejecting management's own system of comparative assessment.

The distinction between Fijian earnings (based on cash and non-cash variables) and those of other groups (based only on cash returns) masked various ways in which Part-European and European wages were also supplemented in kind. Unmarried Part-Europeans and Rotumans were accommodated in barracks without charge, while the house rentals for married Europeans, Part-Europeans and Rotumans were heavily subsidised. The companies' accounts, moreover, showed that Rotumans paid less rent than the inflated value placed on inferior Fijian housing. A large part of the cost of European messing (board and lodging) was also borne by the group,[13] while crib meals valued at a per capita average of 6d. per shift were issued not just to Fijians but to all mill and mine shiftworkers with the exception of Europeans.

Quite apart from these anomalies, the mines' own composition of Fijian earnings was not always consistent. The assessment of overtime, for example, was not, like that for other racial/ethnic categories of labour, based on total emoluments: that is, it did not include the value of rations and housing. So, too, Fijians who

---

[13] In 1963 the gross cost of the European mess totalled £7106 10s. 9d. (or £9 7s. per man per week), only £3496 5s. 9d. (or £4 12s. per man per week) of which was recovered in board and lodging payments. This meant that each man was subsidised at the rate of nearly £5 per week. Cost & Revenue Statement European Mess year ending 12 June 1963, Vat./Items given to N. E. Nilsen during visits.

returned to their villages during their annual (paid) holidays did not receive their rations or the equivalent in cash. Not until December 1949 did the companies agree, under pressure from the mineworkers' union, to permit rations to be claimed. Even then this 'privilege' was enjoyed only by those who returned from holiday and who collected them within a stipulated period of ten days.

To some extent the early decision to ration Fijian mine labour was influenced by the isolation of the gold-fields from the coastal towns and markets. Theodore insisted that 'it would not be possible to keep Fijian labour here in this non-food growing area unless rations are provided by the Company'. 'Native foodstuffs' had to be transported from distant areas, such as the Wainibuka; but bulk purchase of these as well as other food items, such as sugar, bought wholesale from the CSR, and tea, flour, etc. from the companies' agent and retail supplier, Morris Hedstrom, enabled purchases to be made fairly cheaply. The group was, moreover, free to determine the 'market value' of the rations it charged against Fijian labour costs.

Francis Wilson has suggested in respect of the South African goldmines that rationing labour also ensured that a work-force was 'fit enough' to undertake heavy tasks in physically trying conditions.[14] If this was the intention at Vatukoula, it was a fanciful one. Rations did not in fact safeguard workers against malnourishment. Indeed, their poor quality and the heavy concentration of unfamiliar European foodstuffs almost certainly contributed to low standards of health. As a paternalistic system, rationing helped to regulate the lives of mine labour, to determine what and when it was to eat. It kept the overall cost of Fijian labour low; and it was used to justify repeated refusals to improve cash incomes (including cost-of-living bonuses) on the grounds that most of the increase in living costs was borne by the companies themselves.[15]

As a device of labour control the lower cash returns to labour reduced its capacity to exercise free and independent choices over income disposal. Remittances to meet recurring cultural obligations at home could not be as easily fulfilled; and the system virtually obviated the prospect of accumulating savings. Rations were thus a form of truck that could be of critical assistance to the group in tackling the turnover problem induced by non-contract or 'free' labour. As Wilson and others point out, the constraints on saving posed by rationing prolonged employment, thus exacerbating conditions of labour dependence. While no comparable data is available in Fiji, the effects on African remittances of the rationing system in the South African goldmining industry are clear: unlike the diamond industry, where non-rationed labour sent 36% of earnings home, only 18% of earnings was repatriated by rationed goldmining labour.[16]

Rationing was particularly attractive as a less expensive alternative to higher wages, and married workers were cheaper to feed in spite of their extra half (family) ration because they were obliged to bear the cost of firewood, and their

---

[14]   Wilson 1972 : 56.
[15]   Johnstone 1976 : 188–90 offers a similar defence by South African mining interests for depriving African workers of inflation-based wage adjustments.
[16]   E. J. B. Jewel, 'Native Labour and Payment on Premier Diamond Mine', Papers and Discussions of the Association of Mine Managers of South Africa (TCM Johannesburg, 1960-61), cited in Wilson 1972 : 57.

wives the (labour-time) burden of cooking.[17] Rations represented only a small proportion of the total cost of Fijian labour, amounting to only 26% of the total cost of 'native' labour at the Emperor mine between 1938 and 1939, for example. The average daily and weekly costs of Fijian labour (i.e. including rations) worked out at a little over 3s. and £1 respectively. The inclusion of housing in the structure of Fijian earnings had a similar purpose. As Nilsen explained in 1947, 'We consider that it is more profitable to provide employees with reasonably comfortable living quarters, than to be constantly faced with increasing wages.'[18] That rations and housing insulated workers from the inflationary spiral of living costs was also a favourite argument of the South African Chamber of Mines.[19]

Another paternalistic convention with its roots in nineteenth-century Fijian labour legislation intensified the effects of rationing. The practice of deferred pay was applied exclusively to Fijian mine labour, assuming extreme proportions where recruits were brought to the mines under informal group arrangements. In such cases a substantial portion (if not the total) of monies held until the end of three- to 12-month contracts might bypass workers altogether. While initiative for the system of direct payment to the provinces (i.e. to local chiefs) and other arrangements regarding restrictions on personal remuneration appear to have originated with the chiefs, there were obvious advantages for mine employers. Above all the system, by precluding virtually any measure of economic independence, made it difficult, if not impossible, for labour to abscond. As an additional mechanism of labour control this variant of pay deferment was particularly relevant in the conditions of high labour mobility that prevailed in the 1930s.[20]

Occupational benefits such as sick pay, annual holidays and superannuation were, like earnings, not uniform, but conformed to the general pattern of racial differentiation and cost control, and to low-cost Fijian labour in particular. They added weight to the financial burden of supporting an élite component within the work-force. Until the early 1940s only Europeans were given allowances for time away from work on account of illness, this for one day of each month of service (12 days maximum p.a.), so long as it did not arise out of 'misconduct', 'intoxication' or while a worker was away from the mines. In 1943 sick pay at the rate of half a day per month of service was awarded to Part-Europeans, Indians and Rotumans with the Part-European entitlement raised to 12 days per annum in 1946. Fijians were guaranteed only the continued supply of their rations up to one month (thereafter at the discretion of management) while workers injured off the field were charged for the cost of rations supplied to them during their absence from work. The higher costs of reproducing non-Fijian labour were also manifest in the workings of the group's medical benefit fund established in 1935. This offered medical insurance only to European and Part-European

---

[17] In 1949 the extra half (family) ration cost the mining companies 6s. 3/4d. per day while the cost of cooking for a single worker was estimated at 1s. 4d. per day.
[18] Nilsen to Chairman of Directors, 18 Aug. 1947, Vat./Emperor Budget Estimates, Finance, etc. Current File.
[19] Southall 1983 : 80.
[20] For a discussion of the nineteenth-century practices of deferred pay and truck as labour control mechanisms, see Bain 1988 : 130-1; Graves 1983 : 121.

workers (though not to Rotumans), with both groups paying 1s. 3d. per week to the fund, their contributions being subsidised at the rate of £1 for £1. Hospital care for workers and their families was carried by the fund; and the weekly services of a local doctor were provided at company cost.

Annual leave benefits similarly varied according to racial or ethnic classification. For a brief time Part-Europeans enjoyed parity with European workers—one day for each 'completed month of service'. But in October 1936 a new employment schedule reduced their leave entitlement to six days, restricting the maximum amount to those employed for at least six months. This established equality between Part-European and Fijian leave and applied the same proviso that holiday pay would be granted only to workers who returned after the Christmas break. By the early 1940s Indians, Rotumans and Part-Europeans were entitled to one day a month, as European leave was upgraded to two weeks after three years' service. The privilege of a paid bonus holiday was extended to Part-Europeans in 1946 and raised along with the European entitlement to three weeks a year. At the same time, annual Part-European leave was increased to two weeks, while Fijian holidays remained at the original rate of six days.

Blatant though this discrimination was, and in spite of a formal protest on behalf of Fijian workers, management categorically denied 'any intimation of discrimination between the various sections of our employees'. Over the leave question, denial gave way to defence:

> We do not think the comparison of holidays between our European and Fijian employees a suitable one and consider that if comparisons are to be made in this matter they should be made between holidays to Fijians employed by the Mining Companies and holidays given by all other employers of Fijian labour in the Colony.

A flimsy defence, it was enough to snuff out any hint of sympathy within the administration for the Fijian plaintiffs. 'It is difficult', the Commissioner of Labour observed, 'to criticize what are *today better* conditions of employment than Government gives to its own employees.' Non-intervention gave the group free rein to continue and even extend the practice in later years. Not until 1965 were Fijian leave benefits put on an equal footing with those of other ethnic categories of labour.

Additional labour costs were incurred through subsidising and administering a superannuation scheme that offered death and pension benefits to mineworkers and staff. As with the medical benefit fund, the group matched members' contributions; and where, in the case of death, the minimum year's salary could not be met from the fund's savings, it paid the balance. Until late 1946 European employees enjoyed exclusive protection under the scheme, thereafter being joined by their Part-European counterparts. The first Rotumans were selected for membership in 1951. Although a 'canvass' of Fijian opinion immediately after the Second World War indicated that '20-25% of employees would join the scheme if made available to them', no Fijian was admitted until 1961. The policy reflected a largely unchanged ideological climate. It also indicated that in spite of a considerable degree of labour stabilisation and permanency among Fijian mineworkers, the burden of supporting them once they were no longer productive was still to be borne by the traditional social system.

CLASSIFICATIONS, THE WAGE COLOUR BAR AND OTHER DEVICES

The classification of Fijians as general labour, distinguished primarily by whether they worked on the surface or underground, was an important device to keep labour costs to a minimum. The standardisation of jobs and official classifications concealed considerable employment in work demanding specialised skills. The service record cards of Fijian mineworkers provide illuminating evidence of this devaluation of skills. Ascribed classifications were diverse, but they shared one striking characteristic: with few exceptions (e.g. carpenters and a handful of other tradesmen), they commanded only the minimum rates that applied to unskilled labour. Men classified as underground and surface miners, miner truckers, mine labour, machine hands, diamond and churn drill labour, mine timbermen, sample boys, assay boys, fitter assistants, bracemen, electrician labour, mill labour, general labour (allocated to different departments), flotation assistants, cooks and waiters alike, were all paid a basic daily rate of 2s. (surface) or 2s. 6d. (underground) until 1943. At least until the early 1970s Fijians were classified as 'helpers' or 'labour' (diamond drill helpers or labour, for example) rather than 'operators' (diamond drillers).

The efficiency of Fijians in skilled jobs belied their persistently subordinate status. As early as 1937 Theodore informed Melbourne shareholders that 'Most of the work, including the operation of the rock drills, air compressor, pumps and winches has been performed by Fijians, from whom very excellent service has been maintained'. Later, with greater mechanisation, shaft sinking and level development drew further on Fijians for skilled work, for jobs including drilling (by handheld jackhammers), blasting, mucking (by mechanical loaders), pumping and timbering as well as mining by driving, cross-cutting and rising in scattered and narrow orebodies.[21] The situation bore some resemblance to the Gold Coast, where Africans were by the late 1920s being employed in skilled occupations that in South Africa were the exclusive preserve of whites.[22]

Income differentials between different categories of labour bore little relation to the distribution of skills; and where Fijian skills or experience were formally acknowledged and classifications resembled or coincided with others, the ideo-logical basis of a discriminatory wage structure was especially conspicuous. Of 196 Fijians officially entitled 'underground miners' at Emperor in 1948, 66% received wages between 3s. and 4s. a day (the ceiling being 8s. 6d.). This was scarcely more than the minimum rate paid to unskilled underground labour, and in the case of the 33% on 3s., no higher. Although the wages of certain tradesmen tended to be more generous, the wage colour bar was directed with equal vigour towards such occupations.

Acclaimed performance made no impact on institutionalised discrimination, although the iniquity of the system was sometimes questioned within the ranks

---

[21] Mitchell 1953 : 53–78.
[22] Crisp 1984 : xvi.

of company management. An internal memorandum from Emperor's chief engineer to Theodore in 1939 on the case of a Fijian fitter offered one such reservation:

> This man is in receipt of 10s 0d per day plus rations. He is the best all round fitter we have on the mines. He speaks English equally as well as Fijian and has full control of his gang. I have actually stood by a job for 24 hours and seen this man working side by side with European fitters in receipt of £1 per day, and in my opinion this man, by his ability to work and his clear idea of the requirement has easily proved himself a 25% better tradesman than those in receipt of 100% more wages.[23]

The unbending wage colour bar delivered a particularly harsh sentence to another Fijian worker. Accidentally classified as a Part-European in 1939, the man received for four years the Part-European wage for his work as a pipe fitter and plate-layer. In 1944 his true ethnic identity was discovered, whereupon he was promptly reclassified as a 'Fijian' pipe fitter with a wage rate reduced by over 30% to 5s. 6d. per day.

Table 3.2 reveals some of the main characteristics of the wage colour bar applied in the mining industry, showing how in spite of comparable levels of skill, experience or even formal job classifications, the scale of Fijian earnings was noticeably lower than that which applied to Part-European workers. From 1940 an increase in Part-European earnings widened the gap, when the wage range for miners (from learner to leading hand) was raised to between 7s. and 14s. Improvements made to the Fijian basic wage in 1943 were also offset by a lowering of the starting rates of assistants to carpenters, blacksmiths, electricians, engine and pump attendants, samplers, greasers, and assayers' assistants.[24] As the table illustrates, jobs performed by Europeans and Fijians rarely shared the same classification, and Europeans alone occupied the higher-paying positions. There were, however, a few cases of common occupation where a comparison of earnings can more easily be drawn. In such instances, the gulf in earnings was visibly greater than that prevailing between Fijians and Part-Europeans.[25]

The tighter restrictions placed on the occupational mobility of Fijians in contrast to Part-Europeans proved an enduring practice, particularly in respect of the more responsible jobs. By 1940 Part-Europeans were eligible for the position of shift boss, while the most senior jobs open to a Fijian mineworker until well into the 1950s were boss boy, head boy or leading hand miner. This signalled one crucial way in which Fijians were subject to a greater degree of exploitation: the consolidation of skills increased the efficiency of long-service workers, but the barriers to mobility remained. The cost benefits of this discrimination were no mystery, although the system was draped in the cloak of acceptable prejudice. As the mine superintendent surmised in 1948, 'by careful selection and training

---

[23] Potter, Chief Engineer to Managing Director, 19 June 1939, Vat./unclassified.

[24] EGM Co. Ltd, Loloma, TPP, FMD Euronesian Employees' Rates and Conditions of Pay Oct. 1940; Associated Mining Companies Wage Rates and Conditions of Employment for Fijians Dec. 1943.

[25] Wage data for the Zambian copperbelt demonstrates some similarity in the discrepancy between black and white earnings. In 1942 the Rhodesian Selection Trust, which, along with Anglo-American, dominated the Copperbelt, paid its unskilled workers at its Mufulira mine 1s. 9d. per day and its unskilled white workers between 7s. 6d. and 10s. Parpart 1986 : 38 n. 10.

Table 3.2 Comparison of wage rates and job classifications for Fijian, Part-European and European mineworkers, 1936–43*

Race	Requirements	Classification	Wage rate per shift
Fijian		Surface labour	2s.
		Underground labour	2s. 6d. (+ 2s. bonus per week for unbroken and satisfactory service).
Part-European	1st grade	Unskilled workers	6s.
	2nd grade	—helpers & assistants to tradesmen	5s.
Fijian	Beginner—without previous experience	Underground mine labourer	2s. 6d.
Part-European	Beginner—without previous experience	Learner miner	6s.
European (1941)	Beginner—without previous experience	Learner miner	£4 10s. to £5 (p.w.)
Fijian	6 months' continuous service underground	Miner	3s. 4d.
Part-European	6 months' satisfactory progress in mines	Learner miner	7s.
Fijian	12 months' continuous service underground	Miner	3s. 10d.
Part-European	12 months' satisfactory progress in mines	Learner miner	8s.
Fijian	18 months' service underground and with special approval of mine manager	Fijian boss boy	4s. 4d.
Part-European	18 months' satisfactory progress	Learner miner or miner	9s. / 10s.
Fijian	Showing special skills, with ability to take charge of various kinds of work in mine		5s.
Part-European	After one year	Leading hand miner	11s. to 12s.
European		Leading hand miner	£6 (p.w.)
		Miner	£5 (p.w.)
Fijian	1st 6 months' service	Winch drivers & hoistmen	3s. 10d.
	After 6 months' service		4s. 4d.
Part-European	Further promotion on special approval of manager	Winch driver & hoistmen	5s.
	1st year	Winch driver & hoistmen	8s.
	2nd year	Engine driver	9s.
	After 2 years		10s.
European (1940)		Winder engine driver	Av. £6 (p.w.)

Table 3.2 (cont'd)

Race	Requirements	Classification	Wage rate per shift
Fijian	1st 6 months' service	Assistants to fitters, blacksmiths, electricians & other artisans	3s. 4d.
	After 6 months' service		3s. 10d.
	Further promotion on special approval of manager		4s. 4d.
Part-European	3rd grade	Assistants to mechanics (i.e. pipe fitters, lathe men, plumbers, pipe fitters, electrical assistants)	6s.
	2nd grade		7s.
	1st grade		8s.
European (1935)		Fitter's assistant	£3 (p.w.)
		Assistant blacksmith	£5 (p.w.)
Fijian	1st 6 months' service	Samplers & greasers (mill & surface)	3s. 4d.
	After 6 months' service		3s. 10d.
	Further promotion on special approval of manager		4s. 4d.
Part-European	3rd grade	Samplers & greasers	6s.
	2nd grade		7s.
	1st grade		8s.
Fijian	1st 6 months' service	Engine attendants Pump attendants	3s. 4d.
	After 6 months' service		3s. 10d.
	Further promotion on special approval of manager		4s. 4d.
Part-European	3rd grade	Engine attendants Pump attendants	6s.
	2nd grade		7s.
	1st grade		8s.

Table 3.2 (cont'd)

Race	Requirements	Classification	Wage rate per shift
Fijian	1st 6 months' service	Truck drivers	3s. 10d.
	After 6 months' service		4s. 4d.
	Further promotion on special approval of manager (If special qualifications or experience, can be placed at higher rate subject to manager's approval.)		
Part-European	2nd grade	Truck drivers	8s.
	1st grade		10s.
	Working more than ordinary hours		£3 5s. (p.w.)
Fijian		†Churn drill assistant (labour or helper)	2s. to 2s. 6d.
European (1939)		Assistant churn drill operator	£4–£6 (p.w.)
Fijian	1st 6 months' service	Diamond drill head boy	3s. 4d.
	After 6 months' service		3s. 10d.
	Further promotion on special approval of manager		4s. 4d.
European (1941)		Diamond drill operator	£4 10s. to £6 (p.w.)
European (1941)		Churn drill operator	£4 10s. to £6 (p.w.)

* These wage rates apply to the period 1936–43 for Fijians only. For Part-Europeans, they apply to the years 1936–40; and for Europeans to 1936 only unless otherwise specified.

† This work category is not listed in 1936 or 1943 Fijian schedules but from the company service record cards it appears as a common occupation.

Source: Data compiled from Emperor, Loloma and Koroere Mines & TPP Co. Ltd 'Wages, Rates and Conditions of Employment for Fijians and Part-European Employees, Oct. 1936', CSO F10/6 Pt 6; Emperor Gold Mining Co. Ltd Rates of Pay Allowances and Conditions (European Employees) Wages Staff only, 1936, CSO F36/29; Vat./ Confidential to 1940; Vat./General Correspondence Aug.–Dec. 1939; Vat./Loloma Mine Employees, Insurance etc; Vat./Emperor General Correspondence Mar.–Dec. 1935; Service Record Cards of Fijian and Part-European Employees, Associated Mining Companies of Vatukoula.

many have become skilful and reliable but Fijians have not yet been able to accept responsibility in the mines greater than that of leading hand'.[26]

The history of a miner from Kadavu provides a typical example of this form of cost control. Sixteen years of experience underground, broken only by a three-month period of illness, saw him promoted to the position of leading hand by 1952. At 8s. a day, this commanded less than 50% of the European rate that had applied in 1936 for the equivalent position.

The mobility of Fijian wages was subject to similarly stringent control. Except for select tradesmen, truck drivers and engine drivers, who were eligible for higher rates, the schedules applied to all underground and surface Fijian workers, until the mid-1940s fixed a ceiling of 5s. per shift. In contrast, the 1936 schedules for Part-Europeans and Europeans stipulated ceilings of 14s. per day and £7 per week respectively. The maximum Fijian wage thus corresponded to the minimum Part-European wage. Comparative wage scales were themselves a measure of the constraints on Fijian earnings: a range of 9s. per day applied to Part-Europeans, £3 per week to Europeans, but only 3s. per day to Fijians. The implications of this discrepancy emerge very clearly in the case of a Fijian carpenter employed in 1936. Over 12 years of continuous employment (December 1936 to January 1949), his daily wage rose only from 7s. to 9s.[27]

Charles Perrings shows how the upgrading of selected African labour to semi-skilled and skilled jobs in order to reduce the dependence of the Central African copperbelt companies on the expensive skilled market of South Africa led to 'widening the wage differentials between skilled and unskilled black employees'. To this end, minimum rates were lowered in the early 1930s and maximum rates raised.[28] The strategy throws light on similar developments at Vatukoula more than a decade later where a higher ceiling benefited only a handful of workers. From Table 3.3 it is evident that of 955 Fijians employed in December 1947, 49% received between 2s. 6d. and 3s. 6d.; as many as 89.6% were paid between 2s. 6d. and 5s.; and only 4% scored the upper level scale of 7s. to 12s. The ceiling of 12s. was achieved by a single worker. In addition, it seems likely that the corresponding lowering of rates for certain skilled jobs was probably a deskilling initiative linked to their increased allocation to Fijians.

The practice of transferring workers between different departments, so breaking their continuity of employment, was one obstacle to wage increases. Transfers were commonly authorised for Fijians and undoubtedly reduced their capacity to develop work skills. For those moved from underground to the surface or other lower-status work, transfers also meant a lower rate of pay. Yet a more compelling explanation for why so many men were engaged at the same rate or received such small increases over a long period appeared to be that wage criteria took scant account of experience.

In 1936 Theodore emphatically rejected a request from Fijian mineworkers that a wage rise be automatically granted after six months' service. Ten years

---

[26]   Mitchell 1953 : 91.
[27]   Service record cards of Fijian employees, Associated Mining Companies of Vatukoula.
[28]   Perrings 1979 : 116.

Table 3.3   Distribution of wages and total earnings for Fijian mine labour, 1947 (shillings and pence)

Number of employees	Basic rate per day	Cost of living bonus	Rations	Housing	Total emoluments
175	2s. 6d.	1s.	2s. 9d.	9d.	7s.
293	3s.	1s.	2s. 9d.	9d.	7s. 6d.
135	3s. 6d.	1s.	2s. 9d.	9d.	8s.
87	4s.	1s.	2s. 9d.	9d.	8s. 6d.
89	4s. 6d.	1s.	2s. 9d.	9d.	9s.
77	5s.	1s.	2s. 9d.	9d.	9s. 6d.
22	5s. 6d.	1s.	2s. 9d.	9d.	10s.
35	6s.	1s.	2s. 9d.	9d.	10s. 6d.
6	6s. 6d.	1s.	2s. 9d.	9d.	11s.
13	7s.	1s.	2s. 9d.	9d.	11s. 6d.
6	7s. 6d.	1s.	2s. 9d.	9d.	12s.
4	8s.	1s.	2s. 9d.	9d.	12s. 6d.
2	8s.	1s.	2s. 9d.	9d.	12s.10d.
2	8s. 6d.	1s.	2s. 9d.	9d.	13s.
3	9s.	1s.	2s. 9d.	9d.	13s. 6d.
5	10s.	1s.	2s. 9d.	9d.	14s. 6d.
1	12s.	1s.	2s. 9d.	9d.	16s. 6d.
Total 955	Av. Rate 3s. 9d.				

Source: Vat./Associated Companies of Vatukoula Rates of Pay and Emoluments for Fijian Employees as at 17 Dec. 1947.

later, evidence of 'increased skill and capacity for work' was still a precondition of wage adjustments. In the absence of trade testing, rulings on improvements in skill, knowledge or ability were entirely at the discretion of management. For those assigned to 'ordinary surface work', the prospect of incomes rising above the basic rate was especially remote: no guidelines (even discretionary) based on length of service were laid down at all.

Managerial discretion proved less obstructive to European and Part-European mineworkers, who enjoyed fairly regular improvements to their wages and salaries. Ironically, Theodore reasoned that it was precisely the cumulative experience of European supervisors that justified their annual increases: 'the responsibility of the position and the value of the man occupying it may continue to increase year by year, and to retain such men we must recognise their enhanced value'.[29]

But the group was acutely aware of the scarcity value of these two sources of mine labour, particularly during the war years; and they were for this reason more sensitive to the effect of higher living costs on dwindling labour reserves. Early in 1940 Theodore urged a pre-emptive wage increase in order 'to allay any growing unrest arising from the wages schedules now in force', and to postpone having to concede overtime at penalty rates. A 10% increase was granted to all but Fijian mineworkers, and a 5% bonus paid to executive and salaried staff to meet the increased cost of living. At least three other adjustments were made to European staff salaries before 1947. For Part-European and European workers,

---

[29]   Managing Director to Nilsen, 16 Nov. 1940, Vat./Loloma.

cost-of-living allowances rose from 10% to 20% (to a maximum of £1 10s. per week) in 1943 and again to 30% (to a maximum of £2 per week) in 1947.[30]

Until December 1943 Fijian mineworkers received no compensation at all for the steady erosion of their purchasing power, and on the whole little was done to maintain the value of their wages until 1950, by which time the (Indian-based) cost of living index had risen by as much as 143% over the 1939 base year. Rations had to be supplemented especially in the case of married workers with families, and increases in the cost of clothing (including boots), school fees and other necessities had also to be met out of wages.

The failure to make any adjustment to the Fijian schedule before 1943 resulted in an absolute decline in wages; it widened the gap between earnings of Fijians and other ethnic categories of labour; and it intensified the exploitation and dependence of Fijian mineworkers. Their dependence was reinforced by wage deductions, which whittled away cash earnings. By the late 1930s compulsory levies for educational facilities and sporting activities had been added to deductions for tobacco purchases, taxes and rations (Table 3.4). Special fund-raising ventures brought further hardship to low-income-earners since donations were often compulsory, as in the case of the government's Malta Appeal of 1942.[31]

Table 3.4   Comparison between gross and net earnings Emperor Gold Mining Co. Ltd, Tavua, Fiji

Native pay envelope
Period 15 April–12 May 1937

Name Tomasi Number 654	£	s.	d.
Wages (Ai sau)—			
24 shifts @ 2s.	2	8	0
(Veisau) OT		13	9
Bonus 4 weeks @ 2s		8	0
(Bonisi)			
Total wages	3	9	9
(Levu ni sau)			
Deductions—			
(A dinau)			
Tobacco		4	6
Taxes (Lau)	2	11	
Rations			
Total deductions	2	15	6
Net cash		14	3
(Kemu i sau)			

Source: SNA N44/15/8.

---

[30]   Cost of living was calculated separately for Europeans and Indians, reflecting the prevailing wisdom that the two communities shared neither the same standard of living nor similar consumer preferences. The effect of inflation on Fijian workers was evidently not considered serious enough (given the expected buffer role of the traditional economy) even to warrant the collection and analysis of price data.

[31]   The Vatukoula companies demanded a minimum 1s. donation from all their employees towards the Malta Appeal. Those who refused to volunteer this amount had it deducted from their wages, although they could (theoretically) register their objections with management. Community Officer to General Manager re. Meeting with Emperor Fijian Committee on 24–25 June 1942, Vat./Department Memos 1941–May 1944.

The first increase for Fijian mineworkers was authorised in April 1943, bringing the basic surface rate up from 2s. to 2s. 6d. and the underground rate from 2s. 6d. to 3s., just 7d. more a shift than the wage of a black South African miner.[32] A further 6d. wage rise was conceded in 1944 and two cost-of-living bonuses aggregating 1s. were granted by 1950. The increases were a belated response to inclement conditions in the labour market. The protective shield of an interventionist state was preoccupied with other battles, not least the war effort. So it could not be relied on. Prodding from official quarters to approve concessions sufficient to regain the pre-war value of wages and to bridge the gulf with other industrial earnings clinched things.

There were other devices to strengthen company control. Just as annual holiday pay was withheld until the first pay day after the Christmas break, it was the practice to pay (four weeks) wages due before the three annual holidays of Christmas, Easter and the Vatukoula Sports Day in August only if men returned to the mines after the holidays. The companies also inflicted a penalty of 2s. (raised to 3s. in 1948) on workers coming back to the mines after 'unauthorised absence'. Married men with dependants were hardest hit by this, for unlike single men housed in barracks, they could not rely on cooked rations as a means of relief, but had to meet the cost of kitchen firewood out of wages. From 1944, men who overstayed their leave or left the mines for unacceptable reasons were re-engaged at a lower rate. Fijians were downgraded by a daily minimum of 6d. and Part-Europeans by 1s., while penalties for European offenders were prescribed at the discretion of management.[33]

The zeal with which the policy was applied to Fijian mineworkers was evident in the frequency and duration of wage reductions. Its consequences in the long term were horrifying: as skills and efficiency increased, wage rates could actually decrease. An experienced miner trucker on 3s. 6d. in 1944, for example, had his wage cut twice to 2s. 6d. following two short spells of 'unauthorised absence'. By the end of 1945 his rate had climbed back to 3s., only to be reduced again to 2s. early the following year. Another way of penalising Fijians for absenteeism was to downgrade their classifications on return to work. An official inquiry into an underground accident in 1967 indicated that this was still being done by this late date. In this instance, an acting leading hand miner with four years' experience was dismissed on account of three days' absence without leave. He was taken back as an unskilled learner on the minimum daily rate.[34]

The shortage of data on aggregate labour costs unfortunately makes it impossible to monitor the changing racial or ethnic proportions of the wages and salaries bill while taking account of fluctuations in the composition of the work-force. A breakdown of the Emperor mine's labour cost structure for the year 1940 to 1941, however, reveals the grossly disproportionate amount of total wages and salaries paid to Fijian workers and their contribution to the overall minimisation of labour costs. In that year European employees numbering 101 (or 8.3% of

[32] First 1982 : 19.
[33] Minutes of Dept Managers' Meeting, 28 Jan. 1944, Vat./Meetings of Executives Current File.
[34] EGM Underground Safety Officer to Production Manager memo, 20 Jan. 1967, MR/Bunch 20, M541/1 Pt 3.

the work-force) received 32.2% of the total wages and salaries bill. By contrast, 857 Fijians (comprising 70.5% of a work-force of 1215) claimed only 42% of the wages and salaries bill. This represented less than 7% of the value of production.

EARLY REORGANISATION

The high price (and attendant shortages) of Australian skilled miners, technicians and supervisors was a major determinant of early changes to the mines' occupational structure. One effect of the war was to lay claim to Vatukoula's few skilled European workers. After 1945 the situation deteriorated further, with acute shortages of expatriate tradesmen (fitters and turners), churn drillers and other skilled workers, as well as mill and mine shaft bosses being experienced.

The aptitude, behaviour and militancy of European mineworkers were also factors that led the Emperor group to review its employment policy as early as 1935. Recruits were often poor workers, inexperienced (one did not know how to charge a hole, Theodore scoffed in 1935), heavy drinkers or 'grumblers'. Nilsen's private correspondence with Theodore during the war revealed his growing dislike of Australian workers, some of whom were agitators 'for the formation of Unions even for the Fijians'. Early manifestations of European 'insubordination' had drawn attention to the stark contrast between low-paid and unorganised Fijians, and Europeans drawn from a relatively indulgent market and well-versed in industrial bargaining. In October 1935 European miners employed at Emperor and Loloma delivered a petition demanding higher wages, a 44-hour week, overtime and other penalty rates. Four years later a number of defecting workers intercepted by the police complained of unsafe and unhealthy underground conditions.

Disenchanted, perhaps, Nilsen was not unduly alarmed by such exhibitions of truculence:

> when they start thinking they can run this show they are making a big mistake and can easily be sent back to Australia, where they are probably not so hot. A few of the local Europeans have been blowing off a bit of steam too lately. I know what we will do with them and told them so.[35]

Industrial troubles in Australia after the war were observed with greater apprehension. The possibility that these might upset local labour conditions was very real and, for Nilsen, pointed to only one solution:

> Conditions in Australia in recent years have given the workers a tendency and complex to be always 'agin the company' and we do not want this kind of agitation to exist amongst our peaceful Euronesian and native employees. Therefore I feel that the less Australian workers we have, the better. Possibly a few more New Zealanders would be a better policy.[36]

In 1948 agitation among local European shift bosses for a 40-hour week brought the threat of upheaval even closer to home.

---

[35] Nilsen to Theodore, 14 Feb. 1942, Vat./Correspondence EGT/NEN July 1942–Nov. 1944.
[36] Nilsen to Theodore, 6 Jan. 1947, Vat./Correspondence EGT/NEN July 1942–Nov. 1944.

As observed earlier, the Fiji mining industry differed in one important respect from the South African. It was relatively free of the pressures exerted by a local white working class and, skills permitting, could afford to rid itself of recalcitrants. As Marks and Rathbone observe of South Africa, the industry had some ability to control the numbers and distribution of white workers. Not so wages, at least not to the same extent.[37] In Fiji the industry could do both more easily. The expatriate status of nearly all its white workers and proximity to Australia were possible explanations for this. The reliance on a colour-bar convention rather than legislated job reservation was another. According to Marks and Rathbone, white miners in South Africa suffered from 'extreme structural insecurity'. In Fiji the situation was arguably worse.

The local labour market offered Part-Europeans as suitable and cheaper substitutes. Like Fijian agriculturalists and plantation labourers they had been hit by depressed commodity prices during the 1930s. By the latter part of the decade the misfortunes of the copra industry had driven hundreds of them on to the labour market. The group's early experiments in training them as miners, mill labour (riveters and riveters' assistants), carpenters, engine attendants, and mechanics, had showed them to be 'steady, good workers and intelligent'. Theodore had been optimistic that

> By picking the best of these . . . we can get together a good underground staff which in the long run will be better than the European miners. If the experiment proves satisfactory, the number will be increased and no further importation of European miners will be made except to keep up a small force of leading hands and shift bosses.[38]

Within a few years, management resolved to train many more Part-Europeans with a view 'to keep[ing] the number of Europeans down to a minimum'. By the 1940s it was decided that they should be groomed for the 'key positions'.

Labour substitution proved extremely economical, bringing savings of around 60% per worker. European miners received between £5 and £6 a week and a Part-European 'learner miner trucker' 7s. a shift or about £2 a week. Even the maximum wage of 12s. a shift or £3 12s. per week payable until 1940 to a 'class one half-caste miner' represented a large saving over the lowest weekly wage of his European counterpart. The cost of labour dropped still further by the replacement of European by Part-European winder engine drivers.

More important, income differentials remained even as Part-Europeans became more experienced, and wage data demonstrate that these increased considerably during the 1940s. In 1940 the average differential between Part-European and European miners was about 9s. a day. By 1948 this had nearly doubled. A further disadvantage of retaining large numbers of European workers during the war was the cost of subsidising their wages (up to 50%) once they were recruited into the military forces. The same concession was available to Part-Europeans

---

[37] Marks & Rathbone 1982 : 17.
[38] Managing Director Theodore to Legal Manager EML, 28 Oct. 1935, Vat./Loloma Correspondence & Reports Jan. 1936–Feb. 1938.

(though not to Fijians), but because of the discrepancy in wage rates this incurred a smaller liability.

The success of Theodore's 'experiment' with local substitution was evident in correspondence to head office; in the early use of Part-Europeans as leading hand miners and then shift bosses; and in the group's reluctance to re-engage Europeans after the war in some of the jobs reallocated during their absence. The substitution of Part-European for European shift bosses reduced the per capita cost of a fairly senior supervisor from £14 to £8 5s. per week by 1951. But such manoeuvres were more than a drive for economy, and their success could also be measured in political terms. More especially, the changes were important for the friction and polarisation they promoted among non-European workers. From the earliest years of the industry the racial demarcation of jobs and wages militated against solidarity based on shared class relations. Faced with the rumblings of unionism among Fijian mineworkers in the post-war period, the group could see that the consolidation of Part-European (and Rotuman) status and earnings offered a decoy that would align the interests of these two groups more closely with management. As one company official remarked later, their appointment as shift bosses drew them into the 'managerial structure of the Company':

> They therefore would not and could not be expected to have divided loyalties between Union and Company. They were Company men. Because of this the Company had the unassailable right to promote or discipline them without any redress to the Union.[39]

The strategy was then as much an inspired instrument of labour control as it was an appropriate formula for reducing labour costs. As we shall see later, its impact on the pattern of industrial relations and on the development of the mineworkers' union in particular, was dramatic.

Despite what appeared to be significant occupational changes, the principles of labour division by race and ethnicity were not in fact compromised. The structure of mine earnings remained unchanged. Further, the intransigence of racialist attitudes provided the driving ideological force behind continuing restrictions on the mobility of non-Europeans. It cemented the discriminatory system of wages as well as the unbroken tradition of reserving an élite European presence at the apex of the occupational pyramid. In a private letter to Theodore in 1947, Nilsen reflected:

> If the native is prepared to work in proportion to what he eats he can do a lot more work and we will pay him money, or if he works half as hard as he plays we could operate this mine with half the number of men we are employing today. Whatever way you look at it it is most essential that we have experienced and trained supervision in all departments.[40]

Nilsen's crude paternalism articulated a stubborn belief that Fijian mineworkers were destined to be subordinate in the work-place. In the case of Part-Europeans,

[39] Minutes of Joint Consultative Council, 6 March 1967, Vat./Goldmining Joint Consultative Council Meetings.
[40] Nilsen to Theodore, 6 Jan. 1947, Vat./Correspondence EGT/NEN.

he lamented, the main 'drawback' was that '[they] continue(s) to marry back into the native race and the children are more native than Euronesian'. Although succeeded as general manager by men less brazen and outspoken, Nilsen's bigotry typified the attitude of the mines' management. It continued to enjoy a currency and so to legitimise the structures of occupational and wage discrimination for many years.

4   Life and Work on the Frontier 1934–50

STATE PERSPECTIVES

Conditions of work and the physical and social environment outside the work-place offered further evidence of a rationalised system of cheap and controlled labour. Sparing investment was made in the health and safety of mineworkers; housing, recreational, education and medical services shared the characteristics of cost discrimination applied to earnings; and the mining town's infrastructure was shaped by principles of institutionalised racial segregation and control.[1]

The state's acceptance of the need for low-cost labour logically entailed its support for corporate control of expenditure on welfare as of any other return to labour. As an employer itself, government policies were directly influenced by the imperatives of economic stringency. It was no coincidence, then, that in the aftermath of Indian labour indenture, inspections of labour conditions gradually lapsed and that 'during the period 1930–1940 . . . there was less super-vision of labour conditions than at any previous period of the colony's history'. The human costs of this laxity proved enormous. Of the notorious lines on the island of Taveuni, the Commissioner of Labour admitted in 1944 that

> it would probably be fair to suggest that the absence of latrines has been responsible for deaths of young children; that the lack of ventilation and the damp conditions

---

[1]   Discussion in the following sections on the living conditions of plantation and mine labour, and of the various perspectives of medical, labour and other officers of the colonial administration, is largely based on correspondence contained in CSO files F48/137, F36/30 & F48/222; confidential CSO files; PRO CO83 series/215 & /218; and the Mining Board correspondence files of the Dept of Mineral Resources. In respect of mine labour, company sources include internal memoranda, budget and worker compensation reports, correspondence with the colonial government and Basilio Mata, Secretary Fiji Mineworkers' Union, and minutes of management meetings with the Fijian Labour Committee, all of which are scattered through a large number of classified and unclassified company files.

arising from failure to maintain sleeping huts in weather-proof order have led to tuberculosis; and that other diseases have resulted from conditions of squalor and filth that have to be seen to be believed.[2]

Two conflicting arguments emerged to explain this situation. For government medical officers, it was the inappropriate or outmoded legislation that governed the living conditions of wage labour, specifically its failure to demand sufficiently high standards of housing, hygiene or rations, and to extend substantive legal protection to plantation workers. A like argument was advanced in respect of the mining industry, where barracks allegedly conformed to the per capita air space prescribed by public health law. According to the Medical Officer Health Northern:

> The housing of the single Fijian labourers is, I consider, very bad. Although legally the huts are not overcrowded the general impression one gets of human beings put away on shelves till further required is not a good one.[3]

The deficiencies of the law were not confined to mine housing. In the area of industrial hygiene and safety, official regulations were anachronistic. By the early 1950s, it was admitted that they were comparable with those that had applied to the Queensland mining industry prior to 1936. The response of the Labour Department to model legislation from the Colonial Office on accidents and occupational diseases in 1950 threw some light on this anomaly. The ordinance, it was argued, might prove 'irritating' to Fiji's employers.

For others in the colonial administration, public health and labour laws gave ample direction and powers for the regulation of labour conditions. The root of the problem was the state's failure to enforce these and officers were brutally frank about the sensitive political issues that lay behind this. The poor standard of government housing—the 'PWD labour lines (e.g. Lautoka) exceed[ing] in squalor anything in the vicinity' according to the Acting Director of Medical Services—was a major constraint. So too was the government's long-tolerant view of conditions on European plantations. As the Director put it bluntly:

> ... our position is greatly weakened by the fact that we have ourselves connived for so long at the arrangement under which the Regulations were, by mutual consent, kept in cold storage.

More important was the political leverage of employers, particularly the estate owners, which inhibited local authorities from insisting that 'large concerns' comply with the law. Sanitary inspectors hesitated even to inspect estate quarters, and following unsuccessful attempts of the Labour Department to introduce an improved rations schedule, the administration resigned itself to the intransigence of the estates. In general, the Medical Department laconically observed, '... where the interests of the Taveuni planter and labourer conflict, those of the former have almost invariably prevailed, even in a court of justice'. Indeed, as Sir Henry Scott

---

[2] C/L Reay to CS minute, 7 Dec. 1944, CSO F36/30 Pt 1.
[3] Medical Officer of Health Northern (James Taylor) to DMS, Report for May 1939, 10 June 1939, CSO F48/137.

had urged during debate in the Legislative Council in 1935, the administration of the Public Health Ordinance was 'tempered with sweet reasonableness'.

A similar pattern of employer influence over official policy could be detected in the mining industry. The mining regulations empowered the Inspector of Mines to stipulate items of clothing and equipment necessary for the safety and health of underground workers. But such requirements were rarely specified or enforced. A comment by the Inspector of Mines in 1935 that he had on two occasions seen beer bottles lying around where 'barefooted' Fijians worked did not appear to justify a ruling for the compulsory supply of boots.

In general, government labour inspectors were looked upon with suspicion, even outright hostility, by the mines management. In 1940 plans by Fiji's first Industrial Relations Officer, C. S. de Reay, to investigate working and living conditions were angrily opposed. Even the intervention of Colonial Secretary Barton in an attempt to dispel fears of mischievous official probing, drew a blank from Theodore:

> The relations between our companies and their employees is, at present, harmonious and satisfactory; but I believe could easily be upset if it became known to the large body of employees here that an authoritative Government Officer is here to enquire into real or fancied grievances.[4]

Theodore similarly resisted pressure to improve the nutritional quality of mine rations.

Emerging from the turbulent years of the 1930s and 1940s was a growing belief that labour conditions in certain parts of the country could no longer be sanctioned. International labour conventions, labour 'disturbances' in a number of colonies, and a post-war Labour government in Britain were all prominent external influences on colonial policy. A Memorandum on Colonial Mining Policy circulated to Britain's mining colonies in 1946 urged greater vigilance over labour conditions and welfare in mining communities. Closer to home the unsettling effect of the Pacific war on industrial relations also led the local government to question the efficacy of existing industrial legislation as a means of labour control, and the prudence of continued resistance to reform.

Externally induced changes included the Minimum Wage Ordinance of 1935, the Workmen's Compensation Ordinances of 1940 and 1946, the Labour (Welfare) Ordinance of 1941, the Labour Ordinance of 1947 (abolishing penal sanctions), the appointment of an Industrial Relations Officer and the establishment of a Labour Department. On the whole, labour legislation was not introduced without fierce opposition from the leading commercial interests; and the state was well aware that it had the invidious alternative of yielding to pressure or inviting the 'odium' of 'a section [of the community] whose co-operation in the tasks of administration we so badly need'. An ambivalent attitude to active intervention in labour welfare persisted, and legislative reforms proved less effective in practice than they appeared in print.

---

[4]   Theodore to Barton, 22 June 1940, Vat./Emperor General Correspondence Dec. 1939-June 1940.

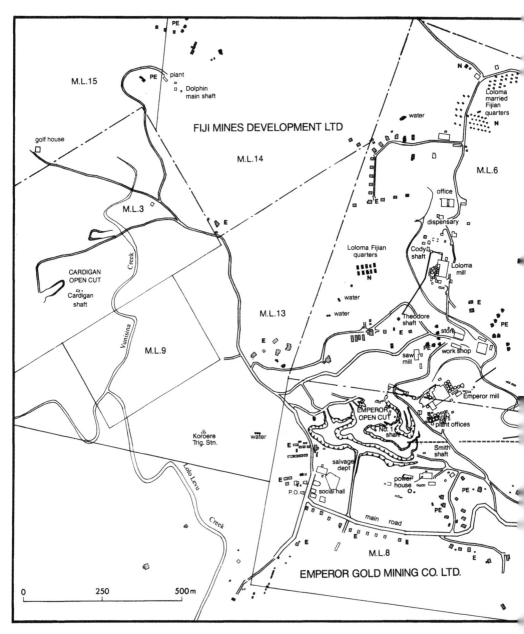

Vatukoula General Property Plan, 1940

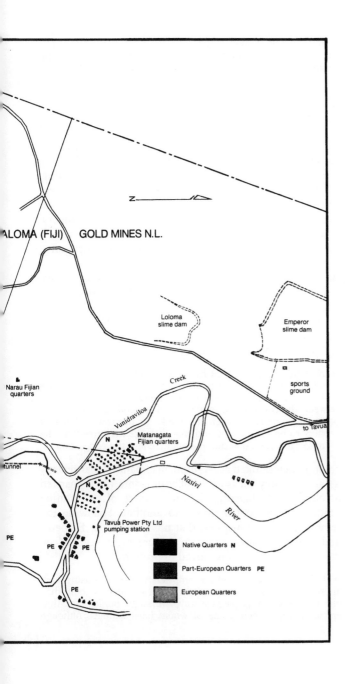

LOMA (FIJI) GOLD MINES N.L.

Loloma
slime dam

Emperor
slime dam

Creek

Narau Fijian
quarters

Vunidraviloa

sports
ground

to Tavua

Matanagata
Fijian quarters

N

Nasivi

tunnel

N

River

Tavua Power Pty Ltd
pumping station

PE

PE   PE

Native Quarters N

Part-European Quarters PE

PE

European Quarters

HOUSING, SANITATION AND HEALTH CARE

> When I joined the union I felt very strongly about the segregated housing. I talked with the welfare chap and he said it was because Fijians weren't educated. The company couldn't give them decent homes because they'd drink grog and spit everywhere. It was the same thing with toilets. [Part-European fitter & turner, Suva, Aug. 1982]

Standards of housing, dining and sanitation at Vatukoula reflected the principles of stratification in the work-place and its underlying racialist ideology. Wooden-floored, ceiled, fly-proof and supplied with electric light, the quarters for unmarried European mineworkers offered accommodation of 60 square feet per person in addition to 'suitable bathing and sanitary facilities'. There were generally only two men allocated to a room, and both were provided with a bed, bedding, a wardrobe and a chair. The room also had a table. Part-European barracks were (in the early years) earthen floored, giving each man a canvas stretcher and a space of 40 square feet. Accommodating between 24 to 36 men in theory, the badly ventilated iron and wooden barracks for Fijian labour confined each worker to an area of just 15 square feet with only a wooden bunk without a mattress for each man.

Fijian labour was organised into provincially demarcated barracks, a divisive practice defended as merely complying with the wishes of workers. In an industry that operated continuously, this arrangement deprived afternoon and night shift workers of sufficient undisturbed sleep during the day. In April 1935, following the outbreak of the first dysentery epidemic, a graphic description of Theodore's 'native' camp was given by the Chief Medical Officer:

> About 48 labour [sic] were living in two huts 24 by 16 feet, and there are 12 bunks on each side 6 upper and 6 lower. The space between the upper and lower bunks is about 3 feet. There is very little vacant space in this building, as there is only a main passage way between the two lines of bunks which is about 2' 6" and there is only a space of about a foot or so between the bunks in the row. I consider the ventilation in these huts to be insufficient and that they are overcrowded. The authorities in charge promised to build an additional hut to relieve the congestion.[5]

Far from abating, the situation deteriorated as recruitment expanded, particularly once the group began as an economy measure to allocate some of its married workers (with wives and children) to barracks. In the absence of partitioning walls, each family area more or less spilled over into another. Following the first major strike in November 1938, it transpired that numbers in the Emperor barracks had doubled, reducing per capita space to a mere eight square feet. The Acting Deputy Commissioner of Police was moved to protest:

> I am not qualified, nor do I desire, to question the proprietary [sic] of housing such a number of men in these huts, but I was astounded to find in some of them that, by fixing a plank in the narrow dividing passage way, two single bunks were thus converted into quarters for married men, some of whom have families. Although

---

[5]   Chief Medical Officer to Acting CS memo, 17 April 1935, CSO F48/137.

in each of these huts a number of single men continued in residence it was left to the occupants of these palatial quarters to devise means whereby they may obtain even the slightest degree of privacy. On visiting these huts at night I was disgusted to find the interior infested with vermin.[6]

The qualms of local officers matched the reformist sentiments emerging in other parts of the British Empire. In 1937 a Parliamentary Commission of Enquiry into labour 'disturbances' in Trinidad and Tobago expressed strong disapproval against the longstanding tradition of accommodating labourers in barracks, which seriously compromised the 'mental', 'moral' and 'physical' condition of workers. Five years later in Fiji, it was similarly recommended that after the war the mines' barracks should 'give way to houses for not more than 12 men'. Sir Alexander Grantham, appointed Governor in 1944, pressed the point further, advising against the construction of any more labour lines and urging that they be replaced by individual housing. It was not to be.

Corrective measures taken in respect of married workers were short-lived, with families again being placed in barrack accommodation in the post-war years. Overcrowding prevented even the inside storage of cooking utensils and strained the already limited bathing facilities and drinking-water supply. By September 1951 the companies' own community and welfare department confirmed that 'from the Public Health point of view', the congestion in the family barracks 'definitely constitutes one of the public nuisances'.

A very different situation prevailed for married European workers. Wooden cottages boasted four or five rooms, comfortable furnishings and, at least until 1944, cooking utensils. Many were situated on the hilltops where they commanded splendid panoramas of the surrounding countryside. In 1936 their cost varied between £350 and £1500, but ten years later had risen threefold to £1000 for the average-sized house with a maximum tag of £3600. Where married Fijian workers were fortunate enough to escape the nightmare of the barracks, they were sentenced to an unfurnished single room (18 feet by 12 feet) without bathing, toilet, food storage or lighting facilities. Houses were located in the valleys, had unceiled roofs, and were built out of corrugated iron rather than wood, which made them vulnerable to temperature changes and leaking in wet weather. Even in Sukuna's opinion, the houses were 'unlivable' in the daytime, while 'towards morning they drip with moisture'.[7] Their cost in 1936 was a modest £70, rising to £200 by 1946.

The poor standard of dining and kitchen facilities for Fijian miners also contrasted with the more congenial environment of the European messes. By the 1960s the dining-room for single Fijian men was still without walls ('as it is intended purely as a shelter not as a "room"') and had an unceiled roof and a concrete ungraded floor to facilitate hosing down. This meant that water collected underfoot. Men had to supply their own plates or bowls. Kitchens in the married barracks had dirt floors, which during the wet months were always muddy.

---

[6]   Acting Dep. Commissioner of Police, 16 Nov. 1938, CSO F36/39/1.
[7]   Sukuna to CS, 16 May 1944, CSO F28/126 Pt1.

The paucity of bathing and washing facilities required Fijian miners and their families to use the river and creeks that flowed through the settlements. The same untreated water was used for cooking and drinking. Health risks were apparent in the outbreaks of typhoid and dysentery, serious enough in 1938 to require an isolation camp on the field after workers had been hospitalised in the main towns along the north and west coasts of Viti Levu. Dysentery recurred through the 1940s, particularly affecting children; and, as we shall see later, deteriorating standards of housing and sanitation catapulted the number of casualties to alarming proportions during the 1950s and 1960s.

Cyanide pollution of the water supply posed a particularly virulent hazard. As early as 1935, following a complaint by the CSR to the Mining Board, a concentration of 0.096 parts per million was detected in the Tavua water supply from spillage of the mines' tailings dam. Observations of cyanide contamination were recorded over the next four years by the local District Commissioner, and in 1942 a senior medical officer charged that the mines' domestic water supply was unfit for human consumption if it remained untreated. The dangerous exposure of local farmers and other residents to industrial sludge was also repeatedly criticised by Indian members of the Legislative Council, and on at least three occasions the filtration and/or chlorination of river water was recommended by government officials as the only viable (if costly) solution.

The mining regulations prohibited the discharge of 'any chemical or other substance deleterious to animal or vegetable life' into a 'water-course', but intervention to enforce these was half-hearted, tempered by a sensitivity to the cost. Available records do not suggest that the companies were ever prosecuted; this in spite of the fact that protective measures extended little beyond approval of (state-funded) anti-typhoid inoculation, controlling bathing and washing near the pump-house, and urging Fijian and Part-European families to improve their own living conditions.

Until 1940 only European housing was provided with toilet facilities serviced by individual septic tanks. For Fijian workers, there were earth latrines to which no sewerage system could be attached. This exposed them to soil infestations by ankylostoma and other worm larvae as well as heightening the risk of dysentery or typhoid. An outbreak of ringworm and tropical sores among workers in 1936 was followed three years later by one of only a handful of health surveys in the industry. This revealed an extraordinarily high incidence (about 80% of Fijians examined) of ankylostomiasis or hookworm, due largely to 'haphazard defecation' on the surface, and many cases of other worm infestation, notably whipworm, roundworm, threadworm and a species of tapeworm.

The twice-weekly salting of the underground workings, a ban on 'underground defecation', and other sanitary measures, such as fly-proof septic tanks and, from 1946, the provision of boots, helped to contain the spread of the disease and to confine it to the surface. They were not enough to eradicate it or to prevent underground contamination by the late 1940s. In the absence of regular testing the incidence surged to new heights among both Fijian and Part-European labour, probably spurred on by the fact that hookworm was not listed as an occupational disease on the grounds that it was endemic to the colony as a whole.

The debilitating effects of hookworm were immense: the disease reduced work efficiency and productivity, and made workers more susceptible to other illnesses. Management conceded that it was 'undoubtedly . . . the underlying cause of much of the ill-health they experience' although curiously it did 'not appear to *inconvenience* the natives'[8] (my emphasis). An unbalanced diet deficient in essential vitamins made matters worse, as the 1939 medical survey argued. In the interests of productivity the Colonial Office, like the local government nutrition committee, also pushed for dietary supplementation for men engaged in mine and other heavy work (Table 4.1).

Table 4.1   Ration scale proposed for Fijian mineworkers* by government nutrition committee, 1938

Daily

1 lb.	bread	
2 lb.	Fijian vegetables (dalo, yam or breadfruit) OR	
1 lb.	rice (rice not to be substituted for root crops on more than 3 days weekly)	
½ lb.	fresh meat, OR	
½ lb.	of tinned beef (on not more than 2 days weekly) OR	
½ lb.	of fresh fish or tinned salmon (on not *less* than 2 days weekly)	
½ lb.	sugar	
½ pint	fresh milk	
6 oz.	uncooked green vegetables (including cabbage, beans, dalo leaves for 'rourou', etc.) OR	
2 oz.	onions (on not more than 3 days weekly)	

Weekly

2 oz. tobacco	4 oz. tea
4 oz. soap	8 oz. salt

And a weekly helping of seasonal fresh fruit (bananas, pineapples, oranges, etc.)

* Extra half-ration for a married indentured worker accompanied by wife and family until the company provides land for the cultivation of native crops.

Source: Ration Scale for Fijian Workers in the Gold Mines in Fiji, CSO F48/222.

Such pressure brought no tangible improvements to the pre-war ration scale of Vatukoula's miners, save an increase in the quantity of root crops offered as an alternative to rice. With inconvenience and cost the major grounds for objection, neither fruit nor vegetables was ever added to a diet heavy in carbohydrates and sugar (Table 4.2). While a limited amount of planting land was available to families, this was prey to the contaminating by-products of gold milling.

Medical facilities at the mines were at best rudimentary. By 1941 the population of Vatukoula stood at around 3000 and it was generally agreed that 'the most outstanding need is to provide hospital accommodation'. But in spite of the stabilisation of labour during the 1940s and the attendant expansion of the town, company services remained that of a small dispensary with a skeleton staff. Unwilling to commit shareholders' capital to building a hospital on the field, the group embarked on a long-drawn-out struggle to extract government finance.

[8]   Safety Officer to GM, 10 April 1952, Vat./Data From and To other mines.

Table 4.2   Rations supplied to each Fijian employee* by Emperor Gold Mining Co. Ltd, Loloma and TPP Companies, September 1938

Daily

1 lb.	bread
½ lb.	fresh OR corned Beef—OR when meat is not supplied—
1 × 6 oz.	tin of salmon
1 lb.	rice
	OR
2½–3 lbs.	yams, dalo & kumala when available
½ lb.	sugar

Weekly

2 oz. Fijian tobacco	4 oz. tea
4 oz. soap	8 oz. salt

Curry powder, kerosene, matches & sandsoap to each Fijian mess weekly.

* Extra half-ration for married worker accompanied by wife.

Source: Theodore, Managing Director EGM & Loloma to Colonial Secretary, 22 Sept. 1938, CSO F48/222.

Within the administration there was little enthusiasm for this proposition, particularly in view of the practice in Northern Rhodesia and the Gold Coast where mining companies provided their own medical services. The provisions of Fiji's 1891 Labour Medical Care Ordinance and the 1935 Mining Regulations strengthened the case against assistance, notwithstanding Theodore's objection to the first piece of legislation on the technical grounds that it did not cover dependants.

Fiji's medical infrastructure, and specifically its servicing of all 'natives', enabled the mining industry to defray the costs of hospitalising its Fijian and Indian workers. Together with their dependants, both categories of labour were generally treated at a small, poorly serviced government district hospital at Nailaga, Ba or by a government medical officer at the mines. For Part-Europeans and Europeans the facilities of a subsidised cottage hospital owned by the CSR were available at cost. Both hospitals were over 20 miles of unsealed road from Vatukoula; and unlike European and Part-European patients, who were transported by ambulance, Fijians travelled by utility truck and later by bus.

By discharging and sending sick workers home to their villages, the industry passed part of the cost of medical care on to the traditional economy. More insidiously, in the case of contagious diseases such as dysentery, venereal disease, tuberculosis or trachoma, the rural areas (notably the women) were inflicted with more than just the burden of nursing and feeding. The village was a preferred isolation ward to the local hospitals, which because of space problems were often forced to discharge patients prematurely. This obliged the mining companies to meet the cost of rations, transport and follow-up medical care. At no time were such considerations more obviously important than in 1941 when following an outbreak of trachoma it was decided that 'mild' cases would be treated locally and 'serious' cases sent home.[9]

Publicly, management peddled the myth of salubrious conditions. Early in 1951

[9]   Medical Officer Ba to General MP Vatukoula, 18 Aug. 1941, Vat./Department Memos 1941–May 1944.

an oblique reference to unsatisfactory standards in the *Fiji Times and Herald* by one self-titled Na Lokobono drew a slick response from General Manager Cayzer. A further letter from the pen-named correspondent threw out another challenge, but was withheld from publication. It was passed on to Cayzer by Alport Barker, editor and proprietor of the paper and European member of the Legislative Council for the country's Southern Division. In it, Na Lokobono (probably a misprint for *Na yaloka bona* or 'stinking egg') described how the furnishings of Fijian barracks comprised only wooden planks for beds, and how the overcrowded settlement of Lololevu, contrary to Cayzer's account, consisted of traditional *bures*, smaller than specified by law, and built and paid for by the workers and their families. The settlement had no sewerage system or electricity and relied on the polluted Nasivi River as its source of domestic water.[10]

Such a damaging description of conditions at the mines could not be permitted to tarnish the companies' public image. 'Needless to say', Barker bantered, 'I am *not* publishing it—I am not risking a libel action!!' Racist attitudes still ran deep within the European community and Barker was no exception: 'Some of these Fijians are really impossible—Fancy providing the ordinary labour with spring mattresses, tables & chairs! Of course he uses all of these in his own home!'[11]

CONDITIONS OF WORK AND OCCUPATIONAL HEALTH

> It is a different air underground. When you first go down, your breath becomes short and your ears ring. The only way you can tell someone is talking to you is by seeing his mouth move. Men go off sick after two weeks for a few days, maybe up to a month. They cough, get backache and go cold and hot from the change. It is a whole new experience ... They work you very very hard. If you are feeling crook, they swear at you ... One day, I got fed up. I went to get some water. My shift boss asked me what I was doing and swore at me. I shouted at him, 'We are machine. We are animal.' I went to kill him but one boy stop me ... Now I am too old. [Rotuman miner, Vatukoula, July 1982]

The quest for labour cost control was amply demonstrated in the restricted expenditure on underground ventilation, protective clothing and other facilities designed to alleviate conditions of intense heat, humidity and dustiness and to protect miners' health. Underground work was a constant test of physical stamina and mental alacrity. Added to the demand of what was, and still is, generally agreed to be an extraordinarily strenuous and hazardous occupation, was the enervating and noisy environment in which work was undertaken.

As underground mining deepened from the 1950s, temperatures rose to well over 100 degrees Fahrenheit (38°C), but even in earlier years at comparatively shallow depths, they were far from comfortable. This was particularly so when driving and cross-cutting were being undertaken at new levels and in areas away

---

[10] *FT & H* 27 Feb. 1951 and Cayzer to Editor, 6 March 1951; unpublished letter by Na Lokobono to Editor 12 March 1951, Vat./Miscellaneous Correspondence—Secretary.
[11] Alport Barker to Kayzer [sic], 20 March 1951, Vat./Miscellaneous Correspondence—Secretary.

from the working face where air currents were poor. Water seeping in through the rock was hot. Even on the sixth level of Loloma, which was flooded following heavy rain in 1949, '*flood* water [was] just above blood heat—by thermal water' (my emphasis).

Compounding the high temperatures and humidity were the discomfort and health risks resulting from exposure to particles of rock dust and noxious gases, both of which were released in large quantities during blasting. Dust was similarly manufactured underground by activities causing 'impact and friction', such as rockdrilling, shovelling, truck tipping, and the transport of ore and mullock. The physical environment for those assigned to the crushing plant and extraction process on the surface, especially the roaster, was also extremely dusty as well as hot.

The composition of mine dust was held to be the decisive factor determining its pernicious effect on physical health and the cause of the miner's pulmonary disease commonly known as pneumoconiosis or silicosis. At the inception of mining in Fiji the prevailing wisdom of the international mining industry was that silicotic disease was caused only by the fine particles of free silica or quartz contained in mine dust. An alternative theory contested this view, however, claiming that silica combined with alumina into (fibrous) silicate minerals, notably sericite, appeared to 'constitute an equal or even greater danger'. It was largely on the basis of this view, and the presence of sericite in 'very great' quantities at the two principal gold-fields, that the Emperor, Loloma, Koroere and Mt Kasi mines were believed to carry a definite risk of silicotic disease.[12]

Concern to safeguard the industry from the scourge of pulmonary disease was expressed in an impressive range of concrete proposals put forward by Fiji's Mines and Medical departments and endorsed by the Colonial Office. Compulsory pre-employment medical examinations, supported by later checks at regular intervals and assisted by the use of X-ray equipment, formed the thrust of these. Admirable though they were, they failed to move much beyond the ideas stage. Only one government-sponsored investigation in 1939 was made into the 'influence of mine working conditions upon pulmonary complaints'; no legal obligations were imposed on the industry to carry out the recommendations; and comprehensive pre-engagement checks were not introduced for a further fourteen years. Left largely to company discretion, medical examinations were sporadic, confined mainly to long-service (10 years) workers and without automatic X-ray scans.

The 1939 survey was itself neither comprehensive nor conclusive. Some 5% of those Fijians examined were diagnosed as having tuberculosis or severe bronchiectasis, or to be sufficiently ill to require transfer to surface work. But the survey involved only one-third of the industry's work-force, none of whom had been radiologically examined on engagement and it took place in advance of deep level mining. Established wisdom held that the non-European mineworker displayed an 'inherent pulmonary weakness' and that the incidence of tuberculosis in the industry was comparable with the national average. Neither claim was

---

12   For detailed discussion of silicosis, its incidence, analysis and preventive measures, see CSO F48/137; Enclosures No. 2 & 3 in CO 83/215; and 5th Empire Mining and Metallurgy Congress, Ventilation and Hygiene Section Questionnaire, Emperor and Loloma Mines Answers March 1952, Vat./Data From and to Other Mines.

informed by facts, but both served the interests of mining capital, helping to conceal the extent of occupationally derivative disease and thereby minimising corporate health costs.

Official doubts about the industrial propensity of pulmonary disease were supported by the perennial myths of 'discretionary' employment, the 'native' predisposition to pulmonary illnesses, and dubious observations of 'uncrowded living conditions'. Although they also rested more convincingly on the high turnover of mine labour, this argument was stretched beyond the limits of credibility by the mining companies, persisting into the 1950s when the labour market was much less mobile. Moreover, in earlier years, the penalties for being sick (dismissal, transfer to lower-paying surface work or the withdrawal of wages) did not necessarily promote labour turnover and so reduce the dangers of pulmonary infection. Quite the reverse, they probably encouraged many, particularly those with families to support, to continue to work rather than admit to an illness or return home. Reporting to the dispensary ran the risk of forfeiting the only means of supplementing rations, buying clothes and paying school fees.

A good illustration of the speciousness of professional wisdom were the conclusions drawn from the 'exceedingly low' chest expansion of the 691 Fijians measured and weighed during the 1939 survey. Medical opinion did not regard this as a measure of 'any constitutional weakness', preferring to see it as a function of inherent physiological differences between Fijians and Europeans that (conveniently) enabled Fijians to use less physical exertion to perform heavy manual work. A policy that prescribed for indigenous labour a crucial and essentially manual role in the colonial economy was neatly sanctioned.

Good underground ventilation was a generally accepted prophylactic measure against silicosis. The main workings at Vatukoula were serviced by natural air flows, supplemented only by low-pressure piped ventilation around the working face. Once this reached the target area, it 'liberated to mingle with dust, smoke and other gases' such that miners who received the circulating flow en route to the surface exit or as they returned after blasting to cul-de-sac work-places inhaled heavily polluted air.

Poor ventilation exacerbated conditions of extreme humidity. This was evident from the fact that wet bulb recordings tended to be very high in underground stopes and other work-places where air motion was restricted. So considerable was the condensation caused in the 'air lines' and 'receivers' that rockdrilling had often to be undertaken in a thick fog. The deficient ventilation system prompted early proposals from the government mines department for a much higher volume of air, an exhaust system, the use of mechanical fans and close monitoring of dust concentration, air flows and humidity, the costs being justified on expedient as well as moral grounds:

> Apart from the philanthropic motives, the mining companies operating in the Colony must support the introduction of preventive measures for economic reasons, in case the development of an occupational disease should scare the prevailing source of cheap labour out of the mine.[13]

---

[13]   Enclosure No. 3, CO83/215.

Although a dust-count device (Zeiss conimeter) was subsequently introduced, analysis of dust concentration was not very comprehensive due to the absence of technical expertise. High atmospheric counts continued to be recorded 'on occasion', and in 1952 management confessed that dust samples were 'never' collected. Mechanical blowers, too, were installed, but were restricted to development ends. With age, they became less efficient, requiring workers at the face to 'rush back to the shaft for air every five minutes'. They appeared in any case to be unsatisfactory aids, their noise adding to the deafening sound of drilling, loading and other underground activities. This tended to discourage workers from using them at all. As the Inspector of Mines observed in 1940, workers

> frequently prefer to work under humid conditions rather than with the noise of the blower or such like, and, awaiting the departure of the miner in charge, will turn off or restrict the units installed for their comfort.[14]

With miners a convenient scapegoat for 'bad working conditions', the postwar period saw a steady deterioration in underground ventilation and a greater susceptibility to pulmonary conditions. Open-cut mining gave way to more underground stoping on Emperor, all three mines deepened, and the migrant system was gradually replaced by a more permanent work-force. As shafts were sunk to lower levels and new work areas opened up, a proportionately smaller volume of fresh air was provided. By the early 1950s only three of the six levels of the Emperor mine on which stoping or development work was undertaken and two out of the seven levels of the Loloma mine received fresh air flows. The upper levels (three on Emperor and five on Loloma) were ventilated with the same air, euphemistically described by the company safety officer as 'not significantly freshened'.

Unwilling to rectify this situation, the industry proved more receptive to two of the other less costly conventional methods of dust suppression, namely wet drilling and the hosing down of work places. Both practices were of questionable efficiency. The precipitation of dust into mud did not eradicate the dust hazard because in such high temperatures mud quickly dried and was reconstituted as dust. Hosing, on the other hand, tended to unsettle as well as to settle dust. More important, the low silica content of local ores made wet drilling an inappropriate protection against pulmonary infection: sericitic dust (which predominated) could not, like certain other dusts, be moistened. On the contrary, it was possible that the introduction of water in the work-place was even 'prejudicial' to the prevention of silicosis. Not only did an increase in humidity debilitate workers and so reduce 'economic effort', but it exposed them to a higher risk of serious chest disorders such as tuberculosis. This, in turn, made them more susceptible to silicosis.

Available evidence does not make it possible to determine the extent to which artificial humidifiers were, in fact, responsible for the contraction of tuberculosis or for the high incidence of influenza and bronchial conditions that developed at Vatukoula. Because of the natural heat and humidity of the mines, workers

---

[14]   IOM and ME to Director of Mines, 24 April 1940, CSO F48/137.

were already vulnerable to these infections for, endeavouring to keep cool, they would hose themselves down regularly during the shift. Wet drilling merely increased the health risks of a continuous process of wetting and drying. Men stood in several inches, sometimes feet, of water and had water 'blasting into [their] faces'. So, too, the exposure to surface temperatures at the completion of a shift presented a problem because of the absence for some years of change houses, a standard facility of mines designed to offer underground workers a place to shower, change and regulate their body temperatures before going home. Men therefore 'came up wet and with no shirts on walked to their barracks'.[15]

The delay in constructing change houses was decisive in the outbreaks of influenza, consistently one of the main causes of absenteeism among Fijian miners. Like other infectious conditions, influenza was easily transmitted where collective work was undertaken in confined spaces. In 1939 an outbreak caused the Loloma mine to close down; and while the Emperor mine limped along, it endured absentee rates that robbed it on one single day of 450 out of 700 Fijian workers. As well as being associated with the spread of hookworm among underground workers, hosing down and wet drilling carried the risk of sore feet, another chief cause of absenteeism among Fijians. Both conditions were preventable by wearing boots, but this essential item of protective clothing was not made available to workers until 1946, and even then only at cost.

For surface (mill) workers, there were, in addition to dust exposure, the dangers associated with toxic gases that derived from the ore treatment process. Because of its rich telluride composition, the crushed ore had to be roasted at very high temperatures. It was a complicated extraction process uncommon in countries where gold existed in quartz form, and it released sulphur dioxide, a strong-smelling and asphyxiating gas. The cyanidisation of gold following roasting produced hydrogen cyanide, which passed as effluent through the gassing tower. Recording a visit of inspection over the Loloma mill in 1938, the District Commissioner Central made a diary entry which still applied half a century later: 'very interesting but very dusty and fumes from furnaces unbearable, sulphur'.

The inhalation of sulphurous fumes was not confined to roaster workers. They dispersed through other surface work areas as well as the housing settlements. The environmental impact of sulphur contamination was visible in the withered vegetation and food gardens, but perhaps the most disturbing characteristic of the gas was the bronchial or asthmatic condition symptomatic of its toxicity (see Appendix J). Although respirators were at hand in the roaster, these had a maximum efficiency of only 50% to 80% if they fitted well. They were hot and cumbersome and were frequently discarded 'as an encumbrance'. Management disclaimed the detrimental health effects of the gas, conceding only that it was 'unpleasant'. A bonus (of 1s. 6d. per shift) introduced for roaster workers was paid only at the discretion of the mill superintendent and depended, literally,

---

[15] Interviews with mineworkers Vatukoula (July 1982) and Suva (October 1983). The 1934 Mining Regulations required 'sufficient accommodation ... above ground near the principal entrance of the mine ... for enabling the persons employed in the mine conveniently to dry and change their clothes'. The first change house was not built at Vatukoula until 1941, and workers at the Dolphin mine were without a facility until 1948. Emperor Annual Report 1942; Vat./Dolphin Mines Ltd Oct. 1947–May 1951.

on which way the wind was blowing. This arbitrary practice was legitimised on the grounds that the fumes were only 'troublesome' when both roasters were operating and the wind direction was 'wrong'.

The exposure of mill workers to cyanide in both its liquid and gaseous forms caused skin rashes, generically classified as chemical dermatitis. One particularly severe type was caused by fumes in the gassing tower. It resulted 'invariably in a painful rash on the neck, arms and parts of the face etc; and in most cases the men concerned [undergo] treatment for one or two days'. By 1951 the time lost through the affliction stirred the group into experimenting with locally made prophylactic ointments. There was some initial improvement, but on the whole the application of the ointment, the use of gloves and later protective suits met with only 'varying success'.

The extent of respiratory or pulmonary illness among mineworkers cannot be accurately estimated until the 1950s, when the industry began to record the details of worker morbidity more systematically. Company correspondence marked the low incidence of these complaints during the 1930s and 1940s, and the few medical examinations undertaken celebrated the absence of conventional mining disease such as silicosis. But in the absence of regular and thorough examinations, such claims were unreliable. A number of other factors, while perhaps diminishing the risks of silicosis, would also have disguised the toll on the physical health of local mineworkers. Notable among these were the mobility of the mine labour market, the group's policy of dismissing and sending home sick workers, and the reluctance of Fijians to report to the mines' dispensary and preference, if unwell, for returning to their villages if they could.[16]

Despite its illegality under colonial rule, luveniwai vaka viti (traditional healers and medicine) were also sought by many Fijians in preference to going to the European hospital, not inappropriately dubbed vale ni mate or house of death. At least until the late 1940s, when with the aid of the local police, the mines management launched a campaign to root out, dismiss and prosecute offending 'doctors' and 'patients', it was relatively easy for workers and their families to maintain this clandestine habit.[17]

Other factors militated against diagnosis of miners' disease in these early years. The symptoms of silicosis, its slow, cumulative pattern, and its close association with tuberculosis hampered easy detection. This was especially so given the rudimentary and largely clinical training of local medical practitioners working at the mines' dispensary and the lack of radiological equipment at their disposal. Simple or uncomplicated silicosis was not infective and 'rarely fatal'; it was tuberculosis that was the cause of both the contagion and death of most silicotics. During its early stages the disease was evident only in 'a shortness of breath', a condition which in the circumstances might well have been incorrectly diagnosed as an ordinary bronchial condition. Only after some years of dust inhalation

---

[16]   The service record cards of Fijian mineworkers show frequent entries of 'discharged own accord' or 'leave required' owing to ill-health as well as 'discharged (involuntary) through illness/medically unfit'.

[17]   Safety Officer, R. H. Yarrow, 'A brief history of organised safety work on the Vatukoula Goldfield together with an indication of the costs involved and the benefits gained', 19 Nov. 1953, Vat./unclassified; Assistant MP Vatukoula, Aseri Manulevu to DMS, 27 Feb. 1952, Vat./Information supplied to Chief GM 1964-65.

would a worker become incapacitated or die. If local doctors tending to non-European mineworkers were ignorant of the manifestations of this unfamiliar disease, the implications were startling: by the end of the 1940s cases of bronchial congestion and catarrh, fibrositis, tracheobronchitis and pulmonary congestion recurred with disturbing regularity.

SAFETY HAZARDS AND SHORTCUTS

Encouraged by the abundance of unskilled Fijian labour, the migrant system of short-term employment and the reproductive (specifically curative) demands that could be placed upon the traditional social system, a strategy of controlled expenditure in industrial safety also helped to maintain low costs at least for the first decade of mining. While government officials hailed the group's exemplary record of safety, this was difficult to square with the injuries mineworkers sustained on the job. Frequency and severity accident rates (which measured the number of lost-time accidents and shifts lost per 1000 manshifts) were high, especially in respect of hand and foot injuries.

The steady transition to deep-level mining brought increasing dangers, but was overshadowed as a cause of a deteriorating safety record by a number of other factors: the restricted access of miners to protective clothing; the absence of free and formal technical training; and, particularly during the war, the poor quality of supervision at a time of intensified effort to raise productivity levels. Accidents caused by falls and slides of rock, for example, a major cause of accidents during the 1930s and 1940s, generally resulted from inadequate inspection of work-places and the resultant omission on the part of workers to bar down (scale the rock ceiling of loose rock fragments after blasting) properly.

Because treatment to a large extent determined the speed of recovery, a critical influence on the accident severity rate was the poor medical assistance available at Vatukoula. Injuries quickly became infected, particularly since living conditions were often unhygienic and the working environment underground was hot and wet. There was a high incidence of septic wounds, though management claimed that the blame for this lay with workers who failed to get their injuries treated. The verdict of an inquiry into the case of a worker's poisoned foot in 1939 expressed official approval for this extraordinary claim. It was considered irrelevant that the worker had not been wearing boots. The infection was caused by 'his own neglect in not receiving treatment immediately after treading upon a cross-cut saw'.[18]

Rebuking workers for their 'carelessness' and 'thoughtlessness' became common practice as the incidence of hand and foot injuries climbed drastically in the 1940s. In spite of this disturbing trend, the absence of any legal specifications enabled the industry to insist that mineworkers pay for their own boots. Their high cost—more than the basic weekly wage for Fijian workers—deterred many

---

[18] IOM and ME to Chairman Mining Board, 30 Aug. 1939, CSO F111/54.

from complying.[19] The high rate of foot injuries persisted, increasing 'substantially' by 1950. Hand injuries also recurred, but the issue of gloves remained restricted mainly because they were 'too expensive to issue to everybody'. In 1948 the companies cut their orders, deciding to distribute them only to platemen, bracemen and 'those who already had hand injuries'. For other workers, including underground truckers, the message was unsympathetic: 'Those of you who placed so much reliance on gloves for the protection of your hands must now depend more upon increased personal care and forethought in your work.'[20]

Ranking behind accidents to feet and hands were injuries sustained to the eyes, commonly caused by flying scats and splashed chemicals, particularly lime. The issue of eye-shields, compulsory equipment for all except office workers in many of the large American and Canadian mines, was confined to only a few occupations (engineering, for example) and even then not distributed to all workers. Where hospitalisation was required, the increasing pressure on available services led to accident cases, like disease cases, often being discharged prematurely. The problem vexed management, not to mention the victims themselves, for obvious reasons. In the case of foot and leg injuries in particular, the practice led to 'delayed recovery, an increased severity rate, protracted compensation payments and in some cases a higher degree of incapication [sic]'.[21]

The shortage of government personnel qualified to oversee mining operations and to regulate work practices and conditions in accordance with Fiji's broadly defined mining law contributed to the indifference with which the group regarded its legal obligations. It meant, on the Mining Board's own embarrassed admission, that the government 'pull[ed] the Mining Coach in "blinkers" '.[22] Even after the recruitment of an Inspector of Mines, the infrequency of his visits meant that district officers, lacking the necessary expertise, continued to inspect machinery and work-places and to conduct accident inquiries. For the 12 years spanning 1937 to August 1949 not a single inquiry was held by the Inspector of Mines into (non-fatal) serious accidents, the group being obliged only to submit 'brief accounts' of all such cases. For a brief period between 1952 and 1953, when inspections and accident inquiries were in the (part-time) hands of a government geologist, the companies themselves were called upon to be independent accident assessors. It was, according to one angry member of the Legislative Council, a 'farcical business', which 'would not be tolerated in any other part of the world'.[23]

Unilaterally assisted by the mines management and European supervisors, official inquiries not surprisingly blamed workers for accidents, at the very least castigating them for their carelessness, and vindicated management of any charge of criminal negligence. A typical example was an accident inquiry in 1937 after

[19] Between 1947 and 1948 a pair of rather unsatisfactory surplus army boots cost 21s. while regulation (hob-nailed, steel-plated and toe-capped) safety boots varied between 27s. and 29s.
[20] Vat./Mining Dept Bosses' Meetings 23 Feb. 1948, 28 Feb. 1949, 19 June 1950.
[21] Safety Officer to GM, Report for period ending 12 Nov. & 2 Dec. 1952, Vat./Emperor Mine Period Reports 1952-53.
[22] Chairman Mining Board (Holmes) to CS, 19 Dec. 1934, CSO F11/7.
[23] H. M. Scott (European Member for Northwest Division), 4 May 1953, Fiji Leg. Co. Report of Economic Review Committee Debate.

a Fijian miner lost an eye. An underground manager, a mine manager and the District Commissioner offered the unanimous verdict that although the man had not been provided with protective eye-shields, the injury 'was accidently [sic] caused through a small scat of stone flying from a rock which was being spalled into his eye. This is a common occurrence and no blame can be attached to anybody.'

The liberal definition of liability, particularly before 1940, was another anomaly. Compensation was tied to proven negligence or neglect by an employer and paid in full only in cases of proven total negligence. A reduced payment was conceded if the worker was judged to be partly responsible for his own injury; and no gesture at all if an accident occurred as a result of his 'neglect of safety regulations' or his 'serious and wilful misconduct'. The frequency with which accident inquiries found mineworkers culpable was a critical determinant of the low rate of compensation payments; and the discretionary, racially discriminatory formula for worker compensation before 1940 also influenced the low levels.

In the absence of a standardised scale of awards, discretion was exercised in favour of Europeans and Part-Europeans, who alone were unconditionally insured against accidents. In the case of Fijians, compensation (at discriminatory rates) for disability or death arising out of accidents was granted only to (indentured) married workers with their wives at the mines, and those who earned more than the minimum rate. Single men or those on the basic rates (at least 55% of the Fijian workforce) could entertain only the hope that *ex gratia* awards would be made to their families (in the case of fatalities) or to themselves (where injuries were not fatal).

The colonial administration was not oblivious of the iniquity of *ad hoc* arrangements between employers and their workers—and by implication the racialist formula of compensation. It was probable, the Secretary for Native Affairs argued in 1934, 'that some injured employees and some dependents [sic] of employees killed in the performance of their duties are awarded higher compensation than others, whose cases are equally worthy of consideration or more so'.

Indian members of the Legislative Council stressed the need for official intervention, and in September 1936 a resolution of the Council of Chiefs urged the colonial government to make legal provision for the accident (including death) insurance of Fijian mineworkers.

The limits placed on Fijian compensation were, like their low wages, rationalised with a contribution from the traditional economy in mind. In the group's summation the distinction between a married worker accompanied by his wife and one who was not, or who was single, signified permanent or casual status. Discrimination in favour of married men with their families was defended on the grounds that as 'permanent' workers they had relinquished their claims to traditional forms of support. In the event of this category of worker dying, Theodore claimed,

> his wife and family have, in a real sense, lost their breadwinner. In the case of a Fijian whose family remain in their own koro and retain their full communal rights, or in the case of a Fijian who is single, their deaths are not so serious a deprivation to their relatives [sic]; and the smaller amount of compensation which, under the

mining companies' scheme, would be allotted in such cases would be considered quite adequate.[24]

The redistributive and communal principles of village life, then, offered the ideological defence as well as the practical means by which this particular cost variable of Fijian mine labour was controlled. Accordingly, when the question of accident compensation arose in the 1930s, Theodore's submission was that 'any proposed law should be considered with full regard to the peculiar situation of the Fijian worker, and especially of his rights and immunities under his communal system'.

Such 'rights and immunities' were interpreted with a liberal and selective hand. When it came to calculating the distribution of compensation, the definition of dependency was based on a Eurocentric concept of the nuclear family to the exclusion of aged parents and dependent children who were not 'minors' or who were 'illegitimate'. This, of course, reduced the cost of Fijian compensation still further.

Although from 1940 employers were obliged to compensate an injured worker 'irrespective of negligence' unless the injury was attributable to the latter's 'serious and wilful misconduct', corporate liability remained circumscribed. Any injury that did not incapacitate a worker for at least a week (reduced to four days in 1946 thence to three days in 1964) was not compensatable; cases of fatal or serious accidents arising from a worker's 'misconduct' could not be referred for judicial review, a protection specified under the Colonial Office model ordinance; and the discriminatory principles underlying compensation awards remained, albeit covertly, intact, a position not wholly inconsistent with the home government's view that legislation should avoid giving the *appearance* of racial discrimination' (my emphasis).[25] The narrow utilitarian definition of disability was to permit this astonishing ruling some years later: 'While the man's arm is admittedly a bit bent the medical officers at present consider that will not cause any disability and that the arm is quite able to be used fully.'[26]

There were other anomalies, such as a case in 1947 when a Fijian miner was declared to have died from 'heart failure' after being pinned to the ground by a capsized underground truck. A similar diagnosis of death by 'natural causes' was pronounced in 1951 for a 43-year-old worker who collapsed and died while pushing an underground truck.

Overall, compensation payments to Fijian miners remained disproportionately low (see Table 4.3). The calculation of awards on the basis of earnings obviated the need for an explicitly racial index; and the death or incapacitating injuries of Fijian, Part-European and European workers, even where they shared the same job, continued to be evaluated differently. As for standardising maximum rates of compensation (£500 for death and £750 for permanent total incapacity), the legislation made even less impact on the practice of discrimination because low-wage-earners were not eligible for these. Nor did the ceiling payable under the

---

[24]   Managing Director EGM & Loloma (Theodore) to CS, 21 Sept. 1938, CSO F36/3 Pt 2.
[25]   W. Ormsby Gore to Officer Administering the Government of Fiji, 25 Aug. 1937, CSO F 36/3 Pt 2.
[26]   Cayzer GM to Sec. FMWU, 20 April 1953, Vat./unclassified.

Table 4.3 Associated Mining Companies: accidents and compensation, 1947

Race	Occupation	Nature of accident	Date	Days absent	Compensation (£ s. d.)
Fijian	Labourer (u/g)	25% permanent disability	19.8.46	142	58.10. 0
Part-European	Miner (u/g)	Fractured spine, rock fall	14.12.46	316	128.17. 4
Fijian	Labourer (mill)	Lacerated toe	26.2.47	17	1. 5. 6
Indian	Labourer (grass cutting)	Punctured foot—septic	15.3.47	25	3. 2. 6
Indian	Labourer	Simple fracture, left leg	21.3.47	79	9.17. 6
Part-European	Motor mechanic	Lacerated wound on frontal region	4.4.47	19	14. 5. 0
Fijian	Driver mechanic	Lacerated left knee	29.4.47	20	2.15. 0
Fijian	Miner	Compound fracture of right second toe (from steel drill falling on foot)	2.5.47	98	16.19. 0
Fijian	Plateman	Lacerated wound to scalp and shock—electricity short circuit	7.5.47	14	1.11. 6
Fijian	Miner	Cornea ulcer in right eye—flying scat	27.6.47	33	4.19. 0
Fijian	Labourer	Compound fracture of index finger and wounded tendon—saw cut	1.7.47	62	5. 8. 6
Part-European	Miner	Fractured rib—fall of piece of iron	8.7.47	16	5.15. 2
Fijian	Miner	Septic finger—piercing wire	2.8.47	15	1. 6. 3
Fijian	Miner	Loss of 2nd and 3rd phalanges of finger—jammed finger	4.9.47	NA	11. 4. 8
Part-European	Miner	Fractured foot	8.9.47	33½	15. 1. 6
Fijian	Labourer	Fractured left arm (still incapacitated)	22.9.47	88	7. 8. 0 (to 8.1.49)
Fijian	Miner	Fractured finger	10.10.47	24	3. 6. 0
Fijian	Labourer	Lost tip of finger	26.11.47	19	1.13. 3
Indian	Firewood cutter	Lacerated foot	22.10.47	24	3. 6. 0
Rotuman	Miner	Lacerated leg (from stone fall)	29.11.47	16	6.12. 1
Part-European	Miner	Lacerated foot	10.12.47	19	3.10. 2
Indian	Truck driver	Face wound (still incapacitated)	12.12.47	19	4. 8.10 (to 9.1.48)
Fijian	Miner	Lacerated finger	5.11.47	36	4.19. 0
Fijian	Miner	Hand injury from trucking (still incapacitated)	28.11.47	20	2.15. 0 (to 2.1.48)
Part-European	Mechanic	Lacerated hand (by fan)	20.2.46	119	21. 3. 0
Fijian	Labourer	Fractured thumb	7.10.47	47	5. 3. 3
Part-European	Roaster operator	Hand injury	11.11.47	14	5. 0. 1
Fijian	Miner/trucker (u/g)	'Died from heart failure' after being pinned to ground by capsized truck	24.11.47	Death	NIL

Source: Data taken from Associated Mining Companies of Vatukoula Return of Accidents for 12 months ending 31 Dec. 1947, Vat./Govt Mines Dept. CSR Co. etc.

ordinance prevent the group from paying higher rates to its European workers and staff.

Until 1946 no legislation in Fiji acknowledged the health hazards of industrial occupations, specified the nature and types of occupational illness, or determined an employer's liability in cases where a worker's illness or death was caused by working (or living) conditions. The 1946 ordinance specified only one of the many mining-related diseases, silicosis, which had been recognised (though not as a compensatable disease) under public health laws since 1935. It failed, however, to include tuberculosis, which was the actual cause of silicotic fatalities.

Occupational health, unlike safety, was not an issue with a history of metropolitan interest or pressure. Indeed, as the model East and West African legislation demonstrated in the late 1930s, the Colonial Office was discreetly opposed to placing employers 'under a statutory liability to pay compensation'. It was also mindful of the inflationary effect legislation would have on insurance rates because of the 'almost . . . complete absence of any effective regulations . . . designed to minimize the risk of the contraction of (occupational) diseases'. It was music to the ears of the major business interests in Fiji who were represented on a local committee charged with reviewing draft legislation for workers' compensation in 1940.

Recognition of occupational health hazards could therefore be legitimately postponed until after the war. When in 1950 Britain pushed for the adoption in its colonies of comprehensive accident and health legislation, its 'irritating' implications for the colony's employers re-emerged as an argument, this time as a reason for outright rejection. The net result was that the various mining diseases included in the model legislation—ankylostomiasis, tuberculosis, dermatitis, miners' nystagmus, subcutaneous cellulitis of the hand, knee and elbow—continued to be excluded as compensatable diseases in Fiji.[27]

The introduction in 1940 of industrial legislation designed to extend financial compensation to workers who sustained injuries during the course of their employment was a direct response to pressure from the Colonial Office to adopt the reforms of an international labour convention. But 11 years separated the metropolitan initiative and its application in Fiji. This was largely due to the uncompromising opposition of the CSR, the mining companies and other large employers who balked at the prospect of statutory labour protection that would raise both the cost and the political consciousness of local workers. Through direct lobbying and the efforts of political strongmen, Scott and Hedstrom, they were able to retard the introduction, reduce the scope, and finally modify the terms of this and other industrial reforms initiated in the late 1930s and early 1940s. The draft bill of 1940 made clear the sensitivity to the interests of employers:

> the burden must be made one which can be borne by the industries of the Colony. It must not be one which will tend in any way to affect adversely the industries

---

[27] A fuller discussion of the debate over the Colonial Office legislation and the implications of inadequate protective legislation for local miners can be found in Bain 1985 : 319–21.

of the Colony . . . [The compensation rates] must be made reasonable so that the rates of insurance which the employer would have to pay are not too high . . .[28]

The force of these sentiments persisted in the face of subsequent metropolitan interventions. The recommendations of the Colonial Labour Advisory Committee in 1948 that compensation for permanent total incapacity be raised to the equivalent of 48 months' wages (from 36 months) and that lump sums be replaced by pensions were both rejected outright. It took nearly another decade for Colonial Office guidelines to make any substantive impression on local legislation. In the interim, the basis of assessing compensation fell increasingly out of step with soaring living costs, rising wages and the prevailing practice in other British colonies.

SINEWS OF SOCIAL SEGREGATION AND CONTROL

A mining town has a distinctive character. It is generally isolated, concentrated rather than sprawling, artificially built up around the industry and even one employer, gender imbalanced in favour of men, and possessed of both the positive and negative features of the frontier—a social solidarity and a brittle, even hostile, parochialism. The town of Vatukoula shared these characteristics and, consistent with colonial examples elsewhere, bore the additional stamp of ethnic plurality and racism. For most Fijian workers the austere and mutually reinforcing demands of mine work, urban life and industrial discipline created an unprecedented scale of economic and social dislocation.

Leisure or recreational activities offered a reprieve from the oppressive demands of the working day; a psychological flight from material and social deprivation; an opportunity to unburden frustrations. They were a means of diminishing the loneliness and the spiritual foundation of intra-working class loyalty and solidarity. For this reason leisure activities could, paradoxically, intensify rather than divert or reduce feelings of disaffection or hostility, whether these were expressed between different workers or by workers towards management.

Dancing, gambling, sex and drinking represented four such paradoxical pursuits at Vatukoula, and their potential to destabilise the industry (and, in the opinion of some nervous colonial bureaucrats, even the colony at large) elicited decisive and essentially coercive responses. For the state, the problems inherent in a mining town, and particularly the removal of indigenous Fijians from the controls of traditional society, raised the disturbing spectre of social unrest. Dancing, drinking and sexual 'immorality' epitomised the disruptive impact of a novel industrial experience that spread its contaminating tentacles from the earliest

---

[28] Attorney-General, 23 May 1940, Fiji Leg. Co. Debates. The Colonial Office advised that workers and grower representatives be consulted as well as companies operating in the colonies. This was not complied with in Fiji, the only Fijian representative being a chief.

years. Parents, chiefs and native ministers, the Methodist Church lamented, seemed 'powerless to check this revolt against established custom'.

A report of a Methodist Church commission in 1938 displayed this preoccupation with spiritual and moral 'laxity'. It provided a telling backdrop to the state's central role in establishing social control at the mines, as well as highlighting the contradictions of Christian evangelism: at once promoting and bemoaning the effects of the 'civilising' march of European capitalism; at once encouraging and lamenting the demise of traditional values and structures.

> It is to be expected that with the impact of an evolved and aggressive civilization such as ours upon a more or less primitive social structure, there would be serious dislocation and necessary adjustments. The unexpected thing is the rapidity of the change; and herein is the real danger, for the strain upon the moral fabric is such that serious and perhaps irreparable rupture is taking place. The Government is perturbed and admits that it cannot keep pace with the movements; and our Mission, with its moral and spiritual interests, is keenly aware of the dangers that threaten. So rapid is the change that in even a space of three years one feels that a different Fijian has arisen.[29]

Venereal disease was one of the more pernicious consequences of the apparent debunking of Christian and traditional ethics. It was attributed to prostitution and precipitated a selective vendetta against the female culprits. A spate of corrective measures was aimed not just at removing 'infected women' from the mines but at fortifying the barriers to the influx of Fijian women generally. In 1935 the Tavua gold-field was added to a list of urban areas that had been declared prohibited to women under the 1927 Native Courts Code.

Measures to control the movement of Fijian women outside their natal villages originated in the nineteenth century. They sprang from the combined initiatives of the early colonial state and the Fijian chieftaincy, and were couched in a shared social code, which prescribed for women a dependent and disciplined existence within a patriarchal society. An 1887 ordinance had declared it an offence for any woman to be absent from home for one month without 'any just or reasonable cause' or 'the permission' of her local or district chief. Unmarried women, whatever their age, were forbidden to leave without permission from their parents, guardian or *mataqali*. Penal sanctions took the form of culturally styled labour services, such as weaving mats or making *masi* (beaten bark cloth), fishing nets or pottery.

The Native Courts Code of 1927 had strengthened these devices by making written permits obligatory and introducing controls on movement into 'prohibited areas' that included the magisterial district of Suva and the municipality of Levuka. Women who remained in one of these areas without authorisation for more than one month became liable to arrest and repatriation. Second or subsequent offences brought the likelihood of penitential labour services. The exemption of those women accompanied by 'husbands, fathers, or male persons under whose control they are according to native custom' or those in regular employment

---

[29]   Report of Commission to Fiji, Aug. 1938, MMSA Cak A/4 (b) Fiji District Cakaudrove Circuit Correspondence Inwards and Outwards 1938.

in prohibited zones was probably a pragmatic response to the increasing demand for male and female Fijian labour around the 1920s. It did not impair the structure of male dominance and control.

With the establishment of the gold-fields, the colonial administration was faced with disconcerting evidence that certain chiefs were being seduced by the prospect of communal incomes into abetting rather than restraining the illicit traffic. It was not about to tolerate such complicity. From 1935 a woman's permit had to be authorised by higher ranking officials, while liability to prosecution, backed up by the stiffer penalties of a £1 fine or a one-month prison sentence, became effective after two days' unauthorised presence in a prohibited zone. Both penalties were raised to £2 and two months respectively in 1937, and reinforced by the introduction of a £5 fine or three months' imprisonment for second offenders. Privately the Colonial Secretary admitted to the 'draconian' nature of this retribution, but such reservations did not prevent 170 women from being prosecuted (sent home, fined or imprisoned) between 1936 and 1937 alone.[30]

If moral opprobrium and punitive action were directed exclusively at the women who indulged in prostitution, the government's attempts to ferret out the offenders in order to lessen the associated health risks were hampered, at least initially, by the mining companies themselves. The group's assurances that it would be equally attentive to removing 'these undesirables' from the field belied its ambivalence to the whole question of commercial sex. Management was alert to the debilitating effect on health and the reduced work efficiency caused by venereal disease. It was also aware that the presence of 'girls' promoted absenteeism, tending to 'keep the Fijian labourers awake till 2 or 3 in the morning'. There was, on the other hand, a strong temptation to permit European miners to exploit the cheap and accessible source of pleasure afforded by 'native' prostitutes.

This contradictory position appeared, in part, to reflect the scarcity value of skilled European workers in contrast to the dispensable surplus of unskilled Fijian labour. So obviously was female prostitution regarded as an esteemed stabilising service for the white working class that the local superintendent of police suggested in 1936 that the mining companies considered it 'was necessary to retain a certain number of Resident Prostitutes for the use of and abuse by the European Employees [although] Prostitutes were NOT necessary for the retention of Fijian Labour'.[31] It was only one of a number of occasions when the point was pressed, and together with the continuing presence of these working women in contravention of the native regulations, was a sore point for the colonial secretariat.

By the outbreak of the Second World War the Vatukoula management had itself come to regard the *vulagi* (or foreigner) peril of venereal disease as a 'menace'. Residual acceptance of the advantages of female patronage nevertheless persisted, and in the aftermath of the war, when local labour still fell well below requirements, the industry extended this indulgent attitude to its Fijian workers. 'Undesirable women', Ratu Sukuna testified, appeared to have 'a free run' at this time.

---

[30] For interesting similarities in the controls on female mobility and sexuality on the Northern Rhodesian copperbelt, see Parpart 1983, particularly 38-9.
[31] CSO/confidential file.

In the longer term the demands of production, in particular the industry's need for a more stable and productive work-force, and the problem of labour shortages demanded a fresh approach to controlling the influx of women. They dictated greater emphasis on selective female settlement, notably through the policy of married labour recruitment initiated in the late 1930s. These were women who through wedlock became the caretakers and the social and biological reproducers of labour rather than just worker playmates. They were women who could also usefully undertake low-paid domestic work in the homes of the small but growing number of married European personnel.

State regulation of the extra-occupational life of mineworkers was not confined to prostitution. Dancing was one of the more popular recreational activities open to Fijians, but because of its alleged association with the rising tide of 'immorality', it too was subject to scrutiny and control. Prohibition of 'native' dances (including the popular *taralala*) held without a permit went back to the nineteenth century. An offence carried the penalty of a £5 fine or, in default, an imprisonment term of up to one month with the possibility of hard labour. During the early 1930s the CSR was asked to assist in 'suppressing' the *taralala* among its Fijian employees. Management was willing to co-operate and accepted unreservedly the rather dubious medical view which claimed 'a serious increase in venereal disease directly and indirectly due to lewd dancing'.[32] The mining companies similarly complied with official regulations, although their reasons probably had little to do with prevailing Christian dogma. Well into the 1960s Fijian (like Part-European) mineworkers accordingly held dances or convened other social gatherings only with management's consent. The occasions were usually policed.

Gambling and 'sly-grog' dealing were two other 'vices' condemned by colonial morality and forbidden by law. For the mine employers, the consumption of large amounts of alcohol and night-time gambling had a deleterious effect on labour efficiency. The failure of government inspections and the group's own surveillance to suppress either activity led, on Theodore's initiative, to the stationing of a police force at the mines in 1940. The cost of this was shared with the state, which justified the move as the only means of bringing 'the troublesome section of the mining populatoin' under 'control'.[33]

Guided by colonial convention, in particular the practice of the CSR, Theodore was the architect of a township of distinct and virtually self-contained racial and ethnic settlements. A segregated pattern of recreation also helped to regulate community life and to inhibit solidarity between different racial and ethnic groups. Although 'in a system of otherwise naked exploitation', as a South African historian has put it, 'social life could be used as the loin cloth of respectability',[34] company investment in the social welfare of mineworkers conformed to the discriminatory pattern of their earnings. A dearth of recreational opportunities open to Fijians contrasted with a plethora of sporting clubs, holiday cottages and other facilities available to European employees, intended to overcome the isolation and cultural alienation that reputedly inhibited European recruitment.

---

[32]   Lord to Manager Nausori Mill Private, 26 Sept. 1933, CSR 142/2902.
[33]   Governor's Address to Leg. Co., 25 Oct. 1940.
[34]   van Onselen 1976 : 159.

In 1937 a social hall was built at Vatukoula for European workers and their families. This comprised a dance hall, library, billiards room, barber's shop, and a 'talkie theatre'. The group constructed a floodlit tennis court and a nine-hole golf course and club house, which accommodated a bar, changing facilities and a room for dances and other social functions. A bowling green with eight floodlit rinks, described as 'the mecca of many of the European employees' was also serviced by a club house and bar among other facilities. Within a few years a social hall was built for Part-European workers, admittedly after initial refusal by management. Gradually a library, billiards table, refreshment room and a nearby tennis court were added. The European privilege of deep sea fishing by company launch was also extended to Part-Europeans.

Separate halls for the Fijians and Rotuman communities followed, but they were furnished on a much more modest scale. A radio alone was provided in each of the three Fijian halls, and there were 'separate buildings' for their dances or other social functions. European, Rotuman, Part-European and Fijian children celebrated Christmas around separate Christmas trees, while their parents attended segregated film screenings.

Sporting activities, including rugby, soccer, cricket, and later hockey and boxing, were the chief sources of legitimate, company-organised recreation for Fijian and other non-Europeans. A playing ground was built following a request from Fijian workers, and in 1939 a sports council was established to ensure the 'proper conduct and control' of activities. Sport was one area where a certain amount of racial/ethnic mixing was tolerated, and it was the council's responsibility to cater for selected inter-racial activities such as cricket.[35]

The policy was not in fact as permissive as it appeared, for desegregated sporting activities meant only that workers of different racial/ethnic backgrounds were allowed to compete against each other. It did not entail mixed composition of the teams. In fact, promoting inter-ethnic competition was probably conducive to heightening rather than dissipating communal tensions.

The discriminatory basis of corporate investment in recreation was reflected in recurrent expenditure. For the financial year 1941, the group contributed nearly £10,000 to the various sports clubs and associations patronised by mineworkers and staff. Of this amount, barely 15% was allocated to those facilities open to Fijians. The golf, tennis, and bowling clubs, swimming pool, launch, Trout Acclimatisation Society, and European social hall—all except the launch admitting only Europeans—claimed by far the largest proportion of company grants. Part-Europeans won some financial support for their social hall; but funds (worth £300) allocated to the improvement of Fijian sports facilities that year were drawn from an 'Unpaid Wages Account'.

Education was no exception and exemplified the benefits of institutionalised racism. The provision of school facilities for the children of miners was necessary to persuade labour to settle permanently. It was also integral to plans for the reproduction of new generations of mine labour since the acquisition of basic literacy and (English) language skills contributed to occupational efficiency. The

---

[35] Memorandum on Native Sports at Vatukoula, Vat./Emperor General Correspondence March 1938–Sept. 1939.

segregationist principles of the industry could, moreover, be applied to great effect through education. By socialising children into the ruling ideology of racial distinction and hierarchy, and specifically inculcating in Fijian children a code of subservience even to their European peers, the industry's social-control apparatus became at once more pervasive and powerful.[36]

One important feature of the cost structure of Fijian and to a lesser extent European education was the industry's reluctance to accept responsibility. In respect of Fijian education, the group's efforts were directed towards persuading the state to accept full costs and managerial responsibilities. Amid a protracted debate it steadily retreated, effecting in 1948 complete disengagement, a more successful conclusion than parallel lobbying over other areas of its social infra-structure. Disengagement involved the withdrawal of all subsidies towards capital and operating costs.

The years that preceded the government take-over saw Fijian mineworkers and their families deprived on two levels: first, on account of the persistent and acute shortages of classroom space and teachers; and second, because they were obliged to meet a significant proportion of the capital and recurrent costs of education themselves. All Fijians, irrespective of whether they had children of school age at Vatukoula, had an amount (6d. until 1942) compulsorily deducted from their monthly wages. From the beginning of 1941 one-third of the cost of constructing the school buildings was raised by way of an additional levy of 1s. This payment continued as a contribution to school fees after the buildings were completed, and was raised to 2s. in 1944 to enable the group to recover one-third of the cost of extensions. Wage deductions were iniquitous, not only because they were applied indiscriminately, but also because Fijians already paid an education tax to their home provinces. They provoked widespread resentment and sustained opposition within the community, which escalated as overcrowding and inadequate staffing left some hundreds of children without any tuition at all.[37]

Market conditions and the expectations (and demands) of the dominant culture meant that the group attended with greater sensitivity to European school accom-modation and teaching standards. As early as 1937, when numbers totalled only 40, a school run by Marist sisters for European and Part-European children was financed. Running expenses were met out of an annual government grant and school fees, but the companies covered the cost of extensions (in 1946) and any deficits. More important was the heavy cost of segregating European and Part-European education, designed to counteract a racial balance that had shifted noticeably and unacceptably towards a sizeable Part-European majority, including some children who were 'possibly over the borderline'. Faced with rumbling dis-content among its European recruits, most of whom were opting for correspondence courses or boarding establishments in Suva, New Zealand or Australia in preference to the 'mixed' environment of the mines' European school, the companies rejected

36   For a comparison with the role of education on the Rhodesian mines, see van Onselen 1976 : 182-4.
37   Details of Fijian education at Vatukoula are drawn from a number of company files, including Vat./Education, Vat./Department Memos 1941-May 1944; Vat./Meetings of Executives—Current File; and Vat./Period Reports to Melbourne Office 1941.

the alternative of enlarging integrated facilities where there was 'no possible way of keeping children apart'.

The establishment of a separate European school consolidated the privileges of a small expatriate élite. The school accommodated fewer than 20 children at a time when its Fijian counterpart had nearly 500 pupils and was plagued with overcrowding, understaffing and waiting lists. It incurred the combined costs of construction, an annual subsidy and a 25% contribution to teachers' salaries. As well as this, the reorganisation helped to widen the social distance between Part-Europeans and Europeans—a few select Part-European children only being permitted to attend the school. When the government took control of the European school in 1948, there was one penalty: a more liberal policy on the question of mixed education was espoused, at least in theory, since children of 'mixed parentage' were eligible for entry providing they had a high standard of English and could afford school fees of 14s. a term.

The transfers did not signal an end to corporate involvement in education. The group fought to maintain expatriate staffing of the European school; it remained in a strong position to dictate a conservative policy to the Roman Catholic school, which came under its control; and it maintained responsibility for administering payroll deductions from Fijian workers for the running of the Fijian school.

As with the group's employment practices, social policy at the Vatukoula mines contained vital elements of control and discrimination. Its breadth and diversity were redolent of the penetrating power of the company town. Probably the most singular feature of community life was, as in Ghana, that 'the authoritarian nature of the mining workplace was replicated in the authoritarian nature of the mining community, reinforcing the labour repulsive character of work in the mines'.[38] Under such conditions, it should come as little surprise that the grievances articulated by mineworkers were directed as much at issues such as education and sport as at wages and housing: indeed the entire gamut of working and extra-occupational life.

---

[38]   Crisp 1984 : 24.

5   Labour Resistance and Conflict 1935–50*

COMMUNALISM AND THE OTHER FACES OF PROTEST

The system of labour exploitation and control in the mining industry created deep frustrations within the work-force. Resistance, though small-scale until the 1950s, preceded by over a decade the formal organisation of mine labour into a union. It took a variety of forms, expressed not solely in collective assaults on capital but also in passive and unorganised forms of protest. Sporadic outbursts of communal hostility and violence also punctuated a seemingly sluggish industrial landscape. They too were 'an important index of working class frustration and despair',[1] although the resilience of communal loyalties underpinning much of the conflict served to diminish the capacity of mine labour to pose an effective challenge to capital. Over all, the constraints on the consciousness and actions of mineworkers in Fiji, like their counterparts in Africa, mirrored 'a complex of material ideological and power variables'.[2]

The desultory and muted nature of early labour resistance, and the dominance of ethnic rather than class- or worker-consciousness, owed much to the coercive and co-optive strategies that the mining industry and the state deployed to safe-guard a system of cheap labour. The principles of racial discrimination in particular helped to foster cleavages within the working class, making ethnicity a logical foundation of industrial bargaining, and providing the impetus for an exclusively Fijian union in 1948. The privileges of Rotumans and Part-Europeans, including their greater occupational and wage mobility, were explicit forms of material

---

* Some of the material in this chapter has been used in earlier writings. See Bain 1986 : 37–59; 1990 : 232–8.

---

[1]   Phimister & van Onselen 1979 : 1.
[2]   Stichter 1985 : 120.

differentiation, which did not exclude them from the working class, but did mean that their relations with capital were generally less repressive. Promotion during the 1940s into jobs that gave them supervisory and disciplinary rights over Fijian labour drew them, moreover, into the structure of management. This 'aristocratic' status encouraged a loyalty to their employers and a willingness to abstain from industrial action or even act as strike-breakers in order to defend their privileges. Only on a single (unsuccessful) occasion do Part-European workers appear to have come out on strike in significant numbers to object to wage cuts and to fend off an assault on other employment privileges. This took place in 1936.

Alongside the compliant behaviour of Part-Europeans and Rotumans, organised protest by Fijian mineworkers was decidedly more militant, albeit rare in the formative years of mining. Its forms were also decisively shaped by the racial specificity of production relations. The thrust of demands was essentially communal, as was its organisational base. Those who resorted to industrial action articulated an angry rejection of occupational discrimination, directing their energies above all at acquiring for Fijians the wages and other benefits extended to Part-Europeans and Rotumans. While representing an attack on capital, their struggle also brought them into direct confrontation with other categories of workers, especially when they appeared obstructive.

The organisational weakness of Fijian labour and the low level of class-consciousness can also be explained by the structure of the mine labour market and, associated with this, the hegemony of traditional cultural values. The transience and low-skill profile of labour inherent in the migrant system and in contracts of short-term employment did not preclude resistance, but did militate against the mobilisation of a strong and cohesive organisation with a viable leadership. In particular the contract system posed an obstacle to industrial combination for it disqualified a section of the work-force from any kind of legitimate collective bargaining: the terms of employment, once accepted at the outset of contracts generally by chiefs, remained fixed.[3]

The Depression diminished further the bargaining power of unskilled labour. The labour surplus it generated made Fijians insecure and expendable; and because it led to competition for work, discouraged the emergence of a collective identity. Such conditions enabled the industry to dispense with workers on the slightest (even specious) charges of inefficiency or incompetence and aided the expulsion of any branded as 'troublemakers' or 'agitators', as in 1936 and 1938.

Shortages of labour during the gold rush gave Fijian mineworkers a brief advantage in a competitive market. The peppering of collective wage demands and strike action led to considerable disquiet among employers, as the report of the Nasivi (Fiji) Gold Syndicate NL hinted:

> We are striking trouble with our labour. The ruling rate is 2/- a day and food, but the natives are getting shrewd and want 3/- and food. We dare not give it because it will cause trouble elsewhere—the Government only give 1/10 and food.

---

[3]   See Stichter 1985 : 190–4 for a discussion of 'the impact of migrancy on worker consciousness' in colonial Africa.

Theodore struck trouble some time back and gave in to them, raised their wages in order to keep his Mill going. If trouble arises the Government will have to step in and settle it.[4]

Wage collaboration between different forms of capital soon dampened this early show of strength. The monopoly that the Theodore group came to command on the Tavua gold-field from the mid-1930s extinguished it.

Shula Marks and Richard Rathbone argue that 'first-generation [African] proletarians still have a consciousness in part informed by their rural class position'.[5] The description is relevant to other colonial societies, including Fiji, where the indigenous people retained access to land resources and a supporting social system. Further, as in the Northern Rhodesian copperbelt, pre-capitalist values did not meet an early 'natural' death at the hands of the intruding culture. This reprieve was in large measure a function of the role that traditional culture (or at least selective parts of it) was assigned within the mining industry. In particular, imaginative energy was invested in integrating traditional social relations into the structure of labour control. This was nowhere more effectively engineered than in the management of the contract system. As we have seen, chiefs often accompanied groups of these workers, and apart from taking charge of the monthly wage packet, conveniently acted as overseers. This established at little or no extra cost a simple and easily managed system of communication and control premised on a tradition-sanctioned code of social behaviour. As the following sections demonstrate, local chiefs were also used to help defuse unrest, suppress strike action and calm other outbursts of industrial turbulence. They became crucial instruments of labour control, dispatched to the mines at the request of the mining companies and with the blessing of the colonial government.

The establishment of a Fijian labour committee in 1936 institutionalised the role of resident chiefs and elders in the general control of labour. The system had precedents in other colonial mining economies, such as Northern Rhodesia,[6] and it was usefully diversified at Vatukoula to provide for separate representation for the Part-European and Rotuman communities. It enabled the companies to monitor any fermenting grievances and had the related advantages of strengthening an otherwise fragile communication link with the work-force and promoting labour discipline. For the Fijian labour committee at least, a disciplinary function in respect of gambling and alcohol-drinking persisted well beyond the Second World War.

As cultural reference points, the committees were an important means of preserving communal identities, lessening the need for alternative worker representation that was more likely to threaten production relations. In this way they

---

[4] D. C. J. Hill to Dunstan, 17 June 1935, MSE/Nasivi (Fiji) Gold Syndicate NL.
[5] Marks & Rathbone 1982 : 12.
[6] A council of tribal elders was introduced on the copperbelt of Northern Rhodesia in 1931. A. L. Epstein gives a detailed account of a system similarly 'designed to provide a link between the Compound Manager and the African population of the compound', noting its usefulness as a means of communicating policy decisions and of keeping management informed of worker grievances. Despite its lack of legal powers, the council also proved extremely important as 'an agency of social control', because of its adjudicating role in settling petty, mainly domestic, disputes. See Epstein 1958 : 27–8.

provided what the Commissioner of Labour was later to describe as a 'safety valve' calculated to pre-empt the formation of a workers' union.[7] On the positive side for workers, the committees were a 'local anaesthetic', which cushioned the dislocating effects of a labour system that separated men from their families and village life and subjected them to an unfamiliar and dangerous occupation. Inter-ethnic, like intra-ethnic, identities offered a palliative, a sense of dignity and a feeling of security.

But shoring up traditionalism and communalism against the levelling tide of urbanisation and wage labour carried the seeds of a unity that could, in the right circumstances, be mobilised against capital. Yet the policy was not openly resisted by mineworkers, at least not until the 1950s. Indeed, artificial barriers such as the provincial and racial/ethnic segregation of the single men's barracks, family communities, and recreation found willing accomplices, particularly in the early years of mining. In the case of Fijian workers, the system acted as an especially potent mechanism of control, because they were, unlike other workers, subject to two (provincial and racial/ethnic) sets of divisive forces.

Cultural influences were subtle yet powerful. Deference accorded by tradition to chiefs, and the customary constraints on making demands, however legitimate, were adroitly fostered in the quite different circumstances of an industrial labouring community. Under chiefly direction the subservient attitudes of commoners were directed towards both colonial officials and employers. Chiefs encouraged mine-workers to regard the companies as their indulgent benefactors, as their *turaga*, and the colonial state as the valiant defender of their economic interests and general welfare. These fanciful perceptions helped to create a relatively quiescent work-force, particularly during the early years of mining, and were used to great effect to quell striking workers in 1938.

The institutionalisation of traditional cultural values had far-reaching implications for the relationships between Fijian and other ethnic categories of labour. It predisposed Fijians towards seeing themselves as part of a distinct and homogeneous communal group rather than as members of a working class, a tendency accentuated by language differences, especially their sparing command of English. Traditional loyalties had the convenient effect of defusing worker-consciousness while inciting inter-ethnic animosity. But the reinforcement of provincial ties exposed one contradiction in the 'traditionalist' strategy: a sense of cultural exclusivity created divisions not only between Part-European, Rotuman and Fijian workers, but within the Fijian work-force itself.

Clashes between Fijians of different provinces were not uncommon in the 1930s and 1940s, although detailed official and company accounts are restricted to just two incidents. Both of these led to official investigations culminating in consolidated acts of suppression. Some of the intra-Fijian feuds had bloody histories that long predated the mining industry. Nevertheless, 'faction fighting' at the mines, and in particular Vatukoula's pitched battle of 1936 between workers from the provinces of Ra and Tailevu, cannot simply be explained in terms of

---

[7] CSO/confidential file.

traditional rivalries;[8] nor can the inter-ethnic violence of 1947 be reduced to 'innate antipathies or any biological bias',[9] as implied by the government and the mining companies. Hostilities between workers were in large measure a product of a coercive and alienating life. The distinctive social pressures of a company mining town and the system of social and economic discrimination aggravated the tensions intrinsic to the capitalist production process.

Industrial stability and control of Fijian wages during the first decade of mining were significantly disrupted only by the communal clashes of 1936 and the unsuccessful strike of 1938. The industry's own forms of labour control were buttressed by an array of legislative, legal and administrative sanctions, topped by the services of a state police force. State intervention in fact became crucial to the group's ability to stave off any challenge to its profitability. Although worker grievances were sometimes acknowledged as legitimate, state action was directed overwhelmingly at the suppression of resistance, protection of strike-breakers, the prevention of picketing, and the prosecution of strike leaders or other 'agitators'. Ian Phimister and Charles van Onselen claim that the preconditions of state intervention in Southern Rhodesia were the threat to production and the danger of uncontrollable unrest extending beyond the mining compound. The same is to a certain extent true of state initiatives in the Fiji mining industry. One important point of difference, however, was that Fijian mine employers appear to have been less reliant on preserving the existing 'pattern of labour mobilization and control'.[10] A noticeable shift in the provincial-ethnic composition of the mine workforce, for example, followed the 1936-47 incidents.

The diffuseness of labour resistance was evident in what have been variously described as its 'covert', 'hidden' or 'silent' expressions. Passive protests, though often unorganised individual demonstrations, were a measure of disaffection.[11] They were as much a rejection of an authoritarian management as the more explicit attempts to acquire some influence over work relations. Although they may not be deemed 'obvious forms' of worker-consciousness or action, they do need to be recognised as a reflection of how mineworkers themselves perceived their working conditions and habitually translated these perceptions into unco-operative behaviour.[12] As van Onselen suggests in the case of Southern Rhodesia, 'unarticulated, unorganised protest and resistance' were the product of a labour-coercive economy that made it difficult, even impossible, for workers to express their protest in more explicit organised form. So, too, they can be merged into the mainstream of open or articulated protest, for they fuelled antagonistic feelings

[8]   The work of Phimister and van Onselen on 'The Political Economy of Tribal Animosity' underlines the importance of integrating communal conflict and violence into studies of working class struggle. It offers an interesting critique of the view that 'faction fights' were 'manifestations of mindless, irrational "tribal" violence', or, as the Rhodesia Chamber of Mines proposed, 'riots which break out for no apparent reason among savage people'. Phimister and van Onselen 1979 : 40-1 & 43.
[9]   Simons & Simons 1969 : 618. The authors are referring here to 'racial alienation in the [South African] working class'. They discuss (616-18) the effects of the job colour bar on the relationships between African and white workers and working class consciousness.
[10] Phimister & van Onselen 1979 : 3.
[11] van Onselen 1976 : ch. 8; Cohen 1980 : 8-22.
[12] Cohen 1980 : 8-10.

that were sometimes acute and pervasive enough to spark off spontaneous forms of collective protest.[13]

Characteristic responses, all of which brought either wage deductions or more often dismissal, comprised some form of labour withdrawal or came under the category of 'insubordination'. The first of these broad classifications included leaving a job without permission, irregular attendance (particularly failure to work for a few days following pay day), sleeping on the job, absence without leave, overstaying leave especially after the Christmas holidays, arriving late for work or missing shifts, skylarking, carelessness, inattention to a job, or a deliberate slow down (termed laziness). Added and related to these were the 'social' offences of illicit drinking and gambling. The second category of labour responses included 'insolence', refusal to take a transfer or to work overtime, generally disobeying instructions, and, in the post-war period, abusive graffiti, assault, property damage and theft (commonly of dynamite used to catch fish).[14] Neither type of informal protest was the monopoly of Fijian workers. On account of their mainly Australian background, European miners were more commonly associated with organised collective protest. Yet their frequent portrayal by management as querulous, boozing shirkers suggests that there was among them also a high degree of covert resistance. The poor behaviour and performance by white mineworkers in South Africa provides an illuminating analogy.[15]

A number of 'passive' offences came under the generic classification of absenteeism and labour turnover, the high rates of which placed them among the more notable expressions of discontent. As Chapter 2 has shown, the exigencies of communal work and tribute, and the political regulation of migratory labour, promoted a high turnover among Fijian mine labour, especially during the 1930s. But the service record cards of individual workers show that, in addition, 'voluntary' discharge—declared and undeclared—was very common. During isolated spells in the 1940s, when the demand for labour was more competitive and copra prices improved, labour could and did withdraw collectively; but even during less favourable times in the late 1930s, when there was a greater dependence on employment at the mines, batches of recruited labour occasionally returned home soon after beginning their contracts.[16] In general, though, this form of protest was an individual action, and penalty by pay deductions and job downgradings indicate the scale of the problem for the industry.

It has been suggested of African wage-earners that the 'rate of desertion depends on the degree of control exercised, but also, more saliently, on the degree of

[13]   van Onselen 1976 : 227, 243-4.
[14]   Service record cards of Fijian employees, Associated Mining Companies Vatukoula; Vat./Native Affairs Camps Reports 1935- ; Vat./Department Memos 1941-May 1944; Vat./Loloma Period Reports Jan. 1941-June 1944. The refusal of Fijian workers to return immediately to the site of an accident, essentially out of fear and, in the case of fatalities, respect for the deceased, was also a recurring problem for the companies, although it does not appear to have necessarily led to suspension or dismissal.
[15]   Richardson & van Helten 1982 : 92-3.
[16]   In February 1939, for example, a group of 80 indentured men from Lomaiviti refused to work for four days when they found there was no accommodation for them, rations were poor, and other aspects of their contract were unsatisfactory. They finally returned home. Inspector of Police Ba and Tavua to Commissioner of Polic Suva memo, 24 March 1939, CSO F36/39/1.

viability that remains to the pre-capitalist mode of production'.[17] This argument holds only partly true for Fiji. Labour withdrawal occurred principally among 'voluntary' workers, and so its high incidence was probably a function of the limited use of contracts. On the other hand, the viability of the rural economy would not appear to be a reliable litmus test unless assessed in conjunction with other factors, such as the distance between labour supplying (home) districts and the mines, non-economic forms of labour coercion, such as taxation, the imperatives of the traditional (chiefly) social system, and the state of the labour market generally, in particular whether there existed wage-earning opportunities outside the mining industry. All had some bearing on the rate of desertion. For example, in Colo North and Ra, provinces that displayed the highest rate of labour withdrawal at the Tavua gold-fields, the opportunities for commercial agriculture were fewest, their proximity made it easier for workers to run away, and their absconders were less likely to face prohibitive cultural (i.e. chiefly) sanctions.

Similarly, although distinct changes in the 'content' of Fijian protest can, as Sharon Stichter argues in relation to Kenya, be related to stages of proletarianisation (and thus the decline of the pre-capitalist economy), there is not the clear transition that she proposes from a 'permanent withdrawal of labour as a form of protest to withdrawal as a weapon of negotiation'.[18] Elsewhere, she describes the transition in rather broader terms, from 'escaping the wage system to various tactics of survival within it'.[19] Following the establishment at Vatukoula of a permanent work-force during the 1940s, strike action became the predominant mode of protest. But, at the same time, permanent labour withdrawal did not significantly decline. The statistics for 1947, the same year as a massive strike, are instructive in this regard. They show that 67% of Fijians (totalling 417) discharged from the industry left by choice. Equally cautionary is the fact that the early strikes, organisational endeavours and economistic demands (1935–38) took place among workers who were still predominantly transient. Furthermore, it was not unknown for disgruntled fully proletarianised European workers to throw in the towel and 'desert'.

We now turn to the incidents of 1936 and 1947. They are described in some detail for two reasons. First, they highlight the acute provincial and ethnic tensions in the gold town. Second, they demonstrate how communal conflict and violence were in large measure rooted in the social and economic relations characteristic of the mining industry. Both events occasioned important expressions of protest and were symptomatic of a coercive labour system.

THE 1936 'BRAWL' AND ITS AFTERMATH

Some time before midnight on Sunday, 9 February 1936, after a worker from Ra had been caught watching some Tailevu women bathing, the people of Vatukoula

---

[17]   Cohen 1980 : 14.
[18]   Stichter 1975 : 31.
[19]   Stichter 1985 : 192.

were shaken out of their slumber. Violent raids and furious clashes between the segregated labour lines of Ra and Tailevu mineworkers were sparked by an offence against (male) proprietorial rights under custom.[20]

Ra's numerical superiority (4:1) and easier access to reinforcements scored its workers an early victory. 'Armed with drills, sticks and stones', they forced their opponents to retreat into the Koroboya hills behind the gold-fields. The destructive effects of the battle were visible in the number of casualties and damage to personal property, likely to have been greater had it not been for the swift arrival of police contingents from Ba, Tavua and Suva and the intervention of the *roko tui* of both provinces, which brought the fighting under control. Production at the Loloma mine was all but halted, and all Ra labour (numbering nearly 200) and some Tailevu workers were repatriated to their villages. Within the week, the hand of colonial law had fallen heavily on some of the offenders: 26 Ra men were found guilty of unlawful assembly, bringing ten men prison terms with hard labour of one month, and a £5 fine or in default one month of imprisonment with hard labour for 11 others.

The conflict between mineworkers from the two largest labour-supplying provinces raised important questions about their relationship within the industry and their attitudes to a shared occupational discrimination. The dislocating effects of the migrant system were probably most acutely felt at this time. Alcohol consumption, gambling and illicit sex were becoming widespread, and undoubtedly placed under strain a community of mainly single males caught in a system of low wages, congested living conditions and a harsh work routine. The inadequate bathing and toilet facilities available to Fijian workers and their families (women, in particular) denied them the privacy necessary to practise traditional customs and *tabu*. In the work-place, dissatisfaction with the basic wage for underground labour had already become known through an (unsuccessful) demand for 'wet pay' a few months earlier.

Yet official and company accounts of the clashes detailed merely the horrifying drama ignited by a provincial indiscretion. Only cursory reference was made to the stoning of the European barracks; and although one government officer suggested that living conditions at the mines had contributed to provincial tensions, there was little to suggest that officialdom perceived the cause of the incident to be anything more than the longstanding feud between the two provinces.

If the violation of a *tabu* precipitated the 'brawl', other economic and occupational considerations underlay community tensions that exploded into clashes of such intensity. The conditions of rural economic decline (outlined in Chapter 2) created a climate of insecurity and competition for work. Workers from Ra appear to have been passed over in preference to Tailevu men for the more responsible and therefore higher-paying jobs available to Fijians. Even before the February violence the two provinces had come to blows over this occupational discrimination, and it was raised as a bargaining point in the early stages of the 1936

---

[20] Official and company accounts of the incident, some of which conflict, are drawn from diary entries, reports and minutes of meetings in CSO F50/53, F 10/6, F15/5, SNA N16/1/69; *FT & H* and *PIM* Feb. 1936; Minutes of EGM Directors Meeting, Feb. 1936, Vat./Emperor Mines Aug. 1935-Dec. 1939.

dispute, when Ra combatants agreed to return to camp on condition that certain Tailevu men were dismissed.

Phimister and van Onselen conclude of a 'faction fight' in Southern Rhodesia in 1929 that it 'was very largely an expression of competition within the working class about limited job opportunities'. They suggest further that 'faction fights' in general

> can be interpreted as intra-working class eruptions which occur in colonial urban ghettos when there is restructuring of a labour market in which employment, to differing degrees, is 'ethnically' defined by employers and/or by workers. Violence is most likely in recessions or depressions when intra-working class competition for jobs is most intense, and when lumpen and unemployed elements in the ghetto (themselves often with a distinctive ethnic identity) initiate conflict and swell the ranks of the combatants.[21]

The 'most menacing riot' of 1936 on the Tavua gold-field strikes a similar chord, although traditional values also had a direct bearing on attitudes and behaviour. Indeed, in the similar economic conditions of the 1950s and 1960s, when traditional values ceased to claim such pre-eminence, there was no intra-ethnic violence of this scale.

A number of developments in the aftermath of the dispute suggest a gestating worker-consciousness. An October strike by 60 Part-European mineworkers over a revised wages schedule prompted a sympathy strike by 57 Fijian workers following the rejection of their demands, their dismissal and the setting up of police patrols that forced them off the field and guarded against their return. Two less coercive initiatives of the industry and the state addressed the problem of control. Under Theodore's direction, management moved to consider the establishment of separate ethnic labour committees and, prompted by Ratu Sukuna, the colonial administration proposed the appointment of a Fijian of 'rank' (or a respected Fijian-speaking European officer) to investigate and mediate in any similar disputes. A letter from a group of ten workers in September 1936 suggests that the initial impetus for the setting up of a labour committee came from the workers themselves.

With its mandate restricted to 'communal matters', the committee made regular submissions to improve both the working and living conditions of Fijian workers. One of its earliest requests was that work on Sunday be optional rather than 'forced'. A deferential tone combined with a disarming logic:

> As you know Sir, the Catholic and Methodist Missions are very strict in observing the Sabbath. If you look at this matter from our point of view you no doubt will agree that since we have exchanged our old beliefs for the religions brought by the white missionaries we must be true to those new beliefs otherwise we are true to none.[22]

Other matters raised included complaints over wage deductions for poor timekeeping or legitimate absenteeism; criticism of the punitive action taken against women who came to the mines to cook and wash for their male relatives; complaints

---

[21]   Phimister & van Onselen 1979 : 41.
[22]   Chairman Matanagata Committee to Theodore, 17 Sept. 1936, Vat./Native Affairs Camps Reports 1935–

about rations; and proposals to improve water, kitchen, bathing and recreational facilities. Demands were not confined to matters of general welfare or to marginal improvements in the terms of Fijian employment.

Two incidents in particular aired the mounting objections to the iniquity of occupational and wage discrimination. In 1936 the committee demanded details of Part-European work requirements underground, protesting that 'the native have use [sic] the machines and also shovelling and the Half-Caste boys just walk about and do what ever they like'.[23] The following year it organised a deputation of workers to demand a wage increase for all Fijian labour after six months employment. The occasions marked the extent to which Fijians had become aware that as a homogeneous group they bore the brunt of exploitative production demands. They highlighted the objective (economic) considerations that nurtured Fijian hostility towards Part-Europeans. More generally, they sowed the seeds of discontent, which erupted quite suddenly into the strike of 1938.

1938: STRIKING OUT

In November 1938, following 'an undercurrent of discontent' that had been simmering for several months and in the wake of two fatal underground accidents, Fijian workers on the Emperor and Loloma mines staged their first concerted strike. Some 600 men were dismissed in response. The ability to orchestrate a quick and large-scale withdrawal of labour, the restrained dialogue, and the absence of disorder despite the provocation of an armed police presence, distinguished the strike as an early landmark in the history of Fiji goldmining. It confirmed a growing trend towards collective resistance and recognition of strike action as a useful industrial weapon. Though Ra men were held to be responsible for the stoppage, the prominent strike-leaders in fact came from several different regions, including Tailevu, the Yasawa Islands, Vanua Levu, Nadi and Colo North as well as Ra.[24]

The strike brought out a number of economistic grievances, including the ineligibility of most Fijians for accident compensation and the inferior quality of rations at the Emperor mine. Above all, the focal points of attack were the low level of Fijian wages, the mechanics of (Fijian) wage control, and the injustice of income differentials. Management's failure to take account of skills and experience in determining wages was roundly condemned, supported by allegations that despite the recommendations of supervisors, increases prescribed under the employment schedule had not been approved or backdated. The practice of cutting wages or downgrading classifications to penalise workers who went off to their villages similarly came under attack. Skilled workers, the strikers insisted, were

---

[23] Chairman & Sec. Fijian Labour Committee to Acting General Manager, 30 Oct. 1936, Vat./Native Affairs Camps Reports 1935- .

[24] Details of the official (including police) investigation of the 1938 strike are located in CSO F36/39/1. The account here is also based on interviews with mineworkers (undertaken mainly in July 1982), and on the company's own record, in particular Vat./Confidential to 1940.

entitled to be re-engaged as skilled labour. In defence, the companies produced records of authorised increases, evidence which clearly satisfied the investigating police officer, but about which the District Commissioner Central was more circumspect:

> He was very elusive and showed me many records of increases to pay—recommendations for increase of pay from shift bosses that he had approved of. I examined many different pay sheets and there are certainly a fair amount of increases but a good deal with no increases.

The companies' case rested ultimately on the interpretation of 'satisfactory' service, which was their prerogative to determine. The claim cut no ice with the strikers who stressed the contradictions of a discretionary clause: 'if they [Fijian workers] are kept on at the mine *after* their six months' period they have automatically qualified as being satisfactory, otherwise they would have been discharged, and are therefore entitled to their increments'.[25]

The introduction of Rotumans into the work-force was another bone of contention, not *per se*, but because as 'raw recruits' and initially under Fijian instruction and supervision, they were immediately eligible for higher (Part-European) rates of pay. Management's defence of Rotuman privileges was that these workers were engaged in raising (mining undertaken at an inclining angle which required greater skill and was generally more dangerous than horizontal drilling). The conventional charge of racialist stereotypes was pressed. Fijians did not possess the appropriate qualities ('the requisite nerve and steadiness') for raising.

The inquiries of the Inspector of Mines revealed that few Rotumans had in fact been allocated to this work. Despite his criticism of higher wages to Rotumans as indefensible and impolitic, the companies' case was not formally contested. Wage discrimination was even tacitly supported within the colonial secretariat on the grounds that 'a Coy must be allowed to pay according to what it thinks is the best type of labour'. The bald deprecation of Fijian work abilities was also upheld as an apposite bias, for it was 'the general opinion here that Polynesians are more reliable, and often better workers than Melanesians'.

Official debate over Fijian wages left the Mines Inspector (and the Mining Board who endorsed all his proposals) even more out on a limb. A general increase raised the threat of 'repercussions on other industries'; while the suggestion of introducing wage differentials between skilled and unskilled work underground went uncomfortably close to the heart of the industry's cheap labour system. The Inspector proposed that a minimum underground wage of 2s. 6d. should, in accordance with Australian practice, 'apply only to shovellers, truckers, and the like', while those engaged on 'rock drills or in "raising", winzing, stoping, driving [i.e. skilled machine work], and in wet places, should receive slight increases'. It was 'best', Colonial Secretary Barton responded, 'not to tinker with a minimum wage'. 'What we need is not advanced (white) Australian practice but S. African for analysis.'

In the final analysis the strike led to a consolidation of the Fijian wage structure.

---

[25]   IOM to Chairman Mining Board memo, 9 Nov. 1938, CSO F36/39/1.

The proposal to introduce an accident compensation scheme was shelved; little wonder since Barton saw the strikers as 'merely seeking to capitalise an accidental death' and therefore deserving of 'precisely no sympathy'. The government's recommendations were unequivocally modest. The group was instructed to compensate the families of the two fatal accidents at approved rates; to provide a Fijian translation of the 1936 wages schedule; and to investigate their records with a view to approving increases in cases that had been overlooked and where 'skill and length of service' warranted them. In the long term the industry was at liberty to pursue a policy that disregarded 'length of service' as a criterion of wage adjustments, and defined 'skill' on the basis of racialist preconceptions and managerial discretion.

The 1938 strike won no general wage increase, nor did it succeed in dismantling the discriminatory structure of earnings. What it did do was to force the repatriation of the group of Rotumans whose arrival had helped to trigger the strike and to bring an end to further recruitment for many years. The strike failed, not because of any weakness of numbers or determination, but because of the force of the state apparatus used to break it. The 1936 'disturbances' had set the pattern for political intervention, and the 1938 strike was similarly tested against the influence of prominent chiefs as well as an armed constabulary.

State intervention did not occur spontaneously, although it was the timing rather than the principle of intervention that was at issue. 'I am opposed', Barton ruminated, 'to Government interfering between master & servant(s) at this stage.' Fears that the return of dismissed strikers to their provinces might ignite the rural areas soon emphasised the imprudence of remaining aloof. Worse still, a Council of Chiefs meeting in far away Somosomo on the island of Taveuni had stripped all provinces of their senior chiefs. Via coded telegrams, their immediate return was hastily instructed, with the exception of Ratu Isireli Tawake and Ratu Tiale Vuiyasawa, the Roko Tui Tailevu and Ra, who were charged with the delicate mission of travelling to Vatukoula 'to discuss the matters fully with the natives and endeavour to persuade them to return to work', the 'method' and 'procedure' being 'purely those of conciliation'. Together with the European Legislative Council Member for the Northwest Division, the District Commissioner Central, and the redoubtable Hedstrom, they addressed large crowds of disaffected workers, canvassed Fijian opinion, and appealed for an end to the strike.

The chiefs excelled in their task, assuring the strikers that the wages and food available at the mines could not be matched elsewhere on the labour market, and appealing to provincial loyalties and ethnic pride to refrain from shameful displays of bad behaviour. It was, they argued, for the government to investigate whatever grievances they might have. District Commissioner Caldwell did not exhibit blinkered devotion to the company cause and complained of Nilsen's uncompromising attitude and offensive manner. An address to 200 strikers none the less pressed traditional values, a conservative ideology and Caldwell's own belief in the fair play of the colonial administration. The 'correct and gentlemanly' action was, he insisted, 'to return to work and to abide by my advice'.

Significantly, the police arrived at the mines not in response to an outbreak of violence, but following the refusal of Emperor workers to continue at their jobs once their demands had been rejected. Between 31 October and 12 November armed patrols were assembled from Ba, Lautoka and Suva. They were extended to intercept vehicles seeking entry to the mines when it was rumoured that dismissed Ra strikers intended to return to sabotage production at the Emperor mill; and were doubled on some nights to protect those who could be persuaded to return to work. Visibly 'resented' by the strikers, police reinforcements enabled the group to expel 'the majority of agitators' to their villages, and to offer protection to Part-European, European, Rotuman and Fijian strike-bearers as well as a freshly recruited batch of labour from the province of Nadroga. This kept the mills going.

The 'special duty' detachment of police from the capital, and later a small contingent of six constables and an officer, remained at the mines long after the first 150 strikers returned to work on 12 November. Labour returned on the old terms. It capitulated in the face of the political and armed intervention of the state and, no doubt, from sheer economic necessity. Flushed with success, the companies advised their Australian shareholders that following 'negotiations, and with the aid of several of their important influential chiefs, [the strikers] were induced to resume work'.[26]

The 1938 strike signalled an explicit defence of Fijian productivity and skills. Though its thrust was communal, it none the less posed a direct attack on what Richard Hyman terms 'the distribution of . . . product'.[27] It was essentially because this distribution was racially structured that protest took a communal form. The use of Part-Europeans and Rotumans as strike-bearers inflamed Fijian opinion and ensured that the cleavages that had been manufactured would continue to militate against working class unity.

TURBULENT TIMES: THE WAR YEARS AND AFTER

With the production of gold hampered by the shortages of labour and supplies during and immediately after the war, the Theodore group sought to contain the threatened slide in profits by increasing the productivity of workers while simultaneously reducing labour costs. Longer hours were worked and the right to one day's rest a week was withdrawn. A large proportion of the work-force thus worked a compulsory seven-day week with overtime paid only beyond this and at ordinary rates of pay. In addition, wage demands were resisted, a more stringent discipline imposed (or 'a gradual tightening-up' as Nilsen called it), and non-European labour was required to perform more skilled work but at discriminatory rates of pay. Such austerity measures outlasted the war by several years.[28]

---

[26] MSE/LGMNL Report of AGM, 11 Nov. 1938.
[27] Hyman 1975 : 27.
[28] The profile of conditions during the war and post-war years is constructed from various company sources, including unclassified files, and classified files entitled Government Correspondence 1942–March 1944, Dept Memos 1941–May 1944, and Emperor Mine Bosses' Meetings Accident Reports; unpublished official sources, notably SNA N44/1/149, CSO F36/29, F36/125, and several confidential files; and Legislative Council debates and papers.

The tensions resulting from these demands were exacerbated by the sharp rise in living costs and the increase in provincial tax levies, which further diminished the net benefits (as well as the real value) of mine employment. Management, moreover, paid less attention to conditions outside the work-place. In particular, its abandonment of organised sporting activities during the war gave Fijian workers little opportunity for escape from the frustrations of a more repressive work routine. The competition over women, expressed violently and leading on occasion to provincial fights, was aggravated by the manufacture and sale of 'home brew' liquor by Part-Europeans, the influx of American soldiers into the neighbouring district of Nadarivatu and the establishment of an army camp at Vatukoula itself. At least one formal complaint was lodged about the harassment of women by American soldiers. Following demobilisation and the reabsorption of returned soldiers into the industry, the liquor trade expanded and with it the gambling market.

Collective withdrawals of labour during the war were symptomatic of mounting dissatisfaction and unrest. So was the resumption of abusive and blasphemous writing (in the vernacular) on company property. The influence of European (mainly Australian) workers on the attitudes of Fijian mineworkers is not easy to estimate. Certainly the mines management became increasingly nervous of the unsettling effect of association between the two groups, particularly once Europeans began talking of unionisation. There was little doubt that the complaints of this more skilled and politicised section of the work-force about working conditions, overtime rates and the price hikes of consumer goods both during and after the war, as well as Part-European pressure for European wages following relocation to European jobs, sharpened Fijian awareness of the injustice of their own position.[29]

So, too, local tensions were probably heightened by industrial unrest amongst Fijian and Indian wage-earners in other parts of the colony. General discontent over conditions of employment and declining living standards was starkly exposed in a strike of Fijian and Indian workers at the Mt Kasi mine in May 1941, the strike of airport workers in the west of Viti Levu in 1942, a protracted canefarmers strike in 1943, and a successful strike of Fijian labour at the CSR's cattle station at Yaqara in Ra in August 1946.

Labour protest in the mining industry appeared to assume a more articulated form around this time, exemplified in the submissions of Na Viti Cauravou (the Young Fijian Society), founded as a colony-wide organisation in 1920. As in 1938, complaints were directed at the racialist index of mine earnings as well as at the declining value of Fijian wages. In 1943 a meeting of two local branches of the society raised two specific grievances with the colonial government: the fact that Fijians had not been granted a wartime cost-of-living bonus until 1943, over two years after other workers; and that, when finally approved, Fijian holiday pay was discriminatory.[30]

---

[29] For a discussion of the influence of militant European miners on New Guinea mine labour, see Newbury 1975 : 25-38.

[30] Chairman Conjoint Branches (Loloma and Matanagata) of the Young Fijian Society (Ni Viti Cauravou), 6 July 1943, SNA N44/1/149.

The amount of support that the society claimed among Fijian mineworkers is unfortunately not known; nor is the extent to which it formed the basis of union membership a few years later. The society's chairman, Epeli Uluiviti, however, became an executive union officer; and its principal aim of 'promoting the welfare of the Fijian race' expressed the same communal sentiment that lay behind the early activities of the union. The society did not represent wage-earners alone but, as the Commissioner of Labour warned the mining companies, 'it does interest itself in labour conditions of Fijians'.[31] That a younger generation of workers dominated the 1947 strike, which preceded the birth of the union, also suggests that the society was more than likely a focal point of collective organisation and resistance, paving the way for later developments.

The disruptive effects of the war and the threat of combined Fijian and Indian resistance elicited new political initiatives. Two important pieces of legislation, the Industrial Associations and Industrial Disputes (Conciliation and Arbitration) bills, were introduced to the legislature in 1941. They represented the fruition of metropolitan attempts over ten years to win the local government over to a pragmatic industrial policy. Colonial Office policy had been primarily directed at the critical question of labour control, although its tinkering with fashionable international labour reforms had sometimes obscured this. A despatch from the Secretary of State in 1937 described the dangers of obstructing the formation of labour unions although the views had little impact before the turn of the decade.

> It should be realised that the prohibition of trade unions or the subjection of them to disabilities which used to be imposed by the Common Law in England, but which are now altogether obsolete is almost certain to encourage the formation of illegal organisations which may easily develop into 'secret societies' and extend their operations into the political field. A policy of restriction in this respect may therefore give direct encouragement to the formation of extremist associations.[32]

Behind the delays in introducing both pieces of legislation lay the sustained and 'bitter opposition from commercial interests',[33] notably the CSR monopoly and later the mining companies. In a flash of political ingenuity, Theodore pressed the incompatibility of trade union principles with the traditional values of a chiefly society. That the substance of his argument should find favour with the Native (chiefly) Members of the Legislative Council, including Ratu Sukuna, came as less of a surprise than that this erstwhile champion of Australian trade unionism and progressive government should adopt such a compromising position.

For the Secretary of State for the Colonies, Theodore's theoretical posture had little appeal, and the reasons for Fijian opposition to the legislation were all but obvious:

> The idea that the sudden introduction of trade union ideas would forthwith wreck the existing Fijian communal village system is completely incomprehensible to me. The ordinary Fijian villager would not understand what was meant in the least by

---

[31]   C/L (Reay) to Emperor and Loloma Companies, 31 Aug. 1943, SNA N44/1/149.
[32]   Colonial Office Circular to Officer Administering the Government of Fiji, 24 Aug. 1937, CSO F36/29.
[33]   For details of the CSR's opposition to the legislation, see CSR 142/2901; /2902; /1106.

trades unions and there would certainly be no agitation among the Fijian commoners to start one. They are much too feudally minded, and would not dream of taking a 'policy' decision of this kind without definite instructions from their chiefs. Indeed, it may be that here is the explanation of the Fijian members (who are all high chiefs) taking their stand against the legislation. They may feel that, although the immediate danger is small, their privileged position as feudal overlords may ultimately be endangered.[34]

Colonial Office predictions of illicit and uncontrollable organisations looked less like paranoia as the war progressed, and certain unpalatable developments turned the tide against the mining and sugar lobby to defer the legislation until after the war. The airport workers' strike of 1942 confirmed the government's worst suspicions and even raised fears of the potential threat to Fiji's defence if the agitation became more widespread. In the sugar industry, the strength and ideological cohesiveness of the sugar growers' organisation, the Kisan Sangh, also signalled the need to enact both ordinances.

The presentation of the Industrial Associations Bill expressed the metropolitan rationale and language of labour control. It was imperative, the Attorney-General impressed upon the Legislative Council, for 'if such associations are not guided sympathetically along the right lines especially in their initial stages, then there is a danger that they may get into the hands of agitators of different kinds'. A number of provisions underscored the parameters of industrial combination and the greater powers of the state. An association was confined to a particular industry, the definition of which included a general trade or occupation. The Labour Department was well aware that such a narrow classification prevented casual unskilled labour from organising and that confined artisans to small and relatively powerless craft unions.

Following the South African example, union membership (excluding the President and Secretary) was also confined to those 'regularly and normally engaged in the industry'. But 'members of a trade', the Colonial Secretary chuckled, did 'not normally include persons with the knowledge and ability required to organise a trade union'. Both conditions were calculated to pre-empt any attempt by 'politically-minded persons ... to dominate and use our associations to further their own political ends'. Under section 21 of the ordinance, picketing was also made a criminal offence and even what superficially appeared to be bureaucratic formalities placed organised labour within a straitjacket. On this, the Governor communicated a clear message to the Council:

> These measures will give to Government the power which it now lacks to control the formation of industrial associations by requiring registration and the submission of their rules and constitutions and the names of their officers.[35]

Successive amendments in 1943 and 1945 demanded financial accountability to the Registrar of Trade Unions and granted the latter powers of registration, cancellation and expulsion of members. In similar fashion the Industrial Disputes (Conciliation and Arbitration) Ordinance defined boundaries of industrial defence

---

[34]   Trafford Smith minute, 11 Dec. 1941, PRO CO83/237/5020.
[35]   Governor's Address to Leg. Co., 19 Aug. 1942.

aimed at preventing a recurrence of the 1942 (airport strike) fiasco. The ordinance made the decision of an appointed arbitration court 'final and binding' and inflicted penal sanctions of a £50 fine or six months prison term on those who violated it.

'HOOLIGANS' AND 'MOB HYSTERIA'

A massive strike brought production at Vatukoula to a standstill towards the end of 1947. On 9 December, following the dismissal of one Tevita Ratoto, an underground miner from Nailaga in Ba, about 300 workers stopped work. By the following day numbers had swelled to over 1000.[36] The outburst of verbal abuse and physical assaults on property and people was reminiscent of the 1936 fracas. But the explosion this time was attended by massive strike action and an even greater scale of violence and had a broader platform. As in 1938 workers who withdrew their labour had to contend almost immediately with a police force, boosted by contingents from Lautoka and Suva (including armed reinforcements), which brought the total force to nearly one hundred, approximately one for ten strikers.

Paralleling the preoccupations of 1936, the official view of the strike highlighted the strained relations between Part-European and Fijian workers, the violence directed at the Part-European community, and the general 'lawlessness', 'hooliganism' and 'mob hysteria'. The absence of a coherent set of demands for improved conditions of employment lent further credence to the view that the 'ugly' incidents had stemmed, not from industrial, but from social discontent.

Certainly, the separate and unequal administration of boxing practices, surveillance of segregated dances, and the conspicuous collaboration between management and the local police fuelled rising communal tensions in the months prior to the strike. There was much resentment of the paternalistic attitudes of Europeans and the scant attention paid to Fijian needs. But beyond this was a wide range of extra-communal grievances, including foot injuries, overcrowding in the barracks, poor drainage and washing facilities, the sleeping problems of shift workers, and the ubiquity of bedbugs. Living conditions, one government officer conceded, were 'by no means as good as they [were] made out' and were compounded by the 'strict colour bar which [extended] to the Euronesians'. A clear set of demands did emerge in the aftermath of the strike. A request by workers for parity between Fijian and Part-European holidays touched the sensitive nerve of the colour bar. It was rumoured that Fijian workers proposed to demand an end to all discrimination in Part-European/Fijian earnings and to stage a general strike for higher wages after the Christmas break.

If social tensions took a communal form, violence erupted only after management refused to dismiss two Fijian assistants in the community welfare department

---

[36]   The description of the 1947 strike and its background are based on police, government and company officials' reports contained in a large confidential colonial secretariat file; a range of company files including those entitled Correspondence EGT/NEN Chief and Chief GM; Fijian Labour Union, Industrial Association, Labour Unrest 1947; and others that are unclassified; and interviews with (ex) management and mineworkers.

whom the strikers saw as collaborators. Non-Fijian workers proved unwilling to join the strike, enabling essential services to be maintained. Anger and violence were neither exclusively nor indiscriminately communal. While raids were conducted on the Part-European barracks, their furniture 'upturned' and broken, and men assaulted, there was 'no general hostility on the part of the Fijians towards the Part-European community as a whole only towards a small group'. Management personnel, company property, the police and, to a lesser extent, the European community, felt the strikers' vengeance. There was stoning of 'the main offices, garages and trucks, dispensary and ambulance station, and the District Officer's station-wagon breaking windows and holing walls'. According to Nilsen, the men sang a 'victory song' as they went.

Richard Hyman argues that 'the labour market is more than a forum for narrowly economic processes of supply and demand: it involves relations of power and control', and it is in this broader sense that the market influences the forms of conflict that emerge.[37] The 1947 strike at Vatukoula provides a good demonstration of this. Above all, it was an emphatic protest over the authoritarian structure of control, exemplified in the occasion of the strike (the dismissal of a worker) and in the demands of the strikers (for the dismissal of certain company staff, their replacement by men 'acceptable to themselves', and the withdrawal of the community officer's disciplinary powers). Each European staff, it was confessed, had been 'acting as a policeman'; and it was not unheard of for 'wholesale dismissals' to take place 'without reason'.[38]

The physical assaults committed by the strikers targeted the symbols or instruments of managerial control. Attacks on the police in particular reflected a long-standing resentment of these 'servants of the Company' whose task was to 'rid(ding) the field of dismissed employees'—'rail-roading' as it was later described in court. Even in the opinion of one investigating official this was an objectionable collusion, which 'smell[t] strongly of American labour methods by which Company Police enforce discipline among labour, such actions often being backed by State Police'.[39] As Dipesh Chakrabarty notes of industrial conflict in the jute mills of Bengal, protest became 'a ceremony of defiance' and physical violence was itself 'an acknowledgement of the way authority was represented ... In the very nature of defiance was mirrored the nature of authority.'[40]

The organisation of the strike and the tactical skills of its leadership indicated a crystallising group-consciousness. The recent strike by airport workers was believed to have influenced the pattern of events at the mines; and indeed one government officer recorded that 'reference to a forthcoming strike at the Mines was made by the secretary of the Airport [Workers'] Union during the Nadi strike'. Nilsen's opinion was more fanciful: 'strikes', he declared, 'like diseases ... spread without provocation'.[41] The efficiency, calm and speed with which labour was withdrawn suggested careful planning, as this description bears witness:

[37] Hyman 1975 : 30.
[38] Vat./General Manager's Report on Labour Trouble Vatukoula Dec. 1947, 15 Dec. 1947; CSO/confidential file; FT & H 9 Feb. 1948.
[39] CSO/confidential file; FT & H 9 Feb. 1948.
[40] Chakrabarty 1983 : 144 & 146.
[41] Nilsen to Theodore, 23 Dec. 1947, Vat./unclassified.

> Shortly after 1 p.m., the crowd, now augmented by others who had come off duty and numbering about 150-200, went to Emperor Mill and called on a number of men who were working there to stop; this they did. They then followed the same procedure at the Power House, the Construction Dept., and the Fitting Shop. At Loloma shaft they met the shift boys coming up and gathered them in; no boys went on the next shift. The same thing happened at the Wallace Smith shaft at Emperor . . . All this was done in a very orderly manner and at times even a nod of the head would stop a Fijian from continuing his work. As the Fijians stopped work the older hands went straight home while the younger generation swelled the crowds.[42]

Money was also raised by the strikers in the form of two collections, the first of 1s. a head in the early stage of the strike and the second of 5s. on pay day following the return to work. It was believed by 'some reliable sources' that they were to fund a strike for better wages and by others that they were 'intended to brief counsel to form a Union'. Although there was some doubt within the administration as to the 'real' reasons for the levies, the registration of the Fijian Mineworkers' Union some two months later lent credence to two compatible testimonies. The recollections of mineworkers today make it clear that the desire for a union was expressed to Ratu Sukuna during the strike, and that he had agreed 'to make one *soqosoqo* [association] so you can have a voice'.[43]

The leadership of the strike and its support suggest that the events of 1947 were a landmark in the relationship between labour and capital, reflecting above all the changing structure of the mine labour market. The stabilisation of labour created the conditions for industrial organisation and was complemented by the declining influence of traditional values. A new generation of Fijian labour, raised if not necessarily born at the gold-fields, had been socialised outside the village environment. Less easily harnessed by customary ideologies and other controls, it furnished the strike with a less quiescent younger element. In this respect the experience of the war for some workers probably encouraged the questioning of values about chiefly leadership. Significantly, among the 40 men prosecuted following the strike, several were returned servicemen.

The strike exposed a weak link in the traditional system, one that looked capable of draining the influence of its chiefly patrons. The intervention of two prominent chiefs, Ratu George Toganivalu, the Roko Tui Ba, and Ratu Sukuna, now Secretary for Fijian Affairs, helped to end confrontation, but not without their authority being ignominiously questioned. The authority of resident chiefs and elders was challenged even more fiercely. Traditional ceremonies of reconciliation were performed by 46 provincial representatives to Vatukoula's general manager, but as the Acting Deputy Commissioner of Police wryly noted: 'The unfortunate part of this reconciliation is that it was not attended by those who actually took a prominent part in the strike such as the young hooligan element who are so undisciplined.'

Reay added a further cynical note, describing the presentation of a *tabua* to Nilsen as 'a token of reconciliation (not of atonement)'. Visiting the mines soon after, Ratu Sukuna found the men 'unrepentant'.

---

[42]   CSO/confidential file.
[43]   Personal communication from mineworkers, Suva and Vatukoula, Aug. 1982.

The strike produced new leaders, among them a former Methodist preacher from Tailevu, Nemani Waka, an applauded orator (one of the finest speakers ever heard according to Ratu Sukuna), who became the first secretary of the miners' union. Others included Ratu Semi Kolikata whose 'considerable influence' as a progressive Tailevu chief indicated the benefits of integrating feudal elements into the trade union leadership. Two exceptional victories for the strikers were the reinstatement of the dismissed worker and the enforced withdrawal of the police.

Post-strike strategies included the revitalisation of the Fijian labour committee (Fijian Committee) onto which 12 of the strike leaders were co-opted. As a forum for 'requests' the committee could not satisfy the aspirations of mineworkers, having contradictory responsibilities to management and the work-force. With the union's formation, it became even more crucial as an instrument of company control. Nilsen proved not averse to reminding it of its policing portfolio: to report the names of any troublemakers on the field to management.

Apart from stimulating management interest in worker welfare by improving housing and offering more organised 'collective games and native mekes', the overriding concern of the colonial administration was to find the best way of reasserting control at the mines. The 'criminal violence' with which Fijians had 'successfully defied Government' and forced the police to retreat, and the 'entire absence of respect or regard for their own chiefs' raised disturbing questions about the stability and security of the state. 'Communistic' influence on the field was also a bogey typical of the times, reflecting an obstinate refusal to admit to 'native' initiative or radicalism. As Britain's *Financial Times* glumly summed up of industrial unrest in the Gold Coast around the same time: 'Agitation from patently Communist sources has made play with the malleable African mind.'[44]

Nilsen was quick to point out that the challenge to traditional values and the weakness of customary controls were not restricted to the mining town:

> the present young generation of Fijians are drifting away from the control of their native customs and chiefs and Government will be well advised to have a strong force in future to meet the emergency. It would be a very serious problem if the Indians and Fijians had strikes at the same time.[45]

He was not alone in his misgivings. In the opinion of District Commissioner Western the strike had indicated 'the urgent need for more Police in the Western District with adequate training to deal with mobs, either with batons or with firearms if the need should arise'. The Acting Deputy Commissioner of Police took an equally strong stand:

> I am inclined to think that the real trouble is deep-rooted and has not yet been probed; and my opinion is that in the very near future much more strike [action] is to be expected at Vatukoula before matters become serene again and that the only way that this will be attained will be through a show of force.[46]

---

[44] *Financial Times* 17 March 1948.
[45] Nilsen to Theodore, 23 Dec. 1947, Vat./unclassified.
[46] CSO/confidential file.

The perceived gravity of the situation offered useful leverage when the group pressed for full state protection should the need arise in the future. In the meantime, with the most urgent task being to 'bolster up the authority of the Fijian chiefs as much as possible', further visits to the mines were made by the Secretary for Fijian Affairs and the Roko Tui Tailevu and Ba. The secondment as the group's Fijian liaison officer of the Buli Bau (and Governor's *matanivanua*) Ratu Rusiate Komaitai, took the industry a further step towards bringing Fijian miners 'under the control of the Fijian administration'. Sukuna 'strongly' advised the companies

> to have special men (two or three) appointed to see that undesirables who have been dismissed leave the goldfields, that is the property of the Company, within a reasonable time. If they do not, I presume an action for trespass lies.[47]

The prosecution of the strike's leaders and key supporters exemplified the Pyrrhic nature of their victory. A three-day trial for 40 men charged with rioting under the Penal Code delivered sentences of between one and six months with hard labour for 16; and two years' probationary release for 24 (plus a £10 bond and two sureties of £10 each). Even their own choice of counsel (A. D. Patel, Nadi lawyer and prominent Indian Member for the Northwestern Division) was 'over-ruled' by Ratu Sukuna, and another lawyer (Robert Munro) appointed for them. Munro was a New Zealander, long resident in the colony, who shared neither Patel's radical politics nor his close association with the (Indian and Fijian) working class. His selection in 1948 had an important consequence: the Crown's case was not challenged and defence rested merely on a plea for mitigation.

BIRTH OF A UNION

If the formation of a union in March 1948 raised Fijian hopes of a better deal, these were soon dashed. The bid for unionisation was not resisted by the state; on the contrary it received its every encouragement. An astringent analysis of the problems deriving from Fijian proletarianisation and changing requirements of labour control lay behind this. The political implications of the December strike and the militancy and heightened consciousness of a vanguard of mine-workers left the labour secretariat in little doubt that though 'responsible trade unionism' might take time to emerge, the attempts to unionise should be actively encouraged. A realistic appreciation of the industrial climate prompted efforts to convince the mining companies to see likewise. It was 'better that the union should be formed under our aegis than under the aegis of some person whose motives might not be altogether good'.

The intention of the Labour Department was accordingly to 'nurse the new union carefully during its early stages'. Encouragement meant close involvement and supervision, which conspired to place organised resistance within acceptable parameters. Labour Department officials assisted in drafting a constitution and rules, prescribing fees, and laying down the procedure for the election of officers.

---

[47] Sukuna to Nilsen, 16 Jan. 1948, Vat./unclassified.

Concerned to prevent the convicted but discharged caucus of strike-leaders from influencing the infant union, they were also able to steer its *ad hoc* committee away from making the appointments of president and secretary open to outsiders, although this was well within the law. The advantage for company control was not lost on Nilsen. His communications with Theodore stressed management's determination to keep non-employees out of the union and he confidently forecast that in time the union leadership would even be seeking counsel from the company over how to manage their own affairs.[48]

By late February, Governor Freeston could report to the Colonial Office that 'indications at present are that the Union will be controlled by moderate elements'. The presence of three chiefs on the 12-member executive committee may well have contributed to this peace of mind.

Government 'advice' and 'assistance' also took the form of regular visits to the mines, attendance at union meetings, and a close working relationship with management and the police. Management was advised of developments in the union, and, charged with the task of gathering intelligence and monitoring the industrial barometer, the police informed the administration of impending industrial claims. Officials addressing union meetings left no doubt that their 'assistance' was circumscribed by the government's commitment to the expansion of the industry. Indeed, the important ideological function of the colonial state as a propagator of capitalist norms and values was clearly depicted by the urging of workers to co-operate with the companies, to avoid strike action, and to be more productive. As the Acting Commissioner of Labour, Hollister-Short, reported to Nilsen of one such meeting, one of its objects had been to 'generally give [the workers] a pep talk on their responsibilities to the Home and Fijian Governments, and to their employers'. The services of 'Reay's offsider from England' vindicated Nilsen's chosen strategy of 'playing ball' with him; and the latter's hope that it would 'not be long before he is working for the Mining Companies too. (We have handled these Union blokes before)' was not in vain.

The full impact of this manipulative strategy was demonstrated in August 1948, when the union committee was pressed to withdraw wages and the cost-of-living bonus from its agenda for discussion with the companies. Management's refusal to meet the committee, its persistent rejection of a wage rise for Fijian labour without an increase in productivity, and its threat to close down the mine if the issue was not dropped, had already pushed the union into a corner. Hollister-Short now acted on this ultimatum by seeking to persuade the union to see the error of its ways. It is likely that the union's loss of credibility and the rift that later developed between its rank and file and leadership had their roots in these manoeuvres.

In an industry where the structure of Fijian earnings incorporated an important non-cash component in the form of housing and food, the responsibilities of the employer included living as well as working conditions. That the union's platform should similarly trespass into the welfare of its members outside the work-place was the corollary. Consequently, housing and sanitation problems,

---

[48]   Nilsen to Theodore, 8 March 1948, Vat./Correspondence EGT/NEN.

the paucity of rations, and the need for more social venues and recreational facilities (matters raised habitually at meetings of the Fijian Committee), also became the declared prerogative of the union. In turn, the committee continued to raise what were strictly occupational matters.

It might be thought that this expanse of common ground would have strengthened the position of organised mine labour. It did not. Proprietorial rights became an inflammatory issue, leading to fragmentation and friction, mainly because management's determination 'to minimise the influence of the Union' meant that it repeatedly communicated and negotiated with the committee and took full advantage of its chiefly liaison officer for Fijian labour. Overall, union efforts to establish a viable basis for collective bargaining were hampered by this alternative structure. Theodore's advice had clearly been taken to heart:

> the best course of policy in respect to the Mine Workers' Union should be one of masterly inactivity. As the Union can fill no function that could not be filled just as well by the old Fiji Committee I should think the average Fijian worker will get tired of paying a shilling per pay into the Union. I think it will tend to fizzle out.[49]

The restriction of membership to Fijians imposed constraints on the emergence of a powerful union. The communal stamp and consciousness it gave limited its appeal. In May 1949, however, just over a year after its foundation, membership was opened 'to all Fijian, Indian, Polynesian, Euronesian workers "regularly" and "normally" employed by the mining industry and deemed eligible by the Executive Committee'. The decision marked an important step towards an organised industrial front that transcended ethnic divisions. It signified the beginnings of a crucial ideological transition, though Reay preferred to see it as a necessary strategy to compensate for the innate organisational and intellectual deficiencies of Fijian workers:

> Fijian leaders have found themselves, by reason of their own limiting racial characteristics, unable to pursue a sufficiently vigorous policy. The result is that while there are probably a number of difficulties which a trade union elsewhere would have taken up with Management, the union committee at Vatukoula has not had the courage or initiative to do so. The leaders probably find that their members are becoming apathetic in the face of no results, and it may be that they want to introduce more articulate elements into their organisation.

For the Labour Department, at least, the move was not entirely alarming. The inclusion of Indian workers was considered a danger for they tended 'to use a trade union for selfish or political ends rather than for the good of their fellow workers', but the admission of Part-Europeans had advantages all round because of their alleged intellectual superiority. In principle, the department was encouraged by the change, 'convinced' that the companies had 'less to fear from a live Fijian union than from no union at all, or a union which exists only on paper'.[50]

Management was not about to sit back and await confirmation of this wisdom.

---

[49] Bain 1986 : 51.

[50] Reay C/L to Nilsen Confidential, 20 April 1949, Vat./unclassified. Reay's views also sprang from a concern over the recent collapse of the Public Works Department Union. He regarded the absence of 'some channel for the ventilation of differences or potential differences' as 'potentially dangerous'.

The Fijian Committee offered an alternative and more easily controlled 'channel for the ventilation of differences', which became all the more compelling as union demands extended to the more radical bounds of a closed shop. The principles of job and wage discrimination could also be usefully recharged to deflect the threat of industrial organisation along class lines. In particular, the accelerated promotion of Rotumans and Part-Europeans to shift boss status helped to maintain ethnic divisions as well as to minimise union support among these two groups, for the latter were not permitted to enjoy the dual benefits of supervisor/overseer status and union representation. Bluntly put,

> if a man was thought suitable for the position of Shift Boss he was interviewed. It was pointed out to him at this meeting that if he wanted to take the position he would be promoted but not as a member of the Union. No offence was committed as the choice was made by the man himself.

Institutionalised divisions in the work-place deterred non-Fijians from joining the union. Generally employed as skilled workers, Part-Europeans were less disposed to align themselves with an association dominated by unskilled labour and preoccupied with upgrading conditions inferior to their own. Unskilled Part-European workers, on the other hand, although more likely to join, were probably inhibited by a desire to maintain their superior earnings and privileges. Sectional interests were paramount, at least in the early years, and the efforts of skilled (Part-European) workers to form a separate trade union in 1950, while abortive, measured this.

There were other more practical obstacles to the early development of the union. Until late 1948 the group refused to make office space available to the union committee. It relented following the warning of the Acting Commissioner of Labour that there was 'the danger if Union Headquarters are set up outside the Field of reactionaries stepping in and upsetting the whole structure', but charged an exorbitant rent of 25s. a week. The lack of trade union education and training, the limited subscription funds that could be solicited from low-wage-earners, unfamiliarity with Western industrial law and the difficulties of conducting negotiations and interpreting legislation in a second language, provided disastrous support to the strategies devised to keep the union weak and fragmented. The union's failure to comply with the legal requirements of accounting procedure prompted a government inquiry in 1948. One outcome was the dismissal and prosecution of the union secretary for embezzlement.

If high subscriptions deterred workers from becoming active union members, their reduction 'to a sensible level' in November 1948 did not arrest the declining support. Between July 1948 and January 1950, numbers fell from 893 to 547. The dormancy of the union, both a cause and a consequence of dwindling support, was reflected in a spell of industrial peace until early 1949. When this was broken, it measured the disenchantment and militancy of rank-and-file members rather than growing union strength. A spate of unofficial strikes, mainly over unjust dismissals and the poor quality of rations, foreshadowed the industrial conflict of the 1950s. While the lack of union discipline weakened the early struggles of organised mine labour, such spontaneous withdrawals of labour signalled a more acute appreciation of and desire to use 'the power of the strike weapon'.

6   Difficult Years:
Coping and Copping It 1950-70

SHIFTING STRATEGIES: CAUSES AND EFFECTS

The 1950s marked a turning-point in the fortunes of Fiji's goldmining industry. The Vatukoula group faced serious cost inflation in respect of labour, staff, materials and equipment as well as mining problems. A fairly static gold price in domestic currency was alleviated only by two devaluations of sterling in 1949 and 1967, which in turn raised the cost of mining imports and underlay a spate of wage demands in the 1950s and 1960s. After Loloma and Dolphin ceased production, Emperor had also to meet the entire costs of milling, social infrastructure and other overheads previously shared with its partners. The mill required modern-isation to treat a rising proportion of ore now mined from the narrow and flat dipping orebodies known as flatmakes, and open-cut mining gave way almost completely to the costly stoping of underground ore, which became 'the lifeblood of the Emperor Mine'.[1] Between 1950 and 1960 working costs for Emperor rose by more than 100% from around 53s. to 108s. per ton of ore mined. Over the same period the aggregate value of production from all three mines dropped by close to one-third (see Table 6.1 and Appendix B).

The problem of prohibitive working costs in the absence of an open market in gold was by no means unique to Fiji. The post-war years severely affected goldmines as far apart as Southern Africa, the Gold Coast and Australia. No longer payable, some marginal mines were forced to close, abandoning large quantities

---

[1]   Details of Emperor's economic policies, problems and strategies from the early 1950s are located in numerous company files. Of particular interest are EGM Report on Gold Price, Financial Assistance and the Shareholder; Vat./Government 1970/71; and EGM Financial Assistance. The minutes of company staff meetings 1953-55 are also informative. These are located in classified files Community Sundries and Meetings of Executives Current File. Also see Report on the Economics of the Gold Mining Industry at Vatukoula CP No. 26, 1960 and Emperor and Loloma Annual Reports to Shareholders 1948-57.

Table 6.1   Operating costs, Emperor Gold Mining Co. Ltd 1950-70*
(costs per ton mined[†])
Fijian currency (shillings and pence)

Year	Mining	Milling	General	Total Costs per ton
1949/50	19s. 7.3d.	22s. 4.3d.	10s. 10d.	52s. 9.6d.
1950/51	21s. 4d.	23s. 7.7d.	11s. 5.6d.	56s. 5.3d.
1951/52	24s. 2.8d.	24s. 8.5d.	13s. 9.9d.	62s. 9.2d.
1952/53	31s. 6.2d.	27s. 1.7d.	12s. 6d.	71s. 1.9d.
1953/54	32s. 4.3d.	25s. 4.5d.	10s. 5.1d.	68s. 1.9d.
1954/55	38s. 0.5d.	25s. 4.4d.	11s. 7d.	74s. 11.9d.
1955/56	45s.	28s. 10.7d.	14s. 1.4d.	88s. 0.1d.
1956/57	47s. 6.4d.	31s. 10.6d.	14s. 7.9d.	94s. 0.9d.
1957/58	45s. 8d.	29s. 9d.	14s. 7d.	90s.
1958/59	51s. 4d.	33s. 7d.	18s. 2d.	103s. 1d.
1959/60	53s. 10d.	34s. 11d.	19s. 4d.	108s. 1d.
1960/61	49s. 2.5d.	32s. 6.5d.	19s. 7d.	101s. 4d.
1961/62	46s. 1.5d.	23s. 7.25d.	14s. 6d.	84s. 2.75d.
1962/63	44s. 5.25d.	19s. 5.25d.	12s. 3.75d.	76s. 2.25d.
1963/64	44s. 11.75d.	19s. 8.75d.	12s. 5.75d.	77s. 2.25d.
1964/65	44s. 0.5d.	21s. 3.25d.	14s. 6.25d.	79s. 10d.
1965/66	— not available —			
1966/67	44s. 6d.	20s. 7d.	14s. 11d.	80s.
1967/68	39s. 5d.	20s. 11d.	13s. 9d.	74s. 1d.
1968/69‡	$4.50	$2.39	$1.62	$8.51
1969/70	$4.50	$2.17	$1.66	$8.33

* Years run from July to June each year.

† From 1960/61, total costs per ton milled are given following the introduction of ore sorting.

‡ From 1968/69, amounts are in dollars and cents.

Source: Data taken from Report on the Economics of the Gold Mining Industry at Vatukoula (CP No. 26, 1960) and Emperor annual reports 1960-70.

of unexploited ore that high costs had pushed below the pay limit. For richer and more profitable mines able to ride the storm of depressed prices, in South Africa's case mainly because of its uranium resources, operating companies keenly pursued tax and royalty concessions, state subsidies and wage reductions. They also opted for mining higher grade ore at the expense of low grade reserves. Over all, the problems of Australia's goldmining industry were cushioned by tax and royalty exemptions as well as Commonwealth government subsidies, access to less expensive local sources of plant and materials[2] and (because of a cheaper currency) higher returns from its gold sales. More broadly, the serious (world) shortages of gold during the 1950s and 1960s emphasised the need for an upward adjustment in the gold price in order to offset cost increases and stimulate a flagging industry.

In Fiji the early 1950s held little prospect of alleviating the labour problems confronting the industry. A mining boom in base metal and uranium in Australia depleted the ranks of Emperor's European management and skilled workers and

---

2   Tsokhas 1986 : 13-18.

raised the price of an expatriate élite. Fijian dependence on mine employment lessened as copra, sugar, and banana prices became more competitive and co-operative farming more widespread. Additional men were siphoned off as the government set about recruiting an expeditionary force to wage anti-communist war in Malaya. The rising cost of Fijian labour aggravated a situation of shortage. The years between 1950 and 1955 witnessed wage increases that surpassed those of the previous 15 years, a development largely attributable to the growing militancy of an organised work-force. Over all, the trend of the 1950s, like the 1960s, was a spiralling wages and salaries bill out of all proportion to the pattern of gold revenue receipts (see Appendix B).

Yet these developments told but part of a story of a monopoly that within 20 years was transformed from three thriving mines to a single undercapitalised and struggling venture, unable to finance a rate of development that would maintain adequate reserves and scarcely able to break even. The other part of the story was told in the group's own rationalisation. In short, the scarcity of working capital derived less from unprofitable mining than from the massive profit distribution encouraged during the peak years of joint production; the 90% reduction of Emperor's share capital; and Loloma's (Australian) investment policy. Coincidentally, state subsidisation of development work at Vatukoula began within a year of Emperor's final instalment of capital returns to shareholders.

Similarly, behind Loloma's declared operating losses of the mid-1950s was a preference for withdrawal from Fiji mining in favour of uranium and tin mining and other lucrative exploits in Australia.[3] Between 1948 and 1957 the number of Australian companies in which Loloma held shares leapt from 17 to 80, while the total cost value of its investments outside the Fiji mining industry rose from £A664,408 to £A1,325,103. From 1958 the participation of Loloma and Dolphin in mining in Fiji was limited to a one-third interest each held in Emperor's exploration and development programme.

Two years later, faced with a low price for Fiji gold and austere tax and royalty laws, Loloma's directorate finally negotiated a complete merger with Emperor. In return for 234,000 (5s.) shares in Emperor Mines Ltd, the company sold all its mining interests in Fiji to the operating Emperor company. The cessation of mining operations brought total gold production from the mine to 462,000 fine ounces valued at about £A5.5m. Dolphin similarly sold out to Emperor for a consideration of 78,000 (5s.) shares in EML. The less congenial circumstances of the 1950s prompted important shifts in Emperor's production and financial policies. As the only producing mine, the thrust of these was directed at improving output rates and reducing the outflow of surplus funds in order to finance the search for new orebodies and the replenishment of reserves. An unprecedented proportion of capital was reinvested in development and exploration. Between 1955 and 1964 (as in 1967 and 1970) the company did not declare a dividend. Its expenditure on development, on the other hand, rose by nearly 90% from £151,344 to £286,709. By the late 1960s the trend was even more pronounced,

---

[3]   Loloma's published annual reports reveal that the company became an equal partner with United Uranium NL, King Island Scheelite (1947) Ltd in an exploration venture in Australia and 'adjacent territories'. In 1962 Loloma began to investigate the prospects for tin mining in Queensland.

with $5.2m spent on general and special development between 1965 and 1970. A significant 37% of gold revenue was earmarked for development in order to maintain Emperor's reserves by 1970.

The industry's cheap labour system now became crucial to its survival. The group tackled the problem of Fijian labour shortages first by experimenting with more rigorous recruitment. Provincial requests for short-term 'mass engagements' were generally rejected as untenable by the late 1950s: training was costly; transport costs were avoided by employing men individually; and the system was cumbersome to administer. Contracts were acceptable only if labour was engaged for a minimum of 12 months and it was not all withdrawn at once. By the end of the decade the group's market advantage of 'voluntary' replenishments and later a surplus reminiscent of the pre-war years enabled it to turn down requests unconditionally. A reduced demand for labour followed the closure of the Loloma and Dolphin mines, while the services of a new generation of young men at Vatukoula offered an accessible source of in-house labour. Catalysts of surplus labour conditions included the introduction of a copra tax in 1951, a massive increase in provincial rates for Vatukoula's major labour-supplying provinces between 1946 and 1956, a rocketing cost of living, and poor marketing and other conditions in the banana industry. A generally rising rate of urbanisation generated greater unemployment and deteriorating living standards.

A long-term solution to the problems of labour costs and unrest was found in rationalising the mines' employment structure. Adjustments to the racial and ethnic distribution of the work-force and further modification to the hierarchy of jobs were made between the mid-1950s and early 1960s. In essence, these measures increased the strength of Indian and Rotuman labour and lowered the number of Fijians, Europeans and Part-Europeans; upgraded more Rotumans and Part-Europeans to European-dominated jobs following management's decision 'to get rid of . . . European labour of indifferent quality . . . with a minimum of delay'; allocated more Fijians to Part-European and Rotuman jobs; and displaced some Fijians by Indians as unskilled labour. The fall in the number of European employees from 76 to 53 effected a proportional decline of 4.8% to 2.9% of the total work-force between 1958 and 1965. All these changes brought reductions in labour costs.

The attractions of Indian labour at this time were diverse: it was abundant, comparatively stable and cheap. The insecurity of rural families during the post-war years—their limited access to agricultural land, poverty and indebtedness—was congenial to their absorption into the mining industry. By the early 1950s labour dependence took deeper root as farmers endured delays in the demarcation of native reserve land and greater difficulty in acquiring land leases or renewals. Unskilled Indian mine labour tended to be cheaper than Fijian during the 1950s if the value of rations and housing was included. Not until 1959 did Indian mineworkers benefit from the wage increases and other improvements in conditions of work won by the union, although membership was officially open to all ethnic categories of labour from 1949. Further, they were not housed on company property and were themselves responsible for paying the cost of commuting between the mines and home, usually in the surrounding cane district and the township of Tavua. Although their numerical strength was never considerable, it rose appreciably from the late 1940s, increasing proportionately from 6% to 10% between 1949 and 1952. This pattern continued into the 1960s, bringing numbers to around 300 or 18% of the work-force by January 1969.

With the approval of Governor Sir Brian Freeston and the convenience of a doubling of the annual tax levy, the revival of Rotuman recruitment also took effect around 1950. The backlash to the group's earlier experiments was far from forgotten, and plans were accordingly executed with the conspiratorial air of a clandestine operation. Taking great care to introduce men 'by gradual stages so as not to annoy the Fijians', management recruited informally through 'Rotuman boys who go back to their home on leave'.[4] By 1956 numbers averaged no more than 100, the main swell occurring between the mid-1950s and early 1960s when numbers rose proportionately by 9% close to 250. Success in tapping the Rotuman market remained inhibited by its size,[5] the communal (notably chiefly) demands on the island's young and able-bodied, and the small capacity and infrequent services of passenger vessels operating between Rotuma and Fiji. There were, in addition, legislative restrictions on Rotuman emigration, though these had limited practical effect. Fortunately, in the face of pressure from the Rotuma Council of Chiefs for a quota system buttressed by chiefly power of approval and recall as well as time restrictions, the colonial secretariat was guided by a more 'liberal' vision.

While the occupational mobility of non-European workers helped to reduce labour costs, its impact on the racial and ethnic division of jobs and earnings was not in fact very great. Certainly between 1950 and 1970 Fijians earned better wages, received more of the benefits enjoyed by other workers, and moved into high-paying jobs. To some extent, improvements to earnings were inevitable with their greater deployment underground. But against the pattern of improvements, pay differentials based on 'race' were retained; parity of earnings eventuated only after protracted struggle; and the vast majority of the Fijian work-force did not enjoy the privilege of enhanced job mobility. There was no intention to jettison job stratification or to abolish the European monopoly of key supervisory positions. For Fijian workers there remained a virtual ban on jobs more senior than junior boss, as well as restricted access to certain jobs, such as winder engine driving, which allegedly demanded a temperament 'which is unfortunately not possessed by many Fijians'.[6] Where management approved the promotion of non-Europeans, it continued to circumscribe financial gains by discriminatory wages.

As in the past, the failure to dismantle barriers to Fijian and Part-European mobility was legitimised by the ruling (racialist) ideology. Promotion to positions of responsibility, management announced to shareholders in 1952, was successful but only 'within their natural limits'. With the expansion of underground mining it was considered vital that Europeans remain charged with overseeing local labour. It was 'obvious' that local leading hands and junior bosses 'were capable of assuming

---

[4]   Governor (L. B. F. Freeston) to CS minute extract, 8 June 1949, CSO F36/173.
[5]   The estimated Rotuman population in Jan. 1943 was 3200. Of these only 650 were males between the ages of 18 and 50.
[6]   General Manager EGM (Cayzer) to Director, Fiji Employers Consultative Association (FECA), 25 Jan. 1962, FECA EGM Co. Ltd EF1/8.

only a limited degree of responsibility and that they could not be left to act independently for long periods without that personal European supervision'.[7]

The continuing manipulation of job classifications and mobility restrictions were especially significant in view of the higher skill profile of the workforce. The 1956 census of the colony classified 50% of Fijian mineworkers as 'unskilled', 34% as 'semiskilled', and a mere 10% as 'skilled'. In one case in 1961 it transpired that two Fijians had remained leading hand miners for between 12 and 13 years. Another had been appointed junior boss after seven years of underground work, a classification that scarcely matched his acclaim by management as an 'experienced miner' and 'an intelligent resourceful and careful man'.

Institutionalised discrimination remained a focus for union attack, and union views were given a public airing in 1960, when a London firm of mining consultants—John Taylor and Sons Ltd—completed its investigation into Emperor's operations on behalf of the colonial government. The Taylor report noted that of 23 shift bosses in the mining department, 16 were Part-European, four Rotuman, and only three Fijian. It confirmed that Fijian representation in overseer jobs was generally confined to the rank of junior boss.[8] In response, the company made some adjustments; but apart from promoting five more men to the position of shift boss, Fijian labour policy was not modified.

The decision to retain a 'strong nucleus of qualified, experienced and energetic [European] members [of staff]' sprang from the imperatives of control, paternalism and production changes. The heavy emphasis on underground mining demanded a more highly skilled body of miners and technicians as well as superior supervision. That the services of shift bosses and technicians should continue to be supplied by expatriate Europeans was a costly sacrifice in circumstances demanding economies. Regular improvements to European pay and conditions of employment were necessary to compete with Australian employers; and, although the first 15 years of mining had seen European wages and salaries increase at a much faster rate than Fijian wages, their steepest rise came after 1950.

Between 1948 and 1954 the average weekly rate (excluding cost-of-living bonuses) for European fitters, drillers, mechanics and other operators more than doubled: from a range of £6 10s. to £7 10s. to one of £14 to £17. The rise in the cost of European shift bosses followed a similar pattern, and by 1967 all skilled workers commanded wages in the region of £30 a week. Holiday benefits also improved and leave grants were introduced, which cost the company in the region of £10,000 a year by 1961. An annual education grant was paid for each European child over the age of 14 and the company footed the bill for airfares taking children to and from Australian schools. By 1963 the weekly cost of subsidising European messing was nearly £5 per capita.

Such inflationary pressures were a significant factor in the group's expanding wages and salaries bill. Emperor complained in 1957 that a two-year arbitration award to local mineworkers was likely to add about £14,000 to the cost of labour. But as Appendix B shows, the total cost of salaries and wages between 1956

---

[7] Minutes of Staff Luncheon and Meeting, 2 April 1954, Vat./Meetings of Executive Current File.
[8] Report on the Economics of the Gold Mining Industry at Vatukoula, CP No. 26, 1960.

and 1958 rose by over £41,000. Another two-year award to the mineworkers' union in March 1959 was estimated by the company to increase its annual wages bill by £13,000. Again it can be seen that total wages and salaries rose by considerably more, by over £56,000 between 1958 and 1961. Even more telling of the disproportionately high cost of European employees and the low cost of Fijian and other local labour is wage data available for the years from 1963 to 1966. The average wages (i.e. exclusive of salaries) bill for these years was less than £43,000. The wages and salaries bill on the other hand averaged a little under £800,000 for three of those years.

In order to offset the growing cost of European labour and staff, to lower production costs and to combat other rising prices as the gold price remained stubbornly immobile, the exploitation of local labour was heightened. 'Greater and cheaper output per man', Nilsen announced in 1953, 'was vitally necessary and had to be achieved in all sections of the mines.' It was not only by adjusting the occupational structure that a higher rate of surplus value was extracted. Coinciding with efforts to improve productivity, retrenchments of 'native labour' took place on selected occasions during the 1950s and 1960s. Dismissals and wage deductions were inflicted in order to reduce absenteeism; the campaign against absenteeism adopted humiliating devices, such as the public broadcasting of offenders' names; overtime was 'policed'; and more coercive forms of discipline bolstered efforts to make men work harder and faster.[9]

The success of these measures was soon evident in a rising output per man shift, improved underground efficiency and a less runaway cost structure. By the 1960s the rewards were even more spectacular. Between 1960 and 1968, with only a 12% increase in labour strength, production levels rose by an impressive 83% from 179,634 tons to 328,791 tons p.a. (Appendix I) while costs fell by more than 30%. Especially significant was the fact that from 1962 output levels surpassed those aggregated by the three mines during their peak years as producers before the (Pacific) war. By contrast, in Australia, production levels were in decline (see Appendix K). Despite the disruption caused by a labour dispute at Vatukoula in 1964, record output was achieved in that year as in most others during the decade. A team of miners dubbed Macfarlane's Flyers set an Australasian record in 1966 when it completed 1309 feet of driving and 70 feet of stripping in its 'spare' time. Rising at the rate of 724 feet in 14 days—part of special development—scored a world record the following year.[10]

Wage control was no longer as easy as in the years of unorganised labour, but the basic principles of a repressive labour system were sustained. All told, the gains of Fijian mineworkers were notable more for their unprecedented regularity than for their volume. Between 1952 and 1966 increments in the basic wage totalled only 4s. 4d. a shift (representing about 3d. p.a.) while the value of rations rose by 1s. Wages tended to keep abreast of inflation, particularly during the 1950s, when indexation was an accepted principle of industrial bargaining. But wage scales remained small, and the narrow gulf between the

---

[9]   Minutes of Staff Meetings, 27 March 1953, & 21 March 1955, Vat./Meetings of Executives Current File.
[10]   *Talanoa*, Vol. 1, No. 2, 3 June 1966.

wage of an unskilled underground labourer (15s. 10d. per day) and that of a qualified miner (16s. 10d. per day) and a leading hand miner (18s. 10d. per day) in 1965 testified to the continued practice of deskilling. It was still the case that Fijian miners were barely paid what their European counterparts had earned over 30 years before.

Where the industry was forced by arbitration rulings to approve increases, it was often able to demand relief in another quarter, notably through government financial concessions. It also ensured that increments were 'earned' so that the cost incurred would 'not be drawn from the profits of the Companies'. Following an award to Fijian workers in 1955, Nilsen cautioned:

> we must accept the ruling of the court and not retaliate on the Fijians who are now seeking some Industrial status. However the Fijian must be made aware that he cannot expect to enjoy European standards of living as an addition to the standards of living associated with his koro.[11]

The practical effects of these extraordinary asides were that the periodical review of Fijian wages was cut back; no further labour was engaged; and no promotions for long service or wage increases were authorised without tangible evidence of improved output.

The 1960s brought fresh incursions into the fragile independence of Fijian labour, mitigated only by the introduction of compulsory superannuation in 1966. The change in the ration system (to wage deductions for food issued), the access to credit and the high cost of locally retailed goods, deductions for house rentals, electricity, children's education and superannuation mercilessly slashed cash earnings. In 1963 around 100 children attending the Vatukoula Fijian school were sent home because their fees could not be paid. Statutory worker contributions to the National Provident Fund extracted a total of $F257,366 between 1967 and 1970. Many mineworkers were confronted with payroll deductions that aggregated more than 50% of their gross earnings; while in 1969, it transpired that some workers received nothing at all on pay-day.[12] Despite the illegality of this, the government Labour Department appeared loath to take action on the publicised inquiries of Opposition Members of Parliament or its own findings. It criticised practices that contravened sections of the Employment Act, but instituted no prosecutions. It insisted only that Emperor obtain written authorisation from workers before deductions were made for articles purchased on credit, and that monopsonistic prices in the company store be reduced to levels comparable with those charged elsewhere to the general public.[13]

Like direct labour costs, indirect costs, especially those based on services and facilities in the non-productive (community, construction and engineering) sectors of the industry, were subject to 'drastic restriction'. Fijians bore the brunt of welfare cuts, with congestion (and its attendant health hazards) in the barracks

---

[11]   Minutes of Department Managers' Meeting, 5 July 1955, Vat./Meetings of Executives Current File.
[12]   J. F. Wren, Chairman of Directors EGM to Minister of Finance, 14 July 1970, Vat./Government 1970/71; Labour Inspector K. T. Valili to Labour Officer Western, 3 March 1969, Labour Department 36/I/121/16-A.
[13]   Labour Department internal memoranda and correspondence with Emperor over excessive pay deductions and store prices are contained in department file 36/I/21/16-A.

and married settlements reaching grave proportions. The practice of 'shelving' Fijian families in barracks persisted, in spite of repeated complaints by union officials. There was general procrastination in the upgrading of sanitation, kitchen facilities and water supplies, contamination of which was now confirmed by the death of local cattle and fish. By the late 1960s it was officially company policy to consider applications for repair and maintenance work 'on merit'. But while the roofs of many Fijian houses were reported leaking in 1968, management proceeded first with improving furniture in the European houses (replacing beds, chairs and coffee stools, etc. 'with those of more modern design').

Around this time the colonial government exhibited renewed concern over substandard living and eating conditions at Vatukoula, instructing Emperor to attend to rubbish dumps, drainage and unauthorised dwellings. Economic considerations, however, still determined the parameters of humanitarian and even pragmatic health initiatives. Because of the industry's financial plight, government demands for conformity with the standards of the newly enacted Health (Hotels, Restaurants and Refreshment Bars) Regulations were ditched. On the water question the government put on a bolder face, with debate over the new mining bill in 1965 raising questions embarrassing enough to prompt a new spate of health inspections and water sampling. Between 1966 and 1970, at least eight of these confirmed that local water was 'grossly polluted' and unsuitable for human consumption. One analysis of tap water in neighbouring Tavua township revealed a cyanide content of 1.7 parts per million, nearly eight times the limit prescribed by the World Health Organisation. In 1969 there was an outbreak of jaundice (probably indicative of hepatitis A) among miners.[14]

A bold face did not necessarily mean bold deeds. Emperor was reminded of its obligations under the Public Health Ordinance, instructed to ensure that cyanide-bearing effluent did not filter into the Nasivi river, and requested, as some 20 years before, to construct a proper filtration and chlorination plant. Management was more annoyed than receptive to what it called 'the repeated attempts by certain citizens to discredit this Company', and while agreeing to improve its water supply, defiantly withstood pressure to construct a treatment plant on the grounds of cost.[15]

It is probable that the high incidence of intestinal infections, respiratory illnesses and other manifestations of declining health standards during this period were a function of expenditure cuts in 'non-productive' community welfare. Following an epidemic of gastro-enteritis in early 1951, the number of monthly cases reported to the mines dispensary climbed steadily, shooting up by 157% between 1955 and 1963. Company propaganda continued to deny this awesome reality: 'employees in the goldmining industry', General Manager Cayzer boasted to the Labour Department in 1959, 'are probably the best nourished and medically fit groups in Fiji [sic]'.[16]

---

[14] Health Inspector Ba/Ra & Tavua to Emperor, 19 Aug. 1966, 23 May & 1 Aug. 1968, 16 Sept. & 17 Dec. 1969, 11 Aug. & 11 Nov. 1970; Sec. Tavua Rural Health Authority to General Manager, 20 Feb. 1969, Vat./ unclassified; Stigzelius (ESCAP) 1981; SDMO Tavua to Manager, 9 March 1970, Vat./unclassified.
[15] Watson General Manager to Director of Medical Services, 12 March 1968, Vat./unclassified.
[16] Cayzer, General Manager to Commissioner of Labour, 2 Sept. 1959, Vat./unclassified.

In the face of the enduring myth that underground mining in Fiji carried no inherent health risks, there was also a startling rise in respiratory complaints. This coincided with changes in the productive basis of mining and the structure of the workforce, notably the heavier reliance on deep-level mining, the larger-scale treatment by roasting of sulphide ore, and a sharp drop in labour turnover. It was followed by unsuccessful union demands for more realistic allowances for roaster workers. While available evidence unfortunately excludes a register of deaths at the mines, it is worth noting that the company dispensary recorded fatalities due to congestive heart failure, bronchial asthma, bronchial congestion, bronchial pneumonia and acute bronchitis. From the early 1950s reported cases of unspecified bronchitis (consistently classified as a clinical condition) began to run into the thousands each year (see Table 6.2).[17]

A greater concern to reduce the sickness rate among workers had become apparent from the late 1940s, deriving essentially from the declining mobility of Fijian labour and recognition of the economic advantages of a fit work-force. The comprehensive medical survey of 1950, the introduction of pre-engagement examinations in 1951, and the more systematic collection of data on illnesses that followed were a measure of this new thinking. By the late 1960s annual medical examinations on young workers (under 21 years) as recommended by an ILO Convention in 1965, had begun. But the perceived benefits were outweighed by the cost of bearing 'the full burden of lost time'. The colonial government still fell far short of providing adequate protection under its compensation legislation. In 1964 industrial diseases listed in the 1950 Model Ordinance from the Colonial Office were formally acknowledged. There was on the other hand still no account of tuberculosis or ankylostomiasis as occupational diseases. Silicosis (the contraction of which was more likely than before) was curiously withdrawn from the statute books.

By the mid-1960s Emperor's small dispensary (now servicing a work-force of around 1700 and a community of more than 6000) was treating around 200 patients a day. Sick or injured workers, the union complained, had to endure long delays before being treated, and wage deductions for this 'lost time' were common practice. From early 1968 part of the cost of dispensary transport, including a charge for transporting families, was also passed on to workers by way of payroll deductions. When this provoked criticism from the Fiji Employers' Consultative Association (FECA) on the grounds that it violated the Employment (Medical Treatment) Regulations of 1966, the company imposed cash levies on dependants instead.

As observed in Chapter 4, underground mining at deeper levels made mine work more hazardous, and the rising frequency and severity of accidents derived from such factors as the intense pressure on workers to be more productive and the restricted expenditure on accident prevention. Management itself confessed that the increased scale of development and production, the inadequate supervision of expanded underground operations and the abandonment of the safety programme in 1955 were all to be blamed for Emperor's tarnished accident

---

[17]   Vat./Welfare Officer four-weekly reports to General Manager, 1952-68.

Table 6.2 Reported cases of gastro-enteritis, infantile diarrhoea, dysentery, unspecified dysentery, influenza and bronchitis, Vatukoula, 1952–68

Year	Gastro-enteritis		Infantile diarrhoea		Dysentery		Unspecified dysentery		Influenza		Bronchitis	
	Total cases	Average per month	Total cases	Average per month	Total cases	Average per month	Total cases	Average per month	Total cases	Average per month	Total cases	Average per month
1952	670	55.8	None recorded		None recorded		None recorded		1,513	126.0	None recorded	
1953	573	47.7	154	12.8	5				762	63.5	None recorded	
1954	393	32.7	242	20.1	1				640	106.6	1,417	236.1
1955	641	53.4	216	18.0					813	67.7	836	69.6
1956	1,047	87.2	335	27.9					1,766	147.1	1,791	149.2
1957	1,162	96.8	547	45.5			3		6,134	511.1	2,021	168.4
1958†	761	126.8	130	21.6			1		1,409	234.8	637	106.1
1959††	661	110.1	112	18.6					1,792	298.6	1,006	167.6
1960	891	74.2	262	21.8					1,802	150.1	1,386	115.5
1961	1,140	95.0	269	22.4					2,438	203.1	2,210	184.1
1962*	1,098	99.8	136	12.3					3,767	342.4	3,018	274.3
1963	1,646	137.1	107	8.9					2,742	228.5	2,013	167.7
1964	992	82.6	199	16.5					1,319	109.9	1,130	94.1
1965	733	61.0	282	23.5					1,505	125.4	905	75.4
1966	600	50.0	549	45.7					2,069	172.4	1,040	86.6
1967	781	65.0	548	45.6					1,343	111.9	1,199	99.9
1968	352	58.6	536	89.3					1,151	191.8	621	103.5

* Total cases in 1962 excludes September.   † Total cases Jan.–June only.   †† Total cases July–Dec. only.

Source: Data compiled from Vat./Emperor Company's Welfare Officer's Four-weekly Reports (totalling about 220) to General Manager.

record of the 1950s. Government inspectors whose powers were in the opinion of one of them 'almost dictatorial' also failed to enforce the law.

A safety programme at Vatukoula, mainly confined to meetings for supervisors and the display of posters (with public broadcasts explaining these), was finally resumed in 1963. It was not enough to arrest the alarming escalation of frequency and severity rates. By the end of 1965 these peaked at 2.91 and 23.95, an increase of 903% and 397% over the average rates for 1951. The mining department took a particularly heavy toll with the number of shifts lost through accidents climbing from 2744 in 1964 to 4537 in 1966. The incidence of hand injuries (mainly in the form of lacerations, cuts, severe crush injuries and puncture wounds) continued to be especially high.

The economic arguments that had given rise to organised safety work in the 1940s resurfaced in 1966 when Emperor ordered its own investigation into the causes, costs and nature of lost-time accidents. The outcome of this confirmed the wisdom of re-establishing 'a proper, effective, safety programme'. The services of an industrious staff member, R. H. O'Reilly, subsequently appointed to the position of underground safety officer, promised to stir the company into more decisive action. O'Reilly proposed that the wearing of (the now-subsidised) safety-boots and helmets be enforced; that the use of gloves be encouraged among all underground workers; that a first aid course for all shift bosses become compulsory; and that meetings of all underground supervisors be resumed. His task proved a thankless one. There was a reluctance to let mineworkers pay for their safety-helmets in instalments, and protective clothing remained in short supply.

Management's unwillingness to support an active safety campaign was, as O'Reilly pointed out, economically irrational as well as impolitic:

> The opinion of some Senior Supervisors may be that labour is cheap and readily available, but not enough consideration is taken to realise that we are still answerable to the Mines Inspector and Department of Labour and Industry.
> Labour is not in the least cheap as it costs this Company approximately £4.10.0 per day to have an employee (local) off work due to an accident.[18]

The government Mines Department was already alert to the disturbing incidence and type of accidents at Vatukoula. Under the direction of E. M. Kennedy, Inspector of Mines between 1966 and 1970, it contemplated a number of options, among them the possibility of holding publicised accident inquiries to 'embarrass' the company into doing something.[19] Demands, directives and entreaties emanated from the Mines Department. All went unheeded.

By the mid-1950s rising living costs and wages made substantial increases in compensation mandatory. In most other colonies, 48 months' earnings had long been established for total incapacity, and 42 or 36 months for death pensions. Maximum payments had also been raised. With the amendment of its Workmen's Compensation Ordinance in December 1957, Fiji finally adopted 36 and 48 months' earnings as measures for fatality and total incapacitation. It also improved minimum and maximum awards.

---

[18] Underground Safety Officer to Acting General Manager, 21 Aug. 1968, Vat./EGM Safety Campaign.
[19] Kennedy (IOM) to Director of Lands, 28 Feb. 1967, MR/Bunch 20 M541/1 Pt 3.

STATE INVESTMENT CONSOLIDATED

The colonial state played a critical role in attempts to restore gold production to a more secure footing. In addition to co-operation over the management of organised Fijian labour and the general control of mine labour costs, it gave generous patronage to the Vatukoula companies, entering a series of agreements that were highly beneficial to them. Most important of all, perhaps, from 1958 it instigated a controversial pattern of subsidisation. State subsidies and grants absolved the industry of the need to solicit fresh capital. After 1935, when EML was formed, shareholders were not asked to finance development for several decades, shares being issued only in order to purchase the assets of associated ventures.

In 1952 the Emperor group scored exemption from tax on capital expenditure as well as a promise that the port and service tax on bullion exports would be abolished. In return, a minimum £200,000 had to be spent on development and prospecting over the following three years, which could be written off against working profits. The Mining (Amendment) Ordinance of 1952 represented a major coup for the group: broadening the range of items that could be charged as costs against royalty, raising the profit yield ceilings at which royalty was assessed, and reducing the rates themselves. The 'noble' intentions of the Colonial Office were thus seriously compromised if not subverted: after a spectacular rise in government revenue earned from mining royalties between 1949 and 1951, the steady decline in income from 1952 owed much to these concessions.

Subsequent approaches to the administration through the 1950s were sympathetically received. In 1957 Governor Sir Ronald Garvey urged members of the Legislative Council that it was the government's responsibility to search for 'any means in its power at present to assist the industry to find the capital it needs, bearing in mind the undoubted difficulties encountered in persuading Australian capital, accustomed to an economy in which gold mining is virtually exempt from taxation, to flow again into gold mining in Fiji'. Garvey's appeal won the day, and the Income Tax Ordinance was amended to permit tax exemption or reduction for mining companies. Emperor became an immediate beneficiary of this largesse, relieved of all income tax and royalty obligations for 1957 and 1959.

Tax concessions were not enough, and the group pressed for a direct subsidy on gold exports. Government compliance meant that funds were approved in 1958 to finance exploration, further mechanisation, and extensions to the mill. A three-year undertaking was given to pay £2 per fine ounce on annual exports of up to 75,000 ounces of gold. As a subsidy on production the gesture appeared ill-conceived, likely to prolong short-term planning and encourage more intensive exploitation of existing reserves, rather than induce large-scale exploration. The principle of private sector state investment was in any event contentious, especially in this instance, because the industry was not competitive and assistance was earmarked for a monopoly concern. One company alone benefited from the injection of public funds.

The subsidy issue had a broader and controversial history. Predating the first deal in Fiji in the late 1950s, it stemmed from the regimented gold price control system administered by the International Monetary Fund. While the IMF did on occasion approve production subsidies on gold (for example, in regard to Canada in late 1947), it was opposed in principle to state subsidies for marginal or low-grade mines such as those in Southern Rhodesia. Subsidies represented an increase in the price paid for gold over and above the official price of $US35 per ounce. The position of the Colonial Office had also been one of unequivocal opposition ('we have set our faces against that'),[20] and while less able to influence political decisions in the dominions, it had been able to impose its will more freely in Britain's colonies.

Between 1947 and 1948 both Sarawak and Kenya had accordingly come up against the cold shoulder of the Colonial Office as they hustled for support in their efforts to save struggling industries. It was the difficulty of 'square[ing] with our obligations under the International Monetary Fund', coupled with other, economic considerations that proved the main stumbling block. The home government was sympathetic to the problem of an ever-diminishing margin between the fixed market value of gold and the rising costs of extraction and treatment. But it was more disposed towards leaving uneconomic gold in the ground until it became payable and in the meantime promoting the production of other dollar-earning or dollar-saving products (such as sisal or groundnuts in Sarawak) at competitive prices. It was not possible, the Kenyan Governor was instructed, for the colonial government to subsidise 'an industry which has become unprofitable'.[21] By granting producers a value for their gold that was higher than that determined by the par value of sterling, a subsidy also had the effect of devaluing sterling.

Overall, the rationale broadly conformed to the development goals of the Colonial Office's post-war royalty formula, seemingly averse to the rapacious policies of politically influential mining interests, which picked out the eyes of a mine and repatriated the bulk of their profits. As over the royalty question the Colonial Office also had occasion to disagree with the Treasury, which in the cynical view of one officer was 'always tending to fall to the fascination of the glitter of gold' and generally favoured stimulating gold production by whatever means and whatever cost.[22] It was perhaps a little strange that the introduction of a gold subsidy in Fiji should be unhampered by any obstruction from Britain a decade later.

Concessions to the mining industry in Fiji were guided by a number of social and economic imperatives. A central argument was the contribution that gold made to the economy as an earner of foreign exchange. The expansion and stability of gold exports contrasted with the extreme fluctuations in sugar earnings, while the massive drop in sugar prices and the declining production in copra from the mid-1960s highlighted the advantages of a relatively healthy gold price. The termination of gold production would entail the loss of around 10% in export earnings and increase the colony's dependence on a narrow range of exports.

[20]   C. G. Eastwood to J. D. Rankine, 1 April 1948, PRO CO 852/950/2.
[21]   Secretary of State for Colonies to Sir P. Mitchell, Governor of Kenya, 12 Feb. 1948, PRO CO852/950/1.
[22]   Caine minute, 14 Aug. 1947, PRO CO 852/950/2.

Another recurring argument was the employment opportunities created by the industry. A closedown of operations at Vatukoula, it was held, would inflict severe 'social and economic dislocation' upon the 5000 (by the 1960s 6000) strong community. Resettlement and redeployment of local mine labour were not attractive options, especially in circumstances of rising urbanisation and unemployment.

The economic defence of assistance was not as sound as it appeared. After the war, gold did not resume its dominant position as a leading export. It raised an annual average of 14% of total revenue from domestic exports between 1946 and 1955, tipping 20% in 1947 and 1951, but this figure declined to around 9% over the following decade (see Appendix D). There was a sharp decline in direct revenue from the industry as tax contributions from Loloma and Dolphin were phased out, higher development costs were charged against taxable profits, and tax concessions abounded. Paradoxically, state investment in the industry rose as gold became more marginal to the colonial economy (see Appendix E).

Behind the material arguments in favour of official patronage, there was also evidence of what the opposition Federation Party later denounced as 'blackmail' and 'ransom'. Baldly stated, if the colony did not wish Emperor to 'pick out the eyes' of the proven ore, to maximise an immediate return to its shareholders, and to gut the mine, the state was obliged to pick up the tab. The government was evidently not inhibited by the fact that the group's financial and production strategies had deprived itself of sufficient working capital and eroded its reserves.

In 1959 Emperor lodged further submissions: a refund of the port and service tax it had paid on imports (estimated to be worth £75,000) during the three-year subsidy period; extended tenure of the subsidy at a higher rate of £3 per ounce from 1961; and exemption from income tax and royalty between 1962 and 1966. This time, the government's bountiful disposition came under the critical eye of headquarters in London. Urged by the Colonial Office to exercise some caution, the Fiji government hired the consultancy firm John Taylor and Sons Ltd to make a technical assessment of the economic prospects of the mine. The team's final recommendations included the continuance of the current subsidy for a further two years and the government's securing a mortgage debenture or making a loan of £400,000 at 6%. Neither was implemented.

By late 1960 the government was buried in its own financial problems, punctuated by a rising level of unemployment and a credit squeeze by the commercial banks. It also faced a major strike in the sugar industry. The precarious position of the economy compelled the Colonial Office to advise against assistance. This did not stop the government from meeting the company's more modest requests for a port and service tax refund worth £44,031 and for exemption from income tax and royalty until profits reached an unspecified level.

Emperor's failure to win a further subsidy led to a feverish pursuit of higher production, achieving an improvement in revenue and in output levels, which management later confessed went 'beyond what was ... provident as far as the ore reserves were concerned' (see Appendix D). When, in 1965, it launched itself into a new phase of more successful representations to the government, the drastic depletion of its reserves ironically sustained its case for assistance. The arguments were typically fashioned as a bald ultimatum. A three-year subsidy of £3 10s. per ounce was the only way of averting the gutting of the mine in two or three years when shareholders would be paid off at around 6s. a share. It meant that the state would carry about 67% (or £1,050,000) of the total cost of a development and exploration programme, thereby permitting the company to pay a dividend of 3d. a year.

This time the submission was supported by the Colonial Office, which argued that 'it would be a grave mistake to permit the mine to close down'. Locally, scepticism and uncertainty marked some official attitudes, and for the first time questions were provoked about the company's motives. Why, the Financial Secretary (H. P. Ritchie) asked, could capital not be found elsewhere? Management's explanation that high production costs and a fixed gold price had deterred at least four interested parties left Ritchie unconvinced. Smarting at the fact that shareholders had been spared similar exhortations and yet had recently been the recipients of about £90,000 worth of dividends, he surmised that the company had deliberately made the terms unattractive: 'If capital could be obtained elsewhere this would diminish their present shareholders' equity—this was not put in quite this way, but it is what it boils down to.'[23]

The possibility of a loan instead of a subsidy or of government acquiring an equity share as a condition of assistance drew an uncompromising rejection from Emperor: 'Mr Nilsen threw up his hands in horror at both these questions.'[24] While the general impression Nilsen projected was one of support for measures to keep the industry afloat, Ritchie insisted: 'Nevertheless, I think he wants money for nothing if he can get it rather than bringing someone else in as partners'.[25]

The option of government shareholdings in colonial mining companies had been aired about 15 years earlier in the confidential dispatches between the Colonial Office and Britain's colonial governments. In the case of Fiji the initiative had come from a briefly seconded Financial Secretary, who proposed in 1950 that the government take a share in the equity capital of the Emperor group in exchange for waiving royalty payments. The Colonial Office had rejected the scheme, yet two years later had set about encouraging its gold-producing colonies to consider the option when future concessions were being negotiated. Even Fiji was among those approached, but by then, in the aftermath of 'considerable taxation concessions', the immediate opportunity and purpose had been lost. Now, in 1965, it presented itself and was lost again.

Whatever the cynicism of individual officers about the motives of Emperor's management, it was the gamble of committing such a large sum without the assurance that new or extended orebodies would be disclosed that lay behind the government's ambivalence. Ultimately the findings of a local branch of the international firm of chartered accountants Price Waterhouse and Co. tipped the balance in Emperor's favour. Commissioned to give financial advice over the company's submissions, the firm endorsed the claim to penury, but advised against government equity. Instead of a repayable loan or a subsidy on production it recommended three years of annual grants, supported by exemption from income

---

[23]   CSO/confidential file.
[24]   CSO/confidential file.
[25]   Ibid.

tax, royalty and dividends surtax (for shareholders), and permission to maintain profit distribution for the duration of the grants. The production subsidy was rejected on the grounds that

> The only benefit to the Government, apart from averting the re-settlement problem at Vatukoula for the time being, will have been some additional revenue from taxation, whereas the company's shareholders will have received the other benefits. The additional development programme will have been paid for by the Government and shareholders will receive a £30,000 dividend in each of the three years. They will also benefit from ore reserves built up over the three years.

In September 1967 a motion to furnish Emperor with three years of grants totalling £1,020,000 was carried in the Legislative Council. No conditions were laid down regarding the use of this money, and the company was permitted to pay an annual dividend of up to £30,000 during the period of assistance. Unfortunately the three-year gestation period to produce a decision had in the meantime again provoked the mining of 'richer ore than would normally have been considered prudent'.[26]

Around this time there was an important development in Fiji which influenced the pattern and success of lobbying by the Vatukoula mining interests. This was the establishment of a political party system. The ideological foundation of the ruling Alliance Party promised to preserve the class structure of colonial society after self-government. The party strongly favoured large-scale foreign investment to finance industrial development, proclaiming political stability as a priority if this was to be achieved. Practical expression was given to its capital investment leanings in the mid-1960s, when a new mining ordinance and regulations permitted royalties to be remitted in whole or part and offered a comprehensive range of tax-deductible items.

On the negative side the mining industry now had to contend with a vigorous challenge to official mining policy from politicians within the opposition Federation Party. During debate on the 1967 grant proposal the party condemned the ease and frequency with which the government had 'succumbed' to the demands of the mining interests to the neglect of urgent educational, medical, and other social services, and in discrimination against a more seriously afflicted sugar industry, which employed thousands more. It ridiculed the suggestion that capital was ever invested with 'charitable' intentions, exposing Emperor's pretensions of concern for the welfare of its labourers as a divisive 'smokescreen' and 'an instrument of blackmail'.[27] By January 1969 the party's opposition to further aid to the industry had crystallised into a central issue on its electoral platform. It also prompted a bid for nationalisation. With barbed humour, the Indian Member for Northwest Viti Levu, R. D. Patel, proposed the motion to nationalise the goldmining industry:

[26] J. F. Wren, Chairman of Directors EGM to Minister of Finance, 14 Nov. 1970, Vat./Government 1970/71.
[27] R. D. Patel (Indian Member for Northwest Viti Levu), S. M. Koya (Indian Member for Western Viti Levu) and A. D. Patel (Leader of Opposition), Supplementary Estimates, Fiji Leg. Co. Debates Sept. 1967; R. D. Patel, Leg. Co. Debate, 1 Sept. 1967.

This industry has been run at least for the last 17 to 18 years on a partnership basis between the shareholders of this company and the taxpayer of this country, and this partnership is such that it reminds me of a comic I read some years back. Mutt and Jeff are two friends and Mutt asked Jeff, 'Hello Jeff how about purchasing a cow in partnership'. So Jeff being a simple-minded fellow says 'Oh all right Mutt. We'll go into partnership.' Then Jeff asked Mutt, 'How shall we divide the cow?' So Mutt said, 'Oh all right, you take the front and I will take the back, which means that you will feed the cow and I will milk the cow.'[28]

It was of course unlikely that a motion tainted with 'a smattering of communism or socialism', as one Minister put it, would be considered by the Alliance government. Nationalisation, it was charged, was not only inimical to the very notion of a 'free' society but was likely to 'spell doom to the further encouragement of overseas investment'.[29]

Opposition from a less predictable quarter added a rather bizarre dimension to the debate. The executive of the mineworkers' union had since the early 1960s become a new target for the company's mendacity. Sakiasi Waqanivavalagi, juggling his responsibilities as union secretary and Alliance Member for Northwest Viti Levu, undertook to defend the company in the Legislative Council. Seduced by the promise of expanded employment opportunities, he condemned the 'cheap' and 'irresponsible' attempt by the Opposition to mislead the electorate. Company-supplied data on Emperor's labour costs, annual royalty, customs and income tax payments were evidence of the company's contribution to the economy, invalidating Patel's agreement that the allocation of resources to the industry had been excessive and inadequately recompensed.

The case for nationalisation failed. It was laid aside, though not to rest, until its banner was taken up again after independence by the mineworkers' union, under rather different leadership. Much later, in 1986, as a young Fiji Labour Party edged its way to an election victory, the issue became an incendiary device.

CHANGING PATTERNS OF RESISTANCE AND NEW FORMS OF CONTROL

The transition from a predominantly migrant work-force to a stabilised working class was accomplished during the 1950s. By 1960 over 75% of the Fijian work-force was permanent, with at least 5% of all non-European labour having been employed at Vatukoula for as long as 20 years. The development of class-consciousness derived from this, but was neither a steady nor simple process. During the early 1950s the mineworkers' union was concerned above all with the widening gulf between net earnings and what was considered an adequate living wage for Fijian workers. Subsistence needs, now defined more broadly in terms of family support and social security, were the backbone of pressure for wage increases.

---

[28] R. D. Patel, 30 Jan. 1969, Leg. Co. Debate on the Nationalisation of the Gold Mining Industry.
[29] C. A. Stinson, Minister for Communications, Works and Tourism, 31 Jan. 1969, Fiji Leg. Co. Debates.

From the web of disparate concerns relating to living and working conditions, it was also evident that the racialist index of earnings remained a focal point of organised protest. Ethnic as well as provincial fights still occurred, though not of the scale or intensity of earlier clashes. The persistence of occupational discrimination that left Fijians trailing behind Rotumans and Part-Europeans not only in promotion prospects but also in wages, basic leave and sickness benefits provided the key to communal preoccupations. Adding fuel to the fire, the retrenchment of Fijians in the 1950s had the intended effect of paving the way for the absorption of more Rotuman labour.[30]

The possibility of a concerted labour offensive against the powerful mining interests emerged slowly as the grip of ethnic sectarianism weakened. Non-European labour appeared to identify a common struggle, and a budding worker-consciousness found bold expression in inter-ethnic alignments within the union. By the late 1950s the focus of industrial action had shifted noticeably away from the defence of Fijian interests towards improvements in the working conditions of all non-European labour. A dispute submitted for arbitration in 1955 marked this important transition, when for the first time Rotuman and Part-European workers were included in the union's submissions. Two years later the union lodged claims on behalf of Indian tradesmen and drivers and demanded a general wage increase for all non-European workers. In 1959 it pressed for (and won) parity base rates for 'ordinary' Indian and Fijian labour.

Other developments reflected a growing awareness of the process of accumulation and specifically the structures of exploitation and control. The struggle to tie classifications and wage adjustments to length of service continued albeit as unrewardingly as in the 1930s. The desired formula in 1952 was that the definition of a skilled worker be based on 12 months' service. Company allegations of low productivity were refuted by the union and countered by charges that diminished output was a function of the poor standards of European supervision, the absence of a formal training programme, reduced ore reserves and other factors beyond the control of workers. During arbitration in 1955, the union secretary announced:

> I have read the letter from the Company which mentions about the number of labourers in Australia equal to three and four Fijians; there was an uproar from all sides saying that it was not true—saying that Fijians work hard.[31]

Attacks on the arbitrary barriers and on management's complete prerogative, in the absence of job evaluation, to determine the value of labour, struck at the core of the system of earnings. Wage demands for long-service workers similarly drew attention to the continuing rejection of experience as a sufficient criterion

---

[30]   The records of the FMWU offer insight into the concerns and preoccupations of organised labour in the post-war period. Particularly useful for the 1950s and 1960s are correspondence between the union's secretaries (Basilio Mata, Nemani Waka and Sakiasi Waqanivavalagi) and Emperor's management; records of meetings between the FMWU executive and management; union log of claims and records of evidence given in conciliation and arbitration proceedings 1955, 1957 and 1959; and a Board of Inquiry into a dispute between the union and EGM In June 1964.

[31]   Evidence given by Basilio Mata, Record of Arbitration into Mineworkers Dispute, Suva, 30 June 1955, Vat./ unclassified.

for wage determination. The industry's moves to arrest the slide in profits by tighter wage control were openly denounced.

But the ideological thrust of bargaining also extended to demands for a return commensurate with improved productivity (for 'a fair share of the [wealth] they're producing') and for greater control over both work relations and extra-occupational life. This second grievance was directly tackled in the union's battle to curb retrenchment; to participate in decisions about transfers and the general distribution of jobs; and to eliminate the use of obscene language and other forms of harassment by supervisors that were symptomatic of the authoritarian style of management. In 1959 striking workers demanded the dismissal of the company's Fijian liaison officer, a chief. In 1964 the union charged Emperor with flouting the ILO's (1957) Abolition of Forced Labour Convention. Two subsequent strikes over offensive language by supervisors won massive rank-and-file support.

The containment of labour unrest was as crucial to the colonial state as to the mining interests if the industry was to survive. The formation of the mineworkers' union under official auspices had held out some promise of stability. But the leadership's failure to restrain a restive work-force (particularly evident in unofficial work stoppages between 1949 and 1952) and the growing number of registered members from the mid-1950s suggested that the rising 'local barometer' needed new forms of control. The response in August 1952 to an unofficial strike over time-keeping, which brought out over 600 Fijian workers and forced the Emperor mine and mill to a complete halt, recalled the state's heavy-handed interventions of the past. In the absence of violence or any kind of disorder, police patrols were brought into the mine area. A security plan stationed detachments from Nadroga and Nadi in Lautoka and put forces in other centres along the (north and west) coast on alert. The address by a respected high-ranking chief, Ratu George Tuisawau, the Roko Tui Ba, added the government's own message of reproach to those of resident chiefs.

In 1955 another official strike by some 1138 workers was broken, violence averted and essential services maintained by the 'prompt assistance' of the Acting Governor and his staff, the visits of four senior chiefs (Ratu Sukuna, Ratu Edward Cakobau, Ratu George Cakobau and Ratu George Tuisawau) and the 'unassuming organisation of the Police Force'. Some years later the government allocated a number of special constables (generally used as part of a riot or strike force) to the industry. They were dispersed through different departments.[32]

Direct intervention of this kind was effective as an immediate means of resolving conflict at the mines. It was not a long-term solution to the problem of worker disaffection. The swelling ranks of the young and unemployed through the 1960s were having a destabilising influence on the whole community. They were also provoking acts of violence reminiscent of earlier years. The dislocation caused by redundancies, reduced work opportunities and a more oppressive work environment was felt particularly severely by a generation that was much more dependent on work in the industry. For Fijians it was a dependence heightened by progressive weakening of psychological and physical ties with their home

---

[32]   Minutes of Meeting of Department Managers, 5 April 1961, Vat./Meeting of Executives Current File.

villages. The steady trickle of school-leavers unable to find work in other urban centres and having relatives at Vatukoula did little to improve the situation. Cases of property damage, theft, assault and drunkenness were common forms of 'community disturbances'. 'Even such essential items as the shower rooms and lavatories', management complained to the union, 'have been damaged ... showers have been wilfully torn down, kicked off their hinges and electrical fittings wrecked while holes have often been slashed through barrack walls by cane knives.'[33]

Increasingly sensitive to the difficulties of controlling a generation of labour raised in 'a multi-racial industrial community' and no longer showing unquestioned allegiance to chiefly authority,[34] management established a boys' club in 1960. This conveniently engaged the unemployed sons of mineworkers in 'odd jobs' and 'voluntary work'. Five years later it was decided to direct this restive element, now swelled by the influx of young relatives coming in from the outer islands, into full-time paid work. It was also resolved to confine future engagements of Fijian labour to this source. The outcome was beneficial, helping to lower the wage bill and alleviate the housing shortage. Wage rates for youth were graded well below that for unskilled labour and were subject only to small half-yearly increments. Savings were considerable where boys entered the workforce at 14, their pay scale rising from only 8s. to 13s. 11d. per day by the time they turned 18.

Measures taken to strengthen company control in the town extended to the eviction from married accommodation of workers who were not legally married. Under the guise of a census, a witch-hunt for 'jobless parasites' was also instigated. The names of authorised residents in each house were publicised. Management approval had to be given before any non-authorised persons could receive hospitality, a policy that clashed violently with traditional cultural values. Posters distributed among the various settlements carried a clear message of recrimination:

> In Vatukoula today there are many who are living in Company quarters when they have no right to do so. Many of these people are lazy, and of bad character and are like parasites on the backs of the hard working married employees.
> People who are causing this overcrowding will ... be found out and asked to leave.
> All employees are asked to help the Company in carrying out the work of the census. This will benefit all the people who live and work in Vatukoula and will remove from their midst the lazy, jobless persons who are a burden to them.[35]

In an attempt to check the decline in traditional values, to defuse class-based sympathies, and to undermine the credibility of the union, the company also promoted the influence of its ethnic labour committees with recharged vigour. Negotiations with the Fijian Committee, bypassing the union, helped to break the 1952 strike. In 1956 the company formed a welfare department, appointing

---

[33] Cayzer, General Manager to Sec. FMWU, 28 Feb. 1959, Vat./unclassified.
[34] The 1955 strike was a case in point. The colonial administration despatched Ratu Sukuna and Ratu Edward Cakobau to the mines in an attempt to persuade workers to await arbitration, but a secret ballot declared an overwhelming majority in favour of strike action.
[35] Management proposed that authority cards be issued to each family. Every person would then be required to give proof of his/her right to be on the field, and charges of trespassing would be laid against unauthorised persons. These more drastic measures were not, in the end, introduced. Minutes JCC meetings, 23 April 1965 & 13 Jan. 1967, Vat./Gold Mining Joint Consultative Council.

a Rotuman officer and posting eleven *turaga-ni-koro* (appointed headmen) throughout the Fijian and Part-European settlements.

Perturbed by the seeming lack of discipline and control of the union rank and file, the colonial government withdrew from its earlier position of enthusiastic sponsorship of mining unionism. Disenchantment was quickly followed by tacit support for the union-breaking initiatives of management. One measure was formal approval of the distinction between industrial and welfare matters, which since the inception of the union had been used by management to legitimise its refusal to dismantle the committee system. A conciliation board ruling in 1952 limited the union's bargaining domain by recognising it as the 'sole' representative of only Fijian labour, endorsing the Fijian Committee as the forum responsible for all matters considered non-industrial. Recognition of the union was subject to review and was 'conditional upon [it] being able to speak for its full membership and enforce discipline'. It could be 'repudiated' if members took 'unauthorised actions outside the Union'.

On the whole, segregation proved remarkably durable. Fijians were reminded in 1955 that they were 'forbidden to enter the [Part-European] Hall except on the occasion of wedding parties or religious functions, and only then by invitation'. Single Rotumans were moved out of Part-European barracks shortly afterwards. In both cases the proposal allegedly came from the workers themselves, but management was not loath to oblige. The 'segregation of the single Rotuman employees', it reflected, 'will greatly assist in the closer supervision of the Rotuman community as a whole'.

Union demands for desegregration in the late 1960s did not lead to dismantling of the system. The replacement of a 'racial' by a 'financial' qualification for club membership, for example, permitted certain higher income-earning local workers (mainly Rotumans and Part-Europeans) to penetrate the corridors of European privilege. This helped the company deflect charges of discrimination and provided a more respectable means for the continued exclusion of the vast majority of Fijians (and some Rotuman and Part-Europeans) from the more salubrious recreational venues.

The attempts of the resident Catholic Church to have European children readmitted to its school were more openly resisted. It was 'not fair to the European child', management protested, 'to dissociate it from its own race and subject it to constant contact with others of different outlook and standards'.[36] Only by the late 1960s was the convent open to children of all ethnic origins and integration in Vatukoula's two primary schools approved.

Other initiatives helped to muzzle union radicalism. The conciliation and arbitration machinery provided an efficient mechanism of labour and wage control. Compulsory arbitration under the 1941 legislation did not make an industrial stoppage illegal, but, by channelling the union leadership into more 'constructive' conciliatory pursuits, it tended to pre-empt or suspend strike action. The Essential Services (Arbitration) Ordinance of 1954 explicitly prohibited strike action by workers assigned to winder engine driving or pumping. Pumping was arguably

---

[36]   C. W. Cayzer to Sister Malachy, Head Teacher Convent, 24 July 1957, RCAF 11/6/2 Vatukoula 1936-58.

not a service 'concerned with amenities, a stoppage of which was likely to have an immediate and serious effect on the life and health of the community', the 'test' of an essential service recommended by colonial heads of labour departments in London late in 1951. Yet it was, along with water, electricity, health and sanitary services, conveniently netted as an 'essential' occupation in the industrial agreements of the 1960s. The union was bound over to safeguard these from any disruption.

The union's acceptance of 'responsible' bargaining through arbitration meant that wage and other demands became subordinated to 'national' considerations. This was because the industry's 'ability to pay' became the guiding principle of arbitration settlements. The union did not relinquish its responsibility to improve earnings and working conditions. But there were obvious contradictions in its support for a policy aimed at shielding industry from interference with production, and its participation in an institution that, above all else, agonised over the financial predicaments of employers.[37]

The collective agreements between Emperor and the union were conspicuously styled on co-option, self-discipline and compromise. During the tenure of an agreement, any claims 'involving directly or indirectly any financial commitment ... [by] the employer' were renounced. The union was duty-bound to 'co-operate' with management 'in maintaining discipline', in promoting worker productivity and efficiency, and in 'actively' discouraging legitimate forms of protest such as walkouts, slow downs, mass 'sickness' or absenteeism as well as unofficial strikes. The union's right to represent the work-force precluded all apprentices, staff members and probationers.

Arbitration imposed additional constraints on organised labour. Charged with ensuring that its members complied with court rulings, the union leadership was implicitly required to take punitive action against recalcitrants within its own rank and file. This disciplinary role set the seal on a process of assimilation (or rather co-option), which sapped the union's ability to maintain a strong opposition to its employer. It was a fate not dissimilar to that of many Western trade unions, which, as two Indian sociologists have put it, became 'the policemen of the capitalist' and the 'managers of discontent ... fully incorporated into the structure of capitalism'.[38]

Under increasing pressure to remove the longstanding inequities in mine earnings and to improve working hours and benefits, state arbitration tribunals approved concessions necessary to contain dissatisfaction. In the main, however, they staved off challenges to the structural basis of discrimination. Although rulings in 1957 and 1959 recommended that job evaluation and trade testing be looked into, it was not until 1961 that this became mandatory. The system did not unduly destabilise the structure of mine earnings because it failed to dispense with wage differentials 'based on different racial living standards'. There were other tell-tale signs. No sanctions existed to compel the company to consult

---

[37] For a development of this argument and discussion of arbitration as a political device to control organised resistance in Australia, see Fieldes 1976 and Higgins 1974 : 165, who argues that compulsory arbitration reduces trade unions to 'state appendages'.
[38] Ramaswamy & Ramaswamy 1981 : 148–9.

the union; after two years, only 1.9% of the workforce had benefited from 'merit payments'; and the remuneration prescribed for evaluated jobs had to be 'commensurate with the overall capacity of the industry to pay'. This of course contradicted the purpose of the system.

The substitution of voluntary for compulsory arbitration in 1958 complied with the critical view of penal sanctions taken by the International Labour Organisation (ILO) and the Colonial Office. It was also based on the realisation that the existence of sanctions did not necessarily prevent strike action. While viewed with alarm by Emperor's management, the change had no appreciable effect on industrial relations in the mining industry. Under the 'great arbitration illusion' as it has been called, whereby it was believed 'possible under capitalism to have an impartial dispenser of justice between employers and their employees',[39] union leadership continued to accept the parameters of protest laid down in the original wartime legislation. It showed itself willing through the 1960s to make voluntary sacrifices in the 'national interest'.

Acceptance of indexation as the basis of wage increases undermined the force of the union's opposition to Emperor in a specific way. As management announced with alacrity, it 'removed their scope for demanding further increases unless there is a very considerable rise in the index'.[40] Indexation, indeed, proved the main defence against wage demands in 1953, 1954 and 1959. On the positive side, of course, it enabled mineworkers to regain the purchasing power of their wages. But even in this respect it was anomalous. First, where a rise in living costs required wage adjustments, the tenure of awards (usually two to three years) or the union's agreement to defer or waive claims, meant that mineworkers suffered at least short-term falls in real earnings. Second, indexation soon became circumscribed by what, in the government's opinion, the industry could afford to pay. The 1963 award was a case in point: in spite of a wage pause effective from 1959, a 5.7% rise in living costs since 1960, an increase in provincial taxation, and evidence of improved productivity, a general wage increase and many other demands were whittled away, largely because of Emperor's declared operating loss of £82,000.

The legislative controls governing the registration, membership and conduct of trade unions were also consolidated around this time. The 1962 Industrial Associations (Amendment) Ordinance granted the Registrar the right to suspend office-bearers; it increased his powers to expel members; and it raised the penalties for contravention of the ordinance. Two years later, under the Trades Union Ordinance, the full weight of state control was foisted upon the trade union movement in an assortment of regulations. The grounds on which the Registrar could refuse registration were broadened to cover failure to enshrine constitutionally arrangements for the 'custody, distribution, investment of and payment' of union funds. His powers to cancel or suspend registration were increased. Influence over the leadership, membership and conduct of the union extended to the right to disqualify an elected secretary or treasurer if, in the Registrar's opinion,

---

[39] Hutson 1966 : 199 cited in Fieldes 1976.
[40] Cayzer to Local Sec. EGM, 14 Oct. 1952, Vat./unclassified.

the officer did not possess a sufficiently high standard of literacy. Under-age workers could be deprived of voting and committee membership rights. The use of union funds could be circumscribed.

When amendments in 1969 tightened the grip of state control still further, the Alliance government became the butt of sharp criticism in the Legislative Council, in particular because there was a complete lack of corresponding regulations governing the employers' association (FECA), other social organisations or any other body entrusted with public funds. Summing up, the Leader of the Opposition, A. D. Patel, pinpointed the effect of the legislation: 'If the labourers in this colony stay silent it is not because they are contented, it is not because they are satisfied with the conditions and the wages they get but it is because they feel helpless . . .'

At times, management played a conciliatory game. The union's claim of 1960, for example, was held to be 'unrealistic', yet it was given a hearing and a few small concessions were approved. This was no capitulation, but rather a tactical move to forestall an anticipated swing to a more militant leadership. It was also calculated to enhance the company's public image and to court government favours. As Nilsen put it bluntly: 'it would be most unwise, particularly at this time, to close the door to negotiations, more so as I feel the Fiji Government is most anxious to help us with our own financial problems'.[41]

Strike action in the sugar industry a few years earlier had in the opinion of prominent chief and politician Ratu Edward Cakobau demonstrated 'the explosive nature of industrial Fijians'. Against a background of escalating unemployment and declining real wages, the turbulence of the massive 1959 oil workers' strike and riots in the capital had taught another even more salutary lesson. Concessions were clearly advisable in order to prevent rank-and-file workers from 'going completely haywire, even to the extent of dumping Nemani and taking on fellows like Tora or Anthony as their leader'.[42]

The establishment in 1961 of a forum for 'joint consultation' between the mineworkers' union and management reflected a similiar rationale. It offered the union greater accessibility to management as well as a platform. It also enabled it to feel some sense of achievement. The erection of a social hall for single Fijians living in barracks, the devolution of some responsibility to shop stewards, and the introduction of more protective clothing were among the successful submissions. On the whole, though, the Joint Consultative Council (JCC) merely confirmed the weakness of the union's position. There was little pretence of industrial democracy in a mandate that excluded 'wages or conditions of employment' from discussions, and which gave the union an 'advisory' role. Further, talk of 'highest level liaison' and concern about worker welfare paled into insignificance alongside the 'joint' efforts to improve 'efficiency' and the importance

---

[41]   Nilsen to Cayzer, 30 March 1960, Vat./FMWU Arbitration Proceedings.
[42]   Nilsen (Melbourne) to C. W. Cayzer, 21 March 1960, Vat./FMWU—Arbitration Proceedings Aug./Sept. 1957 and March/May 1959. James Anthony and Apisai Tora were protagonists of the 1959 strike, analysis of which can be found in Hempenstall & Rutherford 1984 : 73–86; Sutherland 1984 : 286–99; and the Commission of Enquiry into the Disturbances in Suva in December 1959, CP No. 10, 1960.

attached to discussions about output, accident prevention, discipline and training.[43]

The company's perception of the council as a means of communicating and enforcing its own unilateral policy decisions recalled the disciplinary task it demanded of the ethnic labour committees. It was intended to (and did) perform the useful task of 'ironing out difficulties', 'avoiding unnecessary strikes' and reducing the items appearing on the union's log of claims, because certain grievances could be discussed, though not necessarily redressed, in council meetings.[44] Until 1968, when the JCC was formally detached from union business and membership, meetings proved irregular. They lapsed entirely between 1962 and 1964. The constitutional changes of the late 1960s gave it a complexion and mission not dissimilar to the earlier labour forums.

The appointment of Sakiasi Waqanivavalagi as union secretary in 1962 signalled another development in the combined efforts of the colonial state and the industry to influence union politics. With yet another of its secretaries charged with embezzlement, the union appeared to be in disarray. At the invitation of its executive the colonial administration intervened, suggesting Waqanivavalagi as successor. The appointment was significant. For the first time, miners were led by an outsider who was unfamiliar with the harsh demands of their trade and who had been taught the principles of 'responsible' trade unionism at Oxford and Harvard.

Evidently, management now shared Reay's pragmatic view of a 'live' union. It welcomed the appointment, observing that union affairs 'were restored to normal so that it now constitutes once more a body capable of negotiating and of properly controlling its membership'. It was probably this confidence in the moderate and 'responsible' leadership of the union that permitted Emperor to make the tactful gesture of abolishing the position of Fijian liaison officer the following year. 'In view of the changing times', it announced somewhat obliquely, 'the company no longer considers this position necessary.'

The massive surplus of mine labour during the 1960s gave the union little bargaining power. It was difficult to spurn demands for 'self-abnegation' when this sacrifice was presented as the key to the industry's survival and therefore the only guarantee of continued employment. Rank-and-file unrest, demonstrated in a number of unofficial strikes (four in 1960 alone) and in declining support for the union, appeared a response to the conservatism of the leadership. By 1962, following the union's agreement to a wage pause in exchange for job evaluation, membership figures reached their lowest ebb at 600. An industrial agreement the following year scored a victory for the company that fuelled the discontent. Following protracted negotiations, workers found themselves in receipt of only a nominal concession of 4d.-8d. per shift. Significantly, management recorded that 'certain outside forces would have gained support on the field

[43] Minutes of JCC Meetings June 1961, Aug. & Sept. 1964, March & Oct. 1965, March 1969, Vat./unclassified; and Vat./E. B. Turner Joint Consultative Council Notes.
[44] Personal communication, ex-executive member FMWU & JCC representative, Suva, August 1982.

and we could have had serious trouble' had the agreement not been signed so quickly.[45]

Union support was reactivated by the second half of the decade, but the failure to bring appreciable improvements to wages and conditions of employment (in spite of higher output and revenue) strained internal relations to the point of explosion. As complaints were voiced about Waqanivavalagi's leadership, Apisai Tora, President of a strong Airport Workers' Union, prominent leader of the 1959 Suva strike and candidate of the opposition Federation Party emerged as a favourite for the position of secretary. The leadership challenge testified to a radical swing in worker expectations as well as to the prominence of younger militants within the union. It also indicated a more pronounced political dimension in the industrial struggle. The push by Fijian mineworkers for alignment with a predominantly Indian workers' and farmers' party appeared a significant measure of class unity and consciousness. It showed the extent to which communal loyalties had dissipated, and it spelt a rejection both of traditional authority and the alliance between European capital and the Fijian chiefs on which the governing Alliance Party was founded.

Tora's nomination was invalidated in 1967 under section 31 of the Trades Union Ordinance, which prohibited any person from holding office in more than one union. The radical forces were not to be outdone. By the end of the decade, the election of a young underground miner, Navitalai Raqona, paved the way for a dramatic change in the pattern and temper of organised resistance. Its militant tenor was to be stoked by a change in Emperor's management in 1970. Otherwise the colonial era came to an unremarkable close. Vatukoula's distinctive ethos as a company mining town and its discriminatory structures remained intact, albeit weathered by changing times and the struggles of organised labour.

---

[45]   Memorandum of Interview between Nilsen and FMWU (Barawai and Waqanivavalagi), 13 July 1963, Vat./ Items Given to N. E. Nilsen During Visits.

7   'Whoever has the gold makes the rules'

THE POLITICAL ECONOMY OF MINING IN INDEPENDENT FIJI

Rising mineral exploration in Fiji following independence in 1970 (in base metals as well as gold) reflected a general trend of intensifying foreign investment and control in the Pacific region from the late 1960s. In the case of gold, trading on an open market was a stimulus to activity, but the resurgence of interest in Fiji almost certainly owed something to the more generous mining licence and lease arrangements legislated in the twilight years of colonial rule. Fiji's post-colonial governments were generally committed to promoting foreign investment, private enterprise and industrialisation, and in the mining sector to further developing the country's mineral potential. There was a fair degree of continuity with colonial mining policy, notably in the preference for (and concessions to) larger-scale international capital.

The proliferation of exploration persisted through the 1970s into the following decade, curtailed periodically by uneconomic gold prices, the small-scale and broken nature of identified deposits, or high development costs. Ironically, the fervour coincided with a decline in the industry's contribution to the national economy. Negative growth was recorded throughout most of the 1970s, with average annual rates plummeting to lows of −17% in 1971, −22% in 1977 and −43% in 1978 (see Table 7.1). The pattern contrasted with developments in the economy at large, which, in spite of being hit by recession in the mid-1970s, managed to maintain an average 4-5% growth in real GDP.

Low and declining gold exports were punctuated by a huge drop in gold production around 1978 and a massive 77% fall overall between 1970 and 1980. It was not until 1986 that gold output again began to approach levels typical

Table 7.1   Contribution of the mining industry to Gross Domestic Product and annual growth rates 1970-90*

Year	Mining and quarrying GDP $'000	Total GDP all sectors $'000	Mining and quarrying as a proportion of GDP (%)	Annual growth rate of mining and quarrying sector (%)
1970	2900	148,700	2.0	16.0
1971	2400	157,600	1.5	−17.2
1972	2300	170,000	1.4	−4.2
1973	2200	191,600	1.1	−4.3
1974	1900	196,600	1.0	−13.6
1975	1900	196,800	1.0	0.0
1976	1800	201,800	0.9	−5.3
1977	682	605,726	0.7	22.1
1978	388	616,612	0.1	−43.1
1979	410	690,903	0.1	5.7
1980	344	679,329	0.1	−16.1
1981	427	710,278	0.1	24.1
1982	632	712,152	0.1	48.0
1983	554	683,865	0.1	−12.3
1984	670	741,348	0.1	20.9
1985	829	703,672	0.1	23.7
1986	1269	761,876	0.2	53.1
1987	1272	715,598	0.2	0.2
1988	1898	721,343	0.3	49.2
1989	1875	811,159	0.2	−1.2
1990	1839(p)	854,285(p)	0.2(p)	−2.0(p)

* 1970-76 data (and growth rate for 1977) are based on factor cost at constant 1968 prices.
1977-90 data are based on factor cost at constant 1977 prices.
(p) provisional.

Source: Compiled and calculated from Current Economic Statistics (published and unpublished for 1989-90); Report of Financial Review Committees 1979, 1985.

of the colonial period for the three sisters and achieved at the outset of independence by Emperor alone. A protracted crisis was averted only by generous adjustments to the world gold price, particularly during the early 1970s and at the turn of the 1970-80 decade. Fortuitously, as gold output levels plunged from over 100,000 fine ounces in 1970 to around 25,000 fine ounces in 1980, high premiums realised a near fourfold increase in the value of exports from about $3.5 to $12.5 million.

Fluctuating fortunes in the early 1980s led to a general decline in exploration activities, forcing a number of foreign companies to reduce or wind up their operations. However, price movements were sufficiently favourable (not dropping below $300 an ounce) to help push export receipts to $38.6 million by 1986, an all-time record for the fifth year in succession (see Appendix D) This buoyancy in the gold market, along with other factors, such as poor copra prices, acted as a buffer for mining within Fiji's economy. The industry remained one of the country's highest-ranking exports.

Yet gold's importance to the national economy was all too easily exaggerated. The relative volume of gold earnings depicted a less attractive situation. From

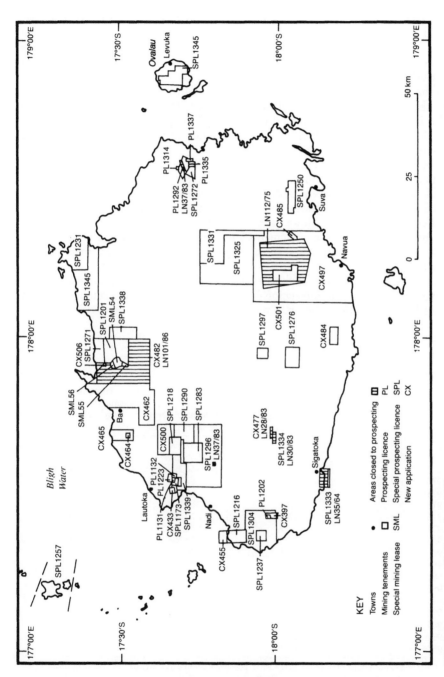

Fiji mining tenements, Viti Levu, June 1991

an average 8.5% of total domestic exports in the last decade of colonial rule, gold receipts dropped to an average 7% between 1970 and 1983, including what was probably an all-time low of 3.9% in 1979 (see Appendix D). The industry's share of GDP, whose estimate of value retained and spent within the local economy included wages and repatriated profits, was still less impressive. In the first half of the 1970s, mining at no stage claimed more than 1.5%, even with the inclusion of the nominal contribution of quarrying. From the late 1970s until well into the 1980s it stabilised at around 0.1% of GDP in spite of improved production levels and a dramatic 26% average growth rate between 1981 and 1986 (see Table 7.1).

In terms of employment, goldmining (as distinct from quarrying and other mining) accounted for an annual average of less than 2% of the total wage- and salary-earners between 1970 and 1983. Moreover, in contrast with the general pattern of employment growth, both its numbers and its share of total employment suffered decline during those years. This was especially so in the crisis years of the late 1970s, when retrenchments forced employment figures down to around 600–700, and the industry's share of employment dropped to less than 1% (see Table 7.2).

A conspicuous feature of the penetration of foreign mining capital was the involvement of several transnational giants. These included the southern African based Anglo-American Group, Consolidated Gold Fields, and Rio Tinto Zinc;

Table 7.2   Employment in the goldmining industry, 1970–87

Year	No. wage & salary earners in goldmining & processing	Total no. Fiji wage & salary earners*	Proportion of total employment contributed by goldmining industry (%)
1970	1694	51,590	3.3
1971	1396	56,210	2.5
1972	1401	58,399	2.4
1973	1454	61,476	2.4
1974	1705	66,998	2.5
1975	1568	69,976	2.2
1976	1381	70,174	2.0
1977	NA	72,383	
1978	699	76,584	0.9
1979	599	78,539	0.8
1980	811	80,484	1.0
1981	811	81,406	1.0
1982	915	78,289	1.2
1983	993	80,075	1.2
1984	1104	78,602	1.4
1985	1114	81,082	1.4
1986	1093	79,854	1.4
1987	1258	78,159	1.6

* These totals underestimate the 'economically active' population because they exclude a number of income-earning categories, as well as non-earning subsistence and other workers.

Source: Data compiled and calculated from Annual Employment Surveys, Fiji Bureau of Statistics 1970–87.

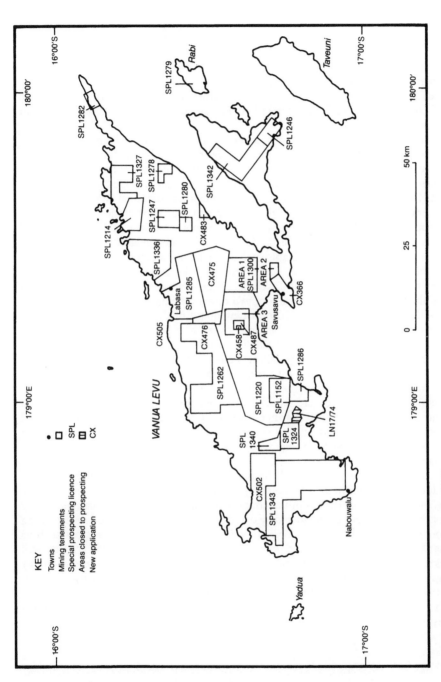

Fiji mining tenements, Vanua Levu, June 1991

American Metal Climax (AMAX), whose wide-ranging mineral interests included a sizeable stake in the Zambian copper industry and operations in Australia, the Philippines, Indonesia and Papua New Guinea; United States Steel Corporation—involved in manganese mining in South Africa and connected with Anglo-American; and the Canadian-incorporated Placer Development Ltd, which also had an interest in the mining industry of Papua New Guinea. With the exception of United States Steel, all operated in Fiji as subsidiaries of Australian parent or holding companies.

Anglo and AMAX were among several companies with which Emperor embarked on joint exploration ventures outside the Tavua basin. Tenement holdings were often massive, and there was a noticeable concentration of prospecting titles in a handful of companies. Anglo's exploration included gold at the old Mt Kasi mine in partnership with the American transnational Newmont Pty Ltd. Operations were conducted through four separate subsidiaries, reflecting the group's decentralised structure and inconspicuous profile.[1] In 1978 Anglo held title, through two of its Fiji subsidiaries, to nearly half a million acres of land.

The operations of mining giants such as Anglo did not entail the marginalisation of the much smaller Emperor, which remained the country's only gold producer and retained its control of the Tavua field. Corporate reorganisation strengthened its ability to safeguard this position, two developments being particularly critical. The first was the birth in 1970 of a new board of directors, which pushed out the old guard, including the Theodore, Wren and Nilsen families, and brought in a fresh controlling group of Australian and New Zealand shareholders headed by New Zealand stockbroker Jeffrey Reid. The second development was the clinching of an eight-year joint venture with Western Mining Corporation, one of Australia's largest companies, with interests ranging from bauxite, iron ore, uranium and nickel to gold, and whose operations extended to North America and Brazil. Emperor's new partner purchased 20% equity in its mine, assumed responsibility for managing all operations at Vatukoula, and embarked on a joint 50:50 exploration venture. Both gold production and profitability improved dramatically.

Australia's pre-eminence in the exploitation of Fiji's mineral resources acquired added significance in the context of Fiji's emerging neo-colonial economy. Singular features of this were the continuing dominance of foreign capital and an increasing external dependence punctuated by deteriorating trade balances and an escalating foreign debt. High levels of foreign ownership persisted in key sectors such as banking/finance (93.2%) and tourism (excluding restaurants) (81.8%) as well as mining and quarrying (99.6%). By the mid-1980s, over 70% of the economy was still estimated to be under foreign control. Australia's near-century-old monopoly of the sugar industry came to an end in 1973, but its position within the Fiji economy became more, rather than less, prominent. It contributed a rising proportion of total foreign investment in the 1960s and 1970s, and by

---

[1]   Innes 1984 : 229-37. Innes's research (1984 : 234) shows that by 1976, Anglo-American 'was involved in over 250 different companies which were active in mining in at least 22 different countries of the world'.

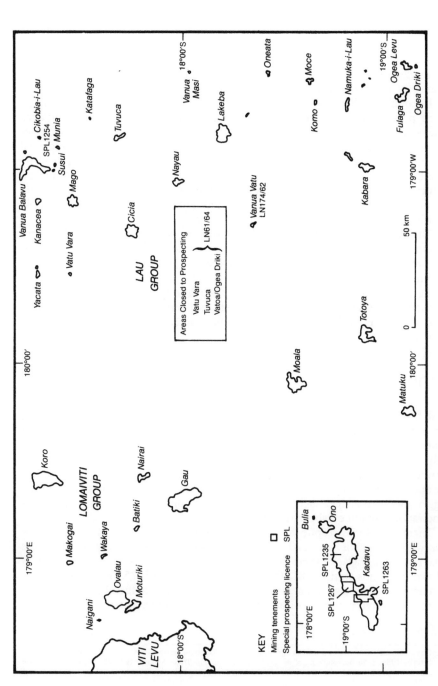

Fiji mining tenements, Lau Group and Kadavu, June 1991

the early 1980s claimed as much as 38% of the total value of Fiji's imports compared with about 26% a decade earlier.[2]

The transfer of political power to the indigenous ruling class did not appear to threaten relations of production in Fiji's goldmining industry. The ideological stamp of the governing Alliance Party gave the mining interests good reason to be confident. The party was pro-business, its chiefly lieutenants were expanding their personal interests in commercial ventures, and early legislative landmarks included the anti-labour Trade Disputes Act of 1973. A favourably disposed post-colonial state could not, however, be presumed, and distinctive of the post-colonial mining lobby was that it was more sharply directed at the chiefly (particularly the Eastern chiefly) élite, which had acquired a hegemonic position within the system of parliamentary democracy bequeathed by Britain. Vatukoula was one of only a few significant employers of ethnic Fijians and it claimed a sizeable portion of more than one electoral constituency.

The continued mobilisation of chiefly support highlighted one of the more enduring and arguably contradictory features of colonial and neo-colonial capitalism: the preference for retaining and exploiting, rather than dismantling, pre-capitalist structures and relations. Now, in the absence of a colonial state, indigenous feudal relations remained integral to the reproduction of mining capital. Profitability became closely linked to the Alliance Party's control of state resources and patronage, and this spurred the mining interests into an active political role during post-independence elections.

RIDING THE CRISES

The first decade of political independence found Fiji's goldmining sector steeped in a series of financial crises, besieged by the problems of recession in the international gold market, and an inflationary capital cost structure, neither of which could be readily solved. Rising operating costs coincident with sluggish upward movements in the gold price after 1968 underpinned the non-viability of operations. So too did the poor (and through the 1970s declining) ore grades, aggravated by practices such as inefficient grade control, ore-breaking techniques and rationalisation of labour resources.

There was some respite for Emperor during the first half of the 1970s as the workings of the free gold market set in motion a period of price increases that rescued its balance sheet from financial loss and even permitted the payment of two dividends worth $F817,000 to EML in 1974 and 1975.[3] Previously uneconomic areas were also opened up to mining. But the benefits of price upswings were significantly eroded by escalating fuel, labour and other material costs. Between

[2] Discussion on these broader trends in Fiji's economy is based on Sutherland 1984 : 336-58; Taylor 1986 : 49-84; Utrecht 1984 : 3-58; Rokotuivuna et al. 1973 : 10-87; and Fiji Trade Reports 1974/75, 1983/84. The trade reports reveal the steady decline in the United Kingdom's proportion of the import bill between 1960 and 1983.
[3] Report of the Committee Appointed to Examine the Economics of the Gold Mining Industry at Vatukoula 1977 (hereafter Report of Enquiry 1977) Appendix H.

1970 and 1976 the company's fuel bill rose from $283,526 to $1,244,654, while its wages and salaries bill shot up from $1,775,240 to $5,255,000. A steady decline in gold production (as much as 35% between 1970 and 1975) and the costly purchase of new plant, both of which resulted from the depletion of higher grade reserves, also militated against a return to sustainable profit margins.

Any hope that company operations could be restored to long-term profitability turned to pure fantasy by the second half of the decade, as gold prices slumped, ore grades deteriorated, production plummeted to spectacular lows, and cost inflation raced away. Between 1976 and 1978 Emperor sustained net operating losses aggregating close to $F5 million. Fiji was not alone, and recession in the Australian goldmining industry took a heavy toll as well, forcing several mines to close. Although Emperor shared in the good fortune of dramatic price surges from the late 1970s, peaking at $US850 in January 1980, two years of profitable operations were constrained by increased expenditure on exploration and development as well as a decision to mine a larger proportion of very low-grade ore from the old Loloma open-cut. From an annual average of 15–20%, the contribution of open-cut mining to tonnage rose to 60%, depressing Emperor's average grade in 1980 to 3.68 g/ton, the lowest in its history.[4] Another price slump in the early 1980s combined with continuing cost increases to incur two successive years of heavy losses for both Emperor's operating and parent companies.

One response to this precarious situation was the restructuring of capital. This involved the formation of several new subsidiaries. As in the 1930s, diversification offered a means of reducing the mining company's dependence on expensive imports. Although investment in ancillary industries diverted financial resources from gold production and development, and several operations later proved unviable, it created a potential source of self-generating local revenue. A major purpose and benefit perceived by Emperor was that it helped to 'spread equity interests' in such a way as to best exploit the group's 'assets and skills'.[5] Comfortable profit margins in the timber, trading and drilling/blasting companies as well as the longer-established electrical power company helped to cushion the mining company's crises in the 1970s. Large losses between 1976 and 1978 were offset by consolidated group profits amounting to over $A2.5m for 1977 and 1978. For three successive years prior to the crisis, profits worth $1.8m in dividends were repatriated to Melbourne.[6]

In this respect the group's decentralised capital structure tended to obscure the extent of EGM's viability during the stranglehold years of recession. Certain factors make it reasonable to assess the company's economic position in the context of group holdings and operations rather than in isolation. As a network of separately managed but (with the exception of one) wholly-owned companies with interlocking directorships, Emperor's subsidiaries formed an integral part of mining operations through their supply of essential goods and services. A

---

[4] Mineral Resources Division 1979, PP 31, 1981; Mineral Resources Dept Annual Report 1980, PP. 50, 1982.
[5] Directors' Report, EML Annual Report 1972. Apart from the mining company, EML's Fiji-incorporated subsidiaries were Emperor Drilling Co Ltd, Emperor Forest Development Ltd, Emperor Timber Industries Ltd, Emperor Trading Co. Ltd and Tavua Power Ltd.
[6] Report of Enquiry 1977 : 15 & Appendix H.

single bank account that housed the group's liquid assets and financed major running costs, such as wages and salaries for all subsidiaries, emphasised this mutuality of interests as well as the concentration of financial control.

Group linkages facilitated transfer pricing. Civil and mechanical engineering, electrical power, welfare and administration were among the services Emperor provided at subsidised rates to its fellow subsidiaries. While the full financial impact of its accounting procedure cannot be assessed, what is known is that the practice of absorbing the cost of 'under-recoveries' from sister companies caused a revenue shortfall for the mining company of at least $160,000 p.a. in the mid-1970s.[7] In 1980 the Mines Department was sufficiently disturbed by the loss of government revenue through 'arms-length transactions' by Emperor to urge the closing of 'tax loopholes involving liaison or transfers with non-mining assets or subsidiaries'. Curiously, neither the interdependence of the companies nor the group's common funding pool, which gave Emperor ready access to liquid capital, inhibited state subsidisation of company operations. The Alliance Government absorbed 80% of planning and construction costs of Vatukoula's 120-acre industrial estate and the full cost of maintaining access roads, water supply, drainage and the disposal of industrial waste. Lengthy tax holidays were among other concessions.

Emperor was able to secure additional financial support from the post-colonial state. Aside from a $2 million government grant that straddled independence, the company received over $356,000 in direct grants and more than $2.5 million in loans on highly favourable terms between 1970 and 1978. Income tax and royalty levies were reduced either as a result of declared losses or on account of exemptions. No company tax was paid between 1970 and 1972 and between 1976 and 1979. Returns in company and export tax between 1970 and 1979 totalled only $793,945 and $284,862 respectively (see Appendix E).

Other concessions helped to shelter corporate profits. An increasingly generous and flexible royalty system extracted payments in only five of the 14 years following independence. Their total value was $621,827, a mere 0.5% of the value of gold earnings (see Appendix E). Changes to the mining law in the late 1960s had permitted, at the Minister's discretion, a yield/profit formula to replace the fixed 5% (f.o.b.) levy on the value of production. The alternative system demanded a basic payment of only 10% of a mine's yield (the difference between operating costs and sales value), and allowed for payments to be deferred until the end of the financial year rather than at the time of export. The switch lowered Emperor's levy from $607,328 to $244,074 in 1980; from $632,823 to nil in 1981; and from $771,016 to nil in 1982.[8] And more was to come.

Confidential tax and lease agreements between Emperor and the Alliance Government in 1983, as the company clinched its joint venture with Western Mining, exemplified the political influence that it still commanded. The issue of four 21-year leases gave the joint venture exclusive rights over more than 3000 acres into the twenty-first century, which contrasted sharply with the usual

---

[7]   Ibid. 15.
[8]   Mineral Resources Dept Annual Report 1984, pp. 72, 1985.

practice of approving annual renewable leases, designed to ensure accountability from mining operators. A bilateral tax agreement extended further favours, notably a seven-year tax holiday on new mines; exemption from (loan) interest withholding tax, fiscal duty on imports and stamp duties; and royalty on the basis of a maximum 2.5% of taxable income, which made payments 'completely independent of annual production level and sales value'. The royalty concession forfeited the country nearly $13 million between 1983 and 1989 alone, raising a mere 0.1% of gold revenue.[9] The seven-year income tax reprieve applied to the rich Nasomo prospect from 1987 stood to lose it even more.

In general, the newly independent Fijian state demonstrated a willingness and capacity to respond to Emperor's crises. The draining of domestic capital reserves this involved consolidated the process of economic underdevelopment that had its roots in the foundation years of the industry. As Fiji's second English-language daily laconically reflected in 1982: 'Large chunks of money sorely needed for development projects elsewhere have had to be diverted to keep Vatukoula operational.'

Other recovery strategies offered further evidence of distorted development, and emphasised the fragile basis on which the mining industry rested. Preferred economy measures of the company included curtailed development and high grading, policies conducive to accelerating rather than arresting the run-down of the mine. Selective and 'pure' mining depleted ore reserves, especially those of higher grade, during the often-prolonged price slumps. Indeed, within two years of independence, Emperor's reserves had dissipated to a point where the mill was deprived of sufficient underground ore of cut-off grade (from 6 to 8 dwt/ton) and was forced to rely on very low-grade open-cut ore to maintain necessary tonnage levels. The 'neglect' of underground exploration provoked stern criticism from a government mining engineer in 1982. What was probably the most important basis of a sound and lasting industry continued to function on an *ad hoc* and irregular basis, 'to whatever extent money happens to be available in any particular year' rather than systematically 'calculated to maintain the ore reserves'.[10]

LABOUR OFFENSIVES AND THE VATUKOULA LAAGER

Another key strategy in Emperor's efforts to deal with the crisis was an assault on labour costs. The mining industry was not alone in transferring losses to its work-force, and company labour policies reflected the state's own austerity measures in the face of the world oil crisis, declining economic growth and a recessionary swing.[11] With few exceptions, the trend in the first decade of independence was for mean wages in mining and quarrying to lag behind those

9   Royalty data supplied by Department of Mineral Resources and Energy, 6 March 1991. Also see Auditor-General's Report, 1989.
10   J. C. Erskine to Minister for Minerals & Energy, 9 Nov. 1982, Dept of Mineral Resources/CY 8 Pt 2.
11   Sutherland 1984 : 335–6; Howard 1985 : 129.

in several other (including lower skilled) sectors, notably construction, transport, service and, a little less consistently, electricity. Only in respect of the agricultural sector were mine wages consistently and markedly superior. This reversed the general pattern of superior or parity earnings compared with most other sectors during the latter half of the 1960s.[12] Moreover, in spite of radical improvements in the gold price, the inferior status of mine earnings persisted into the 1980s, with manufacturing and most other sector earnings surging further ahead. Between 1980 and 1983, the shortfall in mine wages from the industrial average nearly doubled, topping 18% in 1983 (see Table 7.3). This development was undoubtedly a function of an emasculated mineworkers' union, more than once a casualty of deregistration and the withdrawal of company recognition. The position remained largely uncorrected following the imposition of a protracted national wage freeze in 1984. Late in 1986 the companies publicised an hourly base rate for mineworkers of $1.11, about one-third less than the average minimum rate paid to unionised manufacturing workers.[13] In 1987, as gold prices continued to climb (peaking at $633.54 in 1988), daily mean wages in the mining sector of $11.36 fell 10% short of the industrial average.

The pattern of wage distribution told a similar tale. In 1980, 44.5% of wage-earners in the mining sector earned less than $1 per hour. With the exception of agriculture, this was a much higher proportion than most other sectors (22.4% manufacturing; 14.5% construction; 2.5% electricity, gas, water). A large (78%) majority earned less than $1.20, the heaviest concentration for all sectors of the economy. In the higher wage brackets the industry also fared poorly, with only 17.5% of workers earning between $1.20 and $1.60, the lowest proportion for all sectors. A mere 4.2% of mineworkers received between $1.60 and the ceiling of $1.99. The early 1980s brought an upward adjustment in the threshold of mine earnings and witnessed some improvement in their relative status, particularly in the lower levels. For higher-wage earners, however, relative conditions deteriorated.[14]

Mineworkers fell foul of company salvage operations in other ways. Periodic retrenchments, commonly justified as the only alternative to the mine's closure, hit more than 1300 workers (including men of 20-30 years' service) by 1978. For those who held on to their jobs, a pattern of enforced extended leave, transfers and reduced working hours bolstered calls to forgo wage claims or accept wage cuts.[15] Simultaneously, management redoubled its efforts to improve productivity, seeking inspiration for 'increasing mine production and efficiency' in a tour of South African mines. In spite of the retrenchments, impressive tonnages were milled through the early 1970s. Indeed, in 1976, in the throes of financial crisis,

---

[12]   Ministry of Labour Annual Report 1973, Table 8.
[13]   FS Open Letter to Dr Bavadra, 20 Nov. 1986.
[14]   All calculations in respect of wage distribution are based on data provided in Fiji Bureau of Statistics Annual Employment Survey Reports 1980/83.
[15]   General Manager (O. H. Marshall) to Sec. FMWU, 13 Aug. 1970; P. J. Schmidt, Group Manager to S. Waqanivavalagi, Minister for Lands & Mineral Resources, 24 Nov. 1975; P. A. Samuelson, Sec. & Manager of Administration to Ag Sec. FMWU, 21 Dec. 1970; Assistant Labour officer to Ag SLO, 29 Jan. 1971, Labour Dept 36/I/21/16-A.

Table 7.3 Daily mean wages of wage-earners by industry groups, 1960-87

Year	Agriculture	Mining	Manufacturing	Electricity	Construction	Commerce	Transport	Service	All industries
1960	1.27	1.64	1.85	1.81	1.58	1.58	1.86	1.72	1.67
1961	1.32	1.83	1.90	2.03	1.56	1.48	1.89	1.84	1.73
1962	1.30	1.77	1.85	1.74	1.57	1.48	1.85	1.79	1.70
1963	1.42	1.81	1.99	1.95	1.60	1.65	1.87	1.81	1.76
1964	1.50	1.53	2.03	1.91	1.83	1.49	1.81	1.61	1.79
1965	1.48	1.92	1.98	2.04	1.71	1.84	1.83	1.76	1.83
1966	1.61	1.98	2.13	2.24	2.06	1.94	1.97	1.83	1.96
1967	1.62	1.99	2.20	2.33	2.14	1.89	1.97	1.87	2.01
1968	1.58	2.37	2.28	2.78	2.24	2.11	2.23	2.22	2.20
1969	1.78	2.38	2.44	2.41	2.40	2.19	2.21	2.38	2.32
1970	1.97	2.63	2.55	2.53	2.71	2.35	2.52	2.59	2.47
1971	2.13	2.76	2.69	2.99	2.88	2.47	2.86	3.02	2.72
1972	2.39	3.06	3.21	2.99	3.21	3.09	3.38	3.12	3.08
1973	3.12	3.96	3.78	4.22	4.11	4.05	4.11	4.05	3.98
1974	4.49	5.06	4.82	5.01	5.06	4.91	5.28	5.09	4.89
1975	4.98	5.16	6.19	6.41	6.37	5.68	6.35	5.96	5.97
1976	5.03	7.27	6.64	7.22	7.16	6.54	7.04	6.48	6.68
1977	5.76	7.01	6.87	7.97	7.70	6.89	7.69	7.16	7.11
1978	6.67	7.22	8.10	8.98	8.21	7.26	8.46	7.94	7.89
1979	6.88	7.32	8.48	9.42	8.69	7.85	9.10	8.29	8.48
1980	7.44	8.40	9.52	9.12	9.36	8.88	9.76	9.72	9.28
1981	6.24	8.48	10.56	10.96	10.40	10.24	10.56	10.44	10.16
1982	6.16	9.28	11.20	12.96	12.00	10.32	11.76	11.04	10.96
1983	6.96	9.60	11.92	14.64	11.84	11.04	12.24	12.24	11.68
1984	8.64	10.56	12.00	14.56	11.92	11.20	12.56	11.76	11.84
1985	8.32	10.48	12.16	14.96	12.24	11.36	13.20	12.08	12.00
1986	8.24	10.72	11.84	15.20	12.40	11.28	13.20	12.08	12.00
1987	8.26	11.36	12.32	16.16	13.28	11.68	14.08	12.72	12.64

Source: Current Economic Statistics 1960-July 1990.

the company proudly recorded its success in 'outperform(ing) its goldmining counterparts in Australia'.

Vatukoula's contract bonus system was also adjusted and expanded to cover a larger proportion of the work-force. Special productivity schemes were tried, one of which was aimed at raising output per manshift from 1.77 to 2.2 tons and four-weekly throughput from 21,000 to 26,000 tons. Contract bonuses, converted to an exclusive contract system for miners in the late 1970s, gave workers the opportunity to raise the level of their basic wages or, as in the 1977 scheme, to offset the hardship of a wage reduction. But in the shift to payment according to productivity the system also offered the company a means of extracting a higher labour surplus. Rewards to workers were not necessarily commensurate with higher productivity, as earnings were partly determined by factors beyond their control, such as the type of ground being drilled and productivity formulas, including bonus thresholds, were determined unilaterally by the company. 'One stoping bonus . . . would appear to be little more than an over-award payment', observed a company of mining consultants in 1972.

Moreover, the raising of bonus thresholds could put the higher bonuses out of reach for even the most industrious workers, while for spells of illness, authorised leave or production delays, workers' pay reverted to the hourly rate. The absence from worker pay-slips of basic information relating to job description (which management described as 'completely superfluous') and hours of work/absences (an 'unnecessary workload') generated additional frustrations about the contract system.

A diverse range of wage regulatory devices, many of them colonial in origin, persisted to some extent. Experience was still not a significant determinant of wages, and job classifications, including categories such as 'boy' (as in head boy, shift boy, survey boy, toolroom boy), 'hand', 'helper' or 'assistant' continued to minimise distinctions between ordinary labouring and specialised mining jobs as well as generally to depress wage levels. In 1970 qualified miners, truck drivers and leading hand timbermen, pipe fitters, plate layers, riggers and grizzly operators were categorised as semi-skilled; and at 30 cents (surface) and 34.5 cents (underground) an hour, the highest-grade workers were paid only 5 cents an hour (or $2 a week) more than those on the basic unskilled rate. While wider wage differentials sustained a gulf of well over 50% between leading hands and labourers by later in the decade, Emperor's wage system still maintained nominal distinctions between qualified miners and unskilled labourers. By 1977 a grade 1 open-cut miner was paid only 9 cents an hour (or $3.82 a week) more than a new (unskilled) recruit or trainee carpenter.[16]

In the post-colonial era, training and localisation occurred on a larger scale at higher occupational levels, but supervisor-, like worker-training still took place essentially on the job, a situation corrected only partially by the introduction of a formal apprenticeship scheme for tradesmen. Overall, mobility, particularly for Fijians, remained limited, and, in spite of the cost, the mining company retained its preference for a colonial division of labour which kept the repre-

---

[16]   Vat./Goldmining Industrial Agreement, 1970; Vat./Group Personnel Dept Classifications & Rates 30 May 1977.

sentation of Fijians in supervisory and salaried positions to a minimum. In 1977 a commission of inquiry into the industry noted that Vatukoula's racial division of labour had been marginally reformed in the 'lower middle levels' only. 'Management's promised endeavours have wrought little change in the middle and upper echelons . . . localisation has not made much progress over the past seventeen years.'[17] And the pattern persisted much later. While the Joint Venture's Fijian and Indian workers comprised 83% of total employees in 1990, only 14% of them occupied salaried staff positions, with 3% classified as senior staff.[18]

Steady inflation not only reduced disposable incomes from the mid-1970s but caused real wages to decline until a wage award in 1981. Gross earnings were also corroded by mandatory contributions to the cost of protective clothing, worker insurance premiums, education, superannuation and medical care, electricity and, from 1972, housing (rent and, for the minority able to respond to the offer of home ownership, loan repayments). Deductions depressed take-home pay, even for higher-earning contract workers, to levels below subsistence, and paved the way for a dependence on advances and credit from the company supermarket. The credit system ensnared workers within the debt-trap of truck and monopsonistic retail prices, and was a useful avenue through which the company recouped a significant portion of its wages bill. In many respects the system resembled the settler plantations of the nineteenth century.

The persistence of unsound working conditions underground and in the mill was another product of cost-cutting. These came under fire from the 1977 government inquiry, 'appalled' by the 'noxious [roaster] fumes' and 'high humidity and temperature in the lower levels of the mine', which pushed wet and dry bulb recordings to a parity of more than 100 degrees and temperatures to above 97 degrees Fahrenheit. Poor air-circulation, particularly in confined stoping heads where touring committee members found conditions 'literally unbearable', aggravated the discomfort of the underground working environment as did the 'staccato pounding of the eardrums' by pneumatic drilling. Four years later the 'poor ventilation' on sub-levels and stopes at depths of between 1300 feet and 1400 feet warranted an official compliance order for the provision of additional ventilation equipment.

Community living standards remained as much a product of discriminatory policies as of cost-effective initiatives. Housing, like organised recreation, was no longer explicitly organised around ethnicity or race, but the distribution of family accommodation, like access to the bowling and golf clubs, could and did achieve much the same purpose by being a function of occupational status. In the area of recreation, a staff qualification for club membership excluded the majority of Fijians by virtue of their ranking as hourly-paid workers.

With the exception of the barracks where Fijian, Rotuman and Part-European workers could be found in mixed accommodation, the segregated pattern of housing along with its widely varying standards were also abandoned really only in name. For most Fijian families, village settlements still comprised the crude

---

[17] Report of Enquiry 1977 : 28 & 32. Also see FMWU Final Submission to Board of Enquiry 1974.
[18] Wages and housing data are provided in the company supplement, *FT* 9 March 1990.

iron and timber structures of pre- and post-war years, ever plagued by the problems
of poor maintenance, inadequate roofing, toilet, cooking and washing facilities,
as well as polluted water supplies. Even company data acknowledged in 1990
that 72% of Fijians in company accommodation occupied the smallest and poorest-
quality houses. The long-discredited use of the single men's barracks for family
accommodation was also still in evidence with the two remaining barracks in
1992, cramming whole families into 18 feet by 12 feet single rooms. Women
cooked outside on open fires sheltered by fragile corrugated-iron lean-tos. A handful
of open, unpartitioned showers and toilet cubicles in a single block gave no
privacy to male and female barrack occupants. They were dilapidated, unhygienic
and dirty.[19]

In August 1985, following two reported cases of typhoid in the mining town
the previous year, government health inspectors drew fresh attention to the serious
health hazards posed by a contaminated river water supply. They called for an
urgent upgrading of water facilities if 'an epidemic outbreak' of typhoid or cholera
was to be averted. Water sampling revealed that untreated water, on which
mineworkers and their families were dependent, was 'unfit for human consumption'
and contained 'extremely dangerous' levels of toxic waste. There were 'occasions
when up to eight parts per million of the poisonous gas cyanide had seeped
into the river'. In 1990 traces of cyanide were found in hundreds of dead fish
in the Nasivi river, and a World Health Organisation report confirmed a cyanide
concentration as high as 40 mg/l in creek water downstream from one of Emperor's
tailings dam where workers and their families bathed, washed and fished.[20]

An institutionalised paternalism bore witness to the resilience of colonial
structures, with Emperor retaining considerable discretion over the lives of its
employees and their families. Today, direct or indirect involvement in the financial
and administrative affairs of Vatukoula's four schools, two churches, four clubs,
and sports fields underscores the residual trappings of a company-run town.
Emperor is landlord, doctor, creditor, water supplier and rubbish collector for
a large proportion of its employees. Its influence is typified in its relationship
with the town's only secondary school, appropriately named after Nils Nilsen,
Emperor's longest-serving and most imposing of managers: its management of
the school's financial affairs, its grants, its role as financial guarantor, and its
appointment of the school trustees in whom responsibility for financial policy
and control of school property is vested.

In post-colonial times a mining town operating on racialist and authoritarian
principles was a source of political embarrassment. Official criticism of the
'anachronism' of a company town policy that tended to 'frustrate self-determination
and depress self-respect' echoed the winds of political change. So did the calls
for 'emancipating social control'.[21] None of these pressures was enough, however,
to elicit decisive action.

[19] Personal inspections, Dec. 1989 and Jan. 1992.
[20] FT 17 Aug. 1985; H. J. Bavor, WHO Assignment Report 20 Nov.–10 Dec. 1989, 19 Feb. 1990.
[21] Report of Enquiry 1977 : 27.

MORE RESISTANCE

In the aftermath of independence, sustained waves of conflict characterised labour-capital relations in the mining industry.[22] Between 1977 and 1978 they reached a peak with the close of the Emperor mine and mass retrenchments. The first year of independence gave a taste of what was to come: over a period of six months between 1970 and 1971 a total of eight work stoppages brought 1144 men out, costing the industry 6881 work hours. Numerous unofficial strikes featured in 1972 and another peak followed in 1975 when 36,476 man-days were lost. While the nagging issue of employment conditions was a prominent catalyst of industrial conflict, three related concerns emerged centre stage, particularly from the second half of the 1970s: the right to work, the right of association, and the right to union recognition.

Growing labour militancy was not peculiar to the mining industry, but it mirrored a highly charged industrial climate in both the public and private sectors. The 1973 Trade Disputes Act substantially increased state control over the trade union movement, reactivating—for the first time since 1958—compulsory arbitration and 'binding' awards. With its accompanying penal sanctions, compulsory arbitration threw Fiji well out of step with twenty-year-old international labour standards. The legislation also outlawed strikes in various instances, for example, 'sympathy' strike action, where either settlement procedures had not been 'exhausted' or the tenure of an agreement or award had not run its course. The definition of essential services was broadened, thereby narrowing the parameters of legitimate strike action and erecting novel mechanisms of labour (and thus wage) control. Buttressing these controls were penalties more severe than any pre-existing sanctions.

The Fiji Trades Union Congress (FTUC) secured a few concessions through active opposition, which tipped the country's strike record at an average 60 strikes a year in the mid-late 1970s. But the constraints of both the new labour legislation and the establishment in 1977 of the Tripartite Forum soon began to take their toll. The establishment of tripartism, the formal structure promoting dialogue and conciliation between employers, government and organised labour, could perhaps be seen as an apogee of longstanding colonial and post-colonial initiatives to neutralise organised labour and to substitute conciliation for conflict.

The radical swing of the mineworkers' union was derived from conditions of hardship and alienation as well as from a more assertive leadership in the face of an authoritarian management. The temperaments and attitudes of the union general secretary, Navitilai Raqona, and Emperor's chairman, Jeffrey Reid, added a crucial element of instability to day-to-day industrial relations. Spontaneous

---

[22] Unless otherwise indicated, discussion in this section is based on primary source material contained in the correspondence files of the Labour Department (series 36/1/16-A) and the FTUC; Annual Reports of the Labour Department 1970-83; Arbitration proceedings of July 1980 between EGM and the NUM, which the writer attended; and company and union documents (including log of claims and log of counter-claims). The two national newspapers (*Fiji Times* and *Fiji Sun*) provide quite extensive coverage of developments at Vatukoula over the years under review. Interviews between 1980 and 1990 with management, union officials and workers were also instructive.

strike threats, many of which were later withdrawn, were issued regularly. They led to counter-demands from the company for apologies and retractions, as well as retaliatory threats. Reid's opposition to trade unionism was stated quite openly. And on his office desk was prominently displayed a plaque inscribed with the words 'Remember the golden rule: Whoever has the gold makes the rules.'

Hyman argues that in spite of the success with which labour unions have been drawn into managing and disciplining rank-and-file workers, the struggle of the working class continues to be directed at circumscribing or checking managerial control.[23] Such a claim is firmly supported by evidence in the Fiji mining industry, where strikes and other industrial action were commonly prompted by unilateral management decisions over worker transfers, retrenchments, union recognition, and disciplinary action against workers, particularly suspensions. The 1980 industrial agreement, for example, specified that two warnings within a year for 'lateness', 'incompetence', 'absenteeism' or 'malingering' rendered a worker 'liable for dismissal for the third offence'. A recurring demand of Raqona was that the union be consulted over such issues. It was a significant attempt to democratise decision-making in the work process and, to this end, to broaden the scope of company recognition of the union as the legitimate representative of worker interests.

But the militancy of Vatukoula miners was also symptomatic of dissipating traditional values, a process that had its roots in colonial times. Worker submission to managerial authority had been closely linked to cultural mores of obedience to chiefs. A powerful ideological barrier against unionism and industrial and political organisation on class lines had been constructed from this, although the tenuous basis of commoner loyalties to chiefs and their colonial benefactors had at times been exposed. Post-independence developments, however, particularly the rising levels of urbanisation, wage employment, urban unemployment and Western education, hastened the decline of customary values and controls, in particular the unquestioned allegiance to chiefs. They fed a growing restiveness, if not disaffection within the Fijian working class.

While post-colonial industrial legislation continued to contain labour resistance within 'responsible' parameters, it was not necessarily crippling. Nor did organised mine labour perceive it as such. The union frequently appealed for industrial relations machinery to be activated and showed a willingness to discipline its members and to play a role in the wider process of social control. The union scored a few important victories from arbitration and conciliation rulings, which may have convinced its leadership to stick to the well-trodden path of institutionalised dialogue and negotiation. However restrictive, the machinery offered mineworkers a degree of legal protection or security and a sanctuary from the hazards of solitary confrontation with their employer.

Vatukoula reached a critical juncture in February 1977, when for the first time operations ceased and Emperor's board ordered the closure of the mine following the breakdown of conciliation proceedings and a resulting strike. An official inquiry proved sympathetic to union charges of racial discrimination and labour ex-

---

[23]   Hyman 1972 : 98.

ploitation, tracing the causes of hardening relations, in particular the hostility between Reid and Raqona, to shortcomings in company administration and policy. Emperor was castigated for its poor system of internal communication, its anti-unionism, and its autocratic and paternalistic management. The chances of 'true industrial peace' emerging were firmly discounted so long as the company remained 'the largest determinant in deciding, for good or ill, social policy'.[24]

But the 1977 committee of inquiry also reiterated the ideology of responsible trade unionism, implicit in which were that industrial demands should be circumscribed by the 'national interest'; that the union should exercise its power 'responsibly'; and that it should ensure that it never 'betrayed' the trust placed in it. Moral pressures such as these were reinforced by the economic sacrifices demanded of union members, notably a 5% wage cut for unskilled (hourly paid) workers—the company's condition for resuming operations.

Far from improving worker/management relations, the inquiry thrust the industry into further conflict. Emperor's failure to implement its recommendations, save the wage cut, became a festering grievance. It paved the way for the outbreak of a protracted and bitter strike early in 1978, when, in a bid to arrest a continuing profit crisis, the company announced its intention to scale down operations and lay off up to 1000 workers. For the first time the miners pressed the case for nationalisation. And, for a while, the possibility of a government purchase of the mine was seriously entertained.

The task of mounting a successful strike was formidable. The union was faced with well-tested strike-breaking tactics, the pressure of visiting Alliance parliamentarians, and the absence of a strike fund. In the circumstances, a three-month withdrawal, which secured Emperor's agreement to participate in conciliation talks and to reinstate about half the 200–300 laid-off strikers, was no mean achievement. But it could scarcely be construed as a victory. Overall, the 1978 strike sapped the union of its energy and morale, ending with numbers badly depleted and a large debt. Its two telephones were disconnected for failure to pay bills, and it was forced to take its four permanent staff off the payroll. In May the union's clubhouse was gutted by fire, causing some $40,000 worth of damage.

Losing the battle for nationalisation was another mark of the union's failure. So was its inability to get more than a proportion of the retrenched workers reinstated. By November 1978 some 2000 Vatukoula residents—men, women and children—were being prepared for repatriation to their home villages or for resettlement outside Vatukoula. Nearly two years later, fewer than 20% of the workers had been reabsorbed into the industry. Amid allegations that he had mismanaged union funds, Raqona left for England to undertake a two-year course of study in industrial law at Oxford, leaving the mantle of union leadership to revert to his predecessor, Alliance parliamentarian Sakiasi Waqanivavalagi. A few months later the legacy of colonial labour policy dealt the *coup de grâce*. In the rigorous controls of the Trade Union Act was found a case for the union's deregistration.

---

[24]   Report of Enquiry 1977 : 27.

The reincarnation of the miners' union, as the National Union of Mineworkers (NUM), in 1979 sparked off one of the most furious and prolonged battles in Vatukoula's history over company recognition. Ultimately it became an issue for the national trade union body, prompting an FTUC black ban on all Emperor's operations. A compulsory recognition order was followed by a request for voluntary conciliation and (when this failed) compulsory arbitration, which awarded a 10.5% rise in the basic wage along with other benefits. Emperor's claim that the strike was illegal was rejected by the state, and another official investigation into the problems of Vatukoula's miners was mooted.

The 1980 dispute and its outcome confirmed the legitimacy of union grievances, but exposed the weaknesses of organised mine labour. They laid bare the contradictions and biases inherent in the industrial conciliation process. The compulsory recognition order was issued but not enforced. None of the sanctions available to the Tripartite Forum was applied against the mining company for its failure to comply with voluntary recognition guidelines. As in earlier years, conciliation proceedings and compulsory arbitration, while often welcomed by organised mine labour, were symbols of state control over the working class. Compulsory arbitration automatically demanded that striking workers return to work pending the outcome of deliberations. Further, the state's prosecution of essential workers and strike leaders under the Trade Disputes Act looked incongruous alongside its failure to investigate, under provisions of the same legislation, union charges of company victimisation and intimidation of strikers or strike sympathisers.

Emperor boycotted the conciliation talks, withdrew from arbitration, and did not take immediate steps to implement the award. It pulled out of the Tripartite Forum, contested the validity of the compulsory arbitration order, and refused to reinstate all striking workers. While subsequently overturned in the Fiji Court of Appeal, the company's Supreme Court challenge postponed deliberations by nearly a year. By the time the arbitration award of September 1981 confirmed the union's right to recognition, more than two years had elapsed. That period proved crucial. It placed the company in a position to withdraw recognition legitimately, confident that even if the tribunal ruled in favour of the union, its dwindling support had deprived it of the 50% of eligible members necessary to challenge the withdrawal. It was a vicious cycle.

The industrial backdrop against which Emperor entered the concluding stages of its new lease and tax negotiations with the Fiji government in 1983 (and clinched its joint-venture deal with Western Mining) was therefore quite favourable. A crippled union limped along, stripped of recognition and with its financial membership well short of 50%. It was unable to persuade management to look at a log of claims. The union operated out of a run-down office, did not maintain proper financial records and was extremely low in both funds and morale. There was not to be another strike until 1991, more than ten years later. In one of many ironic twists in Vatukoula's history, the scenario was to be almost a repeat performance of 1980.

EPILOGUE: OF MINING AND MILITARY MIGHT

The complexities of events immediately preceding and following two military coups in 1987 cannot be done justice in an overview of developments in post-colonial Fiji. However, certain observations relevant to the current study should be made. The birth in 1985 of the multi-ethnic Fiji Labour Party committed to a broad programme of social welfare and reform, which challenged neo-colonial structures of privilege, patronage and power, was an historical first in the decade following Emperor's crisis years of the mid-1970s. So was that Party's surprise election victory (as part of a coalition) two years later, and its forcible removal from office after a month by a military coup.

All of these events had a direct bearing on Fiji's goldmining industry, with company sensitivities heightened by the Labour Party's specific plans for the mining industry, including support for the miners' union, a proposed independent inquiry, and, for a while, a nationalisation policy that embraced an ownership and management stake for workers. Labour's support for the Nasomo landowners who were locked in battle with both the Joint Venture and the government over mining under their land was more grist to the mill. The rich Nasomo ore promised a prosperity that would match the heyday of the three Emperor, Loloma and Dolphin mines. A legal challenge by indigenous landowners was therefore more than just an embarrassment for them. Public allegations of a role in the pre-coup destabilisation process were a small price to pay for regaining a preferred political environment. More significantly, perhaps, a case for Reid's deportation based on illegal political activities did not survive the overthrow of the new government, led by Timoci Bavadra.[25]

In terms of the profitability of company operations, the 1987 military coups did not appear unduly dislocating. Unlike most major exports, including sugar, copra and coconut oil, whose output fell in the year following the coups, gold production rose by a substantial 38% to 4,128,877 grams. Coupled with the beneficial effects of two devaluations of the Fiji dollar, which enhanced the value of gold sales, this performance offset a small drop in the gold price between 1987 and 1988 to produce $F84 million in foreign exchange. In relative terms, gold exports rose appreciably to 19% of total domestic exports, although the sector's contribution to GDP remained low at around 0.3%.

Still unresolved, the struggle of the Nasomo landowners evokes haunting echoes from the past.[26] The alienation of around 1000 acres of their land in a 21-year special mining lease to the Joint Venture took place without prior consultation and in spite of written objections. The conditions of the lease gave the mining companies rights to mine in the vicinity of their village, in an area that accom-

---

[25] Personal communication, Joeli Kalou, Coalition Minister for Labour & Immigration, 7 May 1990.

[26] The analysis that follows is based on written (including legal) documentation that forms part of a private collection of papers belonging to the late Prime Minister and Labour-NFP Coalition Leader, Dr T. U. Bavadra; discussions with Nasomo elders and villagers in March 1988 and December 1989; numerous discussions between 1985 and 1989 with Dr Bavadra and Tevita Fa, legal counsel to the plaintiffs; and attendance at a Supreme Court hearing of the case in Lautoka on 11 March 1988.

modated a burial ground, a water catchment area, streams and farming land.[27]

The dispute is already complicated by the state's challenge to the legal status of the Nasomo villagers as landowners. The people's case argues that the Constitution as well as mining and land laws have been violated by the co-defendants; that there have been breaches of faith, acts of trespass, unlawful dispossession and appropriation of extracted minerals, physical danger and environmental damage. The essence of the landowners' plea is: that the 1983 mining lease to the Joint Venture should be declared 'null and void'; and that the mining companies should be required either to reimburse the owners for all revenue derived from the sale of their resources or to pay compensation worth $10 million.

A historic case, the Nasomo struggle draws attention to the conflicting concepts of land tenure inherent in Western land law and traditional Fijian culture. Hegemonic Western values have their roots in the period before the First World War: in the illegal 'squatter' status ascribed to the first Nasomo settlers and the state's attempts to remove them from CSR freehold. They are also a product of early amendments to colonial mining law that contrived the (non-traditional) distinction between surface and subterranean tenure; vested sovereignty over all subterranean mineral wealth in the Crown; and decisively undermined the protection of native land-rights prescribed by colonial land law.

As the blueprint for colonial mining economies, such proprietorial claims by the state have not always been relinquished following political independence. Nor are they exercised uniformly. For Fiji's mineral-rich neighbour, Papua New Guinea, for example, where similar contradictions between customary and colonial land law have underpinned an exceptionally violent struggle on the island of Bougainville, successive governments have developed a system, however contentious, of redistributing a portion of royalty revenue to native landowners. They have also acquired their own equity in foreign mining ventures. More recently, the Papua New Guinea state has shown signs of 'moving towards a concept of land ownership which includes the subterranean minerals'.[28] Unlike Papua New Guinea, the more centralised post-colonial governments of Fiji have never ascribed to local landowners, or even to local government, any rights over the division of mining revenue, notably royalties—at least not before the Labour Party put this on its agenda. Nor have any avenues for participating in the formulation of mining policy been open to them.

˙ Ironically, the purported paramountcy of indigenous rights in post-coup Fiji has made little impact on the country's mining law, which continues to do violence to customary land-rights, and to render the prerogatives of the *taukei* subordinate to those of the state. This is exemplified in the continued reservation to the Crown of all minerals regardless of land ownership or tenure and in the fact that ownership rights extend only to 15 metres below the surface. The state is empowered to overrule the right of owners or occupiers to withhold their

[27] Writ and Statement of Claim, Supreme Court, Lautoka, 25 March 1986; Plaintiffs—Isimeli Naivitu, Serevi Naitokatoka, Solomoni Vuki, Taniela Koto, Apisai Leone, all of Nasomo Village, Vatukoula and Timoci Uluivuda Bavadra of Laucala Beach Estate, Suva; and Defendants—The Attorney-General, EGM Co. Ltd, Western Mining Corporation (Fiji) Ltd; Special Mining Lease No. 55, Reg. No. 15102, 25 March 1983.
[28] Standish 1989 : FA13.

consent to mining or prospecting operations in certain areas. And while the new 1990 Constitution proposes that an undefined proportion of mining royalties may henceforth accrue to landowners, this is only in respect of *future* mining agreements. Emperor's operations—the most lucrative of which is on Nasomo land—are implicitly exempted, at least until the 1983 agreements expire. In the case of Nasomo, a 'new' mine, this will not be until 2011. If royalties are introduced for the *taukei*, distribution would almost certainly replicate the surface rental system, whose principal beneficiaries are the chiefs.

But there is another anomaly, which may prove a more serious liability to the country in the long term. The Constitution makes no distinction between native and other landowners in prescribing royalties; and, with the exception of the disputed Nasomo property, all of Emperor's mining continues to take place on company freehold. Should the new royalty provisions be applied to Vatukoula in the future, it could, ironically, mean absolving the company (as the landowner) from at least a part of the royalty levy, thereby reducing its already nominal contribution to national revenue.

As for the Aboriginal people of Australia, the Maoris of New Zealand, and the native Indians of North and South America as well as Canada, the encroachments into indigenous land-rights have inflicted greater deprivation because of a traditional ideology which emphasises a non-material, spiritual affinity with the land. While the freehold status of Nasomo land technically distinguishes it from an ancestral homeland, denying the dispute the status of a customary land matter, over 60 years of occupation of the area have significantly narrowed the conceptual divide. At least two generations have been born, raised and buried in Nasomo, and the migration of the first settlers is firmly grounded in ancestral bidding and prophecy. From these special circumstances have sprung a consciousness and sentimental attachment to the land that no amount of deftly contrived legal arguments can erase.

For the Nasomo people, there is no wholesale rejection of mining, and the opportunities it can provide to improve living standards, through employment and infrastructural development, are keenly recognised. There is a very simple desire for a greater degree of control over the means of production and the distribution of mining benefits. Broad parallels can be drawn with the Bougainville landowners at the Panguna mine where, behind the actions of a revolutionary army, have lain deepseated frustrations over increasing landlessness, poverty and marginalisation. At the heart of these is dissatisfaction over the system of distribution.

Retrospect and ahead

The capitalisation of Fiji's mineral wealth represents a major development in the country's economic history. In 1990 the value of its gold exports fell just short of $F70 million, 12% of Fiji's total export income. Annual production in the late 1980s was in the region of 600,000 tonnes per annum deriving from open-cut as well as deep-level mining to below 2000 feet, and yielding around 4000 kg of unrefined gold. Between 1983 and 1988 the country's third-ranking revenue-earner achieved an annual average growth rate of 30%.

But the story is not all romantic. An extractive primary industry aimed solely at the international market and controlled and fully owned by a foreign monopoly now operating out of the Isle of Man tax haven evokes images of economic imperialism in its classic form. High export earnings and respectable growth rates mean little in terms of real and sustainable development unless they are evaluated alongside corporate production, financial and labour policies, or even government taxation of the industry. Similarly, the channelling of indigenous labour reserves out of a redistributive subsistence economy into an austere industrial environment for little reward recalls the well-trodden path of mining capitalism in other parts of the Third World. The joint venture's wages bill of $8.45 million for 1989 claimed just 12% of gold earnings, 16% if we include the earnings of salaried staff who form part of management.[29] These and many other features of Fiji's goldmining experience must inevitably raise questions about the nature and beneficiaries of mining development. They are questions all the more pertinent at a time when Fiji and the Pacific region at large are experiencing a resurgence of interest by foreign companies in their mineral (particularly gold and copper) resources.

In the Third World the large-scale use and abuse of productive land resources by mining companies is one manifestation of the deleterious environmental impact and general unsustainability of mining 'development'. The Pacific's tiny phosphate islands of Nauru, Banaba and Makatea (like Papua New Guinea's copper- and gold-rich island of Bougainville and nickel-rich New Caledonia) bear the ugly scars of depredation. On Bougainville, prior to closure in 1989, no less than 135,000 tons of toxic tailings were dumped into the river, thence to the sea, each day. More recent disclosures of the contamination of water supplies and marine life by the BHP-managed Ok Tedi gold and copper mine provide another piece of this depressing mosaic. Australia too is not exempt from such destructive development.[30]

Nor is Fiji. The Vatukoula example may not be as extreme, but it is significant that the operations of Emperor and its associates currently tie up more than 15,000 acres of land in mining leases, while their tailings dams (all with outlets into the main river system and creeks and occupying over 600 acres of good land) are situated upstream from the principal water catchment area for the several thousand people who live in and around the nearby Tavua township.

Notwithstanding the modest beginnings of minting legal tender gold coins by a new Emperor subsidiary, Pacific Sovereign Mint Ltd, the current system of exporting Fiji gold in an unrefined state (bullion bars having a purity of just over 80%) is consistent with the general pattern of transnational operations. As Crough and Wheelwright observe, the global organisation of the production process by TNCs is rationalised according to the maximisation of corporate profits rather than the interests of host countries.[31] Heavy reliance on imported sources of capital equipment, technology and senior management and technical skills is also a product of transnational control over Fiji's mining sector. In conjunction

---

[29] 'The Facts About Vatukoula', four-page advertising supplement of Vatukoula Joint Venture, FT 9 March 1990.
[30] Hughes & Sullivan 1989 : 38–9; Viviani 1970; Crough & Wheelwright 1982 : 84.
[31] Ibid. 82.

with mechanisms such as transfer pricing, both processes constitute leakages out of the country's share of its mineral wealth. Both, directly or indirectly, aggravate Fiji's trade deficit and consolidate its economic dependence.

Crough and Wheelwright make the point in respect of Australia that it is 'not coincidental . . . that [it] remains as a large producer of minerals but accounts for only a very small proportion of the world production of processed minerals'.[32] Similarly, Norman Girvan's observations of corporate imperialism would appear to hold true for the Fiji mining industry: 'the possibilities of utilizing the resource as a basis of backward and forward linkages within the national economy are restricted by its already existing use as a basis of backward and forward linkages within the corporate economy.'[33]

Employment and incomes represent tangible benefits from mining, but their importance relative to national employment statistics and gold earnings has been consistently small. Since the birth of the industry, employment figures for the Vatukoula companies have hovered between 1000 and 2000, with prolonged spells when work-force contractions forced numbers down into the hundreds. While output levels are higher today, workers number far fewer (closer to 1000) than they did in the 1930s. Gross employment figures also conceal the structural peculiarities of job and wage distribution, notably the limited penetration of senior and higher-paying jobs by nationals (particularly Fijians and Indians). The tradition of retaining an expensive nucleus of expatriate staff and skilled workers is as old as the industry.

Today, the average miner's gross annual earnings, inclusive of overtime, are around $8000. An élite group of contract miners command between $50–$60 an eight-hour shift, and some of what the company calls its 'better' miners earn in excess of $10,000. But hourly wages for experienced leading hands and tradesmen peak at $3.65 an hour, with the unskilled base rate at just $1.55.[34] Productivity rates (i.e. the rate of pay per ton of ore broken), like gross earnings for contract miners, fall well short of those for Western Mining's Australian miners. Company-controlled pay deductions continue to reduce net earnings substantially (see Table 7.4), compounding the ill-effects of a decline in real wages caused by post-coup (government) wage controls, a 33% devalued currency, and inflation, and, more recently, the imposition of an indirect tax on goods and services (VAT).

There are still the problems of an exceptionally hazardous occupation that has seen 10 accident fatalities between 1985 and 1990. The Vatukoula community is also far from healthy. The most common types of illness or disease are infections of the skin (scabies, ringworm, dermatitis), respiratory tract (bronchitis, bronchial asthma), and the intestine (diarrhoea). Between 1987 and 1988, medical opinion put diseases of the respiratory tract at a conservative 10,000 cases a year. These almost certainly derive from the low standards of industrial and domestic hygiene, including water and atmospheric pollution. Management refers to the condition with vicarious affection as 'the Vatukoula cough'. It is merely a matter of 'learning

[32] Ibid. 81.
[33] Girvan 1976 cited in ibid.
[34] 'The Facts about Vatukoula' FT 9 March 1990; FT 6 March 1991; Daily Post 21 March 1991.

Table 7.4   Western Mining Corporation, Vatukoula fortnightly pay-slip, trainee miner, 1989

		Total due	Deducted
Gross pay	$202.30		
Contract bonus	$202.30		
Provident Fund	$14.14		
Basic Tax	$5.05		
PAYE Tax	$50.59		
Deductions	$38.70		
	Rent	$2.00	$2.00
	Electricity	$3.00	$3.00
	Salary Advance	$43.97	$26.37
	Vatukoula Medical		
	Benefit Fund	$0.72	$0.00
	* Emperor Presentation	$3.00	$3.00
	Insurance LIC	$4.33	$4.33
			$38.70
Actual Pay	$93.82		
Net pay	$94.00		

* A misnomer, this constitutes a loan to the worker for funeral expenses.

Supermarket credit allowance for next pay period—$29.19.

Note: Other deductions not made on this sample, but applied as a rule, include safety boots (after the free issue of two pairs p.a.), overalls, tools and explosives.

the art of shallow breathing'! In the case of an eczema-type condition of the foot prevalent among miners, the humidity and heat of the underground working environment (exacerbated by the absence of adequate changing facilities and safety boot issues) are chief culprits. The high incidence of malnutrition among children, on the other hand, bears depressing witness to poverty.[35]

The social and economic impact of goldmining in Fiji transcends the political boundary of colonialism and independence. It is possible to discern a marked continuity in the perspectives and functioning of the colonial and post-colonial states, the dominant ideologies, the process of labour subordination, and the symbiotic relationship between the state, mining capital and members of the traditional chiefly class whose rôle as recruiters and controllers of indigenous mine labour has been a crucial link in the reproductive cycle of mining capitalism and in the continuing dominance of foreign capital. An important aspect of the role of the state has been to encourage foreign investment and to safeguard conditions for capital accumulation. It has functioned as a vehicle of public finance approving its assistance in the name of 'national development', albeit servicing the needs not of the industry but of a single and foreign corporate group. An interventionist political function has been based mainly on its regulating and policing roles in the mine labour market and in its application of conservative mining and industrial law.

---

[35] Personal communication, private medical practitioner, Tavua, 16 Dec. 1989.

A historic strike sustained since February 1991 is the latest reminder of this general pattern. The strike has dislocated Australian share prices, gold production and exports, and brought the industry to the edge of yet another precipice. In their bid for improved conditions of employment and union recognition, Fijian miners have been caught in a maze of legal and procedural obstacles, including a struggle for union registration. The interventions of riot police on the picket lines and in the homes of strikers evicted by the company have been reminiscent of the early colonial strikes when security forces were mobilised in the absence of any violence or serious civil disorder.[36] A fresh batch of presidential labour decrees in 1991 included the Protection of the National Economy Decree No. 19, 1991, apparently aimed at clipping the wings of militant mine strikers. Subsequently suspended, though not revoked, along with a similar decree targeted at the sugar industry, the national economy decree prescribed a mandatory 14-year prison sentence (at least double the penalty for manslaughter) or a $10,000 fine (or both) on any person found guilty of 'any act or any . . . omission that harms the operation of any major industry which threatens or is likely to threaten the economic life of Fiji'. Goldmining was identified as one of eight such 'major' industries.

The militarisation of Fijian society introduced a unique dimension to the politics of the Pacific region. The effects of the political and constitutional crisis created by the 'neutralisation' of an elected government in May 1987 have probably been more traumatic than at any other time in the country's history. These effects are now well documented, and they stretch from the collapse of the economy and the continuing mass emigration of skills to the general decline in living standards, assaults on the labour movement and violations of human rights.[37] The banner of extremist ethnic Fijian nationalism, which is closely associated with a belligerent Christian fundamentalism based on Old Testament Methodism, has added a virulent dimension to the new order. Implicit in both are demands for socio-political paramountcy.

But the populist imagery disguises a rather more complex situation and many contradictions, central to which has been a strategy aimed at mobilising a united Fijian front in defence of a weakening chiefly system. As such it continues to represent a significant, if obtuse and increasingly unpopular, instrument of working-class domination. The new republican Constitution tips the balance of power decisively in favour of the chiefs, and racially discriminatory provisions and a communal franchise will discourage cross-cultural solidarity along class lines. Official trade union policy also encapsulates the assault on the Fijian working class, punctuated by bans, detentions, the ubiquitous decree, and, latterly, the new 'labour reforms', as well as the less obvious strategy of ethnic division. In the mining industry there has been little in the actions and policies of the post-coup regime during the 1991–92 strike to suggest that the new nationalism embraces the Fijian working class.

---

[36]   *FT* 5 and 4 March 1991; and visit to strike site, Vatukoula 3 March 1991.
[37]   See Prasad 1988; Robertson & Tamanisau 1988; and Knapman 1988 : 157–90; Barr 1990 : 115, 119–21, 132–43; Bain & Baba 1990 : 376–8.

On the other hand, there are a few indications that organised mine labour could meet with greater success in the years ahead. Certain problems that plagued the union in the past either no longer exist or are not as intractable. In its task of forging a collective consciousness and solidarity out of ethnic communities that have been differentially incorporated into the labour process, the union has demonstrated remarkable success. The stumbling blocks of an itinerant labour market and competing traditional values and allegiances are no longer such critical issues. The hardships, sacrifices and other collective privations inflicted by the 1991–92 strike have forged a steely determination and solidarity. For the first time women (some of them striking workers, but the majority wives of miners) have played a prominent and active role in an industrial dispute in the mining town.[38]

Against this, employer opposition to unionism in the industry has hardened. In the past the paternalism and self-interest of the colonial government dictated some accommodation of unionism. Management attitudes were at times conspicuous more for their begrudging acceptance of a necessary evil than for outright suppression. While today's home-ownership and trust-fund schemes for higher-paid workers to an extent reflect ongoing strategies of 'incorporation', official and company labour policies are unreservedly anti-union. The increasing importance of the mining industry to the national economy prefigures a strengthening of state support for company labour policies, however questionable they may be. A fivefold increase in the value of gold sales between 1983 and 1988 was an auspicious turn of fate that is unlikely to be jeopardised by the adoption of more sympathetic labour policies.

For the mineworkers the problems of state and employer opposition are aggravated by insecurities that stem from a glutted labour market and more capital-intensive mining operations. These conditions make for a higher degree of economic dependence and job competition and thus a greater susceptibility to friction, factionalism and co-option. The interdependence of jobs and extra-occupational life inherent in a company-run town further exacerbate worker dependence. For the hundreds who have faced retrenchment since the 1970s, and the 400-odd strikers who have been dismissed by the company as a result of strike action in 1991, the loss of jobs has not only withdrawn the means of livelihood, but also the source of shelter and social reproduction, including the education of their children.

Kosmas Tsokhas has argued that the returns to mineworkers in Australia depend largely on the level of control they have in the workplace, including the extent to which they are able to influence changes in labour practices, technology and work processes. They are a function of their effectiveness as organised labour and in turn of the extent of their ideological and organisational unity.[39] This may well be so, but the peculiarities of Vatukoula suggest a more complex problem. Certainly the powerlessness of the mineworkers springs partly from circumstances similar to those found in Australia, where 'an industry [is] often built around

---

[38]   See Emberson-Bain 1992 : 161–2 and video 1992.
[39]   Tsokhas 1986 : 243–7.

a company town with few opportunities for alternative employment'.[40] But in its lifespan of over half a century the town's pattern of racial and ethnic inequalities has produced tensions and hostilities that extend beyond the usual strains of a company town. Worker dependence at Vatukoula is also intensified by the additional handicaps of much lower earnings and the absence of any other operating goldmine in the country. As a study in 1970 noted, it is only really the artisan component of the work-force for whom there are alternative work opportunities. 'For an important segment ... the kinds of skills developed in the mine are not likely to be very relevant to those parts of the economy most likely to expand in coming years ... To all intents and purposes, their skills become redundant.'[41]

Nationalisation, once again being mooted by the mineworkers' union, would seem an improbable option, largely for political reasons. This of course raises a number of questions: first, whether in fact nationalisation would necessarily deliver significant improvements in the returns to mine labour; second, whether it would transform production relations; and, finally, whether it would promote a more sustainable, socially conscious model of development. The short answer to all these questions is 'no' and we need look no farther afield than Fiji's phosphate-rich neighbour, Nauru, to see why.[42] Among the tell-tale signs within Fiji itself is the fact that post-colonial governments (with the exception of the ill-fated Coalition) stand firm in their support for capitalist and chiefly class interests.

But the operative word is 'necessarily'. At the risk of appearing utopian, it would seem reasonable to suggest that Fiji is, in fact, in a position to demand a greater degree of control over the production and distribution of its mineral wealth. A form of state participation that allowed for local management, industrial democracy and worker equity was envisaged by the deposed, Labour-led Coalition Government, and it is this kind of arrangement that is again being promoted by elements within the miners' union and the trade union movement generally. Such a formula could offer a conduit of change, and it has a successful precedent in the aviation industry. But it does of course require a political will and appropriate political structures.

Five years after the military coups the rumblings of economic nationalism and the serious dislocation wrought by a protracted strike may be enough to nudge a nationalisation package along. On the other hand, there is little to suggest that Vatukoula's corporate interests are losing their political influence. They handle their public relations with skill, and are well-practised in arguing their case to government, and using the generally pro-employer legal process to full advantage. Corporate confidence is reflected in the candour with which management declares its opposition to a miners' union, and in the open hospitality it extended to

---

[40]   Ibid. 246.

[41]   L. V. Castles, 'The Emperor Goldmining and the Fiji Economy' [sic] n.d. (c. 1970), Vat./unclassified.

[42]   See Howard 1988 : 126–52. Hyman (1975 : 133) usefully recalls Engels's argument (1958 : 147–9) that nationalisation is 'in no sense a socialistic measure'. On the contrary, 'the more it [the capitalist state] proceeds to the taking over of the productive forces, the more does it actually become the national capitalist, the more citizens does it exploit. The workers remain wage workers—proletarians. The capitalist relation is not done away with. It is rather brought to a head.' For a more optimistic and recent assessment of the nationalisation option in respect of the Caribbean, see Girvan 1971 : 217–40.

police officers stationed at the mine during the 1991–92 strike. The personal relationships nurtured over two decades with well-placed members of the Fijian hierarchy seem unlikely to come unstuck, notwithstanding the company's litigation against the post-coup government in connection with the dispute. A symbolic reminder of the bond is Reid's CBE honour from the Alliance Government.

When John Maynard Keynes scoffed at gold as 'this barbarous relic', his main concern was the high economic cost of sustaining gold as an anchor of the international monetary system. Vatukoula's story must surely prompt us to ponder whether in Fiji, at least, the human as well as the developmental costs have been too high a price to pay for the exploitation of the country's gold resources. Labour's prescription for Vatukoula was never ministered, so it would be folly to perceive it as a certain panacea. But the alternatives for a Third World island-state are few, and the situation in Fiji's gold town could well deteriorate if it remains uncorrected. A day of violent clashes between riot police and strikers that ended in the death of a court bailiff marked the rising industrial barometer in early 1992. In time, the human volcano that engulfs the 'face of the snake' could erupt with devastating and tragic consequences.

8   Vatukoula: A Photo Essay

VATUKOULA GOLD-FIELD

An aerial view of the Vatukoula gold-field shows the foothills of the Nakauvadra mountain range in the background and two tailings dams in the foreground, 1947. (*Photo: Ministry of Information*)

The Emperor open-cut mine, 1946. (*Photo: Ministry of Information*)

What was once the manicured golf course of Vatukoula is today a tailings dam. At the centre a pipe-line spills out slurry tailings into the dam. (*Photo: Anokh Kumar*, Fiji Times)

THE WORKING ENVIRONMENT

Fijian mineworkers at the Wallace Smith brace (shaft surface), 1946. The group on the right is waiting to be conveyed underground by the cage (at centre) for the start of their shift. The workers on the left are emerging at the end of a shift. An expatriate supervisor (head obscured) operates the command signals to the winder driver (cage operator). The miners are carrying their enamel bowls/plates for the underground 'crib' meal, which is provided by the company. Not all men are wearing hard hats and boots. (*Photo: Ministry of Information*)

A mined-out orebody in the Loloma mine, 1946. Artificial timber supports (stulls) erected by timbermen in lieu of natural rock pillars support low backs (hanging wall or rock ceiling). The slightly bent stull on the left and the ground failure (collapse of the ceiling) on the right indicate the pressure on the stulls. (*Photo: Ministry of Information*)

A mined-out, very narrow, horizontal orebody in the rich Dolphin mine dips up to the right. The hanging wall is supported by timber stulls. The narrowness of the orebody indicates that rock extraction was designed to ensure maximum ore grade (with no grade dilution). Such a practice meant very difficult working conditions for miners and timbermen. (*Photo: Ministry of Information*)

A group of Fijian miners work in a development drive in the Emperor mine, 1946. The old drill being used is heavy, cumbersome and with limited flexibility compared with today's drills. The men are standing in sludge and their only source of light is a small carbide light on the left. They have no personal helmet lights, and two of them are without boots. The mist to the right of the picture is caused by exhausted compressed air combined with fine droplets of oil from the drill. (*Photo: Ministry of Information*)

An open stope down in the Emperor mine with square timber sets holding up the rock ceiling on the right, 1946. The miner holding the long, pointed steel bar is scaling the rock ceiling of loose rock fragments (barring down) after blasting. The broken rock is hauled in by winch (operated by scraper driver seated at front). The lamp at the left hand side is the only source of light for the workers. (*Photo: Ministry of Information*)

Fijian miner putting in rock bolts in underground (decline) tunnel in the Emperor mine, 1989. Installed rock bolts can be seen supporting the rock ceiling. (*Photo: Asaeli Lave*, Fiji Times)

Two Fijian miners work in a typical flatmake stope of the Emperor mine.
From the use of personal cap lamps, gloves and a later model rock drill, it
seems likely that the photo was taken in the early 1960s. (*Photo:
Department of Mineral Resources*)

A crib room (underground dining-room) for underground mineworkers, 1946. The notice at top right
(in Fijian) instructs workers to keep the crib room clean and tidy, and to place their scraps in the
rubbish bin (at centre). (*Photo: Ministry of Information*)

Ore is trammed by hand from underground chutes (above) to the shaft, 1946. Each hand-pulled rail trolley or truck holds close to one ton of dry ore. Today (below), ore is transferred from underground stockpiles to the shaft by either battery-powered locomotives or large dump trucks. (*Photos: Ministry of Information and Asaeli Lave*, Fiji Times)

FAMILY HOUSING FOR FIJIAN MINERS

A Fijian miner's wife cooks the family meal on an open wood fire in the family 'kitchen', at Loloma Fijian settlement, 1990. (*Photo: Asaeli Lave*, Fiji Times)

A grandmother and grandchild eat outdoors on a mat, Loloma, 1991.

Inside a miner's home, Loloma Fijian settlement, Vatukoula, 1990. (*Photo: Asaeli Lave*)

As in the 1930s, the ordinary miner's home in Vatukoula today is not equipped with a bathroom. Each of the four shower cubicles, toilets (out of view) and wash tubs service between three and five families, and are located some distance from the houses. (*Photo: Asaeli Lave*, Fiji Times)

Housing for married Fijian mineworkers built in the 1930s is still in use today in Matanagata Fijian settlement. A house consists of a single (18 by 12 foot) room with corrugated-iron walls and unceiled roof. There are no inside cooking or bathroom facilities. (*Photos: Ministry of Information, 1946, and Ann Livingstone for the author, 1980*)

Housing built at Loloma after the Second World War is still in use. A house consists of the original 18 by 12 foot living quarters and an extension wing. Fijian miners and their families continue to live in these crude corrugated-iron and timber structures. (*Photos: Ministry of Information*, 1946, *and Asaeli Lave*, Fiji Times)

The communal tap alongside the bathroom and washing block in the Loloma Fijian settlement is used by miners' wives for preparing vegetables, cleaning fish, washing dishes and bathing children. Before the wash tubs were built in the 1980s, it was the only facility, apart from the river, available for washing clothes. (*Photo: Asaeli Lave*, Fiji Times, 1990)

BARRACK ACCOMMODATION 1989–1990

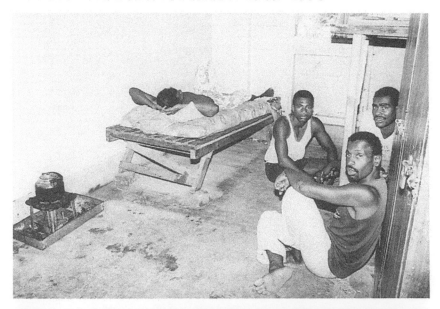

Sleeping quarters in the Narau barracks today still comprise bare, wooden bunks. All furnishings, including mattresses and primus stoves (in picture above), are supplied by the workers themselves. As in the past, a family may be accommodated in such a single room. (*Photos: Asaeli Lave*, Fiji Times, 1990, *and the author*, 1989)

These wooden shacks are the kitchens where women living in the barracks cook on open fires. (*Photo: the author*, 1989)

Communal showers and toilets afford little privacy for the women, men and children living in the barracks. (*Photos: the author*, 1989)

COMMUNITY

Senior staff of Emperor and Loloma mining companies, 1946. Seated in the middle of the front row is N. E. Nilsen, General Manager and Chief General Manager of Emperor, Loloma and Dolphin mining companies, 1936–70. (*Photo: Ministry of Information*)

Overlooking the mining town of Vatukoula is the home of E. G. Theodore, Managing Director of Emperor, Loloma and Dolphin mining companies, 1934–50. (*Photo: Ministry of Information*)

The Vatukoula company dispensary (foreground) and general mine administration offices (background), 1946. (*Photo: Ministry of Information*)

The Vatukoula Fijian school, 1946. (*Photo: Ministry of Information*)

The Vatukoula community cinema (top floor) and library (ground floor), mid-1970s. (*Photo: Asaeli Lave*, Fiji Times)

THE INDUSTRIAL SCENE

Jeffrey Reid, Managing Director, Emperor Mines Ltd, 1970–92. (*Photo: Anokh Kumar*, Fiji Times)

Striking mineworkers forcibly evicted from company housing by Fijian riot police in early 1992. Violent clashes left a court bailiff dead. (*Photo: Anokh Kumar*, Fiji Times)

Striking miners picketing outside the Philip shaft, Vatukoula, April 1991. (*Photo: Anokh Kumar*, Fiji Times)

Police riot squad stand guard having evicted picketers from the Philip shaft during the 1991 strike at Vatukoula. (*Photo: Anokh Kumar*, Fiji Times)

Appendices

Appendix A
Average annual values of Fiji gold, 1936-90

Year	Export gold price per fine ounce (Fiji currency) £ s. d.	$	Gold price per fine ounce London (Fiji currency) $
1936	7 13 10		
1937	7 15 0		
1938	7 17 0		
1939	8 11 7		
1940	9 11 0		
1941	9 11 6		
1942	9 7 3		
1943	9 4 2		
1944	9 10 9		
1945	9 11 1		
1946	9 11 0		
1947	9 11 1		
1948	9 11 4		
1949	10 15 9		
1950	13 15 6		27.75
1951	13 16 9		27.75
1952	14 11 10		27.75
1953	14 2 0		27.75
1954	13 16 0		27.75
1955	13 17 6		27.75
1956	13 19 11		27.75
1957	14 0 6		27.75
1958	14 1 2		27.75
1959	14 0 0		27.75
1960	13 19 10		27.75

(continues)

236

Appendix A   (cont'd)

Year	Export gold price per fine ounce (Fiji currency) £ s. d.			$	Gold price per fine ounce London (Fiji currency) $
1961	12	12	2		27.75
1962	14	0	0		27.75
1963	14	0	0		27.82
1964	13	16	7		27.75
1965	13	15	7		27.75
1966				27.61	27.75
1967				27.92	27.96
1968				32.32	33.64
1969				35.25	35.77
1970				31.11	31.30
1971				30.55	35.02
1972				48.97	47.96
1973				76.94	77.25
1974				125.14	128.26
1975				124.84	132.21
1976				110.25	111.16
1977				134.27	135.46
1978				191.44	163.61
1979				223.29	256.24
1980				496.10	496.94
1981				421.79	392.24
1982				339.86	350.14
1983				423.92	429.25
1984				386.27	389.58
1985				364.31	365.58
1986				414.43	416.21
1987				525.58	546.34
1988				633.54	625.04
1989				556.86	565.93
1990				565.35	

London market prices are included for comparison with the prices received by Fiji for its gold. They are calculated from the US price per fine ounce and average annual exchange rates. Prices recorded for the period 1950-62 are estimated on the basis of a frozen official price of $US35 per fine ounce and a fixed exchange rate between the US dollar and the Fiji pound (1.2613).

Source: Compiled and calculated from Fiji Trade Reports; Fiji Current Economic Statistics; and IMF International Financial Statistics.

Appendix B
Wages and salaries as a proportion of revenue, 1938-70

Year	Value of gold & silver production for Emperor, Loloma & Dolphin mines £ (F) for 1938-65	Total salaries & wages paid by Emperor, Loloma & Dolphin companies £ (F) (1938-65)	Real unit labour costs as a % of the value of production
1938	669,451	121,610	18.1
1939	869,217	140,241	16.1
1940	970,646	167,300	17.2
1941	1,054,585	161,847	15.3
1942	771,288	115,899	15.0
1943	556,734	107,284	19.2
1944	391,342	120,634	30.8
1945	911,918	138,163	15.1
1946	784,113	166,036	21.1
1947	910,283	220,165	24.1
1948	904,931	255,221	28.2
1949	1,141,593	255,595	22.4
1950	1,441,982	277,136	19.2
1951	1,331,987	338,790	25.4
1952	1,200,766	390,741	32.5
1953	1,101,089	376,394	34.2
1954	90,539	399,532	40.3
1955	1,037,227	437,752	42.2
1956	943,316	490,627	52.0
1957	1,105,254	531,923	48.1
1958	1,143,924	532,270	46.5
1959	1,006,059	75,834	57.2
1960	1,004,188	545,640	54.3
1961	1,158,312	588,463	50.8
1962	1,209,898	625,049	51.7
1963	1,498,247	708,004	47.3
1964	1,404,000	729,032	51.9
1965	— not available —		
1965/66*	3,241,768	1,796,260	55.4
1966/67	3,192,312	1,859,764	58.3
1967/68	3,296,608	1,993,416	60.5
1968/69	3,653,293	2,095,323	57.4
1969/70	3,466,559	2,230,822	64.4

* Years run from July to June for the years 1966-70. Values are in Fijian dollars for that period.

Source: Data compiled and calculated from Vat./Statistics relating to Activities of the Associated Companies of Vatukoula from Jan. 1935-Dec. 1964; Vat./Government 1970/71 J. F. Wren, Chairman of Directors, EGM Co. Ltd to Minister of Finance 14 Nov. 1970.

Appendix C
Nominal and relative values of principal exports, 1932-50*

Year	Sugar £	%	Copra £	%	Gold £	%	Bananas £	%
1932	624,310	80.3	170,240	10.6	2,053	0.1	67,237	4.2
1933	1,289,239	NA	195,788	NA	13,500	NA	69,243	NA
1934	1,069,049	79.6	127,941	9.5	7,590	0.6	67,845	5.1
1935	1,314,128	76.2	230,263	13.4	54,019	3.1	66,863	3.9
1936	1,331,701	65.8	406,393	20.1	131,684	6.5	84,548	4.2
1937	1,388,681	65.4	407,354	19.3	166,115	7.8	80,071	3.8
1938	1,338,183	52.8	270,915	10.7	701,272	27.7	73,578	2.9
1939	1,425,704	51.7	204,289	7.4	928,128	34.1	26,411	1.0
1940	1,285,191	51.9	125,063	5.0	1,024,923	41.4	41,747	1.7
1941	942,920	43.3	85,168	3.9	1,128,884	51.8	21,887	1.0
1942	1,761,055	61.3	252,544	8.8	816,385	28.4	42,400	1.5
1943	1,345,286	60.3	318,975	14.3	529,761	23.7	38,508	1.7
1944	1,035,616	56.5	352,492	19.2	426,452	23.3	18,565	1.0
1945	536,201	30.8	469,177	26.9	694,956	39.9	42,954	2.5
1946	2,111,557	58.6	379,760	10.5	657,527	18.2	49,988	1.4
1947	2,840,307	47.2	966,246	15.7	1,288,780	21.0	72,867	1.2
1948	4,265,406	54.8	992,234	12.7	1,011,225	14.0	94,996	1.2
1949	3,205,524	46.8	729,943	10.7	1,123,241	16.4	119,024	1.7
1950	3,750,712	48.0	544,401	17.0	1,420,578	18.2	101,869	1.3

* Relative values for 1940-45 are based on these four exports (making up the bulk but not the total of Fiji's exports) because of restrictions on publicising data during the war. They would therefore be slightly inflated for all four items.

Source: Data compiled from Fiji Trade Reports; Mining Board and Mines Department Annual Reports; Fiji Colonial Reports 1947-50.

Appendix D
Value of gold exports, 1936-90

Year	Quantity fine ounces unrefined gold	Value of gold exports £ (F) (1935-65) $ (F) (1966-90)	Value of total domestic exports £ (F) (1935-65) $ (F) (1966-90)	Gold as a % of domestic exports
1936	17,107	131,684	2,023,496	6.5
1937	21,407	166,115	2,121,920	7.8
1938	89,354	701,272	2,458,797	28.5
1939	108,114	928,128	2,659,858	34.9
1940	107,332	1,024,923	2,577,711	39.8
1941	117,903	1,128,884	2,577,711	49.3
1942	87,206	816,385	2,961,958	27.6
1943	57,533	529,761	2,312,454	22.9
1944	44,712	426,452	1,935,564	22.0
1945	72,725	694,956	2,092,559	33.2
1946	68,859	657,527	3,441,268	19.1
1947	134,922	1,288,780	5,816,331	22.2
1948	105,712	1,011,225	7,372,295	13.7
1949	104,115	1,123,241	6,419,501	17.5
1950	103,111	1,420,578	7,104,630	15.8
1951	93,700	1,296,403	6,413,576	20.2

(continues)

Appendix D   (cont'd)

Year	Quantity fine ounces unrefined gold	Value of gold exports £ (F) (1935-65) $ (F) (1966-90)	Value of total domestic exports £ (F) (1935-65) $ (F) (1966-90)	Gold as a % of domestic exports
1952	80,189	1,170,247	9,870,750	11.8
1953	70,467	993,698	12,010,689	8.2
1954	78,411	1,081,915	9,962,962	10.8
1955	73,989	1,027,538	11,428,502	8.9
1956	67,130	937,769	9,681,788	9.6
1957	76,620	1,074,768	13,505,459	7.9
1958	81,120	1,140,348	12,245,098	9.3
1959	70,719	990,208	11,403,955	8.6
1960	71,677	1,002,655	12,780,486	7.8
1961	95,349	1,202,022	10,434,546	11.5
1962	84,926	1,189,011	12,492,790	9.5
1963	111,260	1,557,633	19,391,972	8.0
1964	100,193	1,385,745	23,120,846	6.0
1965	112,060	1,544,494	17,805,875	8.7
1966	109,732	3,029,966	32,233,681	9.4
1967	112,698	3,146,996	35,359,506	8.9
1968	106,784	3,451,732	39,224,227	8.8
1969	95,346	3,361,287	43,547,740	7.7
1970	107,632	3,349,068	49,254,404	6.8
1971	87,630	2,677,939	48,854,932	5.5
1972	81,269	3,979,467	51,785,373	7.7
1973	79,606	6,124,821	52,373,136	11.7
1974	68,890	8,621,188	95,369,484	9.0
1975	68,756	8,583,604	115,948,396	7.4
1976	65,757	7,249,954	89,439,735	8.1
1977*	48,846 (1,519,106)	6,558,765	124,484,329	5.3
1978	25,869 (804,513)	4,952,325	121,885,648	4.1
1979	29,072 (904,143)	6,491,551	167,586,256	3.9
1980	25,015 (777,982)	12,410,041	229,655,592	5.4
1981	28,146 (875,356)	11,871,658	193,735,392	6.1
1982	45,838 (1,425,561)	15,578,602	181,198,894	8.6
1983	39,781 (1,237,175)	16,864,014	177,875,300	9.5
1984	53,065 (1,650,315)	20,497,440	197,869,148	10.4
1985	59,896 (1,862,758)	21,820,904	190,630,294	11.4
1986	93,216 (2,899,003)	38,631,655	241,864,916	16.0
1987	96,193 (2,992,000)	50,557,000	334,091,228	15.1
1988	132,743 (4,128,877)	84,097,535	437,378,998	19.2
1989	127,084 (3,952,835)	70,767,996	479,581,508	14.7
1990	121,182 (3,769,273)	68,510,320	581,491,052	11.7

* From 1977 the quantity of gold exports is also given in grams.

Source: Data compiled and calculated from (published and unpublished) Fiji Trade & Overseas Trade Reports, 1936-90.

Appendix E
Associated Mining Companies' royalty, duty and other direct tax payments, 1938–89

Year	Royalty on gold*	Port & service tax on gold	Duty & tax on direct imports	Income (company) tax	Export tax (2% on gold sales) £ (F) (1938–65) $ (F) (1966–89)	Total	Value of gold exports	Gold tax as % of export revenue
1938	33,155	6,623	11,549	16,398	Nil	67,725	701,272	9.7
1939	42,846	8,546	10,326	18,836	Nil	80,564	928,128	8.7
1940	48,029	9,625	15,738	40,192	Nil	113,584	1,024,923	11.1
1941	51,606	10,340	14,400	37,149	Nil	113,495	1,128,884	10.1
1942	38,054	7,623	7,974	66,071	Nil	119,722	816,385	14.7
1943	27,287	5,472	5,688	66,192	Nil	104,639	529,761	19.8
1944	19,538	3,951	6,257	20,835	Nil	50,581	426,452	11.9
1945	45,546	9,109	9,646	63,849	Nil	128,150	694,956	18.5
1946	38,999	7,800	18,448	102,840	Nil	168,087	657,527	25.6
1947	45,263	9,052	18,560	104,689	Nil	177,564	1,288,780	13.8
1948	44,654	8,930	14,559	78,142	Nil	146,285	1,011,225	14.5
1949	25,454	11,299	5,779	109,193	Nil	151,725	1,123,241	13.5
1950	132,192	14,332	6,376	159,055	Nil	311,955	1,420,578	22.0
1951	127,331	9,489	12,658	160,612	Nil	310,090	1,296,403	23.9
1952	44,476	Nil	19,471	122,621	Nil	186,568	1,170,247	15.9
1953	23,541	Nil	7,607	75,408	Nil	106,556	993,698	10.7
1954	13,116	Nil	5,933	50,892	Nil	69,941	1,081,915	6.5
1955	10,271	Nil	7,086	38,489	Nil	56,846	1,027,538	5.5
1956	4,318	Nil	9,868	18,235	Nil	32,421	937,769	3.5
1957	183	Nil	10,036	Nil	Nil	10,219	1,074,768	1.0
1958	Nil	Nil	18,230	Nil	Nil	18,230	1,140,348	1.6
1959	899	Nil	29,155	2,156	Nil	32,210	990,208	3.3
1960	1,457	Nil	17,167	4,090	Nil	22,714	1,002,655	2.3
1961	Nil	Nil	26,311	Nil	Nil	26,311	1,202,022	2.2
1962	3,861	Nil	31,564	11,957	Nil	47,382	1,189,011	4.0
1963	2,264	Nil	30,053	9,435	Nil	41,752	1,557,633	2.1
1964	3,170†	Nil	26,479	10,653	Nil	40,302	1,385,745	2.9
1965	4,418†	Nil	NA	15,296	Nil	—	1,544,494	—
1966†	4,774	Nil	30,008	14,354	Nil	49,136	3,029,966	
1967–69			Not available					
1970	Nil	Nil	NA	Nil (loss)	Nil	Nil	3,349,068	0
1971	Nil‡	Nil	NA	Nil (loss)	Nil	Nil	2,677,939	0
1972	Nil	Nil	NA	Nil (loss)	Nil	Nil	3,979,467	0
1973	57,380	Nil	NA	110,555	Nil	167,935	6,124,821	2.8
1974	190,567	Nil	NA	390,851	Nil	581,418	8,621,188	6.1
1975	96,357	Nil	NA	292,539	117,657	506,553	8,583,604	5.9
1976	Nil	Nil	NA	Nil (loss)	167,205	167,205	7,249,954	2.3
1977	Nil‡	Nil	NA	Nil (loss)	Nil	Nil	6,558,765	0
1978	Nil	Nil	NA	Nil (tax rebate)	Nil	Nil	4,952,325	0
1979	Nil	Nil	NA	¶61,810	Nil	—	6,491,551	0
1980	Nil	Nil	NA	¶66,343	NA	—	12,410,041	—
1981	21,124	Nil	NA	¶ 7,835	NA	—	11,871,658	—
1982	Nil	Nil	NA	¶42,278	NA	—	15,578,602	—
1983	250,399	Nil	NA	¶23,340	NA	—	16,864,014	—
1984	Nil	Nil	NA	¶16,904	NA	—	20,497,440	—
1985	80	NA	NA	¶ 9,864	NA	—	21,820,904	**0
1986	23,913	NA	NA	NA	NA	—	38,631,655	**0.1

(continues)

Appendix E   (cont'd)

Year	Royalty on gold*	Port & service tax on gold	Duty & tax on direct imports	Income tax (company) tax £ (F) (1938–65)	Export tax (2% on gold sales)	Total	Value of gold exports	Gold tax as % of export revenue
1987	110,794	NA	NA	NA	NA	—	50,557,000	**0.2
1988	18,728	NA	NA	NA	NA	—	84,097,535	**0.02
1989	501,300	NA	NA	NA	NA	—	70,767,996	**0.7

NA   Not available.
*   For the years 1970-84, royalty revenue is for both gold and silver.
†   Years run from July to June.
‡   Royalty waived.
¶   Total company tax paid by the mining and quarrying sector. This represents more than the Vatukoula companies would have paid in any single year.
**   % total export revenue from gold paid in royalties.

Source: Vat./Statistics Relating to Activities of the Associated Companies Jan. 1935–Dec. 1964; Emperor Annual Reports 1965-66; Fiji Leg. Co. Debates Supplementary Estimates Sept. 1967; Department of Mineral Resources Annual Reports 1970-84; & MR/CY8E.

Appendix F
Prospecting licences in the Yanawai district, 1909–39

P.L.	30	The Fiji Prospecting & Mining Syndicate
(no.)	43	J. Malcolm
	50	J. H. Jamieson
	51	J. H. Jamieson
	52	J. H. Jamieson
	53	E. F. Powell & J. H. Jamieson
	67	F. B. Spaeth
	70	F. A. Archibald, W. H. Creighton & H. J. Wright
	91	F. B. Spaeth
	92	D. G. S. Whalley
	94	J. I. Dods
	95	J. I. Dods
	97	W. H. Creighton & J. H. Wright
	98	E. Cresswell
	104	J. I. Dods
	105	J. I. Dods
	107	F. J. Evetts
	108	E. Cresswell
	109	J. A. Muir & G. Whalen
	111	M. J. Dods
	112	F. A. Archibald
	127	W. V. Terry
	139	J. E. Michelmore
	140	B. E. Archibald
	141	M. W. Gordon
	142	J. L. Gordon
	143	A. O. MacKenzie
	144	G. P. Donovan
	148	W. V. Terry

(continues)

Appendix F   (cont'd)

149	M. Cameron
150	J. L. Stark
154	D. Cameron
155	F. B. Spaeth
156	C. B. du Pertuis
158	A. T. Acton
159	C. L. N. Bentley (transferred to Vatukaisia Mining Co. Ltd; transferred to Mount Kasi Mining Co. NL)
160	R. C. Kerkham (transferred to I. R. Cameron transferred to F. B. Brown)
161	O. E. Provis (transferred to C. T. Griffiths)
162	F. G. Spaeth
163	F. B. Spaeth
165	E. MacKenzie
166	A. O. MacKenzie
167	G. P. Donovan
169	M. Cameron
170	J. L. Stark
172	W. V. Terry
173	D. Cameron
174	L. W. G. Williams
175	A. T. Acton
176	Mt Kasi Mining Co. NL
177	F. B. Brown (transferred to G. Mitchell)
181	C. T. Griffiths
182	F. G. Spaeth
183	F. B. Spaeth
205	A. O. MacKenzie
206	G. P. Donovan
211	D. Cameron
212	F. A. Smith
226	J. L. Stark
227	Mt Kasi Mining Co. NL
228	G. Mitchell
229	W. Mitchell
231	F. A. Smith
233	C. T. Griffiths
239	Mount Kasi Mines Ltd
240	Mount Kasi Mines Ltd
275	Vatukaisia Mining Co. Ltd
276	Vatukaisia Mining Co. Ltd
279	East Reefs Consolidated NL
280	East Reefs Consolidated NL
290	Vatukaisia Mining Co. Ltd
293	East Reefs Consolidated NL
305	Kasi Development Ltd
309	East Reefs Consolidated NL
316	Vatukaisia Mining Co. Ltd
317	Vatukaisia Mining Co. Ltd
320	Mineral Developments (Fiji) Ltd
321	Mineral Developments (Fiji) Ltd
322	Mineral Developments (Fiji) Ltd
333	Vatukaisia Mining Co. Ltd
334	Vatukaisia Mining Co. Ltd
335	Kasi Development Ltd
356	Mineral Developments (Fiji) Ltd

(continues)

Appendix F   (cont'd)

357	Mineral Developments (Fiji) Ltd
358	Mineral Developments (Fiji) Ltd
359	Vatukaisia Mining Co. Ltd
368	Vatukaisia Mining Co. Ltd
369	Kasi Developments Ltd
370	Vatukaisia Mining Co. Ltd
373	E. Hathaway
374	Vatukaisia Mining Co. Ltd
377	E. Hathaway

Source: MR 30/ . . . /377/ML2-1.

Appendix G
Prospecting licences in the Tavua area, 1933-36

P.L.	207	P. Costello
(no.)	208	G. C. Foulis
	209	H. L. Morton
	210	J. H. H. Millett
	213	A. Aitken
	214	A. F. Thompson
	215	W. E. Goodsir
	216	W. B. Ragg
	217	R. A. Brooks (transferred to E. G. Theodore)
	218	W. G. Lawler
	219	H. B. Morton (Jr)
	220	J. H. Davies (transferred to W. C. Nicholson)
	221	R. H. Roskelly
	222	J. H. H. Millett, F. A. Archibald, E. S. G. Ruthven
	223	T. H. Coster
	224	V. S. Ruthven
	236	E. G. Theodore
	247	E. G. Theodore
	250	Tavua Gold Developments Ltd
	251	Tavua Gold Developments Ltd
	252	Mineral Developments (Fiji) Ltd
	253	Tavua Gold Developments Ltd
	254	Mineral Developments (Fiji) Ltd
	255	Mineral Developments (Fiji) Ltd
	256	Mineral Developments (Fiji) Ltd
	257	Mineral Developments (Fiji) Ltd
	258	Mineral Developments (Fiji) Ltd
	260	Mineral Developments (Fiji) Ltd
	261	Mineral Developments (Fiji) Ltd
	262	Mineral Developments (Fiji) Ltd
	263	Mineral Developments (Fiji) Ltd
	264	Tavua Gold Developments Ltd
	265	Tavua Gold Developments Ltd
	272	Gold Mines of Fiji NL
	273	Gold Mines of Fiji NL
	281	Fiji Gold NL

(continues)

Appendix G   (cont'd)

282	Fiji Gold NL
288	H. H. Ragg
291	Loloma West Ltd
294	W. C. Nicholson & C. C. Fenton
295	Pacific Gold Syndicate
298	Gold Mines of Fiji NL
299	Gold Mines of Fiji NL
300	P. Costello
301	Pacific Gold NL
302	Pacific Gold NL

Source: MR 207/ . . . 302/ML1/3 to 5-1.

Appendix H
Emperor Gold Mining Co. Ltd Memorandum of Agreement under the Masters and Servants Ordinance, 1936

MEMORANDUM of AGREEMENT under The Masters and Servants Ordinance, 1890, made the .... day of .... 1936. BETWEEN the Emperor Gold Mining Company Limited, of Tavua Goldfield, Colo North, in the Colony of Fiji, (hereinafter called the "Company") of the one part and .... of .... (hereinafter called the "worker") of the other part.

1. The said worker shall for the term of .... months from the date hereof serve the said Emperor Gold Mining Company Limited as ....

Note: Insert here: Surface or U/ground Worker, Underground Worker, Surface Worker, OR, as the case may be,

2. The said Emperor Gold Mining Company Limited shall during the continuance of this agreement pay to the said worker on the regular pay day on every fourth Saturday, wages for each day worked by him at the rate of ....

Provided that if the wages rate for the worker as set out in this clause does not exceed two shillings and sixpence per day then, in addition to the daily wages agreed to in this clause, the Company shall pay a bonus of two shillings for each completed week of service when the Company, in its discretion, considers the work performed is satisfactory.

3. In addition to the wages provided for in Clause 2 hereof rations on the following scale shall be provided:

Daily

Bread, 1 lb.
Fresh or Corned Beef, ½ lb. or, when meat is not supplied, 1 tin of Salmon.
Rice 1 lb. When Yams, Dalo or other native vegetables are issued in sufficient
    quantities rice ration is to be reduced to half a pound.
Sugar, ½ lb.

(continues)

Appendix H   (cont'd)

Weekly

```
Tobacco  ..............................  2 ozs
Soap  ..................................  4 ozs
Tea  ...................................  4 ozs
Salt  ..................................  8 ozs
```

4. The ordinary hours of labour for the said worker shall be forty-eight hours in each week divided, so far as practicable, in the discretion of the Company, evenly over the six ordinary working days.

When more than 48 hours in one week are worked by the worker he shall be entitled to be paid at ordinary rates for the extra time worked, or, in the alternative, shall be entitled to equivalent time off in a subsequent week.

When the worker is required to work on Sunday he shall be entitled to equivalent time off in a subsequent week.

5. The Company shall during the continuance of this agreement provide the worker with proper lodging in accordance with the provisions of the Fijian Labour Ordinance of 1895, and shall provide medical care as if Section 17 of the Labourers Medical Care Ordinance of 1891 were applicable to the worker.

6. If the worker is married and brings his wife and family (if any) to the place of employment the Company shall provide suitable house accommodation for such married worker and his wife and family (if any), and, until garden land is provided for cultivation of native food by such married worker, shall issue to him for his wife and family (if any), in addition to his ordinary rations, rations equal to one-half the ordinary rations.

7. Upon completion of service under this agreement the Company shall provide the worker with a return passage to the place whence he first embarked for the purpose of his engagement with the Company, namely

....

8. The said worker shall at all times during the continuance of this agreement faithfully and diligently employ his whole time in the service of the Company and obey the lawful commands of the Company's representatives.

Signed by the Employer
in the presence of: _____   EMPLOYER

Signed by the Worker
in the presence of: _____   WORKER

District Commissioner

Source: Vat./Native Affairs Camps Reports 1935-.

Appendix I
Comparative trends in wages/salaries and labour productivity, Vatukoula, 1938–70

Year	Tonnage of ore treated on Emperor, Loloma & Dolphin*	Average no. employed on Emperor, Loloma & Dolphin mines†	Per capita output (tons p.a.)	Wages and salaries bill for Emperor, Loloma and Dolphin mines £ (F)
1938	195,497	1,390	140.6	121,610
1939	204,719	1,554	131.7	140,241
1940	190,970	1,645	116.0	167,300
1941	190,729	1,506	126.6	161,847
1942	145,887	961	151.8	115,899
1943	157,179	801	196.2	107,284
1944	158,775	893	177.7	120,634
1945	158,923	1,030	154.2	138,163
1946	173,246	1,244	139.2	166,036
1947	159,285	1,274	125.0	220,165
1948	170,426	1,383	123.2	255,221
1949	165,992	1,313	126.4	255,595
1950	173,212	1,340	129.3	277,136
1951	184,247	1,460	126.2	338,790
1952	181,957	1,539	118.2	390,741
1953	186,117	1,333	139.6	376,394
1954	179,787	1,348	133.4	399,532
1955	179,053	1,412	126.8	437,752
1956	165,987	1,426	116.4	490,627
1957	187,507	1,478	126.9	531,923
1958	191,739	1,465	130.9	532,270
1959	172,393	1,539	112.0	575,834
1960	179,634	1,464	122.1	545,640
1961	200,293	1,416	141.4	588,463
1962	247,185	1,527	161.9	625,049
1963	290,077	1,592	182.2	708,004
1964	269,961	1,626	166.0	729,032
1965	291,588	1,705	171.0	NA
1966	291,126	1,757	165.7	$F1,796,260
1967	313,723	1,682	186.5	$F1,859,764
1968	328,791	1,644	199.9	$F1,993,416
1969	NA	1,640	—	$F2,095,323
1970	327,374	NA	—	$F2,230,822

*   Years run from January to December except for 1965–70 when they end in June each year.
†   Average number of employees for the years 1965–69 are calculated from totals in January, June and December each year.

Source: Data compiled and calculated from Vat./Statistics relating to Activities of the Associated Companies of Vatukoula from Jan. 1935–Dec. 1964; Emperor Annual Reports 1965–70; Vat./Monthly Returns of Employees Vatukoula Associated Companies 1965–69.

Appendix J
Health hazards of industrial gases

SULPHUR DIOXIDE
Colourless gas with a distinctive odour; . . . somewhat soluble in water.
TOXIC BY INHALATION
IRRITATING TO SKIN, EYES AND RESPIRATORY SYSTEM
Avoid inhalation of gas. TLV 5 ppm (13 mg per m^3).

Toxic effects:
The vapour irritates the respiratory system and may cause bronchitis and asphyxia. High concentrations of vapour irritate the eyes and may cause conjunctivitis.

HYDROGEN CYANIDE (hydrocyanic acid gas)
Colourless liquid or gas with faint odour of bitter almonds; bp 26°C; very soluble in water, the solution being only weakly acidic.
EXTREMELY POISONOUS GAS AND LIQUID
POISONOUS BY SKIN ABSORPTION
HIGHLY INFLAMMABLE
Prevent inhalation of gas. Prevent contact with skin and eyes. TLV (skin) 10 ppm (11 mg per m^3).

Toxic effects:
Inhalation of high concentration leads to shortness of breath, paralysis, unconsciousness, convulsions and death by respiratory failure. With lethal concentrations, death is extremely rapid although breathing may continue for some time. With low concentrations the effects are likely to be headache, vertigo, nausea and vomiting. Chronic exposure over long periods may induce fatigue and weakness. The average fatal dose is 55 mg, which can also be assimilated by skin contact with the liquid.

TLV = Threshold Limiting Value;
bp = boiling point.

Source: G. O. Muir, *Hazards in the Chemical Laboratory*, 2nd ed., London: The Chemical Society, 1977 cited in Herman Stigzelius, *Environmental Impact of Gold Mining at Vatukoula in Fiji*, ESCAP Regional Mineral Resources Development Centre Report, No. 146, Bandung, Oct. 1981.

Appendix K
Comparative gold production, Fiji and Australia, 1960–70

Place	Company	1960	1965	1970
			(fine ounces)	
Western Australia				
Kalgoorlie	Gold Mines of Kalgoorlie (Aust) Ltd	150,300	155,000	137,300
Kalgoorlie	Lake View and Star Ltd	174,200	152,000	101,700
Kalgoorlie	North Kalgurlie (1912) Ltd	87,800	76,000	53,200
Kalgoorlie	Great Boulder Gold Mines Ltd	123,900	92,300	9,100
Norseman	Central Norseman Gold Corp. NL	101,300	95,100	60,000
Mount Magnet	Hill 50 Gold Mine NL	83,000	54,200	15,400
Northern Territory				
Tennant Creek	Peko-Wallsend Ltd	11,700	30,000	92,300
Noble's Nob	Australian Development NL	56,600	47,300	32,000
Queensland				
Mount Morgan	Peko-Wallsend Ltd	64,200	80,000	60,000
Other Australian gold and by-product producers		233,000	95,900	56,000
Vatukoula	Emperor Gold Mines Ltd	71,677	112,060	107,632

Source: Data on these Australian mines is taken from I. Coghill, *Australia's Mineral Wealth*, Melbourne: Sorrett Publishing Pty Ltd, 1971 : 85.

Appendix L
Fiji Trades Union Congress resolution on Vatukoula mineworkers, 1990

This 33rd Biennial Delegates' Conference of the FTUC meeting at Suva, 2 June 1990, resolves as follows:

Resolution 7	*Mineworkers*
Applauding:	efforts by FTUC Organising Unit to organise mine workers at Vatukoula;
Deplores:	the sub-human, degrading and oppressive working and living conditions at the Vatukoula Mines and highly exploitative rates of pay;
Notes:	that serious negligence of environmental, health and safety conditions at the mines have had a detrimental effect on the health, safety and welfare of workers and their families; and that there is an urgent need for the review, amendment and better enforcement of existing legislation covering these issues;
Condemning:	the inordinate delay on the part of authorities to register a Mineworkers Union without any legitimate reasons;
Urges:	the Interim Administration to recognise the right of mineworkers to organise; and further
Requests:	the Interim Administration to set up a high powered tripartite committee to investigate and make recommendations to improve the working and living conditions and the minimum rates of pay of the mine workers;
and further calls:	upon the Interim Administration to set up a Wages Council for the mining industry.

Bibliography

The following provides summaries of primary and secondary materials used during research for this book. The private archival records of the principal mining companies operating at Vatukoula, most of which have never been previously researched, provided the most crucial source of empirical evidence. These records were supported by data from the vast volume of colonial government archives located in Fiji, Australia and the U.K. as well as other sources, including the testimonies of mineworkers, cited below. Only the names of primary source collections are provided, not individual files or papers. These are far too many to list individually, and many appear in the references. With respect to secondary references, only those cited in the text are listed.

1. OFFICIAL MANUSCRIPT MATERIAL

Records (open and confidential files, minute papers, internal reports and official diaries) of the
- Colonial Secretary's Office, National Archives of Fiji, Suva
- Secretariat of Native Affairs, National Archives of Fiji, Suva
- Ministry of Labour, Government of Fiji, Suva (series 36/I/21/16-A)
- Ministry of Mineral Resources, Government of Fiji, Suva (series Bunch 20 M541/1; AP 1; 30/...377/ML 2-2; 296/...857/ML 10/18-1; Bunch 2, MB7/136; 207/.../302/ML 1/3 to 5-1).

Colonial Office correspondence with the Government of Fiji, National Library of Australia, Canberra (series CO83) and National Archives of Fiji, Suva.

Correspondence files, minute papers, etc. of Colonial Office, Treasury and Bank of England, Public Record Office, Kew, England.

Proceedings of the Council of Chiefs, National Archives of Fiji, Suva.

Provincial Council Reports for Colo North & East, Ra, Tailevu, Naitasiri, Lau, Macuatu, Bua, Cakaudrove, Lomaiviti, Rewa, Ba, Kadavu, Namosi and Serua, National Archives of Fiji, Suva.

Records of the proceedings and awards of Fiji Government-appointed conciliation and arbitration regarding industrial disputes between the Fiji Mineworkers' Union and the Associated Mining Companies, Vatukoula, 1952–69, and 1980, Vatukoula.

2. UNOFFICIAL MANUSCRIPT MATERIAL

(i) Company records

(a) Associated Mining Companies of Vatukoula: correspondence files; internal memoranda; reports and minutes of meetings held by staff/executive, departmental managers', bosses, and Joint Consultative Council; four-weekly Safety Officer and Welfare Officer reports; records of government conciliation and arbitration proceedings, and industrial inquiries; employment (including job classification), salaries/wages and financial data; employee service record cards (approx 5000).

(b) Colonial Sugar Refining Co. Ltd Archives, Deposit 142, Archives of Business and Labour, Australian National University, Canberra, and CSR Head Office, Sydney.

(c) Research Library, Sydney Stock Exchange for Mt Kasi Mines Ltd, Kasi Development Ltd and Vatukaisia Mining Co Ltd: correspondence, shareholdings lists, agreements and annual reports, Deposit M 145.

(d) Melbourne Stock Exchange Mining Collection, Melbourne University Archives of Business and Labour: correspondence files and annual reports to shareholders/statements of accounts for Emperor Gold Mines Ltd, Loloma Gold Mines NL, Mt Kasi Mines Ltd, Koroere Gold NL, Fiji Mines Development Ltd, Mt Morgan Developments Ltd, Mineral Developments (Fiji) Ltd, Gold Search (Fiji) Ltd Tavua, Natalau Gold Prospecting Syndicate, Whitehall Exploration Ltd, Tavua Gold Developments Ltd, Pacific Gold NL, Kasi Developments Ltd, Fiji Mining Corporation, East Reefs Consolidated, Aloha Central, Loloma West, Vatukaisia Mining Co. Ltd, Fiji Gold NL, Tavua Gold Options Ltd, Vuda Prospecting Syndicate, Homeward Bound Syndicate, Nasivi (Fiji) Gold Syndicate NL, Western Mining Corporation.

(ii) Trade union/employers' association records

(a) Emperor Gold Mining Co. Ltd holdings, Vatukoula: correspondence and minutes of meetings between Fiji Mineworkers' Union (FMWU) and Associated Mining Companies, Vatukoula; FMWU logs of claims and submissions to government conciliation and arbitration proceedings, collective labour agreements between EGM and FMWU.

(b) Registrar of Companies and Trade Unions, Government of Fiji, Suva, holdings: FMWU constitution and rules, office-bearers, and audited financial statements.

(c) Fiji Trades Union Congress, Suva: FMWU correspondence files.

(d) Fiji Employers' Consultative Association (FECA), Suva: FMWU correspondence files (cited only as a confidential source).

(iii) Private collections

(a) Sir Colin Fraser Papers, Melbourne University Archives of Business and Labour.

(b) Stanmore Papers, Mitchell Library, Sydney.

(c) Timoci Bavadra private papers on Nasomo dispute with Emperor Gold Mining Co. and Western Mining Corporation, Suva.

(d) With regard to E. G. Theodore, the following collections held in the National Library of Australia were consulted:
• F. Giblin collection, MS 365/5/1-88 General Correspondence 1896-1935;
• Henry E. Boote collection, MS 2070/1/42-113 Correspondence 1918-33;
• King O'Malley Papers, MS 460/5249-50/5251/5291, Edward J. Ward collection, MS 2396 10/1, 10/2-3, 10/598.

(iv) Other collections

Methodist Missionary Society of Australasia: Fiji District collection, Fiji National Archives, Suva.

Roman Catholic Archives of Fiji, Series 7.17 Vatukoula and 11/6/2 Vatukoula 1936-58, Suva.

3. OFFICIAL PRINTED MATERIAL

(i) Fiji

Fiji Blue Books.

Fiji Government Civil Lists.

Fiji Bureau of Statistics Annual Employment Survey Reports, Census of Industrial Production, and Current Economic Statistics.

Fiji Census Reports 1901-86.

Fiji Colonial Reports.

Fiji Government Ordinances, Laws and Regulations regarding labour, land, mining, public health, Indian immigration, industrial matters, income tax, native/ Fijian affairs and taxes.

Fiji Legislative Council (pre-1970) and Parliamentary (post-1970) Debates.

Fiji Legislative Council and Parliamentary Papers for Department/Ministry of Labour, District Commissioners, Mining Board, Mines Department/Lands and Mineral Resources Ministry, Secretary for Native (and Fijian) Affairs, published annually.

Fiji Republic Decrees 1987-91.

Fiji Trade Reports.

Native Lands Commission, Vol. II, 1927, Final Report on the Provinces of Lomaiviti, Ra and Tailevu South; Vol. III, 1958, Final Report on the Provinces of Ba, Nadroga, Colo West, Colo North, Serua and Namosi.

Sir Alan Burns, T. Y. Watson & A. T. Peacock, 'Report of the Commission of Enquiry into the Natural Resources and Population Trends of the Colony of Fiji, 1959', CP No. 1, 1960.

R. S. McDougall, 'Report on Fijian Administration Finances', CP No. 35, 1957.

C. O. O'Loughlin, 'The Pattern of the Fiji Economy: The National Income 1950–1953', CP No. 44, 1956.

Price & Waterhouse, 'Private and Confidential Report on Emperor Gold Mining Co. request for assistance from the Government of Fiji', 31 Aug. 1966 (cited as confidential source).

Report of the Board of Enquiry into the Trade Dispute between the FMWU and EGM Co. Ltd, 1974.

Report of the Committee Appointed to Examine the Economics of the Gold Mining Industry at Vatukoula, Suva, April 1977.

Report of Commission of Enquiry into the Disturbances in Suva in December 1959, CP No. 10, 1960.

Report on the Economics of the Gold Mining Industry at Vatukoula, CP No. 26, 1960.

O. H. K. Spate, 'The Fijian People: Economic Problems and Prospects', CP No. 13, 1959.

Herman Stigzelius, 'Environmental Impact of Gold Mining at Vatukoula in Fiji', Economic and Social Commission for Asia and the Pacific (ESCAP) Regional Mineral Resources Development Centre Report No. 146, Bandung, Oct. 1981.

H. J. Bavor, World Health Organisation (WHO) West Pacific Regional Centre for the Promotion of Environment Planning & Applied Studies, Community Water Supply & Sanitation Project 005, Feb. 1990.

(ii) Australia

Commonwealth Government of Australia, Inter-State Commission of Australia Report on South Pacific Trade, 1918.

New South Wales Workers' Compensation (Silicosis) Committee Report, New South Wales State Archives, Sydney.

(iii) Other

International Labour Conventions, ILO, Geneva.
House of Lords Debates, United Kingdom.

4. PRIVATE PRINTED MATERIAL

H. H. Dunkin, *A General Description of Community Life and Safety Work in Vatukoula Fiji*, Vatukoula, 1947.

R. H. Yarrow, *A Brief History of Organised Safety Work on the Vatukoula Gold Field, together with an indication of the costs involved and the benefits gained*, Vatukoula, 1953.

C. W. Marshall & Associates Confidential Report on Vatukoula Emperor Gold Mine to Ratu Penaia Ganilau, Minister for Home Affairs, May 1972.

FTUC/FMWU Submission to Board of Enquiry, Nov. 1974.

FMWU Final Submission to Board of Enquiry, Nov. 1974.

5. NEWSPAPERS AND PERIODICALS

The Australian.
Canberra Times.
Daily Telegraph.
Fiji Sun.
Fiji Times.
Fiji Times and Herald.
Daily Post.
Financial Times.
Pacific Islands Monthly.
Sydney Morning Herald.
Talanoa (Associated Mining Companies, Vatukoula publication).
The Australian Worker.
The Brisbane Courier.
The Daily Standard (Brisbane).
The Herald (Melbourne).
The Queenslander.
The Worker (Official Journal of the Federated Workers of Queensland).

6. INTERVIEWS

A wide range of informal interviews and discussions were carried out with mine-workers previously and currently employed with the Vatukoula mining companies in Vatukoula, Suva, and Lautoka, Fiji; elders and villagers of Nasomo village; incumbent and ex-management personnel; (colonial and post-colonial) government officers (including Mines Department personnel); politicians; and union officials in Vatukoula and Suva, Fiji, and Sydney, Australia.

7. PUBLISHED WORKS, UNPUBLISHED THESES AND PAPERS

Adam, H., 1971. *Modernising racial domination: South Africa's political dynamics*, Berkeley: University of California Press.

Ali, A., 1980. *Plantation to politics: studies on Fiji Indians*, Suva: University of the South Pacific & the Fiji Times & Herald.

Aliber, Robert Z., 1977. *The international money game*, 2nd ed., London: Macmillan.

Arrighi, Giovanni, 1973. 'Labour supply in historical perspective: a study of the proletarianisation of the African peasantry in Rhodesia', in G. Arrighi & J. S. Saul, *Essays on the political economy of Africa*, New York: Monthly Review Press.

Bain, 'A., 1985. 'Vatukoula—Rock of Gold: labour in the goldmining industry of Fiji, 1930-1970', Ph.D thesis, Canberra: Australian National University.

—— 1986. 'Labour protest and control in the goldmining industry of Fiji, 1930-1970', *South Pacific Forum*, Vol. 3, No. 1 (April).

—— 1988. 'A protective labour policy?: An alternative interpretation of early colonial labour policy in Fiji', *Journal of Pacific History*, Vol. 23, No. 2, (Oct.)

—— 1990. 'Class, communalism and the 1947 Fiji Mineworkers Strike', in C. Moore, J. Leckie & D. Munro (eds), *Labour in the South Pacific*, Townsville: James Cook University of North Queensland.

Bain, 'A. & Baba, T. (eds), 1990. *Bavadra: prime minister, statesman, man of the people: selection of speeches and writings, 1985-1989*, Nadi: Sunrise Press.

Barr, K. J., 1990. *Poverty in Fiji*, Suva: Fiji Forum for Justice, Peace and the Integrity of Creation.

Belshaw, Cyril, 1964. *Under the ivi tree: society and economic growth in rural Fiji*, London: Routledge & Kegan Paul.

Bennett, J. A., 1987. *Wealth of the Solomons: a history of a Pacific archipelago, 1800-1978*, Honolulu: University of Hawaii Press.

Bienefeld, M., 1984. *Work and Income for the people of Fiji: a strategy for more than just survival. The final report of the Fiji Employment and Development Mission*, Suva: Government Printer.

Burawoy, M., 1976. 'The functions and reproduction of migrant labor: comparative material from Southern Africa and the United States', *American Journal of Sociology*, Vol. 81, No. 5.

Callick, Rowan, 1989. 'Behind the trouble on Bougainville', *Islands Business* Mar./Apr.

Chakrabarty, Dipesh, 1983. 'On deifying and defying authority: managers and workers in the jute mills of Bengal circa 1890-1940', *Past and Present*, No. 100 (Aug.).

Chapman, J. K., 1964. *The Career of Arthur Hamilton Gordon First Lord Stanmore 1829-1912*, Toronto: University of Toronto Press.

Coghill, Ian, 1971. *Australia's mineral wealth*, Melbourne: Sorrett Publishing Pty Ltd.

Cohen, Robin, 1980. 'Resistance and hidden forms of consciousness amongst African workers', *Review of African Political Economy*, No. 19, (Sept.-Dec.).

Connell, J., 1977. 'The decline of local government councils and the rise of village government', in J. Connell (ed.), *Local government councils in Bougainville*, Christchurch: Bougainville Special Publication No. 3.

Crisp, Jeff, 1984. *The story of an African working class: Ghanaian miners' struggles 1870-1980*, London: Zed Books.

Cross, Malcolm, 1971. 'On Conflict, race relations and the theory of the plural society', *Race*, Vol. XII, No. 4.

Crough, E. J. & Wheelwright, E. L., 1982. 'Australia the client state: a case study of the mineral industry', in E. J. Harman & B. W. Head, *State, capital and resources in the north and west of Australia*, Perth: University of Western Australia Press.

Curtain, R., 1984. 'The migrant labour system and class formation in Papua New Guinea', *South Pacific Forum*, Vol. 1, No. 2.

Deere, C. D., 1976. 'Rural Women's Subsistence Production in the capitalist periphery', *Review of Radical Political Economy*, Vol. 8, No. 1 (Spring).

Denoon, D., 1973. *People's History*, Inaugural lecture, Port Moresby: University of Papua New Guinea.

Derrick, R. A., 1950. *A History of Fiji*, Vol. 1, 2nd ed., Suva: Printing & Stationery Department.

Dunkin, H. H., 1947-48. 'Gold mining at Vatukoula, Fiji, parts I-VII', *Chemical Engineering and Mining Review*, July 1947-Jan. 1948.

Durutalo, S., 1983. 'The Liberation of the Pacific Island Intellectual', *Review*, Suva: University of the South Pacific, Vol. 4, No. 10 (Sept.).

—— 1985. 'Buccaneers and Chiefly Historians', *Journal of Pacific Studies*, Vol. 11.

Emberson-Bain, 'A., 1992. 'Fiji: women, poverty and post-coup pressure', in D. Robie (ed.), *Tu galala: social change in the Pacific*, Sydney: Bridget Williams Books/ Pluto Press.

—— 1992. *Na Ma'e! Na Ma'e! We Stand Until We Die!* (video).

See also entries under Bain, 'A.

Epstein, A. L., 1958. *Politics in an urban African community*, London: J. Nicholson.

Fieldes, Diane, 1976. 'Pains and penalties: the penal powers of arbitration 1956-1970', BA (Hons) thesis, Canberra: Australian National University.

First, Ruth, 1982. 'The gold of migrant labour', *Review of African Political Economy*, No. 25, (Sept.-Dec.).

France, Peter, 1969. *The charter of the land: custom and colonization in Fiji*, Melbourne: OUP.

Furnivall, J. S., 1948. *Colonial policy and practice: a comparative study of Burma and Netherlands India*, Cambridge: CUP.

Gillion, K. L., 1962. *Fiji's Indian migrants: a history to the end of indenture in 1920*, Melbourne: OUP.

—— 1977. *The Fiji Indians: challenge to European dominance 1920-1946*, Canberra, ANU Press.

Girvan, Norman, 1971. 'Why we need to nationalize bauxite, and how', *New World Jamaica Pamphlet* No. 6 (1971), reprinted in Norman Girvan & Owen Jefferson, *Readings in the Political Economy of the Caribbean*, Caribbean: New World Publications, n.d.

—— 1976. *Corporate imperialism: conflict and expropriation*, New York: Monthly Review Press.

Graves, Adrian, 1983. 'Truck and gifts: Melanesian immigrants and the trade box system in colonial Queensland', *Past and Present*, Vol. 101.

Griffen, J., Nelson, H. & Firth, S., 1979. *Papua New Guinea: a political history*, Melbourne: Heinemann.

Hardy, Frank, 1975. *Power without glory*, St Albans, Herts: Panther Books Ltd.

Hempenstall, P. J., 1978. *Pacific Islanders under German rule: a study in the meaning of colonial resistance*, Canberra: ANU Press.

Hempenstall, P. J. & Rutherford, N., 1984. *Protest and dissent in the colonial Pacific*, Suva: University of the South Pacific.

Higgins, W., 1974. 'Reconstituting Australian communism', in R. Miliband & J. Saville (eds), *The Socialist Register*, London: Merlin Press.

Horwitz, R., 1967. *The political economy of South Africa*, London: Weidenfeld & Nicolson.

Houghton, D. H., 1967. *The South African economy* Cape Town: OUP.

Howard, M. C., 1985. 'The evolution of industrial relations in Fiji and the reaction of public employees' unions to the current economic crisis', *South Pacific Forum*, Vol. 2, No. 2.

—— 1986. 'History and industrial relations in the South Pacific', *South Pacific Forum*, Vol. 3, No. 1 (April).

—— 1988. *The impact of the international mining industry on native peoples*, Sydney: Transnational Corporations Research Project, University of Sydney.

Howard, M. C., Plange, Nii-K., Durutalo, S. & Witton, R., 1983. *The political economy of the South Pacific*, Townsville: James Cook University of North Queensland.

Howe, K. R., 1979. 'Pacific islands history in the 1980s: new directions or monograph myopia?' *Pacific Studies*, Vol. 3, No. 1 (Fall).

—— 1984. *Where the waves fall: a new South Sea islands history from first settlement to colonial rule*, Sydney: Allen & Unwin.

Hughes, P. & Sullivan, M., 1989. 'Environmental impact assessment in Papua New Guinea: lessons for the wider Pacific region', *Pacific Viewpoint*, Vol. 30 (1).

Hutson, J., 1966. *Penal Colony to Penal Powers*, Sydney: Amalgamated Engineering Union.

Hyman, Richard, 1972. *Strikes*, London: Fontana.

—— 1975. *Industrial relations: a Marxist introduction*, London: Macmillan.

Innes, D., 1984. *Anglo-American and the rise of modern South Africa*, New York: Monthly Review Press.

Johnstone, F. A., 1976. *Class, race and gold: a study of class relations and racial discrimination in South Africa*, London: Routledge & Kegan Paul.

Knapman, B., 1987. *Fiji's economic history, 1874–1939: studies of capitalist colonial development*, Canberra: National Centre for Development Studies, ANU.

—— 1988. 'The economic consequences of the coups', in R. T. Robertson & A. Tamanisau, *Fiji: shattered coups*, Sydney: Pluto Press in association with the Australian Council for Overseas Aid & the Fiji Independent News Service.

Kuper, Leo, 1971. 'Political change in plural societies: problems in racial pluralism', *International Social Science Journal*, Vol. 23, No. 4.

Kuper, Leo & Smith, M. G. (eds), 1969. *Pluralism in Africa*, Berkeley: University of California Press.

Lal, B. V., 1988. *Power and prejudice: the making of the Fiji coup*, Wellington: New Zealand Institute of International Affairs.

Leckie, J., 1983. 'Towards a review of history in the South Pacific', *Journal of Pacific Studies*, Vol. 9.

—— 1987. 'Introduction—Women and Work in the South Pacific', *Journal of Pacific Studies*, Vol. 13.

—— 1988. 'Confrontation with the state: industrial conflict and the Fiji Public Service Association during the 1970s and 1980s', *South Pacific Forum*, Vol. 4, No. 2 (April).

Leftwich, Adrian, 1974. 'The constitution and continuity of South African inequality: some conceptual questions', in Adrian Leftwich (ed.), *South Africa: economic growth and political change*, Great Britain: Anchor Press.

Legassick, M., 1974. 'South Africa: capital accumulation and violence', *Economy and Society*, Vol. 3, No. 3.

—— 1977. 'Gold, agriculture, and secondary industry in South Africa 1885-1970: from periphery to sub-metropole as a forced labour system', in R. Palmer & N. Parsons (eds), *The Roots of Rural Poverty in Central and Southern Africa*, London: Heinemann Educational.

Legassick, M. & Wolpe, H., 1977. 'The bantustans and capital accumulation in South Africa', *Review of African Political Economy*, No. 7.

Legge, J. D., 1958. *Britain in Fiji 1858–1880*, London: Macmillan.

Lum, J., 1985. 'Fiji', *Mining Annual Review*.

—— 1987. 'Fiji', *Mining Annual Review*.

Macdonald, B. K., 1982. *Cinderellas of the Empire: towards a history of Kiribati and Tuvalu*, Canberra: ANU Press.

Macnaught, T. J., 1974. 'Chiefly civil servants? Ambiguity in district administration and the preservation of a Fijian way of life, 1896-1940', *Journal of Pacific History*, Vol. 9.

—— 1982. *The Fijian colonial experience: a study of the neo-traditional order under British colonial rule prior to World War II*, Pacific Research Monograph No. 7, Canberra: ANU Press.

Mamdani, M., 1976. *Politics and class formation in Uganda*, London: Heinemann Educational.

Marks, S. & Rathbone, R. (eds), 1982. *Industrialisation and social change in South Africa: African class formation, culture and consciousness 1870–1930*, London & New York: Longman Group Ltd.

Marx, K., 1901. *Capital*, Vol. 1, London: Swan Sonnenschein.

Marx, K. & Engels, F., 1958. *Selected Works*, Vol. 1, London: Foreign Languages Publishing House.

McConville, Chris, 1981. 'John Wren: machine boss, Irish chieftain or meddling millionaire?', *Labour History*, No. 40 (May).

Meillassoux, C., 1981. *Maidens, meal and money: capitalism and the domestic community*, Cambridge: CUP.

Meleisea, M. & Schoeffel, P., 1984. 'Saving Pacific Islanders from themselves: Eurocentric bias in Marxist social theory', *Journal of Pacific Studies*, Vol. 10.

Mies, M., 1984. 'Capitalism and Subsistence: Rural women in India', *Development: Seeds of Change*, Vol. 4.

Mitchell, D. T., 1953. *A general description of mining operations at Vatukoula Fiji*, Australian Institute of Mining & Metallurgy, Proceedings No. 168-169.

Moore, C., Leckie, J. & Munro, D. (eds), 1990. *Labour in the South Pacific*, Townsville: James Cook University of North Queensland.

Muir, G. O., 1977. 'Hazards in the Chemical Laboratory', 2nd ed., London: The Chemical Society.

Murphy, D. J., 1978. 'Edward Granville Theodore: Ideal and reality', in D. J. Murphy & R. B. Joyce, *Queensland political portraits 1859–1952*, St Lucia, Qld: University of Queensland Press.

Narsey, Wadan, 1986. 'Fiji's colonial monetary system and export of colonial capital: some questions for the theories of the Currency Board system and colonial underdevelopment', *Journal of Pacific Studies*, Vol. 12.

—— 1988. 'A reinterpretation of the history and theory of colonial currency systems,' unpublished Ph.D. thesis, University of Sussex.

Nathan, Dev, 1987. 'Structure of the working class in India', *Economic and Political Weekly*, Vol. XXII, No. 8 (May).

Nayacakalou, R. R., 1975. *Leadership in Fiji*, Melbourne: OUP.

Newbury, Colin, 1975. 'Colour bar and labour conflict on the New Guinea goldfields 1935–41', *Australian Journal of Politics & History*, Vol. 21, No. 3.

—— 1980. 'The Melanesian labor reserve: some reflections on Pacific labor markets in the nineteenth century', *Pacific Studies*, Vol. IV, No. 1 (Fall).

O'Faircheallaigh, Ciaran, 1983. 'Mining in the Papua New Guinea economy, 1880–1980', unpublished paper, Research School of Pacific Studies, Canberra: ANU.

Oxaal, I., Barnett, T. & Booth, D. (eds), 1975. *Beyond the sociology of development: economy and society in Latin America and Africa*, London: Routledge & Kegan Paul.

Parpart, Jane L., 1983. *Labor and capital on the African Copperbelt*, Philadelphia: Temple University Press.

—— 1986. 'The household and the mine shaft: gender and class struggles on the Zambian Copperbelt, 1924–64', *Journal of Southern African Studies*, Vol. 13, No. 1.

Perham, Margery, 1960. *Lugard: the years of authority 1895–1945*, London: Collins.

Perrings, Charles, 1979. *Black mineworkers in Central Africa: industrial strategies and the evolution of an African proletariat in the Copperbelt, 1911–41*, London: Heinemann Educational.

Phillips, Anne, 1977. 'The concept of "development" ', *Review of African Political Economy*, No. 8, (Jan.–April).

Phimister, Ian & van Onselen, Charles, 1979. 'The political economy of tribal animosity: a case study of the 1929 Bulawayo location "faction fight" ', *Journal of Southern African Studies*, Vol. 6, No. 1 (Oct.).

Plange, N.-K., 1985. 'Coming in from the cold: gold mining and proletarianization of Fijians, 1920–1985, *Labour, Capital and Society*, Vol. 18, No. 1 (April).

Prasad, S. (ed.), 1988. *Coup and crisis: Fiji a year later*, Victoria: Arena Publications.

Ralston, C., 1977. *Grass huts and warehouses: Pacific beach communities of the nineteenth century*, Canberra: ANU Press.

Ramaswamy, E. A. & Ramaswamy, Uma, 1981. *Industry and labour: an introduction*, New Delhi: OUP.

Rex, J., 1959. 'The plural society in sociological theory', *British Journal of Sociology*, Vol. 10.

—— 1971. 'The plural society: the South African case', *Race*, Vol. XII, No. 4 (April).

Richardson, P. & van Helten, J. J., 1982. 'Labour in the South African gold mining industry 1886–1914', in S. Marks & R. Rathbone (eds), *Industrialisation and social change in South Africa: African class formation, culture and consciousness 1870–1930*, London & New York: Longman Group Ltd.

Robertson, R. T., 1985. 'Nationalism, protest and dialectic of development', *Journal of Pacific Studies*, Vol. 11.

Robertson, R. T. & Tamanisau, A., 1988. *Fiji: shattered coups*, Sydney: Pluto Press in association with the Australian Council for Overseas Aid & the Fiji Independent News Service.

Robie, David (ed.), 1992. *Tu galala: social change in the Pacific*, Sydney: Bridget Williams Books/Pluto Press.

Rodney, Walter, 1977a. 'Immigrants and racial attitudes in Guyanese history', unpublished paper, Institute of Commonwealth Studies, University of London, May.

—— 1977b. 'Subject races and class contradictions in Guyanese history', unpublished paper, Institute of Commonwealth Studies, University of London, May.

Rokotuivuna, A., Dakuvula, J., Narsey, W., Howie, I., Annear, P., Mahoney, D., Fong, A., Slatter, C. & Noone, B., 1973. *Fiji, a developing Australian colony*, Melbourne: International Development Action.

Sayers, R. S., 1976. *The Bank of England 1891–1944*, Vol. II, Cambridge: CUP.

Scarr, D. A., 1984. *Fiji: a short history*, Sydney: George Allen & Unwin.

Shineberg, Dorothy, 1967. *They came for sandalwood: a study of the sandalwood trade in the south-west Pacific, 1830–1865*, Melbourne: Melbourne University Press.

Shivja, Issa, 1975. 'Peasants and class alliances', *Review of African Political Economy*, No. 3 (May–Oct.).

Simons, H. J. & Simons, R. E., 1969. *Class and colour in South Africa 1850–1950*, Harmondsworth (UK): Penguin.

Smith, M. G., 1965. *The plural society in the British West Indies*, Berkeley: University of California Press.

Southall, Roger, 1983. *South Africa's Transkei: the political economy of an 'independent' bantustan*, New York: Monthly Review Press.

Spate, O. H. K., 1978. 'The Pacific as an artifact', in Niel Gunson (ed.), *The changing Pacific: essays in honour of H. E. Maude*, Melbourne: OUP.

—— 1979. *The Pacific since Magellan I, The Spanish lake*, Canberra: ANU Press.

—— 1983. *The Pacific since Magellan II, Monopolists and freebooters*, Canberra: ANU Press.

—— 1988. *The Pacific since Magellan III, Paradise found and lost*, Canberra: ANU Press.

Standish, B., 1989. 'Bougainville: undermining the state in Papua New Guinea', background paper, Foreign Affairs Group, Commonwealth of Australia Parliament (Oct.).

Stanner, W. E. H., 1953. *The South Seas in transition: a study of post-war rehabilitation and reconstruction in three British Pacific dependencies*, Sydney: Australasian Publishing Co.

Stavenhagen, Rodolfo, 1975. *Social classes in agrarian societies*, New York: Anchor Press.

Stichter, Sharon, 1975. 'The formation of a working class in Kenya', in Richard Sandbrook & Robin Cohen (eds), *The development of an African working class:*

studies in class formation and action, London: Longman Group Ltd.

—— 1985. *Migrant Laborers*, Cambridge: CUP.

Sutherland, W. M., 1984. 'The state and capitalist development in Fiji', Ph.D. thesis, University of Canterbury, Christchurch, New Zealand.

Taylor, M., 1986. 'Multinationals, business organisations and the development of the Fiji economy', in M. Taylor & N. Thrift, *Multinationals and the restructuring of the world economy*, London: Croom Helm.

Thompson, E. P., 1980. *The making of the English working class*, Harmondsworth (UK): Penguin.

Trapido, S., 1971. 'South Africa in a comparative study of industrialization', *Journal of Development Studies*, Vol. 7, No. 3 (April).

Tsokhas, Kosmas, 1986. *Beyond dependence: companies, labour processes and Australian mining*, Melbourne: OUP.

Utrecht, E. (ed.), 1984. *Fiji: client state of Australasia?*, Sydney: Transnational Corporations Research Project, University of Sydney.

van Onselen, Charles, 1976. *Chibaro: African mine labour in Southern Rhodesia 1900–1933*, London: Pluto Press.

van den Berghe, P. L., 1967. *South Africa, a study in conflict*, Berkeley: University of California Press.

—— 1969. 'Pluralism and the polity: a theoretical exploration', Leo Kuper & M. G. Smith (eds), *Pluralism in Africa*, Berkeley, University of California Press.

van Helten, J. J., 1978. 'British capital, the British state and economic investment in South Africa, 1886–1914', unpublished paper, Institute of Commonwealth Studies, University of London, June.

Viviani, N., 1970. *Nauru: phosphate and political progress*, Canberra: ANU Press.

Ward, R. G., 1972. 'The Pacific bêche-de-mer trade with special reference to Fiji', in R. G. Ward (ed.), *Man in the Pacific Islands: essays on geographical change in the Pacific Islands*, Oxford: Clarendon Press.

Index

Note. Numbers in italics refer to illustrations.

For EU product safety concerns, contact us at Calle de José Abascal, 56–1°,
28003 Madrid, Spain or eugpsr@cambridge.org.

 www.ingramcontent.com/pod-product-compliance
Ingram Content Group UK Ltd.
Pitfield, Milton Keynes, MK11 3LW, UK
UKHW042316180425
457623UK00005B/24